CHARLESTON

UNIVERSITY PRESS OF FLORIDA

Florida A&M University, Tallahassee
Florida Atlantic University, Boca Raton
Florida Gulf Coast University, Ft. Myers
Florida International University, Miami
Florida State University, Tallahassee
New College of Florida, Sarasota
University of Central Florida, Orlando
University of Florida, Gainesville
University of North Florida, Jacksonville
University of South Florida, Tampa
University of West Florida, Pensacola

CHARLESTON

An Archaeology of Life in a Coastal Community

MARTHA A. ZIERDEN
AND ELIZABETH J. REITZ

Foreword by Joseph P. Riley Jr., Mayor of Charleston

University Press of Florida
Gainesville · Tallahassee · Tampa · Boca Raton
Pensacola · Orlando · Miami · Jacksonville · Ft. Myers · Sarasota

Cover: *Charleston Square* by Charles J. Hamilton, 1862. Courtesy of Colonial Williamsburg Foundation, Museum Purchase.

First cloth printing, 2016
First paperback printing, 2024

29 28 27 26 25 24   6 5 4 3 2 1

Library of Congress Cataloging-in-Publication Data
Names: Zierden, Martha A., author. | Reitz, Elizabeth Jean, 1946– author. |
   Riley, Joseph P., 1943– author of foreword.
Title: Charleston : an archaeology of life in a coastal community / Martha A.
   Zierden and Elizabeth J. Reitz ; foreword by Joseph P. Riley Jr., Mayor of
   Charleston.
Description: Gainesville : University Press of Florida, [2016] | Includes
   bibliographical references and index.
Identifiers: LCCN 2016015346 | ISBN 9780813062907 (cloth) | ISBN 9780813080819 (pbk.)
Subjects: LCSH: Archaeology and history—South Carolina—Charleston. |
   Excavations (Archaeology)—South Carolina—Charleston. | Historic
   buildings—South Carolina—Charleston. | Charleston (S.C.)—Antiquities. |
   Charleston (S.C.)—History. | Charleston (S.C.)—Buildings, structures,
   etc.
Classification: LCC F279.C447 Z54 2016 | DDC 975.7/91501—dc23
LC record available at https://lccn.loc.gov/2016015346

The University Press of Florida is the scholarly publishing agency for the State University System of Florida, comprising Florida A&M University, Florida Atlantic University, Florida Gulf Coast University, Florida International University, Florida State University, New College of Florida, University of Central Florida, University of Florida, University of North Florida, University of South Florida, and University of West Florida.

University Press of Florida
2046 NE Waldo Road
Suite 2100
Gainesville, FL 32609
http://upress.ufl.edu

For Kathy Deagan
Who taught us

CONTENTS

ILLUSTRATIONS

Figures

Plates *(following page 202)*

FOREWORD

The importance of archaeology and The Charleston Museum in understanding the history and development of Charleston is difficult to overstate. Charleston has undergone a revitalization in the last few decades that has attracted many new residents and visitors from the United States and beyond. Our emphasis has been on achieving excellence in design and construction, enhancing the public realm, and respecting the rich history of this city, founded in 1670.

Martha Zierden and The Charleston Museum have worked hand-in-hand with the City of Charleston in this renaissance, leading the way to document and illustrate our rich mosaic of history. In the process, they have developed methods and approaches with national significance. One of the first lessons we laypeople learned to appreciate from the Museum's work on city projects was that the written record tends to emphasize the activities of a small number of citizens, the most wealthy and powerful.

What The Charleston Museum's work opened up for us was the record of the whole population, rich and poor, painting through urban archaeology a more accurate picture of a bustling, teeming, complex settlement. Elizabeth Reitz's groundbreaking work in documenting the food supply of this city, from its early history until the end of the nineteenth century, enhanced our understanding of how this city worked, lived, and changed over such a long period.

The stories of the excavations read like detective fiction and are exciting for that reason alone. But their deeper importance, in making possible a richer understanding of our past, is that they are guideposts for how we treat this city in the future. The Charleston Museum has been a wonderful partner, and Charleston is much the better for this collaboration.

Joseph P. Riley Jr.
Mayor, City of Charleston
1975–2015

PREFACE

For over 30 years, we have enjoyed the good fortune of studying one of America's most historic cities, a vital urban area and the birthplace of the nation's historic preservation movement. Visitors to Charleston, South Carolina, are attracted to the innumerable historic homes, public buildings, and museums. Decorative arts made and used in the city grace historic house museums and private homes. The dirty, broken, mundane fragments of pottery, nails, glass, bricks, and other objects retrieved by archaeologists from beneath the modern ground surface offer only a glimpse of the finery for which the town is so well known. These below-ground materials, however, tell about the daily challenges and the grittiness of life experienced by many in the city.

We first met in 1979. Martha was a graduate student at Florida State University, studying under Dr. Kathleen Deagan. Betsy was a graduate student at the University of Florida, studying with Dr. Elizabeth Wing. At the time, Kathy was researching sixteenth-century Spanish sites in St. Augustine, Florida, with a grant from the National Endowment for the Humanities, and Betsy was writing her dissertation on the animal bones recovered by that project. Kathy was a member of both of our graduate committees. She invited her field school students, among them Martha, to a meeting of the specialists working on the grant project. Martha and her fellow students listened carefully to the discussion among the scholars, answering the occasional question put their way. Leaving the meeting, Kathy reminded them that faunal studies, and other special studies, should always be part of any archaeological research project.

A few years later Martha began working with Dr. Elaine Herold at The Charleston Museum. Martha became responsible for the Museum's historical archaeology program after Elaine left the Museum when her husband, the Museum's director, took a position with the Buffalo Museum of Science.

When Martha's first small field project, at McCrady's Tavern, yielded well-preserved animal remains, she did what Kathy told her to do: she called Betsy, by that time at the University of Georgia. Betsy quickly agreed to look at the material. That first sample of bone was small by most standards; but the materials were interesting, and so our work began. Project after project produced additional faunal remains, soon merged into a sample of significant size.

The animal bones are an important part of the archaeological story. When combined with the written record and other artifacts of human life, such as ceramics, glass, and metal objects, bones help us draw a lively picture of life in the city. Charleston's archaeological heritage enables our interpretive reach to extend beyond the elegant townhouses to include many aspects of urban life in the historic city, from the first decades of the Carolina colony to the end of the nineteenth century. The Charleston Museum featured our work in two exhibits entitled "The Bountiful Coast," in 1988 and 2004. As our work continued we realized that this was more than a title. The colony succeeded in part because of the bounty of the lowcountry. A rich range of natural and cultivated resources meant that food was readily available; this bounty later provided wealth to some. The bountiful coast is an important part of Charleston's story.

As the years passed, we shared our enthusiasm and findings with our historic-preservation and museum colleagues. Most importantly, our findings were shared with historic-house docents and with the public. On several occasions, highly visible excavations became focal points in the daily chatter of Charleston's horse-drawn carriage tours. All of this work was supported by archaeological mitigation and historic-preservation projects funded by the City, public preservation organizations, and private property owners. Their backing reflects Charlestonians' interest in all aspects of local history and pride in their city. Our primary stimulus in writing this book is to share with them what we have learned with their help. We could not have done this without them.

ACKNOWLEDGMENTS

The first question we ask of prospective archaeology students is "Are you a team player?" Successful archaeological research is a group effort, often a large group effort. Research that has spanned so many years, and relied upon the knowledge and skills of so many disciplines, of necessity has required the support of many people and institutions. Over the decades, hundreds of learned and dedicated individuals have contributed to the archaeological study of Charleston, from volunteers washing artifacts to colleagues debating interpretations and answering odd questions. We endeavor here to recognize their contributions; if we have omitted anyone, please be assured that the omission is inadvertent.

Special recognition is due to the citizens of Charleston, whose interest in their city's heritage has supported this work in both tangible and intangible ways. We are very grateful to the City of Charleston, particularly to Mayor Joseph P. Riley Jr., whose vision for a livable city included preservation and study of its archaeological heritage. The Charleston Museum, founded in 1773, has a long history of embracing archaeology. The Museum supported development of a historical archaeology program under Elaine Herold. Two previous directors of The Charleston Museum, Donald Herold (1973–1984) and John Brumgardt (1984–2013), encouraged the archaeology department to engage in research and excavation and to include archaeological data in museum programs. Museum director Carl Borick continues this legacy with enthusiasm. Carl's support made this volume possible.

Dr. Elaine Bluhm Herold created the historical archaeology program at The Charleston Museum, and her work of the 1970s figures prominently in the Charleston database. Elaine lost her long battle with Alzheimer's disease as this volume was being submitted to the press. We are proud to build on the foundation created by her research and advocacy.

Present and former staff of the City of Charleston and Charleston Water Systems assisted in the myriad logistics required to conduct excavations in the city, ranging from administrative oversight to access to public property and use of heavy equipment to facilitate those digs. Beth Brownlee, Laura Cabiness, Matt Compton, Yvonne Fortenberry, Kin Hill, Steve Livingston, Mary Ann Sullivan, and Laurie Thompson made many projects possible.

A number of public and private historical and preservation institutions have supported archaeology through advocacy, project development, and grant funding. We have worked with the Charleston County Library, Historic Charleston Foundation, Old Exchange and Provost Dungeon, the Preservation Society of Charleston, the South Carolina Historical Society, South Carolina Department of Archives and History, South Carolina Institute of Archaeology and Anthropology, and the College of Charleston. Historic Charleston Foundation, particularly through the efforts of Jonathan Poston and Katherine Saunders Pemberton, has been a leader of advocacy and preservation, protecting hundreds of archaeological sites through protective covenants. They also have designed and funded archaeological research on numerous public and private properties.

Several private citizens funded archaeological research on their own properties, on commercial properties, or on sites of special interest to them. We are grateful for the support of Julian Brandt, Ethel Jane Bunting, Hugh C. Lane Sr., Peter and Patti McGee, Catherine Parker, Margaret Thornton, James Werrell, the Mills B. Lane Foundation, the Post and Courier Foundation, and the Seymour H. Knox Foundation. Equally critical were the architects and project managers who facilitated archaeological fieldwork and integrated it into overall site restoration plans. In particular, we worked with Will Evans, Tommy Graham, Glenn Keyes, Richard Marks, Joe Opperman, Katherine Saunders Pemberton, Joe Schmidt, and Sheila Wertimer.

Managers of these properties and projects, both public and private, made us feel welcome and enhanced our on-site experience. These were the go-to people for every detail: Will Evans, Dickie Godley, Lynn Hanlin, Glenn Keyes, Robert Leath, Richard Marks, George McDaniel, Neil Nohrden, Joe Opperman, Allan Parks, Valerie Perry, Jonathan Poston, Russell Rosen, Ernie Schealey, Joe Schmidt, Allan Stello, Linda Walraven, Frankie Webb, Richard Widham, Melanie Wilson, and Tony Youmans.

Much of the fieldwork was conducted by students in archaeological field schools offered through the College of Charleston, directed by Museum archaeologist Ron Anthony and College of Charleston professor Barbara Borg. These and other College of Charleston students worked in the laboratory as interns. Many of the technicians who worked on multiple projects were graduates of this program. We could count on them for superb fieldwork and good company: Andrew Agha, Katie Epps, Margaret Harris, Nicole Isenbarger, Jason Moore, Virginia Pierce, Kim Pyszka, Elizabeth Garrett Ryan, Hayden Smith, Matt Tankersley, Genevieve Brown Taylor, Randall Turner, and Martha Middleton Wallace.

Laboratory analysis of the thousands of artifacts was directed by four Museum archaeologists through the years: Ron Anthony, Kimberly Grimes, Debi Hacker, and Elizabeth Paysinger. They, in turn, guided numerous student interns from the College of Charleston. Laboratory and fieldwork was also supported by countless volunteers. Many joined us for a few hours, or a few days. Others stayed for years, participating in fieldwork or helping in the lab on a weekly basis. These are special friends: Barbara Aldrich, Larry Cadigan, Doris Dann, Harriett Goldenberg, Margaret Harris, Mary Hildebrand, Bob and Maggie Jacobs, Sandy Just, Bill Koob, Myrna Rowland, Lee Stevens, Bill Turner, and Linda Wilson.

Zooarchaeological analysis was conducted by numerous students at the University of Georgia, including Sarah Bergh, Nanny Carder, Carol Colaninno, Maran Little, Gregory Lucas, Kelly Lynn Orr, Barnet Pavao-Zuckerman, Jennifer Webber, and Daniel Weinand. Students in zooarchaeology classes analyzed additional samples.

Historical and documentary research for the various projects was conducted by skilled historians, both at The Charleston Museum and at other institutions. Our site-specific research builds on the work of Suzanne Buckley, Nicholas Butler, Jeanne Calhoun, Ziyadah Kirnon, Charles Philips, and Christine White. Many historians have helped with particular aspects of the development of Charleston and the lowcountry, and their work serves as an anchor for our study: Susan Bates, Dan Bell, Millicent Brown, Richard Côté, Sarah Fick, Myrtle Glascoe, Harlan Greene, Steve Hoffius, Cheves Leland, Suzanne Linder, Charles Philips, Richard Porcher, Bernard Powers, Ted Rosengarten, Hayden Smith, Robert Stockton, and Susan Williams.

As the properties we study contain buildings, both extant and in ruins, our architectural colleagues have been essential to site interpretation. Moreover, they have directed and guided our interdisciplinary excavations on house-museum properties: Susan Buck, Willie Graham, Bernard Herman, Carter L. Hudgins, Carl Lounsbury, Richard Marks, Orlando Ridout, and Matt Webster.

Other colleagues have given generously of their time and expertise and shaped our research. They are almost too numerous to mention. Our zooarchaeological colleagues have provided guidance and comparative samples: Phillip Armitage, Joanne Bowen, Simon Davis, Nick Laracuente, Bruce Manzano, Henry Miller, Barbara Ruff, and Elizabeth S. Wing. We are particularly grateful to Chad Braley and Simon Davis for permission to reprint their images. Studies of soils and botanical remains were conducted by John Foss, John Jones, Lisa Kealhofer, Karl Reinhard, and Michael Trinkley. Guidance on the archaeology of gardens and plants came from C. Allan Brown, James Cothran, Dee Dee Joyce, Bill Kelso, Richard Porcher, Barbara Sarudy, and Tim Trussell. Dan Ksepka, Laurie Reitsema, Daniel Thomas, and Dwight Williams helped us identify the parakeet in the Charles Willson Peale painting of young Miss Proctor and aided our search for the identity of the Heyward-Washington parrot. Guidance from decorative arts and material-culture experts helped us identify many of the fragmentary artifacts recovered on sites and understand their place in the material world; we learned from John Bivins, Jan Hiester, Rob Hunter, Rod Jellico, Jill Koverman, Robert Leath, Chris Loeblein, Grahame Long, Anne Smart Martin, George McDaniel, Maurie McInnis, Louis Nelson, Brad Rauschenberg, Dale Rosengarten, Elizabeth Garrett Ryan, Tom Savage, and Bly Straube. Our interpretations are built on the very broad foundation their studies offered.

Many archaeologists, visiting our sites and working on their own sites, have helped shape our research and place Charleston in a broader context. We have benefited immeasurably from conversations, some brief and some lasting over the decades, with Andrew Agha, David Barker, Chad Braley, Marley Brown, Ashley Chapman, Sarah Stroud Clarke, Brian Crane, David Crass, Pam Cressey, Kathy Deagan, Chester DePratter, Lesley Drucker, Dan Elliott, Leland Ferguson, Carl Halbirt, Lynn Harris, Michael Hartley, Barbara Heath, Nick Honerkamp, Carter C. Hudgins, Carter L. Hudgins, Nicole Isenbarger, Larry James, J. W. Joseph, Chris Judge, Julie King, Jim Legg, Kenneth Lewis, Lynn Lewis, Jon Marcoux, Linda Carnes McNaughton, James Nyman, Eric Poplin, Kim Pyszka, Nan Rothschild, Theresa Singleton, Steve Smith, Stanley South, Carl Steen, Linda Stine, Michael Stoner, Sean Taylor, Diana Wall, and Anne Yentsch. Carol Poplin of History Workshop Inc. turned these interpretations into public exhibits at several sites.

Andrew Agha, Carl Borick, Julie King, Jon Marcoux, Katherine Pemberton, Richard Porcher, Max Reitz, Nan Rothschild, and Susan Williams read drafts of this volume. We are very grateful for their willingness to help us clarify our ideas and improve the volume in countless other ways. Photography by Olga Maria Caballero, Sean Money, Rick Rhodes, and

Terry Richardson enhanced this volume. Susan G. Dusar prepared the present-day maps. The Charleston Museum, Charleston County RMCO Office, Colonial Williamsburg Foundation, the Gibbes Museum of Art, Hammond-Harwood House, Historic Charleston Foundation, South Carolina Historical Society, Southeastern Archaeological Services, University of Oklahoma Press, Winterthur Library, Yale University Press, and Taylor & Francis gave us permission to use images from their collections. We could not have completed this without the help of archivists Virginia Ellison, Karen Emmons, Becca Hiester, Marianne Martin, Jacklyn Penny, and Laurie Perkins. At The Charleston Museum, Jennifer McCormick and Sean Money were invaluable in assembling images. Curators Matt Gibson, Jan Hiester, Grahame Long, and Jessica Peragine provided objects from the collections. We appreciate the able assistance of the staff at University Press of Florida, particularly acquisitions editor Meredith Morris-Babb, project editor Catherine-Nevil Parker, and copyeditor Lisa S. Williams.

Some information about sites and interpretations presented in this volume was previously published in essays by Zierden in books published by the University of South Carolina Press. "Charleston: Archaeology of South Carolina's Colonial Capital" appears in *Archaeology in South Carolina: Exploring the Hidden Heritage of the Palmetto State*, edited by Adam King (2016). "The Archaeological Signature of Eighteenth-Century Charleston" appears in *Material Culture in Anglo-America: Regional Identity and Urbanity in the Tidewater, Lowcountry, and Caribbean*, edited by David S. Shields (2009).

And last, but not least, we recognize that none of this would have been possible without the patience, tolerance, and love of our families.

1

POTS, BONES, AND
THE URBAN LANDSCAPE

In 1761 John Rutledge scandalized his mother by hosting an oyster roast and asking his guests for their vote in his run for assemblyman. Despite the social misstep, Rutledge was elected and went on to an illustrious career in public service. But archaeologists and students of the material world and daily life find the party more interesting than the political career. For we know what he served, and how he was supplied. The menu speaks to the resources available from local woods and waters, the tastes and fashion of Europeans living in the North American colonies, and the trade network of a port city.

Fare for the oyster roast included crayfish in aspic, shrimp, red snapper baked whole in Bordeaux sauce, terrapin stew, and venison patty. The venison was provided by Indian traders. Watercress salad, pudding made of palmetto hearts and yams, and biscuits made from swamp cabbage (palmetto trunk) complemented the meats. Madeira was provided for the gentlemen, and Bordeaux or schnapps for the ladies. Rutledge ordered a number of supplies from merchant Henry Laurens for this event, including the drinks enumerated above (two turns of madeira, four cases of schnapps, and two casks of Bordeaux). He also added four cases of Curacao cordial, 1 barrel of molasses, hardware, muslins, and dried fruit to his order.[1]

Our world is filled with information on what people eat. Friends load our social media accounts with photos of lunch plates piled high. They champion healthy meals and recount epic desserts. Two centuries ago such information was not so easily shared; detailed menus such as Rutledge's are rare. But evidence for food, drink, and the accoutrements of dining, both ordinary and elegant, lies beneath the streets, sidewalks, back yards, and buildings of Charleston, South Carolina. Archaeological excavations produce fragments of wine bottles, china, and cooking vessels. They also provide animal remains in great quantity, from the animals cooked and consumed to those living in close proximity to homes, businesses, and other places within the city. The venison, fish, and terrapin served at Rutledge's oyster roast are regular discoveries on Charleston's archaeological sites. Together, these materials describe daily life in Charleston in ways not found in standard histories, sometimes contradicting those histories and sometimes expanding upon them.

Charleston's place in the real and imagined world is deep and complex. It is first and foremost known as the place where the Civil War began in 1861. Yet the city's history, as a place and as a political entity, began 200 years earlier. Charleston also is the birthplace of the historic preservation movement. The trajectory of preservation and tourism go hand in hand in the city, though the collaboration has not always been smooth or clear. Visitors to Charleston are attracted to the innumerable historic homes, public buildings, and museums, and to the decorative arts that grace these places. Our vision of Charleston, the city, is often inseparable from that of the surrounding lowcountry, a region still dominated by plantations.[2] Carolina was an entrepôt for thousands of Africans brought to North America against their will; for many, a lifetime of servitude began when they arrived in the Charleston Harbor. Gullah culture remains a vibrant part of lowcountry life and of the visitor experience, even as the collective understanding of African American culture in the Carolina lowcountry becomes more complex. Finally, Charleston is a mecca for foodies, with its long-standing seafood industry and an explosion of respected and sought-after restaurants, chefs, and food festivals.

Charleston, for the most part, is not widely known as a world-class archaeological site. Yet it is this aspect of the city's physical and social world that weaves together all of these different images of the city. When most people think of archaeology, they think of the ruins of ancient buildings and, maybe, some old pots. Archaeologists, however, mostly think about the less familiar materials encountered during excavations: dirty, mundane fragments of pottery, nails, glass, bricks, and other objects of daily life lying beneath the modern ground surface. Fragments of plants and animals provide additional details about the way the city looked as it grew over the centuries. These bring Charleston's past to life and lead to our perspective that urban areas are environments that shape and are shaped by the plants, animals, and people who live in them.

This record offers new and sometimes unexpected vignettes of daily life. Below-ground materials are tangible links to the city's past. They offer only a glimpse of the finery for which the town is so well known but testify to the daily challenges and the grittiness of life experienced by many here. This is especially true for the city's poor and less influential residents, about whom written records may be silent.

Animal remains are among the most common artifacts retrieved from beneath modern Charleston. Studies of these remains and the behaviors they represent provide unique and illuminating glimpses into everyday life in the city and the Carolina lowcountry. Most Americans, especially urban dwellers, are largely divorced from contact with animals (with the exception of pets) both domestic and wild; but this is a development of the last century. Pets, work animals, barnyard animals, and wild animals were very much part of Charleston's landscape in the past and are still part of that landscape. Controlling "nuisance" animals, in particular, remains a major challenge to public health and safety.

Just as the contributions animals made to urban life in the past were essential, their analysis today enriches our interpretation of that past when merged with the written record and more familiar archaeological artifacts. They allow us to draw a lively picture of city life beyond the elegant townhouses, from the first decades of the Carolina colony to the end of the nineteenth century. For these reasons, this volume portrays Charleston's archaeological history through the lens of cuisines, foodways, and animals in an urban landscape, as seen from dozens of excavations inside the city and beyond.

Our collaboration began with a week-long testing project in 1982 that produced a small sample of 682 bones and teeth. Now, some three decades later, the Charleston record of animal use ranks among the largest urban assemblages in the country. The Charleston Museum's analyzed samples total some 2,171 individual animals identified from 134,309 specimens weighing almost 1,000 pounds from 55 sites or portions of sites (appendixes 1 and 2). These materials tell us about the lives of Europeans, Africans, Native Americans, and Asians over three centuries. The sites that produced them are residential, commercial, defensive, and public. They sheltered people who could write and those who could not. They housed wealthy, middling, and underprivileged residents of the city. They also sheltered many animals, intentionally and unintentionally.

Surprises

As the site excavations increased and our samples of cultural and environmental artifacts grew in size and complexity, we found that the archaeological record of Charleston diverged from the story told by documents. Charleston's story also differed from traditional archaeological interpretations of colonial life. We were surprised by some of our discoveries.

The first surprise was what people ate. The South, and South Carolina in particular, is often referred to as the "Kingdom of Pork." Pork barbecue and barbecue joints play a central role in southern lore. We expected animal remains from Charleston to be dominated by pigs. Instead, site after site produced more fragments of bones and teeth from cows than from pigs. Beef was more abundant than pork from the earliest site to the latest. Perhaps, like today's trip to the barbecue joint, pork was an occasional treat. We also found that most of the pigs and cattle were young animals, not old ones slaughtered after many years of service.

We were surprised at how quickly Charlestonians and other residents of the Carolina lowcountry took advantage of the area's wild bounty. Projects at seventeenth-century sites reveal that a unique regional diet combining wild and domestic animals developed within the first decade of settlement. Moreover, it was long-lasting; the same suite of resources was used well into the nineteenth century, with only subtle changes. Armed with data from St. Augustine, less than 300 miles to the south, we noted that foodways practiced by people at the Spanish colony were different from those living in the English colony, despite access to similar resources. People in Spanish St. Augustine relied on small estuarine fish; hundreds of small fish bones filled excavation screens in that city. Because we learned our craft in St. Augustine, we expected to retrieve large numbers of small fish in Charleston, too; but they never materialized. Though our screens were filled with bone, we rarely found the concentrations of fish we remembered from our college days.

We were surprised to find no clear-cut distinctions in animal use that could be attributed to status or other social attributes. Historical archaeologists expect that material culture and foodways reflect consumer choices, which reflect in turn status, ethnicity, wealth, and power. Foodways seem good candidates for such studies, but people in Charleston appear to have eaten the same types of food, and the same cuts of meat, whether rich or poor. It is unfortunate that we cannot measure the quantity and quality of food consumed on a daily basis, which may vary widely with status. The

Figure 1.1. Map of the eastern United States showing key cities and archaeological sites. (Prepared by Susan Duser.)

archaeological evidence, however, indicates that ritual, accoutrements, and manners, the components of cuisine—rather than basic foods, the elements of diet served on platters and bowls throughout the city—separated rich and poor.

There are subtle differences among the collections, however. People at sites associated with wealthy households had a more diverse diet, probably reflecting access to broader resources. Surprisingly, this difference was due to wild foods, not domestic ones. City residents, particularly wealthy ones, ate many wild animals. These appear to be preferred foods, listed on party menus of the time and providing dietary richness to those who could afford it. Wild game still highlights celebratory events and some everyday diets in coastal South Carolina.

We also expected that people in the city and people in the country got their food in different ways—that everyone in the city would obtain their food from markets or other commercial outlets. Although we can distinguish between rural and urban collections, we find no clear-cut differences between urban residential and urban market collections. As in other instances, the animal remains are more subtle and more complex—we had to work for results. At site after site, the evidence for raising and butchering large animals on residential properties was compelling. It became increasingly clear that city residents, particularly the wealthy, maintained and slaughtered cattle and other livestock at their homes, despite the presence of markets and vendors. Our interpretation of this through the years went from "possibly" to "probably"; we eventually dropped qualifiers altogether.

The final surprise is that artifacts, especially animal remains, indicate people lived and worked anywhere and everywhere. Wealthy homes and middling ones, commercial sites and residential sites, public venues and private homes—we expected clear-cut differences, definable archaeological signatures of site function. This was never the case. Instead, we have a composite archaeological signature of a vibrant, densely packed landscape, where the lives of people and animals were conducted in close proximity, where social distance did not equate to physical distance, and where multiple activities occurred on the same property.

Our Archaeological Approach

We have chosen to tell the story of Charleston through the lens of foodways and animals. We focus more on the work-yard side of the fence than on the residential side in our discussion of the urban environment; it was in the work yard that people and animals carried on the chores of daily life and interacted most intensely. We broadly describe sites excavated within the city and nearby rural locations and what we have learned from them about urban life, following a generally chronological framework. Our discussion of artifacts is limited to those related to foodways and dining, trade networks, and the urban environment; entire classes of objects are absent from this discussion.[3]

Urban archaeology is the study of material remains of daily living, human behavior, and human perceptions in urban settings.[4] European colonial proprietors encouraged the development of urban centers for protection, community, and commerce; towns played a pivotal role in the development of American life. Urban archaeologists, therefore, study cities,

Figure 1.2. Aerial view of Charleston, facing southwest. Features of the urban environment include dense buildings, small yards, and low-lying lots. (Historic American Buildings Survey [HABS] photograph, 1992, Library of Congress.)

not just people within cities. We use the perspectives of urban archaeology to explore these relationships of daily life and human activity in Charleston. Our focus is on three broad, intertwined topics: the evolution of the urban environment, provisioning the city, and urban foodways and cuisine.

We first consider the evolving urban environment as land modified for human occupation and used as a shared space, growing to serve a community.[5] Urban centers are greatly magnified examples of environmental modifications, and animal remains elaborate upon these modifications. The early-eighteenth-century city resembled small farms clustered inside a protective wall. The late-nineteenth-century city was a mass of multistory buildings, outbuildings, passageways, and small enclosed yards. Yet the two perspectives were more similar to each other than either is to the city of today. The urban environment can be understood only in reference to the greater lowcountry, so environmental information, historical documentation, and selected archaeological sites from rural settings elaborate upon the local resources available to residents of Charleston. Animals and the keeping of animals substantially modified both the rural and the urban environments. Our perspective on Charleston is of an environment shared with animals, of animals contributing in many ways to lowcountry life, and of animals connecting people in Charleston with the lowcountry and beyond.[6]

Combining environmental and archaeological discoveries enables us to explore the ways the city was provisioned. We examine the sources of wild and domestic animals, the local production and importation of food and fuel, transportation of goods to market, distribution to consumers, and social connections that facilitated economic exchange. We also explore the production, distribution, and consumption of goods and services linking the city with its rural neighbors and global markets. External trade routes and imported goods are part of this story, and the merger of local and global provisions is characteristic of the earliest Carolina deposits. Charleston may have been on the frontier, but it was never isolated.[7]

The animal remains recovered from both urban and rural sites tell us about our third topic: urban foodways and cuisine and the unique way in which people took advantage of the bountiful coast. Our study of urban cuisine incorporates all of the artifacts we recover, not just the animal remains. We examine the full range of objects retrieved from our excavations, from fragments of bottle glass to entire houses, from this perspective.

Food is essential to life. Its production, distribution, and consumption form the core of cultural identity and social communication. Animals used as food serve an inherently nutritional role. However, food choices are cultural behavior. Both animals and food have political, social, ritual, and cosmological meanings beyond nutrition. Animals, especially animals used for food, often are used to characterize people, behaviors, and nations favorably or unfavorably regardless of their nutritional value. Foods are used routinely to organize daily activities and define social relationships. The symbolism of the traditional Thanksgiving dinner in the United States, for example, clearly outweighs its nutritional consequences. Though interpreting such symbolic meanings from archaeological remains is difficult, we cannot ignore the social meaning of biological organisms.[8]

We distinguish among nutrition, menus, diet, and cuisine. Nutrition is a measure of the physiological adequacy of foods (including beverages) in terms of fundamental biological requirements for growth, repair, and reproduction. We have basic nutritional requirements, but these can be met in many ways. Menus are the lists of food items available, whether or not they are known to be edible or are used. Diets consist of the food and beverages consumed. Many different choices are made about how foods are procured, distributed, prepared, and served. The results of these choices constitute culturally distinctive foodways and cuisines.[9]

Foodways are formed by the cultural, social, and economic choices involved as nutrition is mediated through diets. Diets distinguish the resources that are preferred from among the many resources available, ranking them from simply edible to highly desirable items that confer prestige upon the consumer. Different foodways may use the same menu items but prepare them in different ways. Opportunities for change are often mediated by a general dietary conservatism, the desire to eat what is familiar and comforting. Foodways and eating habits are influenced by local environmental conditions, by the interactions of different ethnic groups, and by regional, national, and global changes in the production and marketing of food and food-related items.[10]

The term *cuisine* has many meanings. As used here, cuisines are defined by combinations of foods; the manner of preparation; the style of cooking; the social rules governing when, how, and by whom they are prepared and eaten; the accoutrements and ambiance of dining, proper dress, and service; and the circumstances under which food consumption occurs. The social circumstances of cuisine include all of the objects used in food rituals, ranging from snacks to tea ceremonies, formal state dinners, and even ritual sacrifices. Cuisines link many of the ceramic, metal, and glass objects recovered from Charleston's archaeological sites directly to the animal remains recovered from those same contexts. Our archaeological study focuses on the dining and cooking environment and the material accoutrements of those activities. We are not able to propose, or test, the quality and quantity of foods consumed. Nor can we identify the ingredients or recipes that are popularly considered "cuisine," though we use historic recipes to interpret the combinations of ingredients and other resources recovered archaeologically.

Relationships among status, wealth, and food are complex. Age, religious beliefs, gender, ethnic affiliation, authority, and power are communicated through foods consumed or avoided. Anthropologists are always concerned about applying their own cultural biases and stereotypes to the interpretation of animal remains deposited by other cultures. Although tongue might have been the ideal component of a high-status dish in Charleston at one time, for example, it may not symbolize high status to many urbanites today.

Foods and nutrition rarely are linked in consumers' minds. Most of us drink sweetened, caffeinated beverages that we do not consider food,

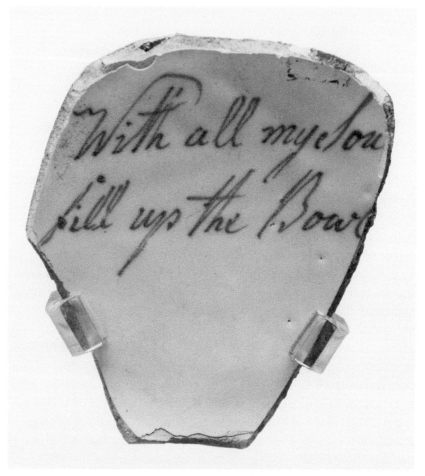

Figure 1.3. Base of a delft punch bowl from the Exchange Building. Punch bowls reflect the celebratory, rather than the nutritional, aspects of communal drinking. (Collections of The Charleston Museum, Charleston, South Carolina.)

regardless of the caloric content. These beverages play important social roles unrelated to nutrition. Likewise, meat has value beyond nutrition. The meat should be tasty, juicy, tender, and have a high fat content. It is not difficult to see that the greater value attached to filet mignon over chicken is not based on nutrition. Michael Jochim suggests that high-prestige meats are obtained from large animals not common locally or the acquisition of which involves high cost or risk. The nutritional value of meat may have little to do with the actual price per pound. Resources that are more costly because they are hard to obtain, have higher prices, require more time, or are more risky in some way often are more prestigious. High-cost foods such as gourmet coffee or caviar may have little to recommend them nutritionally, but they may have high symbolic value because they are rare or expensive. Of course, there are some foods that are rare but not highly valued, and hence not costly. The relationship between market price and a cut of meat is often a social one.[11]

Political, Ethnic, and Geographic Terminology

The focus of this volume is Charleston, in South Carolina. Charleston was founded and occupied within a complex ecological, cultural, and political landscape that changed identity over the centuries. At the risk of oversimplifying complex social dynamics, we place sites and people into the human landscape with reference to the most prominent European claimant for each site: Spain, Great Britain, or France. This broader perspective is necessary because of the diverse sources of goods and people contributing to Charleston's identity.

The major players were the Spanish Empire, or entities that were part of that empire (e.g., the Philippines, the Netherlands, Germany, northern Africa, New Spain, the Canary and Caribbean islands, South America), Great Britain (a union of England, Wales, Ireland, and Scotland formalized in 1707), and France. Many of the sites discussed here were occupied before the United States formed, but each site is referenced by its present geopolitical affiliation. Charles Town is described as being in South Carolina, and St. Augustine in Florida.[12]

The Carolina colony, named in honor of Charles II of England, was founded as a proprietorship in 1663 and became a royal colony in 1719. Carolina was divided into North Carolina and South Carolina provinces in 1729, when the crown bought out all but one of the proprietors. Charleston was originally known as Charles Town and was founded a few miles inland from the Atlantic coast. In 1680 Charles Town was moved downstream to its present location. The town was renamed Charleston in 1783, at the end of the Revolutionary War. To distinguish between the earliest evidence of colonization in South Carolina and later developments, we refer to the first settlement as Charles Town (presently Charles Towne Landing State Historic Site). We use the name Charleston consistently for the second location, regardless of whether it was known officially as Charles Town or Charleston. We refer to the dominant political authority throughout the town's pre-Revolutionary War history as British.

Each colonial population and each site's occupants were much more diverse than the political affiliations imply. Individuals in each colony may have originated in Europe, in Africa, or in colonies claimed by another European power, either directly or indirectly. Some colonists originated at outposts in Spanish, British, and French colonies in the Americas, or elsewhere in the emerging global network. The national boundaries of European colonial powers were themselves in a state of flux. Regional differences existed within each of the "homelands" of the dominant political powers as their present borders and identities developed.[13]

The ethnic affiliation of a site's occupants does not always correspond with the identity of the prevailing political body. Africans were part of the colonial mix from the earliest days, often as slaves, but also as free people of color engaged in the colonial enterprise. Some Africans may have come directly from Africa, others indirectly from other colonial settings. Native Americans, free and enslaved, from across the greater Southeast were associated with Spanish, British, and French colonies. Colonists and Native Americans interacted over a much larger area than our focus, of course. The presence of people from many different parts of the world is likely one of the principal explanations for the flexible and eclectic use of a wide array of indigenous and introduced resources seen in the archaeological record.[14]

All of the sites in this study lie within 20 miles of the Atlantic Ocean or the Gulf of Mexico, in an area known as the Southeast or the southeastern coastal plain. Spanish Florida included the northern Gulf of Mexico, peninsular Florida, the Georgia coast, and the Carolina coast, from the 1500s into the 1700s. British and French authorities claimed much of this same area. Although political boundaries were fluid, they were characterized by a steady retreat of Spanish interests in the face of advancing British ones after the 1670s, French ones after the 1680s, and American ones after 1776.[15]

Organization of This Study

Although our research focus has shifted through the years, our study of Charleston is always cumulative. Old site reports are consulted and old collections are reexamined. Small projects conducted in the early 1980s as well as large-scale explorations of the city's market and the city wall conducted in the early 2000s are merged into an evolving interpretation of Charleston's past through the lens of the archaeological record. Each new site produces information that is added to the existing baseline study, either supporting or changing the prevailing interpretation. After each project a report is prepared (appendix 1). From these studies, we conclude that the city *is* the site. All of the individual properties, whether residential, commercial, or public, are components of this large urban site and linked on a regional scale to rural sites. Charleston's archaeological record is that of a city set within the Carolina lowcountry.[16]

Major political events do not fit easily into the archaeological record, and it is rarely possible to match specific events with specific archaeological deposits. Thus, the time periods used to organize this volume are more general. Like the archaeological records of each site, the city's record is subdivided temporally based on stratigraphy, artifacts, specific site events, and general trends in Charleston's history. For our study, Charleston proveniences and their materials are grouped into six broad time periods, five of which have archaeological assemblages sufficient in scope for reliable analysis. Assignment of specific sites and components of sites to individual time periods reflects the integrity of the sites' stratigraphy, the types of materials recovered, the architectural and documentary record, and the location in the city. Many of the phenomena we study cannot be restricted to a specific event or a single time period.

The time periods for Charleston span the decades from about 1670 through 1900. Archaeological insights into the first decade of the colony (1670–1680), before the town moved to its present location, are limited. The second period (about 1680–1710), and the earliest one for which archaeological evidence is available from Charleston's present location, corresponds to the city's role as a frontier outpost and emerging port city. Archaeological evidence for this period is extremely rare and often indistinguishable from the third time period (about 1710–1750). This third period has a more robust archaeological presence and is associated with economic stability and physical growth of the city and region. The fourth period (1750–1820) encompasses the city's years as a leading seaport and center of wealth. The antebellum era (about 1820 to the 1850s) is the fifth period of study, prior to the political and economic watershed of the Civil War. The sixth period (about 1850–1900) corresponds with the postbellum era, as the city experienced economic stagnation, social upheaval, and physical decline following the Civil War. These periods also correspond to changes in technology and the materials recovered archaeologically.

All of the sites in this volume have been continuously occupied and used from their initial occupation until the present, though the dates of first occupation are variable. All of the sites, therefore, are multicomponent, and most can be subdivided into discrete temporal, physical, and functional components. Details of the excavations and histories of most of the sites are provided in the chapter that corresponds to each site's earliest, or most germane, association. The primary interpretations of topics directly related to animals are discussed where they seem most appropriate, though their relevance is clearly not confined to that specific chapter. We trace the evidence for animal husbandry and butchering strategies in chapter 8, for example, because these are closely linked to townhouse life of the 1750s–1820s, but animal husbandry also informs other time periods and aspects of Charleston's landscape. Many of the sites are revisited in subsequent chapters when pertinent to our three research topics. By the end of the story, we discuss all of the sites in the context of the urban environment, cuisines, and provisioning the city.

Quantification of thousands of fragments, rather than interpretation of individual objects, is the fundamental source of our understanding of city life, and the basis for the themes discussed in these pages. A varied, but finite, range of artifacts is recovered from these sites. We find many of the same types of artifacts—green bottle glass, hand-wrought nails, cooking pottery, teacups—at every site. Artifacts are identified by type and quantified by type and group. Some of the many common artifacts are described in this volume, but our focus is on those related to our exploration of animal use.

In addition to the thousands of common artifacts, there are a few that are rarely preserved or discarded, or are unusually illustrative of past events. Archaeological collections from the city include thousands of fragments of colono ware, for example, but only two fragments of sea grass baskets. Among the thousands of fragments of green glass wine bottles, only a few are embellished with sealed initials that allow us to identify the owner. Such rare materials provide unusual views into daily affairs, and these are highlighted.

John Rutledge's oyster roast may have scandalized his mother, but his menu speaks volumes. It touches on the evolving urban environment, the merger of resources from lowcountry woods and waters, the novel foodways and cuisines created by people living in North American colonies, and the global network that provisioned the growing city of Charleston. Archaeology allows us to study urban life through the discards of daily life, and our work has revealed a great deal about Charleston's evolution from a fledgling frontier outpost to a modern city.

I

THE SETTING

2

URBAN ARCHAEOLOGY IN THE HISTORIC CITY OF CHARLESTON

"Why are these bones in here?" So ask many young students in The Charleston Museum's archaeology programs, as they sort through a representative sample of archaeological artifacts. "Because they are the most interesting things we find" is the reply.

Archaeological methods, artifacts, and environmental materials all offer important insights into the evolution of urban landscapes and cities as sites. Archaeological stratigraphy, the layer cake of deposits on each site, is the key to documenting physical and social changes. Artifacts contribute to studies of consumerism, refinement, social stratification, and ideology. They are used to explore trade and international relations, cultural diversity, and social identity. Environmental materials help us understand modifications to the land, diets, and cuisines. Archaeological evidence for the production, distribution, and consumption of goods and services links the city with its rural neighbors and global markets. The "facts" of history are dynamic rather than stable—and may not be facts at all, but edited realities constructed for political or economic purposes. It is often difficult to identify and interpret "symbolic" history using archaeological evidence, but excavation of historic sites is imperative in order to test accounts offered by the written record.

Charleston's Early Archaeology

Archaeology in Charleston is little more than a half century old. Professional archaeology in the city began in the 1960s with excavations by John Miller, a Charleston Museum research associate. Of particular significance was Miller's excavation in the colonial Exchange, at the foot of Broad Street.

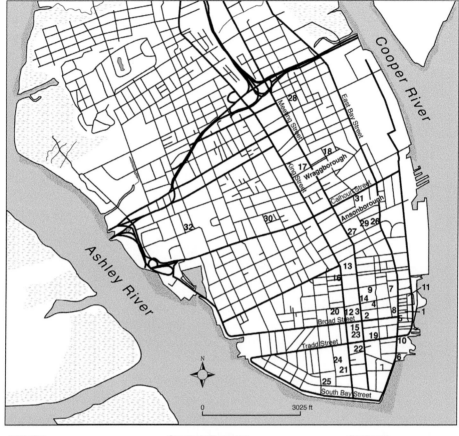

Public Sites

1 Atlantic Wharf
2 Beef Market/City Hall
3 Charleston County Courthouse
4 Dock Street Theatre
5 Exchange Building/Half Moon Battery
6 Granville Bastion/Missroon House
7 Lodge Alley/State Street
8 McCrady's Tavern and Longroom
9 Powder Magazine
10 South Adger's Wharf/Lower Market
11 Vendue/Prioleau

Commercial/Residential

12 Charleston Judicial Center
13 Charleston Place
14 First Trident
15 Hollings Center
16 Saks Building
17 Visitor Reception and Transportation Center

Residences

18 Aiken-Rhett House
19 Heyward-Washington House
20 John Rutledge House
21 Miles Brewton House
22 Nathaniel Russell House
23 Post Office/Courthouse
24 Simmons-Edwards House
25 William Gibbes House
26 Juliana Dupre House
27 Hieronymous-Roper House
28 Jackson House
29 Kohne-Leslie House
30 Sanders House
31 Gaillard Auditorium
32 President Street/MUSC

Figure 2.1. Map of Charleston, South Carolina, showing sites discussed. (Prepared by Susan Duser.)

Figure 2.2. Dr. Elaine Herold mapping features encountered behind 33 Broad Street, 1978. (Collections of The Charleston Museum, Charleston, South Carolina.)

Miller dug in the Exchange Building's basement, sponsored by administrator C. Harrington Bissell. Miller passed away shortly after this excavation, and the artifacts languished on sawhorse tables for decades.

Elaine Herold, an archaeologist trained in prehistory at the University of Chicago, moved to Charleston in 1973 with her husband, the new director of The Charleston Museum. Herold turned her attention to the Museum's Heyward-Washington House. She excavated there on a volunteer basis for four years, producing an impressive array of artifacts and features, including some from two occupations predating the 1772 house. The Heyward-Washington House assemblage remains the largest in the Museum's collections. Dr. Herold also conducted important excavations at the Exchange Building and at sites on Broad Street and Meeting Street.

Work in Charleston proceeded apace with the rest of the United States. Philadelphia witnessed the first National Park Service excavations of an urban site in the 1960s. By the 1970s many archaeologists advocated studying cities systematically. Bert Salwen of New York University suggested that cities "deserve more attention since they were the loci of more human activity." As the largest, and one of the earliest, cities on the East Coast of the United States, New York was the site of path-breaking projects, both in size and scope. Roy Dickens of Georgia State University excavated large

samples from Atlanta, Georgia, for the Metropolitan Atlanta Rapid Transit
Authority (MARTA) project and produced the first edited volume on urban archaeology. Salwen and Dickens were among the first to propose that
individual sites were part of a single urban site and to argue that research
should focus on the process of urbanization. Pamela Cressey and her colleagues responded by developing a long-term, citywide research plan for
Alexandria, Virginia. After a decade of conducting individual digs, Herold
proposed a similar plan for Charleston in 1981.[1]

In the late 1970s and early 1980s, Charleston experienced extensive urban renewal under Mayor Joseph P. Riley Jr. Many of these projects received
federal funding, which required archaeological mitigation. Projects along
the Meeting Street corridor produced small assemblages from complex
sites. The largest project was associated with construction of the Charleston Place hotel complex, which impacted an entire city block. Charleston
Place was the first major archaeological contract project in the city guided
by a series of formal research questions. Monitoring and salvage by The
Charleston Museum followed the controlled excavations by Nicholas Honerkamp of the University of Tennessee–Chattanooga.[2]

A Citywide Research Perspective

In 1981 the City of Charleston provided funds to The Charleston Museum
to produce a citywide research plan. With additional funds from federal
Survey and Planning Grants administered by the South Carolina Department of Archives and History, this two-year survey was based on maps and
documents rather than archaeological digging. We examined social variability of urban residents, the material world and economy of Charleston,
and the physical formation of the urban archaeological record. We suggested that the entire city was an archaeological site. It appeared likely that
all projects, no matter how small, could contribute to thematic research.
Urban animal use and contrasts between rural and urban sites were included in the overall research plan.[3]

"How did these artifacts get here?" This is a question visitors often ask.
It is also a question we ask ourselves every day. Understanding the processes by which sites form is fundamental to archaeological interpretations. Michael Schiffer divides the processes that transform materials from
a living context into an archaeological context into two categories: normal
and abandonment. Each process produces a slightly different assemblage.
Discard is the most common normal process. Deposits created by discard

are dominated by household trash, most of it building debris and artifacts related to food preparation, service, and storage. Sometimes discarded materials are found in clusters next to the main structure on the property, and sometimes they are scattered about the property in a casual form of discard. Losing or hiding objects is another normal discard process, though it is likely that whoever hid the objects intended to retrieve them at some point. Lost or hidden finds are usually small, found in out-of-the-way places: in drains, beneath floors, or in small pits at the back of the property. Abandonment occurs when materials, some of which may still be usable, are discarded after a disaster such as a fire or storm or when a building is remodeled. Such deposits contain objects that normally last a lifetime and seldom would be discarded under normal circumstances. Abandoned objects are often single artifacts such as scissors or swords or clusters of related objects, such as the contents of a medicine chest.[4]

The type of deposit encountered often depends on where archaeologists excavate. Early historical archaeological studies focused on buildings, exposing brick foundations or stains left by wooden posts. Charles Fairbanks was the first historical archaeologist to advocate moving away from buildings into the "back yard," where most trash-producing activities likely occurred. Archaeological refuse from the foundations of townhouses is often different from that found in and around kitchens, stables, and outbuildings. Accurately interpreting a site requires excavating as many of these different types of activity areas as possible.

Site function was another early focus of historical archaeology. Stanley South proposed grouping artifacts from British colonial sites by their household function. South divided artifacts into eight categories that he argued encompassed the normal range of daily human activities. South emphasized the importance of quantifying archaeological remains and using the patterns formed to compare sites across time and space. In Charleston definitions of artifact types and groups are constantly revised, but each study begins by organizing Charleston's collections into functional categories for direct comparison. By combining studies of functional artifact categories with site formation processes, we should be able to see evidence of socioeconomic status and ethnicity among urban residents in architectural elements, material possessions, and animal remains. We also should be able to distinguish between commercial or craft enterprises and residential activities. At least we should be able to do so in theory.[5]

Charleston's dependence on a plantation economy formed the basis for research into differences between the urban and rural lives of people of all social and ethnic classes. Research initiated in 1987 concentrated on issues relating to Black residents, especially in areas of the city settled during the nineteenth century and occupied by an ethnically diverse population. Charleston had a large African American population, both free and enslaved. The lives of Africans in the city, particularly those who were enslaved, were very different from the urban lives of free white residents. Likewise, urban slavery differed in some respects from slavery on plantations. Charleston also housed a small, but significant, population of free blacks for much of the city's history. We anticipated differences between wealthy white residents living in the city and those living in the country, just as the lives of urban slaves differed from those of plantation slaves. The archaeological survey used documents to identify sites occupied by African Americans, and sites where the tools of archaeology could define an archaeological signature for an African American presence.[6]

Interdisciplinary Archaeology in Charleston

The citywide research design was first implemented through a series of small-scale projects in the early 1980s (see appendix 1 for a list of site reports). These focused on nineteenth-century sites along Charleston's commercial corridor. The sites were complex, characterized by combinations of commercial and residential functions, and subject to frequent changes in occupants and activities. Dense concentrations of materials crossed modern property lines, reflecting mixtures of people and activities. Each project was limited to a few test excavations, but these deep sites offered a solid record of urban life. The complexity of these sites mirrored the complexity and congestion of the city, with different activities involving many different people. This meant we could not conduct traditional household studies, which rely on linking individuals or groups whose identities were known with specific materials they had used. We had to think beyond individual property owners and beyond the idea that residential, commercial, and public life were physically separate activities.

In the late 1980s research moved from these multifunction sites to more strictly residential properties throughout the city. Whether large, upperclass townhouses or more moderate single houses, these residential sites were somewhat more straightforward than the multifunction sites. They permitted the assumption that most, if not all, of the refuse recovered was generated by people living at each site and engaged in the activities of daily life. Still, the sites were complex, the shared homes of wealthy and enslaved, black and white, with people, animals, and activities crammed into constricted work spaces.

The first residential projects were at historic house museums, with urban archaeology contributing directly to public interpretation. The established interdisciplinary team of field archaeologists, zooarchaeologists, ethnobotanists, and historians of the early 1980s expanded to include architectural historians, garden historians, palynologists, landscape architects, material culture specialists, and interpreters.

Historic Charleston Foundation and The Charleston Museum led the way in many of these projects, engaging teams of architectural historians to examine extant buildings and produce a detailed analysis of historic structures. A few civic-minded homeowners engaged the same teams to answer questions of past use and style during renovation projects on their private properties. Although the specific areas investigated by archaeologists were largely determined by the property owners' goals, communication among the scholars permitted simultaneous study of issues pertinent to the archaeologists. We excavated next to houses to determine the age and history of the structures, but we also explored work yards and gardens.

Excavations at homes built in the eighteenth and nineteenth centuries by wealthy Charlestonians contributed to our understanding of the city's urban landscape. This was a cultural landscape, land modified according to a set of cultural plans with technological, social, and ideological dimensions. Russell Handsman suggests that creating the urban landscape involved deliberate actions "guided by aesthetics" and accidental actions guided by "the circumstances of ordinary urban life." This landscape approach considered the physical terrain, architectural developments, health and sanitation, and ideology. As animals were actors in all of these arenas, merging studies of animals with studies of other archaeological materials was an obvious choice. Our research on urban life focused on buildings and the spaces between buildings. Much of what we have learned about Charleston is from gardens, work yards, streets, passageways, and public spaces.[7]

Since 2000 our attention has turned to the first decades of the British-sponsored settlement, largely in the late seventeenth century and first decades of the eighteenth century. Thus far, no deposits or sites from the late seventeenth century have been encountered in the city. Our knowledge of these first decades is obtained from partnering with scholars working on nearby seventeenth-century sites. In Charleston we focused on colonial markets and the iconic feature of the early city: the brick seawall. This work returned us to the subject of the first below-ground study in Charleston, the

Granville Bastion and old city wall, conducted in 1929 by architects Albert Simons and Samuel Lapham.

Urban Archaeology

The archaeological record is an independent source of information that augments, expands, and amends interpretations of Charleston and life in it offered by other sources. This applies equally to specific issues on particular properties and to broader historical subjects. Archaeological evidence, as well as architecture, probate inventories, plats, oral histories, photographs, and paint layers, is an important source for interpreting daily life in Charleston.

Archaeological evidence can be divided into three categories: material culture, biological remains, and stratigraphy. Material culture includes all of the cultural items recovered from a site. These are principally objects discarded or abandoned by people who used them. Archaeologists study these artifacts to make broad interpretations of people's lives. Yet a visit to The Charleston Museum reminds us that archaeologists recover only a small portion of the objects used by people in the past. Instead of a coat or a doll, we may find buttons or a small porcelain foot. Some types of material culture are under-represented (e.g., furniture, tools), and others generally are not represented at all (e.g., paintings, baskets).

The other categories of archaeological evidence are seldom displayed in museums. To some, biological remains are the least glamorous evidence, but these are artifacts of human behavior that speak as directly to daily life in Charleston as do pipe stems and goblets. Plant pollen, seeds, and phytoliths (silica particles contained in some plant tissues) recovered from sediments and soils tell us about gardening, fertilization, refuse disposal, animal husbandry, forest cover, wetlands, erosion, and environmental changes. Among the biological remains, those from animals are of particular interest in our own study of Charleston.

Cultural artifacts and biological materials, and the events they represent, are primarily dated and interpreted by their association in the ground. Archaeological sites are deep, dense, and complex. Sediments and soils build up on sites through deliberate actions and inadvertent activities; they reflect the lives of the plants, animals, and people who lived there.

Archaeological sites, the artifacts they contain, and the events they reflect are dated by two basic principles: the law of stratigraphy and *terminus post quem* (time after which). *Stratigraphy* refers to the soils and sediments

Figure 2.3. Soil profile from the interior of the ca. 1749 stable at the Heyward-Washington House. The deepest layer is the humus of the original grade. Above that is a layer of ash from the fire of 1740, followed by soils that accumulated in the 1740s–1750s. A posthole and mold (*left*) and well construction pit (*right*) cut through the layers of soil. (Collections of The Charleston Museum, Charleston, South Carolina.)

that develop or accumulate on a site as people live and work there. Over time, soils and sediments form layers, termed strata. Today, we walk on the current archaeological layer, our soda straws and gum wrappers creating a new archaeological component that will eventually be buried by the same processes that buried the evidence of earlier activities. These layers are keys to determining construction and remodeling sequences for buildings, dating events such as fires, and observing modifications to the urban landscape. The sequence of these layers, the site's stratigraphy, is interpreted using the geological principle that the deepest deposits are the earliest ones. Basically, archaeologists work their way back through time as they excavate deeper and deeper. On urban sites, where people and activities are packed into constricted spaces, these layers and the artifacts they contain often are very deep and may not be neatly organized in chronological order with one layer on top of another.

"Where is the colonial grade or living surface?" is a common question put to archaeologists, particularly by restoration architects. If archaeological layers accumulate over time, why aren't the windows of eighteenth-century houses buried? Where did the first colonist actually stand? Although archaeologists work by defining and dating each layer as it is exposed during excavation, the actual creation of sites is not so simple. We define early layers by subtle differences in color and texture, as well as by the absence of materials found in the later layers. People living and working on a site often impacted deeper, earlier levels, leaving nineteenth-century artifacts mixed in with eighteenth-century ones. What we define as the "top" of a 1760s layer may actually be the surviving bottom of the 1760 layer. Sites also are filled; dirt and debris can be added to a property to increase elevation and promote good drainage. This is common today. Layers of fill mask the original topography and grade. The most common answer to the question "Where is the colonial grade?" is usually "I'm not sure."

The second basic principle is *terminus post quem* (TPQ), which dates each deposit by the artifacts found in it. The TPQ is established by the manufacture date or construction date of the most recent object found in the provenience. None of the levels and associated artifacts can be earlier than the newest, most recent artifact in that deposit. The dates of manufacture are known for many objects recovered from historic sites, and these known dates are used to calculate date of deposition. A deposit containing a sherd (fragment) of transfer-printed pearlware, a ceramic style first manufactured in 1795, was last disturbed no earlier than 1795, though it may have been disturbed more recently.

Archaeological field methods maintain control over the stratigraphy and artifacts in them so that objects from each time period or behavior are separate. Archaeologists largely do this by excavating very carefully, so that changes in stratigraphy and artifacts are noticed promptly. These changes are interpreted in terms of when they occurred, where they occurred, and why they occurred. Archaeologists take pride in the precision with which they can do this, dividing the site into a series of standardized excavation units and maintaining straight, vertical walls and a level, flat floor while excavating. The goal is to avoid mixing material from one context, which represents one event, with that of other contexts and other events. Archaeologists use the term *provenience* to refer to specific contexts from which an object is recovered. Proveniences may be grouped by time period, location, function, social status, ethnicity, or other attributes.

Archaeologists organize their excavation units in order to control the proveniences from which artifacts are recovered by establishing a grid, which controls where units are placed. Although many archaeologists use the metric system to standardize the placement and excavation of their units, those working on British colonial sites often use British standard

Figure 2.4. Excavation units at the Simmons-Edwards House. Three 5×5-foot squares have been excavated; a fourth is being excavated; and adjoining units outlined with string await excavation. (Collections of The Charleston Museum, Charleston, South Carolina.)

measurements, because most of the sites were built according to those standards. The basic excavation unit in Charleston measures 5 × 5 feet, though tight spaces and other aspects of some sites require units of other dimensions. Regardless of their shape, units are generally referred to as *squares*. A single square may be excavated at a site, or a series of adjoining squares may be excavated in a large-scale recovery project. Because urban sites are deep, and full of materials, excavation is time-consuming and costly. A five-foot square can take days to excavate; thus, many sites have been tested with only one or two units.

Archaeologists also manage the recovery of artifacts and other information by passing the excavated dirt through a meshed screen and retaining the artifacts left there. A standard screen size ensures that materials recovered from multiple sites are directly comparable. In Charleston, as at most historic sites, dirt is screened through ¼-inch mesh screens. Occasionally, organically rich deposits are screened through finer mesh, but materials from such deposits must be analyzed separately. Screening is accomplished by shaking the dirt through the screen (dry screening) or running water through materials that accumulate in the screen (water or wet screening).

Screening also ensures that all artifacts are collected, not just those that are colorful, complete, or "interesting." Although this volume is filled with images of the "most interesting" and "most complete" objects, these images represent thousands of less photogenic examples. In the screen, all artifacts are equal.

Archaeologists divide excavated deposits into two broad types, zones and features. Zones are stratigraphic layers that build up gradually, usually through inadvertent activity; they often extend across large areas of the site, onto adjacent properties, or even across the entire city. Zones contain artifacts that accumulate in them over time. Features have distinct physical boundaries and form through specific activities; they may represent a single event. Features often are filled within a relatively short time, and all of the artifacts in them may have been used, lost, or discarded at the same time. An abandoned well would be classified as a feature.

Archaeologists distinguish between primary and secondary deposits, and these may be treated differently during excavation. Objects in primary deposits are those that have not been moved since they were placed there by the people who originally used them. A scatter of pipe stems near a hearth may be evidence of someone smoking by the fire. Other deposits are secondary, places where refuse was discarded after being moved there from another location. An animal may be butchered in a work yard, with

Figure 2.5. A screen full of artifacts, typical of Charleston sites, includes bricks, oyster shells, bottle glass fragments, ceramics, nails, and animal bones. (Collections of The Charleston Museum, Charleston, South Carolina.)

some portions of the butchered animal then dumped into the harbor and other portions discarded along the back of the property. Materials may be moved several times. Most urban archaeological deposits are secondary.

Once a date of deposition is determined for each provenience, the proveniences are grouped by time period. Sometimes dates of archaeological deposits are corroborated by events described in the documentary record. A 1794 coin recovered from an ash layer at the Beef Market corresponds with the 1796 fire that destroyed the market. Mid-eighteenth-century artifacts in a distinct debris-filled layer at the waterfront correlate with the great hurricane of 1752. Ordinarily, however, links between the site's history and artifacts recovered are more difficult to establish. Most deposits are assigned broad dates, such as our 1750–1820 time period. The goal is to interpret the site and its place in the life of the city as precisely as possible, consistent with the evidence recovered.

How do archaeologists know when to stop digging? Typically they stop when all of the artifact-bearing layers have been excavated, when they reach a culturally sterile level. Sterile deposits no longer contain bricks, nails, and fragments of glass. In Charleston culturally sterile levels are usually a yellow to tan sand or clay-sand. More often than not, Charleston excavations cannot reach a sterile level, because the water table is encountered before the lowest level of the site is reached. This water can be temporarily removed by pumping, but it is difficult to maintain control over context in damp deposits. Sea level has been rising since Charleston was founded, plaguing city residents as well as archaeologists.

Careful excavations of urban sites, no matter their size and complexity, are essential for sound interpretations. Individual proveniences must be isolated and excavated separately following the site's stratigraphy. The archaeological record, contained within the stratified layers of the site and defined by the associated artifacts, is part of the total historic fabric, worthy in its own right of preservation. The archaeological component is a nonrenewable resource, damaged or destroyed by any ground-disturbing activity, whether that is constructing a swimming pool, stabilizing a foundation, restoring a historic garden, or excavating the archaeological record.

Often there is not enough time, or money, to conduct a controlled excavation in advance of construction or some other disturbance. Archaeologists may be called to "monitor" a construction project, watching the construction activity and stopping the bulldozer when large, or unexpected, archaeological materials are uncovered. These materials usually must be retrieved hastily, with the result that the collection is not complete and is therefore biased. Diligent citizens may notice artifacts on the ground or in dirt piles and bring these to archaeologists. Without context the mundane and common materials no longer tell their full story. Unusual items may be important for their own sake, however, and expand our knowledge of city life, despite their compromised proveniences.

Zooarchaeology

Much of our study of Charleston draws upon what is called zooarchaeology. Zooarchaeologists examine relationships between people and animals, with particular emphasis on the ways environments, animals, and people influence one another. Animals provide many goods and services, and some occupy prominent places in our lives. Animal remains are often studied for information about diets and economic strategies, but animals play much larger roles in human society. The role of animals in the evolving urban landscape is particularly interesting. Some animals contributed to the poor health and poor sanitation in the city, while others controlled the accumulating garbage. Although many serve important functions, such as enhancing soil productivity or as roving garbage disposals, most are ignored by people. Often only domestic animals or pests get our attention. Nonetheless, even animals that we do not think have economic value may offer important environmental and cultural insights into urban life. Some animals had significant economic value as commodities in provisioning the city and in international trade networks. In some cases the symbolic role of animals in the social lives of human communities and cultural relationships is a compelling part of the story.

It is generally assumed that most of what we want to know about animals introduced during colonization can be learned from written records. Studies of animal remains from archaeological sites, however, expand our understanding of animals and their interactions with people, often contradicting perceived wisdom in important ways. This is particularly the case for Charleston, where the study of animal remains is part of long-term, interdisciplinary research. This long-term perspective and recovery of information from many different types of sites provides details of animals in the city that we would not have known if the work were more limited in scope or duration.

Zooarchaeologists primarily study nonhuman vertebrates (e.g., fishes, amphibians, reptiles, birds, mammals) and the hard tissues of mollusks (e.g., oysters), crustaceans (e.g., crabs), and echinoderms (e.g., sea urchins).

In Charleston we generally focus on vertebrates. Oysters were, and are, important ingredients in lowcountry cuisine as well as in lowcountry architecture. In many cases it is not possible to distinguish oysters used to line garden paths or make mortar from those discarded after an oyster roast; many oysters were used for both.

Although the abundance of oyster shells in Charleston makes excavations challenging, the shells are one of the reasons we enjoy such good bone preservation. As oyster shells decompose, they change the surrounding soil to a more alkaline environment, enabling animal bones and teeth to survive. Lime mortar, composed principally of burned oyster shells, does the same thing. Where oyster shells are rare or lacking, bone is rare or in poor condition. Unfortunately, the very conditions that enhance bone preservation retard the preservation of many plant remains.

The first step in a zooarchaeological study is careful excavation and identification of animal remains from each site. After excavation these remains are washed and sent for further study to zooarchaeology laboratories such as the one at the Georgia Museum of Natural History. There, researchers begin by trying to attribute each fragment to a specific animal by making frequent use of comparative skeletons and publications. Following identification, specimens are counted and weighed to determine how many teeth and bones of each animal were recovered.[8]

Quantification makes intersite comparisons easier and more objective. One approach estimates the number of different types of animals, or taxa (singular: *taxon*), present in a context. Another approach to quantification estimates the Minimum Number of Individuals (MNI) in each collection. This estimate is based on the number of individuals of each species that would be necessary to explain the types of specimens recovered. Two left scapulae of a cow, for example, would imply that portions of two cows were present in that context. The goal is to determine which animals were present at the site and in what proportions. Occasionally estimates are made of the amount of meat (biomass) each animal might have contributed. This is distinct from the number of individuals, in that this estimate does not presume that an entire animal (an individual) was consumed at the site.

Along with identifications, other observations are recorded. Remains of some animals are measured to provide estimates of size. It may be possible to determine whether pigs, cattle, or other animals became larger in Charleston between the mid-1600s and the late 1800s. An increase in size might be due to improved husbandry techniques. The types of bones and teeth recovered make it possible to consider how animals were butchered and who purchased which portions, or to ask whether animals were slaughtered on site instead of purchased from markets or vendors. Small cuts on bones may be evidence that a knife was used in butchering; a straight line across the shaft of a bone may indicate the use of a saw; and irregular, deep nicks suggest a cleaver. Some bones and teeth provide information about the age of animals when they died. From this we can learn whether animals were slaughtered after long lives as draft or dairy animals, or if they were slaughtered at a young age, when the meat was tender and the hide bore fewer scars. If we find that mostly young animals were killed, it is probable that animals were raised specifically for meat. Evidence of gnawing by rodents or dogs tells us that the bones were left exposed to scavengers; an absence of these gnawing marks suggests they were discarded quickly into a trash pit where scavengers could not reach them. All of these choices have significant implications for sanitation and health in the city.

Archaeology of a City

Consistent use of standard archaeological methods to recover and study Charleston's archaeological record enables us to consider the evolution of the city from its inception to the end of the nineteenth century. We have studied many facets of Charleston's evolving landscape, cuisine, and trade networks with neighbors as well as with global trading partners. We have been surprised at the results; these surprises are elaborated upon in the remainder of this volume.

3

THE BOUNTIFUL COAST

"These parts being very well furnished . . . in the Season, [with] good Plenty of Fowl, as Curleus, Gulls, Gannets, and Pellicans, besides Duck and Mallard Geese, Swans, Teal, Widgeons, etc.," so wrote John Lawson from Bulls Island in 1700. Lawson set forth by canoe from Charleston on December 28 on a journey through the Carolinas, in the company of "six English-men, with three Indian men and one woman, wife to our Indian guide." Along the way, he filled his journal with descriptions of animals encountered on his journey.

An early stop was Bulls Island, 20 miles up the Atlantic Coast. "We . . . came Safe into a Creek that is joining to the north end of Bulls Island. . . . On the morrow we went and visited the Easternmost side of this Island, it joining to the Ocean. . . . At our return to our Quarters the Indians had killed two more deer, two wild Hogs, and three Raccoons, all very lean except the Raccoons. We had great Store of Oysters, Conks, and Clamps, a Large sort of Cockles." Lawson's observation of the woods and waters of the lowcountry are mirrored in Charleston's archaeological record.[1]

Colonists in the late seventeenth century encountered a bountiful land, one teeming with fish, game, and other resources. Salt marshes, estuarine waters, coastal islands, pine forests, and freshwater hardwood swamps characterize the Atlantic coastal plain upon which Charleston was built. The rivers traversing the area formed natural harbors and transportation routes. Settlers immediately fanned out from the first settlement, Charles Town, following the Ashley and other river drainages to take advantage of the land's bounty.

The bounty of the lowcountry soon attracted attention in Britain, with artists and naturalists dispatched to record and collect specimens from the region. John Lawson was one of these. He traveled from Charleston to North Carolina in 1700 and wrote comprehensive descriptions of the plants, animals, and people he encountered. Mark Catesby spent the years 1722–25 in Charleston, sending specimens and art to Hans Sloan and other patrons in Britain. Others followed their examples. Specimens collected from the Carolina colony formed core collections at the newly founded British Museum in the mid-1700s. When William Bartram traveled from Charleston to East Florida in the late eighteenth century, the vast tracts of wilderness and diversity of habitats, plants, and animals were still a source of wonder. Bartram also described Native Americans, some of whom still lived on the coast.

Many visitors and residents were impressed with Carolina's resources. Richard Porcher notes that the state supports "some 3,160 species of native and naturalized vascular plants" as well as indigenous and introduced crops and livestock. South Carolina's location between the semitropical and mid-Atlantic climate zones and its wide range of physiographic regions are responsible for this diversity.[2]

Climate and Geography

South Carolina's climate is humid subtropical, with hot summers averaging 80°F and mild winters averaging 44°F, with some below-freezing temperatures. The state averages 49 inches of precipitation annually.[3]

The Carolina lowcountry is part of a low, flat coastal plain of well-drained, gently rolling hills and poorly drained flatwoods that stretches along the eastern Atlantic seaboard. In South Carolina, the coastal plain extends east and south of the Fall Line or Fall Zone, a line of old dunes marking a former shoreline. Although the area is relatively stable tectonically, it did experience a major earthquake in 1886. Three major coastal rivers, the Pee Dee, Santee, and Savannah, originate in the Appalachian Mountains, whereas the Edisto (Pon Pon) River begins at the Fall Line and the Ashley and Cooper Rivers originate on the coastal plain itself. Even during the colonial period, the inner coastal plain was distinguished from the outer, or lower, with most colonial and plantation enterprises located on the latter. The inner coastal plain has elevations about 220–300 feet above mean sea level, whereas the lower coastal plain is relatively flat and low-lying. Many swamps, ponds, lakes, and sluggish, meandering streams traverse the lower coastal plain.

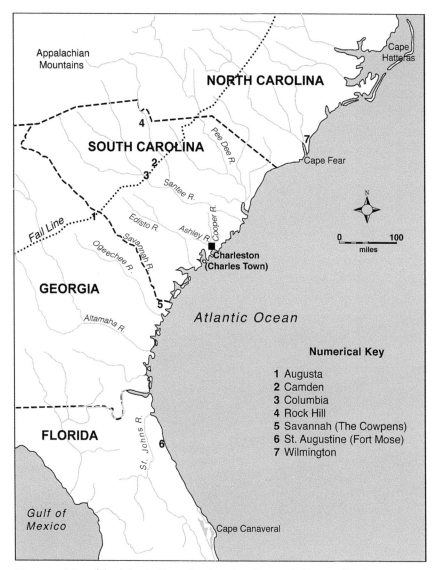

Figure 3.1. Map of the Atlantic Coast showing sites discussed. (Prepared by Susan Duser.)

Rivers of the coastal plain are influenced by daily tides for approximately 10 miles before reaching the sea. This tidewater zone is protected from the Atlantic by a series of barrier, or sea, islands. Marsh islands lie between the barrier islands and the mainland. These islands are important features of the coastline. In the coastal zone fresh waters become increasingly brackish as mainland streams mix with Atlantic waters. This mixture forms estuaries consisting of complex salt marshes and tidal creeks. Freshwater streams may rise and fall in response to tidal influence even though the water itself remains fresh. These streams become increasingly brackish and eventually form the upper reaches of estuaries. The lower reaches are farther from the mainland and experience higher salinities, conditions that extend a short distance offshore. Botanists further distinguish the outermost portion of the coastal zone as the maritime strand, an area of vegetation influenced by "wind-borne salt spray and/or water with significant concentrations of salt."[4] This coastal zone is part of a large embayment known as the Georgia Bight, extending from Cape Fear to Cape Canaveral.

The Plants

The fire-dependent longleaf pine community once dominated the coastal plain but is now largely gone. Today, common plant species on well-drained soils include other types of pines, as well as some longleaf pines, several species of oaks, and a diverse herbaceous understory (appendix 3). Pine savannas are dominated by grasses and canes. On poorly drained soils,

Figure 3.2. Longleaf pine forest in the Francis Marion National Forest in 1930. (Courtesy USDA Forest Service, Francis Marion National Forest.)

known as the pine–saw palmetto flatwoods, trees are primarily longleaf and slash pines, with a dense subcanopy of American hollies, cabbage palmettos, Hercules' clubs, redbays, and saw palmettos. In more open areas, eastern redcedars, wax myrtles, and yaupons are common. Pond pines dominate where the soil is especially poorly drained. These plants are adapted to a humid subtropical climate of mild winters, hot summers, high rainfall, and frequent ground fires.[5]

Hardwood communities flourish along freshwater creeks, in swamps, and in low, fertile areas near the coast. Trees in these communities include cabbage palmettos, hickories, laurel oaks, live oaks, loblolly bays, magnolias, and sweetgums. Bald cypresses, red maples, and water tupelos are common in swamps. The low-lying, swampy forests of the lowcountry feature dense understories of switchcanes or river canes, in addition to other grasses and vines.

Cane is a native bamboo with straight, hollow stems and bunches of narrow leaves. The giant cane of South Carolina could be as high as 30 feet and "grow so close together, there is no penetrating them." Both the giant cane and the smaller switchcane were common on the edges of savannas, along streams and rivers, and in other damp places. Canebrakes were favored foraging grounds for deer and other wild animals. In the historic period they also were favored by cattle and hogs. Burning canebrakes encouraged new growth and improved grazing. Lawson notes that cane "grows in Branches and low Ground . . . their leaves endure the Winter, in which Season our Cattle eat them greedily."[6]

Both Porcher and Mart Stewart note that switchcane did not grow as high or as thick along the Atlantic Coast as it did on the Gulf Coast. Nonetheless, the smaller stands of the lowcountry were valuable for livestock feed. European and African herders, like Native Americans before them, used fire to "green up" the stands and expose fresh growth. Cattle favored the canebrakes year-round, but particularly in summer and winter they headed into the dense "cane swamps" for cover and food.[7]

Lowcountry residents of all backgrounds took advantage of the bounty of the lands and waters of the coastal plain. Mature forests produced nuts in the fall, including acorns, chinquapins, beech nuts, black walnuts, and hickory nuts. In summer, blackberries and blueberries could be gathered from the undergrowth, and saw-palmetto berries were ripe in the fall. Fruits from bayberries, blackgums, cabbage palmettos, grapes, hackberries, mulberries, passionflowers or maypops, persimmons, sumacs, and wild plums and cherries were additional seasonal treats. Edible roots and

Figure 3.3. Switchcane understory at Elmwood in the Francis Marion National Forest. (Photograph by Olga Maria Caballero, courtesy USDA Forest Service, Francis Marion National Forest.)

tubers included greenbriers, groundnuts, and wild onions and garlics. Canarygrasses, fuzzybeans, goosefoots, knotweeds, and pigweeds yielded starchy seeds. Bearsfoots and sunflowers provided oily seeds. Greens, such as pokeweeds and purslanes, were widely available.

Native Americans had hunted, fished, and farmed in the lowcountry for centuries before European-sponsored colonization began. They used many of these same plants and also cultivated corn or maize, beans, and squashes. Maize, beans, and most of the squashes were domesticated elsewhere in the Americas and introduced into the lowcountry long before European colonization. Europeans were particularly attracted to the "old fields" of Native Americans, because these fields were in favorable locations and required little or no work to prepare for planting.

People create and maintain an additional terrestrial plant community: the disturbed habitats of yards, garden plots, garbage dumps, fence rows, cultivated fields, and fallow lands. Early cattle herds and foraging pigs made major changes to the landscape, as did rice cultivation. Swamps were subdivided, ditched, and diked for rice production. Remnants of these banks and ditches still transect lowcountry swamps. Some of these disturbed habitat plants are propagated by humans, and others may be encouraged for easy access to their edible fruits, seeds, and leaves. These include blackberries, goosefoots, knotweeds, passionflowers, pigweeds, purslanes, and wild beans. Some may not have been intentionally planted by colonists but were used nonetheless. Other plants, often termed weeds, voluntarily take advantage of open ground. Some barren-ground colonizers, such as cockleburs, goosegrasses, and spurges, are considered nuisances.

Settlers grew a wide range of fruits and vegetables on the coast, including maize, beans, and squashes originally grown by Native Americans in the lowcountry. They also introduced exotic plants from across the globe. These included okras, peanuts, peas, peppers, and tomatoes. Peanuts, peppers, and tomatoes were domesticated in the tropical Americas, whereas okras and peas were brought from the Old World. Traditional European grains, such as barley and wheat, did not flourish in the lowcountry, but maize did and became the principal grain.

The primary commercial crops grown by colonists were all introduced from elsewhere. These included cotton, indigo, and rice. Upland cotton, the most widely cultivated cotton crop in the United States today, is of South American origin. Sea Island cotton, originally domesticated in the Andes, was brought to the United States from the West Indies in 1785 and was an important crop on barrier islands.

A few decades after the Carolina colony's founding, the environmental and economic success of rice transformed this grain into the foundation of the lowcountry cuisine and its economic prosperity. Rice, originally an Asian crop, was first grown on upland fields, but farmers noticed that it grew better in moister conditions. African slaves working as cattle hunters were already familiar with the bottomland swamps and canebrakes, because cattle and hogs preferred this habitat in the winter. By 1712 rice was grown in flooded rice fields, a practice familiar to many African workers.

Porcher and Judd divide the history of rice cultivation into three phases. The first, called "providence" by Porcher, involved casual, experimental planting on dry ground, relying on rainfall. Porcher notes that the most successful sites were "low moist grounds," so the crop was not truly upland. The "inland swamp" method emerged in the first decades of the eighteenth century. Inland swamp production required a reliable source of water to flood fields and water the crop, which in turn required systems for managing the water. Fields were situated in low, rich, inland swamps and usually depended on rainwater trapped in a reservoir by an earthen dam, the key feature of "reservoir culture." The third phase, "tidal culture," developed in the late eighteenth century and used the natural influence of tides on lowcountry freshwater rivers to irrigate rice fields created by damming and banking streams and swamps. Both reservoir and tidal culture relied on banks and ditches, as well as simple, yet ingenious, trunks (wood culverts with gates) to control the flow of water. All three methods required detailed knowledge of river systems and wetlands where rice was grown.[8]

The rice fields, both inland and tidal, followed a variety of ecological paths after rice production declined in the mid-1800s. Tidal rice fields revert to swamp forest as old field banks erode. Farther upstream, where tidal flow is weak or river levels reduced, a dense mature swamp forest occupies acres of abandoned rice fields. Fields that are still in succession feature trees such as immature bald cypresses, red maples, sweetgums, and swamp tupelos. Where rice field banks are maintained, smartweeds and widgeongrasses grow in the abandoned fields. Such areas are attractive to waterfowl as well as other aquatic animals.

The Animals

South Carolina today supports 70 species of freshwater fishes, 160 species of salt-water fishes, 17 species of turtles, and an astounding variety of birds.

Only those that make an appearance in Charleston's archaeological record are reviewed here. With the exception of the introduced domestic and commensal animals, all of the animals found in Charleston archaeological deposits were used by Native Americans in the lowcountry long before European-sponsored colonization began. Native American farmers, hunters, and gatherers managed the land and waters to encourage game for centuries. They burned forests to reduce undergrowth and encourage preferred plants, thereby creating openings known as savannas. Many of the animals encouraged by these efforts were important sources of raw materials such as hides, feathers, fur, grease, and bone, as well as ingredients in both Native American and Charleston cuisines.[9]

The region's bounty was quickly noted. Writing home from Charleston in 1686, Huguenot Jean Boyd described the flavor of "bear and tigers (wildcat), as well as stags and wild turkeys." He also listed "quantities of ducks, teal, wild geese, woodcocks, two or three types of snipe, sea larks and cormorant," as well as "very good rabbits and hares, and squirrels."

Figure 3.4. Fire burning in longleaf pine forest. Fire was an important tool in clearing forests and improving forage for livestock. Longleaf pine seedlings are fire-resistant. (Courtesy USDA Forest Service, Francis Marion National Forest.)

Boyd reports that "found . . . but a little higher up were wolves, wildcats, leopards, tigers, bears, foxes, raccoons, badgers, otters, beavers and a type of black and white cat which for its only defense pisses on people who pursue it."[10]

Many animals that became part of the lowcountry cuisine are found in salt marshes, tidal creeks, and wetlands. Opossums and raccoons are small, omnivorous, primarily nocturnal mammals found in a variety of habitats. Both forage in coastal marshes, though they commonly raid henhouses, gardens, and garbage cans. Raccoons were considered nourishing and easily obtained, though they were not universally appreciated. Opossums were hunted or captured in traps or nets. If captured alive, they could be "cleaned out" by feeding for several days on milk, bread, and potatoes. Rabbits are vegetarians that feed at dawn and dusk, usually in low-lying damp areas and hedgerows. They commonly raid gardens. Cottontails prefer wooded and open high areas, whereas marsh rabbits are characteristic of marshes and floodplains. Squirrels are active diurnal feeders. Gray squirrels are common in hardwood forests and urban areas, whereas fox squirrels prefer more open conditions, frequently feeding near fields. White-tailed deer feed in forest-edge settings, gardens, orchards, and fields, though occasionally they feed in salt marshes. They are most active at dawn and dusk. The abundance of deer was used as evidence for the bounty of the land by early British settlers in New England, though overhunting for the deerskin trade seriously diminished deer populations by the eighteenth century.[11]

Other animals found in Charleston's archaeological sites reside in or near aquatic habitats and provide valuable furs in addition to food. Beavers are the largest rodents in South Carolina, and the tail is considered a delicacy by many. Otters are the primary mammal found in aquatic environments. These animals were hunted almost to extinction for their soft, thick pelts. Bears yield fur, grease, and meat. Additional fur-bearing animals include woodrats, muskrats, foxes, skunks, minks, mountain lions, and bobcats. Lawson ate many of these animals during his travels, finding most acceptable.[12]

Many birds are featured in the lowcountry cuisine. Herons, ducks, and rails are almost exclusively aquatic. Many wild ducks prefer freshwater marshes, lakes, and estuaries, and some were likely common in flooded rice fields. Canada geese are particularly common in Charleston collections. Hawks, vultures, quails, plovers, sandpipers, gulls, terns, passenger pigeons, and mourning doves also are found in archaeological deposits.

Many of these birds raid gardens and forage in fields. Some also feed on garbage and carrion.

Turkeys are a North American bird, and wild turkeys are common in the southeastern United States, including the lowcountry. Genetic evidence suggests that modern domestic turkeys are related to a subspecies known as the South Mexican turkey, domesticated in Mexico about 800–1200 BC, and it is possible that some turkeys in the American Southwest were domestic as well. After 1492, domestic turkeys were introduced to Europe and quickly spread throughout that continent. They subsequently were reintroduced into North America as domestic animals. Domestic turkeys might have been brought to Charleston from Mexico, from flocks left behind on formerly Spanish Caribbean islands as these became British, or from Europe.[13]

It is difficult to determine whether turkeys recovered from Charleston's archaeological sites are local wild turkeys or domestic birds introduced by colonists. Show standards for turkeys were established by the mid-1800s in North America. In 1851, at the first annual exhibition of poultry held in Charleston, exhibitors showed birds described as "white and wild turkeys." Diseases such as blackhead probably restricted efforts to maintain large numbers of domestic turkeys until the twentieth century, though both tame and domestic populations might have been prevalent in Charleston and on neighboring plantations.[14]

Canada geese pose similar problems. Wild populations are found throughout much of North America. Canada geese were probably non-nesting winter residents in the lowcountry in the past. Today, flocks of these geese graze on lowcountry lawns, golf courses, and fields near water throughout the year. They are particularly attracted to old rice fields but also feed in brackish coastal waters. Show standards for Canada geese also were established by the mid-1800s in North America. The large number of Canada geese in the Charleston archaeological record suggests year-round populations, perhaps sustained by the rice fields and supplemented by other reliable sources of food. Today many are habituated to the human presence, though it seems likely that wild birds in and around Charleston once were more wary, given the extent to which they were consumed.

Mallards also may be wild, tame, or domestic birds. Wild mallards are widespread in temperate eastern North America as well as in Europe and Asia. Wild mallards are winter residents in the lowcountry, where they frequent old rice fields, swamps, and tidal rivers. Many of the domestic duck breeds originated from mallard populations in Europe and Asia, including the all-white Pekin duck. These domestic white mallards were introduced from Europe to North America during the colonial era.[15]

Turkeys, Canada geese, and mallards are examples of how difficult it is to distinguish between wild and domestic forms when both occur in the same place. The presence of bones from juvenile birds and the size of adult bones sometimes aid in distinguishing between them. Large numbers of juvenile individuals are considered indirect evidence that a breeding population was present, suggesting the population was domestic. Domestic chickens, for example, are represented in Charleston collections by large numbers of the porous bones of young birds. Most of the Charleston turkey and Canada goose bones are the well-formed bones characteristic of adult birds, suggesting most of these birds were wild adults.

Another indication of domestication is a change in the ratio between the length and width of bones from the wing or the leg. As a general rule, domestic birds are larger than their wild counterparts and have shorter, stockier bones. Measurements of turkeys and Canada geese in Charleston archaeological collections do not change over time, and all appear to be similar in size and shape to those of wild birds. It seems likely that in the 1600s and 1700s, Charleston's turkeys, Canada geese, and mallards were primarily wild, but that by the mid-1800s some were at least tame if not fully domestic birds.

Wild turkeys, Canada geese, and mallards may have flourished in habitats created or modified by people without becoming dependent upon people, establishing local resident populations if food was adequate. These birds could have been hunted or trapped in the usual way; others may have been captured and pinioned to keep them nearby, either on plantations or in the city. Pinioning involves removing the large primary feathers from the wing, along with the underlying bone. This leaves the bird unable to fly. Pinioned birds do not need to be penned and can range freely, though they are vulnerable to predators. Such local wild birds probably coexisted in the barnyard with fully domestic birds, perhaps interbreeding with them. Eventually they were replaced by domestic breeds.[16]

Passenger pigeons were formerly widespread throughout the temperate zone of eastern North America and abundant as winter residents in South Carolina. They formed large flocks that were easily hunted. Lawson describes them as breaking stout limbs when they roosted; he also describes Indians "bringing away thousands." Overhunting and deforestation contributed to their demise. Their numbers declined steadily during the early

Figure 3.5. Articulated passenger pigeon skeleton prepared by Charleston Museum curator Gabriel Manigault in 1876. (Photo by Sean Money, Collections of The Charleston Museum, Charleston, South Carolina.)

1800s, and the last known passenger pigeon died in captivity in 1914. The few passenger pigeons found in nineteenth-century Charleston deposits may have been among the last of these birds in the lowcountry.[17]

Reptiles are the most diverse class of animals in terms of habits and habitat preferences. Sea turtles feed in estuaries and nest on the seaward side of the sea islands during the summer. Snapping turtles, musk turtles,

Figure 3.6. Articulated yellow-bellied slider skeleton. Prepared by curator Gabriel Manigault in the 1880s. (Photo by Sean Money, Collections of The Charleston Museum, Charleston, South Carolina.)

pond turtles, and softshell turtles are common in freshwater, and some are found in estuarine waters. Most pond turtles are aquatic; many are known as basking turtles, because they sun themselves on logs, rocks, and banks overhanging or adjacent to water. They quickly fall into the water when startled, a habit that leaves them vulnerable to traps set under favored sunning spots. Diamondback terrapins are pond turtles that prefer estuarine waters. Box turtles are small, semiterrestrial members of this family but primarily are found in open woodlands near quiet bodies of water. Alligators frequent fresh and estuarine waters and seaward beaches. During nesting season all of these reptiles may be found on land as they seek places to lay their eggs.[18]

Fresh and coastal waters teemed with fishes. Common along beaches and in the lower reaches of estuaries, rays are found in a variety of salinity conditions. Gars are primarily freshwater carnivores, though longnose gars are sometimes observed in estuarine waters. Gars are air-breathers and linger just below the water's surface in order to quickly breathe at intervals.

They form large schools and are often captured in nets and trawls. They are considered pests by fishermen. Their lack of commercial value is a relatively recent phenomenon, because they were widely consumed in Charleston into the mid-1800s.

Sea catfishes are very common in estuaries. The hardhead catfish is more common than the larger gafftopsail and tolerates a greater range of salinities. Sea catfishes are present inshore year-round, though most leave for deeper waters during cold weather. These are bottom-feeding scavengers, but they may rise to the surface at night to feed. They are easy to catch and attracted to garbage thrown into the harbor. Both were widely consumed in Charleston, despite today's often-held notion that they are poisonous.

Other fishes are widespread in coastal estuaries and prominent in the lowcountry cuisine. Adult sea basses prefer deeper waters, but juvenile black sea basses are common in estuarine sounds and rivers. Sheepsheads are found around jetties, wharfs, and pilings. Their large front teeth enable them to scrape barnacles and other shellfish from pilings. Members of the drum family often are the most common fishes in Charleston collections. Drums include seatrouts, kingfishes, and Atlantic croakers. The two largest are black drums and red drums. Small black drums are present year-round. Red drums spawn in coastal waters near shore and are present inshore year-round. Schools of mullets circulate in mid-channels of larger creeks and bays. Large roe, or striped, mullets make spawning runs along beaches in the fall. Mullets are easily taken with nets but rarely rise to a hook. Flounders are uniquely adapted to life on the bottom of coastal and estuarine waters. They may be taken by net or line but more frequently are taken by gigging. A host of other inshore fishes were less frequently used, such as bluefishes. Bluefishes are seasonal migrants that enter Charleston's estuary during spring and fall migrations but are more abundant offshore.

Freshwaters support a number of fish species. In addition to sturgeons and gars, freshwater fishes include bowfins, suckers, freshwater catfishes, perches, and sunfishes. These inhabit creeks and rivers, and some prefer swamps, flooded rice fields, and drainage ditches. Some are found occasionally in estuaries.

A few of the fishes found occasionally in Charleston collections may not be from local waters. These possibly exotic fishes include groupers, snappers, grunts, and scups. Some of these fishes might be taken locally, from locations farther north or south of Charleston, or from offshore. The parrotfish and queen triggerfish specimens recovered are almost certainly not local fishes. Both fishes are found over tropical reefs, and the few bones recovered from Charleston were probably brought to the city as curios.

Some animals were newly arrived colonists. Prior to the colonial era, dogs were the only widespread domestic animals in North America. Colonists added cats, horses, pigs, cattle, goats, sheep, and chickens to the list. Donkeys and mules likely were brought to the colony, though it is difficult to distinguish among horses, donkeys, and mules from the very few archaeological fragments recovered from Charleston. It also is difficult to distinguish between goats and sheep using archaeological fragments, and these closely related animals frequently are referred to by the subfamily name, Caprinae, anglicized to caprine. These introduced animals can substantially alter local environments. In particular, the feeding behavior of pigs and cows alters plant communities and the animals that live in them, with significant impacts on rural as well as urban landscapes.

Many of the pigs in lowcountry assemblages were probably either feral or free-ranging animals hunted rather than raised in the traditional domestic sense.

> The real American hog is what is termed the wood hog; they are long in the leg, narrow on the back, short in the body, flat on the sides, with a long snout, very rough in their hair, in make more like the fish called a perch than anything I can describe. You may as well think of stopping a crow as those hogs. They will go to a distance from a fence, take a run, and leap through the rails three or four feet from the ground, turning themselves sidewise. These hogs suffer such hardships as no other animal could endure.[19]

Although this description seems unlikely, wild hogs were known as resourceful, dangerous, nocturnal, and gregarious animals. Pigs gain weight rapidly and have a high reproductive rate. These animals prefer moist bottomlands, where they feed on seeds, roots, fruits, nuts, mushrooms, snakes, larvae, worms, eggs, carrion, mice, and small mammals. Pigs frequently raid fields and gardens. Confining pigs to keep them out of gardens can be a challenge. Sixteenth-century reports that listed wild swine as native to the land were probably reporting feral animals, the progeny of pigs that had escaped during earlier exploration and colonization efforts.[20]

In many respects, pigs are ideal urban livestock. They eat table scraps and other refuse and, prior to municipal trash collection, were essentially roving garbage disposals. As such they likely made a positive contribution to urban sanitation and public health, even as they detracted from sanitation and health in other respects. City statutes against "the suffering of Hogs to run about the street" and complaints to the grand jury on this topic are common throughout the eighteenth century, suggesting that pigs were common and disruptive components of the urban landscape. Residents of upper-status sites may have raised pigs as an inexpensive way to feed large households consisting of people of diverse status. Pigs likely remained in the city until an 1837 city ordinance prohibited keeping hogs within the city limits; households in the Charleston Neck were not governed by this law until after 1849.[21]

It is likely that many large households had at least a milk cow in the work yard. Milk cows require the presence of offspring to encourage them to let down the milk, so it is likely that both a cow and her calf lived in many yards. Females provided not only dairy products but fertilizer for the gardens; and oxen provided labor. In the days before refrigeration and mechanized transportation, being able to slaughter livestock near the point of consumption was an important consideration.

Early free-ranging cattle were tough, resourceful, and adapted to hot, humid environments where pasturage was scarce and low in nutrients. Cattle initially had some difficulty adapting to the lowcountry but eventually flourished. Carolina colonists considered the cattle of Spanish Florida superior to British cattle. Complaints that British colonists and their Native American allies stole Spanish cattle from seventeenth-century Spanish Florida were common. The reported superiority of Spanish cattle was not simply hyperbole. Archaeological evidence indicates that cattle from Spanish Florida were larger than cattle in Charleston, though about half the size of their probable Spanish Caribbean ancestors. Free-ranging cattle also raided fields and gardens. Their management was a challenge to Native American farmers unaccustomed to building corrals or fencing fields. This was a constant source of tension between Native Americans and colonists in the Southeast.[22]

Sheep and goats were not as successful in the lowcountry. Colonists in Spanish Florida disliked sheep, because they did not defend themselves against wild dogs and wolves and did not reproduce freely. British colonists probably experienced the same problems. As the preferred animal husbandry technique was to turn animals loose, these were obvious drawbacks. These deficiencies were compounded by biological constraints; male sheep are sterile for about a year after being transferred from a temperate to a tropical setting and do not breed well thereafter. Goats fared better than sheep, because they could defend themselves against carnivores.[23]

Some of the introduced mammals were small. These included European domestic rabbits and South American guinea pigs. Rabbits were raised in Europe for fur and meat and may have served such purposes in Charleston. Guinea pigs were domesticated in the South American Andes about 2500 BC. They were present in the Caribbean by AD 500 and widespread by the fifteenth century. Native Americans in South America and the Caribbean raised guinea pigs primarily as food, but these animals also served ritual and social roles. In his 1526 report on the natural history of the West Indies, Gonzalo F. de Oviedo reported that the islanders ate guinea pigs, which were "very pretty." It is likely that some were taken to Spain about this time, along with turkeys and Muscovy ducks. Guinea pigs reached England by 1574–75. Although it is possible that guinea pigs were consumed in Charleston, the individual identified from an 1820–50 level in the privy at the Heyward-Washington House more likely represents the social role of guinea pigs: that of an exotic pet. The guinea pig demonstrates the broad reach of Charleston's trade routes and direct or indirect ties with Spanish or formerly Spanish colonies, possibly in the Caribbean or perhaps reaching into South America itself.[24]

Muscovy ducks are also domestic birds in Charleston. Wild populations of Muscovy ducks range from southern Mexico to Peru and Argentina, though they originally were domesticated in tropical South America. When the colonial era began, domesticated Muscovy ducks quickly became widespread in the Antilles and elsewhere. They were described by the Italian ornithologist Ulysses Aldrovandus in 1522 and reached England as early as 1550. The Charleston birds could be from Europe rather than from a Spanish or formerly Spanish territory in the Americas. Their presence in Charleston, however, may be additional evidence of ties between Spanish and British America.[25]

Chickens are often cited as animals that should be common in colonial contexts; however, predators took a heavy toll. For protection, free-ranging chickens roost well above the ground and nest in out-of-the-way places. Such behaviors do not facilitate catching chickens for dinner or collecting their eggs. It is possible that chickens are under-represented in zooarchaeological collections if eggs were the primary product, but it is more likely that eggs and chickens were seldom used. Without year-round lighting, most hens lay eggs only in the summer, when daylight is plentiful. Chickens can be kept close by feeding them table scraps; Spaniards fed them shellfish.[26]

Common or rock pigeons are domestic birds introduced from Europe. In many parts of their modern range, formerly domestic pigeons have reverted to a feral state and are considered pests. Although probably native to the Mediterranean, wild or feral birds are widespread in Europe, northern Africa, southern Asia, and the Americas. Wild pigeons roost on cliffs and rock ledges; feral populations use buildings, monuments, and statues instead. In their original range, they may have been commensal wild animals attracted to farms and fields by crops and stored grain. They are known for good flavor (as squabs) and for their homing abilities. Some varieties serve as carrier and racing pigeons. They also are raised as pets for their fancy plumage.[27]

A group of animals is classified in this study as commensal. Commensal animals pose a considerable interpretive problem, because the same animal could fill any number of roles in different cultural traditions. Dogs and horses exemplify the importance of cultural perspectives in determining whether an animal is or is not consumed and the multiple roles animals can play under different circumstances. The term *commensal* specifically refers to "a relationship between two species in which one population is benefited but the other is not affected." For the sake of simplicity, the term is used here to refer to many different roles, not all of them benign or mutually exclusive. Some ethnic traditions would have considered any or all of the animals classified as commensal here as edible or important for other reasons. Almost all of the Charleston "commensals" are considered inedible, or at least famine foods, by most Charlestonians today. This includes dogs, cats, horses, mules, and donkeys. Many of the animals we consider noncommensal wild members of the lowcountry cuisine might have been commensal. Likewise, some animals classified as commensal may have been part of the early lowcountry cuisine and subsequently dropped from the menu.[28]

Some commensal animals are attracted to human-built environments because they offer easy food, safer hiding or nesting places, a more open canopy, or fewer competitors. Commensals, and their prey, may live quiet and unnoticed lives. Others are more visible as they scavenge in refuse heaps, raid crops and henhouses, or infest stored foods. Some cause a great deal of damage to crops and stored goods; others are vectors for disease. When they die, or are killed as vermin, their remains may become part of the archaeological record, requiring archaeologists to determine what their roles in the city might have been. Such animals offer important insights into evolving urban environments.

Chief among the commensal animals were house mice, Norway rats, and black rats. These rodents joined indigenous rodents such as deer mice and Hispid cotton rats. Norway and black rats came to this hemisphere with Christopher Columbus and are present in sixteenth-century St. Augustine deposits as well as in 1670 Charles Town deposits.[29]

Commensals also include other small rodents; owls; perching or song-birds such as crows, bluejays, bobolinks, bluebirds, robins, and cardinals; snakes; frogs; and toads. Songbirds may have been caged birds or wild birds living in the city. Some small birds, such as bobolinks, also known as rice birds, were once part of the colonial cuisine.[30]

Opossums, rabbits, squirrels, and raccoons could have been commensal animals as well, as they live in American cities today. All are familiar to urbanites as pesky raiders of gardens and trash cans. They are also part of the lowcountry cuisine, even today. The single opossum bone recovered from an 1820–50 deposit in a formal garden could be from a random scavenger; but this specimen was found along with the remains of pigs, cows, chickens, turkeys, sea turtles, and fish, remains that otherwise appear to be food refuse discarded in the garden. Thus, the specimen is interpreted as food debris because of its context and known role in the lowcountry diet. Many domestic animals filled similarly ambiguous roles. As the discussion of Canada geese, turkeys, and mallards demonstrates, it is difficult to be confident that some of the animals recovered from Charleston sites were domestic at all. Some probably were feral animals living beyond human ownership, such as dogs, cats, and common pigeons. Common pigeons are interpreted as domestic because colonists introduced them to the region, though at some point individual birds joined the ranks of urban wildlife.

Commensal and noncommensal categories are not mutually exclusive. Most, if not all, of the animals interpreted as commensal could have been consumed, and animals considered wild members of the Charleston cuisine could have been commensal instead of cuisine. If these "wild" animals were not consumed, but simply part of the urban wildlife, they would enlarge the ranks of the wild community in the city even further. Either way, they must be considered in studies of urban foodways and landscapes.

Setting the Stage

The Carolina lowcounty was a bountiful land teeming with fish, game, and other resources. Colonists quickly developed an economy and a cuisine that relied on this bounty. In many instances this new strategy was very similar to that practiced for many years by Native Americans; but colonists expanded upon the local offerings with provisions from around the world. In so doing, colonists modified both the rural and the urban environments and drew upon multiple sources to create a new cultural tradition that was the outcome of dynamic exchanges, reformations, and inventions.

4

DEVELOPMENT OF CHARLESTON AND THE LOWCOUNTRY

Two vistas defined Charleston. First is the harbor, the city's doorway to the transatlantic world. Harbor and city met at the brick wharf wall and the wharves projecting into the Cooper River. Ships loaded with goods, both plain and exotic, and foods, both plain and exotic, rode anchor in the harbor or docked at the wharves, waiting for their cargos to be transported to merchants' shops clustered along the Bay. The second, and broader, vista of the hinterland stretched inland through a maze of marsh, swamp, and flat woodlands. Rivers run finger-like through the landscape, offering a bounty of foods and resources, both wild and cultivated. These wide, flat floodplains and their meandering rivers are known as the lowcountry.[1]

Charleston was forged within the opportunities and hazards of the broader geopolitical conflict that engaged France, Spain, and England and defined much of Carolina's early history. From the Spanish perspective, the lands that became Carolina and Georgia were theirs. British colonists were invaders, and British traders were unwelcome competitors in the Indian trade. Occasionally, tensions between Spain and Britain resulted in actual battles. The extent to which colonists took advantage of the opportunities and prepared against the hazards is very clear in the archaeological record. It is probably not an accident that Charleston was Britain's only walled city in North America and that Spain built the formidable Castillo de San Marcos in St. Augustine. Equally clear is Charleston's rapid transformation into a regional and global center of commerce as Spanish and French threats receded.

Before Charles Town

A permanent European presence was established in the region in 1565, when Spain founded St. Augustine, in what is now Florida in the United States. A second town, Santa Elena, was settled on Parris Island, in Port Royal Sound, in 1566. Santa Elena was the capital of Spanish Florida until 1587. Between 1565 and 1763, Spanish towns, missions, cattle ranches, presidios, and roads were built and abandoned between Parris Island and St. Augustine and westward across northern Florida into Apalachee Province.

Much of the history of domestic animals along the Atlantic and Gulf coasts likely is linked to these Spanish outposts and trade networks. The introduction of livestock often was intentional, sometimes in advance of European settlements. Spanish and French efforts to explore and settle the Atlantic seaboard included livestock, beginning with Juan Ponce de León's 1513 exploration of the Florida peninsula. Some of these animals escaped or otherwise survived. The wild swine observed in 1562 near the St. Johns River, Florida, likely were survivors of one of these expeditions. Cattle ranches flourished in portions of Spanish Florida, particularly in Apalachee Province and between that province and St. Augustine, in the seventeenth century.[2]

France also had colonial ambitions. A 1562 French fort on Parris Island was abandoned before Spain established Santa Elena there, but this was not the only French settlement on the Atlantic seaboard. French colonists primarily spread down the Mississippi River Valley, claiming much of the northern coast of the Gulf of Mexico. By 1702 France had established Old Mobile on the northern Gulf Coast. From these western settlements France competed for the same territory and Indian trade claimed by Spain and England.[3]

British colonization of North America began with the founding of Jamestown in 1607, but it was not until Charles Town was founded in 1670 that interaction with Native Americans intensified in the lowcountry. British merchants competed with Spanish interests for furs and deerskins. Colonists also claimed Native lands. By the early eighteenth century, the British trade network extended throughout the Southeast and was a driving force in the region's economy. Some British traders, and their livestock, lived in Indian communities.

Competition to dominate this trade was intense among Spanish, French, and British traders and their Native American allies. The region was the scene of persistent warfare. Over decades, Spain was forced to abandon most of its outposts, a process intensified by Carolina governor James B. Moore's raids in 1702 and 1704. In 1763 Spain relinquished its Florida territory to Britain, regaining part of Florida in 1783 but yielding it again in 1821, this time to advancing American interests.

Africans used the Anglo-Spanish rivalry to escape bondage in Carolina. Spanish governors offered freedom to escaped slaves if they converted to Catholicism. By 1738 the number of refugees was large enough for a community to be established for them a few miles north of St. Augustine. Known as Gracia Real de Santa Teresa de Mose, it quickly became a refuge for Carolina slaves. This policy helped incite the 1739 Stono Rebellion in the Carolinas.[4]

Charles Town

In 1663 eight British noblemen received a grant of land as a reward for their loyalty to King Charles II. These Lords Proprietors planned to attract as many settlers as possible to the new colony. The expedition that founded the first permanent British settlement in the Carolinas left Britain in three vessels and sailed into Charleston Harbor in April 1670.

The colonists settled upstream on the Ashley River, protecting their settlement with a palisade and four pieces of artillery. Native Americans reported to their Spanish allies in 1672 that 30 small houses were located on the west bank of the Ashley River, and four were on the east bank of a coastal peninsula formed by the confluence of the Ashley and Cooper Rivers. By this time the colony had grown to 268 men, 69 women, and 59 children. African slaves were already among the residents. Seventeenth-century colonists included settlers from British Caribbean islands, particularly Barbados. These experienced colonists brought a cultural model that included political acumen, a drive for social and economic improvement, and familiarity with a plantation system based on slave labor.

Carolina settlers built on lessons learned in earlier colonies and immediately searched for exports. But first the settlers had to become accustomed to the lowcountry environment. Contrary to their expectations, the climate was semitropical rather than tropical, and the colder winters caught them by surprise. Unfamiliarity with the local environment and limited labor hampered the colony's agricultural efforts during the first decade.

Cattle and pigs flourished in the relatively mild climate and grasslands of

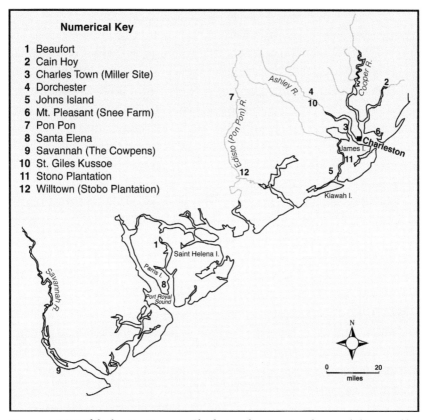

Numerical Key

1 Beaufort
2 Cain Hoy
3 Charles Town (Miller Site)
4 Dorchester
5 Johns Island
6 Mt. Pleasant (Snee Farm)
7 Pon Pon
8 Santa Elena
9 Savannah (The Cowpens)
10 St. Giles Kussoe
11 Stono Plantation
12 Willtown (Stobo Plantation)

Figure 4.1. Map of the lowcountry near Charleston showing sites discussed. (Prepared by Susan Duser.)

the lowcountry. Cattle ranching required little capital or labor. Spurred by the leadership of the Barbadians, Carolina colonists soon shipped beef and pork to Caribbean colonies, where sugar production left little time or space for food production. Ranching was a productive lowcountry enterprise for decades. The search for a profitable crop, however, advanced more slowly. Forty years, and a shift to royal rule, passed before the colony was well situated financially.[5]

The Lords Proprietors devised both an aristocratic and a headright system to distribute property. The latter granted 70 to 75 acres to any free person arriving in the colony, with an additional 50 acres for each accompanying servant or slave. Land was thus acquired with relative ease if you were free, and conditions were ideal for forming large plantations. Colonists soon established farmsteads and plantations along the Ashley River, along the Edisto River to Port Royal, and along the Santee River.

The growing colony never lacked settlers. Englishmen, Scots, New Englanders, Dissenters, and Jews formed the core of this diverse group. The West Indies was an important source of colonists, and a bloc of Barbadian planters known as the Goose Creek men were particularly influential in the colony's political and economic development. Carolina's policy of religious toleration attracted French Huguenots fleeing persecution in their homeland. The Huguenots settled in town and three outlying communities, particularly along the Santee River. A large number of settlers came unwillingly, transported from Africa and the West Indies as slaves to work in cowpens and plantations. Rice cultivation created a voracious demand for labor. By 1708 the majority of lowcountry residents were Africans.[6]

Numerous Native American groups resided in the lowcountry when British settlers arrived; as many as 18 are known by name. Native peoples had already started to move away from the coast due to the Spanish presence, and this retreat increased after Charles Town was founded. By 1682 the Kiawah had moved from the Ashley River to Kiawah Island, for example. The arrival of Scottish settlers in 1683 triggered the displacement of Yamasee and Guale from the Port Royal area. Smallpox and other European diseases also took a toll on the coastal tribes. Small Native American groups, however, remained in the lowcountry as "settlement Indians" or "neighbor Indians."[7]

Efforts by both the Proprietors and the colonial government to control the Indian trade characterized the early Carolina enterprise. A profitable informal trade between planters and neighboring Indians flourished in the seventeenth century. Charleston's access to inland waterways facilitated trade with these groups. Alliances with the Creeks were cemented in 1685 when Henry Woodward arrived in Coweta, the preeminent Muscogulge town. This began a trade that dominated Creek life for the next century. By the eighteenth century Native Americans allied with Charleston included Siouans, Cherokee, Upper and Lower Creeks, Choctaw, and smaller tribes such as the Yamasee, Westo, Yuchi, and Tuscarora.[8]

Flintlock muskets, metal tools, and European textiles were traded for "deerskins, other produce, and captive enemies." Joel Martin notes that the deerskin trade provided Carolina with a badly needed commodity. Moreover, by involving "thousands of native consumers," the trade enabled Charleston merchants to import and sell far more goods than could be purchased by colonists alone. Deerskins soon became Carolina's most profitable export, an enterprise that became larger and more organized as the eighteenth century progressed. Carolina merchants also profited from a trade in Indian slaves.[9]

The Yamasee War of 1715 took an additional toll on Native Americans and displaced many. The war was stimulated by lax regulation of traders and smoldering complaints against them. After two years of fighting, the defeated tribes moved farther inland, and interior trade routes expanded. Long-distance exchange necessitated trading posts and storage facilities. By the end of the proprietary regime, the Native American trade was dominated by a few merchants and planters.[10]

Raising cattle was an early productive enterprise, requiring only land and a small labor force. Cattle hands could be Africans, Europeans, or Native Americans skilled as cattle hunters or herders. From the earliest settlement, enslaved Africans responsible for the cattle herds tended them with little supervision. Peter Wood suggests that the term *cowboy* originated from these circumstances; the term *cow hunter* suggests the wild nature of the animals.[11]

The once-extensive longleaf pine forests of the lowcountry provided other marketable commodities. Forest products supplied the naval stores essential to wooden sailing vessels. Workers burned longleaf pine wood in large earth-covered kilns and collected the rosin. Tar was used to waterproof ship riggings, thereby preventing decay. Pitch (tar refined by boiling) sealed caulking on both the inside and outside of ship hulls. Carolina also shipped pine, cypress, and oak planks, shingles, and staves from lowcountry trees to the West Indies.[12]

It was rice that made many Carolina settlers wealthy and brought enslaved African settlers to the colony in large numbers. Rice was introduced in the late seventeenth century, and by 1730 inland swamp rice production was more profitable than any of the previous exports. African bondsmen, well versed in rice production in their homeland and familiar with the inland swamp environment from their work as cow hunters, cleared the freshwater swamps of trees and stumps and built dams, gates, ditches, and canals to flood and drain fields. Rice production jumped from 8,000 barrels in 1715 to more than 40,000 in the 1730s. Inland swamp cultivation was the major production technique for the remainder of the colonial period. Planters who were wealthy enough to create the necessary infrastructure found even greater profits in tidal rice production after the Revolutionary War.[13]

Indigo was another early commercial success. Indigo produced a deep blue dye prized by British cloth manufacturers. The plant grows on high land, leaving freshwater swamps and lowlands for rice cultivation. The plant itself needs little tending, though producing the dye is "demanding but delicate." Loss of the British indigo subsidy after the Revolution reduced the profit to be made from indigo.[14]

Settling the Peninsula

The Lords Proprietors directed Carolina settlers to "plant in towns." By 1680 Charles Town was moved downstream to the coastal peninsula where some members of the colony already lived. This new site offered relatively high bluffs, a narrow marsh, a good harbor, and a defensible location. More importantly, it was "ideally cituated [sic] for trade." Robert Weir notes, however, that the peninsular location was not ideal and that the town's future was uncertain until the end of the seventeenth century. Mortality rates were high and population growth was slow.[15]

An early plan of Charleston, called the Grand Modell, divided the peninsula into deep, narrow lots and guided development of the city for several decades. The highest land, between Vanderhorst and Daniel Creeks, was the focus of the earliest settlement. This location coincided with the narrowest reach of marshland and overlooked the harbor's deepest waters. The creeks were natural barriers and were enhanced with fortifications. By 1686 an earthen "tranchee" protected a stretch of the Cooper River between two small wooden forts. After years of erosion the General Assembly authorized construction of a brick "wharf wall" or "curtain line," augmented by brick fortifications. Queen Anne's War in 1703 prompted work that subsequently enclosed the entire town in a system of entrenchments, flankers, parapets, bastions, redans (triangular projections in the defensive wall), and a town gate at Meeting and Broad Streets.[16]

Commercial success with deerskins, cattle, rice, timber, and foodstuffs led to slow but steady growth of the port city in the 1700s. Removal of the inefficient proprietary government in 1719 hastened commercial growth. Successful merchants and equally successful planters emerged as the leaders of society. Soon the two groups meshed through economic diversification and intermarriage. Many of Charleston's colonial merchants profited from the deerskin trade. Samuel Eveleigh, Benjamin Stead, James Crockatt, John Gordon, and Henry Laurens managed much of the city's Indian trade and obtained skins from Georgia as well as Carolina. By this time the "infinite deer herds" of the late seventeenth century were greatly diminished.[17]

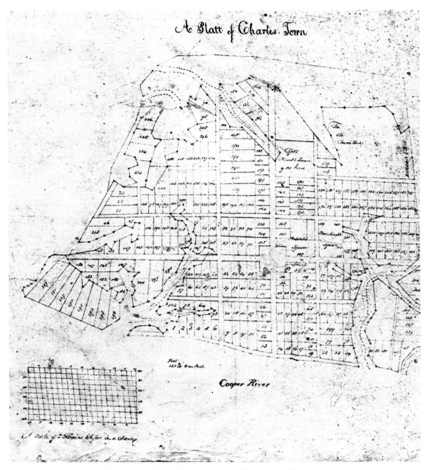

Figure 4.2. The Grand Modell, plan for the second location of Charles Town, on Oyster Point at the confluence of the Ashley and Cooper Rivers. (Courtesy South Carolina Historical Society.)

Though the Indian trade moved inland after the Yamasee War, Native Americans did not disappear from Charleston's colonial landscape. In addition to small enclaves of "settlement Indians" in the coastal region, delegations of Creek, Cherokee, Chickasaw, and others traveled regularly between Charleston and Indian country along well-trodden paths leading into the interior. Travelers camped on plantations and farms along the way, and colonists often were reimbursed for "entertaining Indians."[18]

Charleston's economic expansion generated physical expansion. The city's population grew rapidly in the eighteenth century. The 1739 *Ichnography* shows a city grown well beyond the old city walls. Development was primarily westward, toward the Ashley River, and southward, to the tip of the peninsula. The 1739 *Prospect* shows a densely packed city filled with post-medieval-style, multistory storehouses, dwellings, and shops. The agricultural economy required an increasingly large labor force of African slaves, and the city had a black majority from 1708 until the 1850s. The city encouraged white immigration to offset the dramatic increase in Africans.[19]

The city shown in the *Prospect* did not last. The fire of 1740 leveled 40 percent of the town. The hurricane of 1752 was the largest to hit the city during the eighteenth century, though not the only tempest to do so. The brick seawall suffered considerable damage and required extensive rebuilding. The storm surge overwhelmed the southwestern part of town. The resulting wall of debris caused extensive damage to houses and wharves along East Bay Street.[20]

Despite fires and storms, Charleston's plantation-based economy was thriving by the 1750s and, with it, the relative affluence of its citizens. White per capita income was among the highest in the colonies. Furniture, silver, table wares, textiles, paintings, and other symbols of wealth poured into the colony. These imports were matched by a rise in local craftspeople and their

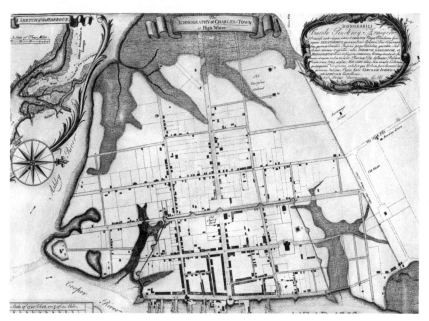

Figure 4.3. *Ichnography of Charles-Town at High Water*, 1739, engraved by B. Roberts and R. Toms. Charleston extended far beyond the city wall by this time. The landward walls had been abandoned, but the brick seawall was still in use. (Print enhanced by Alfred O. Halsey, 1959, Collections of The Charleston Museum, Charleston, South Carolina.)

Figure 4.4. *An Exact Prospect of Charles Town*, by Bishop Roberts, 1739. This engraving does not show the eight wharves that appear on the map by the same artist in 1739. The fire of 1740 destroyed many of the buildings shown in this view. (Published in the *London Magazine* in 1762, Collections of The Charleston Museum, Charleston, South Carolina.)

slaves producing similar finery. Personal displays of wealth were matched by new public and domestic architecture built after each natural disaster.[21]

Monumental public buildings cemented the visual image of Charleston as an economic force and symbolized the prosperity and prestige of the city. The State House, built in 1753, and St. Michael's Episcopal Church, built in 1752, were adjacent to the city square; the intersection of Meeting and Broad Streets was once dominated by the town gate. The Exchange Building was built at the foot of Broad Street in 1771 over the foundation of Half Moon Battery, formerly an important part of the city's defensive wall. Charleston continued to be a fortified city but was no longer a walled city.[22]

If the intersection of Broad and Meeting Streets became the administrative center of the city, the waterfront remained its economic center. Factors, commission merchants, and retailers clustered on the wharves and along East Bay. As the eighteenth century progressed, more and more wharves were built in front of the original brick curtain line. Government officials who thought that breaches in the curtain line left the city vulnerable to attack were overruled by those who argued that closing these passages would impede trade.

Charleston society's wealth and cosmopolitan nature gave rise to some of the colony's earliest public intellectual institutions. The Charleston Library Society, modeled after those in Britain, was founded in 1748. The Charleston Museum was founded in 1773, becoming the nation's first public natural history museum. These institutions galvanized around investigations into the region's natural history, beginning with John Lawson's *New Voyage to Carolina* in 1700.[23]

The Revolutionary War Era and Its Aftermath

On July 4, 1776, 13 British colonies in North America proclaimed their independence from the British Empire. The first British attempt to capture Carolina came in 1776 but was unsuccessful. Warned of another attack in late 1779, General Benjamin Lincoln ordered earthworks to be built. After a lengthy siege, British troops took the city in 1780. The British occupation lasted two years. Homes such as Rebecca Motte's mansion were used to quarter troops. Some Charlestonians were imprisoned, and others were exiled to St. Augustine during that city's brief British occupation. Carolinians also were plundered of "enormous wealth." Occupation forces did, however, clean up the city, hauling rubbish to unknown locations. The British occupation brought other changes, including new imported foodstuffs.[24]

After the Revolution, the bounty on British indigo ended. Planters searched for other crops to grow on their high land. Long a staple, Sea Island cotton emerged as a viable replacement for indigo. The first post-Revolution cotton reached Britain in 1785. Development of the cotton gin by Eli Whitney in 1793 mitigated some of the labor required to cultivate cotton and prepare it for market. Experimentation by the Burden family of Johns Island improved the strain.[25]

The war only briefly interrupted the city's economic growth. The physical and economic destruction of the war offered rice planters an opportunity to begin cultivating in tidal swamps. These swamps were cleared, diked, and ditched. Between the 1760s and 1780, the population of enslaved Africans doubled.[26]

The city was incorporated and renamed Charleston in 1783. At the same time the city limit was moved four blocks north to Boundary (now Calhoun) Street. The ever-growing population was accommodated within this small space by subdividing lots and expanding into the centers of established blocks.[27]

The area known as Charleston Neck, north of the city proper and some distance from the wharves, developed more slowly. King Street, the main road from the backcountry into the city in the eighteenth century, became the city's commercial and retail center. Retail merchants followed their customers up King Street as the residential sections expanded. Residences and workplaces increasingly were separated, and neighborhoods of wealthy planters appeared.[28]

Although the lowcountry economy suffered periodic depressions, planting continued to offer white residents opportunities for amassing fortunes.

Figure 4.5. *Ichnography of Charleston, for the Phoenix Fire Company of London*, 1788, by Edmund Petrie. Most of the creeks that defined the limits of the walled city were filled by this time. (Collections of The Charleston Museum, Charleston, South Carolina.)

By the nineteenth century, prime rice lands were so expensive that most successful rice planters had "old money." As the nineteenth century advanced, Charleston society became increasingly "closed" to outsiders or newcomers, as well as conservative in arts, education, civic improvement, and economic diversification.[29]

Tidal rice and Sea Island cotton production stimulated 20 years of unbridled prosperity for the city. Overproduction of cotton, however, led to a collapse in prices in 1819 and a national depression that was long-lasting. During the 1819 depression, some planters tried to reform wasteful agricultural practices and develop more efficient ways to use land and labor. Dependence on two crops and their international markets left the local economy vulnerable to external forces. Both rice and cotton faced competition from newer agricultural areas in the Mississippian region. Many planters and their slaves moved to these new areas, and by 1850 Charleston had a white majority for the first time since 1708.[30]

Steamships and railroads changed the region's transportation network. The development of the steamboat in 1819 meant that ships no longer needed to follow the trade winds to southern ports. Railroads provided inland planters an efficient way to get their crops to market, and the Gulf

Coast cities of Mobile and New Orleans rapidly became depots for inland cotton. Charleston benefited from neither transportation improvement.[31]

Progressive urban citizens of the early nineteenth century encouraged diversification and industrialization. Many of these new enterprises settled in Charleston's burgeoning suburbs on the Neck. The Neck was home to new Irish and German immigrants who fled to America after 1820, as well as enslaved African Americans living "out," away from their owners. The Neck also housed a large number of the city's free persons of color, a small but influential group of African Americans. The area between Calhoun (Boundary) and Line Streets was annexed into the city in 1849, principally to impose police control over the area.

Slavery was synonymous with labor in nineteenth-century Charleston. Most African American slaves were field hands, laborers, servants, or porters, but some worked as coopers, blacksmiths, and millwrights, particularly in the city. Others were carpenters and brickmakers. Women worked as seamstresses, while men worked as barbers and tailors. Enslaved African Americans dominated the maritime labor force as wharf hands and stevedores. Bernard Powers notes that these skilled positions often involved little direct supervision and a good deal of mobility; urban slaves were relatively well traveled.[32]

Owners routinely "hired out" their enslaved artisans. Slave owners purchased licenses, represented by copper tags, from the City. These permitted slaves to work for others or without supervision. Slave badges for "porters" and "draymen" are common. Badges for vendors, hucksters, and butchers were the most expensive and were heavily legislated. These badges are a reflection of the prevalence of slave hucksters and their de facto control of Charleston's market economy.[33]

The 1819 depression was followed by a purported slave uprising in 1822. Brought to Charleston in the service of a sea captain, Denmark Vesey purchased his freedom with winnings from a lottery and worked in the city as a carpenter. He reportedly masterminded a slave revolt to overthrow white authority and establish Black control over the city. Witnesses testified that between 6,000 and 9,000 slaves joined the cause, some from as far away as plantations on the Santee River. The overall plan is unclear, and some scholars question whether an uprising was in the works at all. Still, the mere possibility of such a revolt intensified white Charlestonians' fears of the large African American population and led to increasingly harsh restrictions on people of color, particularly free African Americans.[34]

Urban environments throughout the nation changed radically in the second quarter of the nineteenth century as industrialization and a national economy replaced local and regional economies. Cities developed centralized business districts; established separate residential, business, and industrial zones; and improved public transportation. Charleston initially kept pace with other cities but eventually lagged behind.[35]

Many legislative adjustments and physical improvements resulted from rebuilding after disasters. Fear of fire, preventing fire, and rebuilding after fire are recurring themes in Charleston's history. Major fires devastated the city in 1740, 1778, 1796, 1835, 1838, and 1861. The 1861 fire, on the eve of the Civil War, was Charleston's largest, and recovery took decades.

The city's location on a narrow, low-lying peninsula traversed by marshes and creeks and almost completely surrounded by water left it vulnerable to both floods and sickness. Storms plagued the city. Standing water from rain and floods contributed to unhealthy conditions. Debris accumulated in creeks, marshes, and low-lying areas of the increasingly congested city. Wealthy residents of the lowcountry spent summers in the mountains, the pine flatwoods, and the seashore, hoping to catch "healthy breezes."

Though the 1850s appeared prosperous in Charleston, Gene Waddell suggests that Charleston's economic standing slowly but steadily declined after 1800. He argues that good agricultural land was already largely under cultivation, and soil fertility in many of these fields was depleted. The concentration of land in the hands of a few was matched by a concentration of human property. Two-thirds of the valued property owned by the planter class was human.[36]

Civil War and Its Aftermath

Looming changes were not apparent to rice and cotton planter families enjoying a credit-bolstered lifestyle. South Carolina led the fiery rhetoric that defended slavery and called for secession from the United States as tensions between the federal government (the Union) and southern, Confederate states intensified. Shots fired on the Union's Fort Sumter from the Charleston battery in April 1861 signaled the onset of the Civil War.

The city felt little of the war's impact for several months after this opening volley. Cotton prices even rebounded. Following the fall of Port Royal in November 1861, however, refugees crowded into the city. By 1863 the city was blockaded and under siege. Repeated bombardments damaged the lower city and drove residents up to the Neck or out of town. By February 1865 the city's capacity to resist was broken, and Confederate general P.G.T. Beauregard ordered the city evacuated. Federal troops entered the city and remained there until 1876.[37]

The refugee status of many white Charleston families continued beyond the war's end in 1865. The lower city, particularly the portion burned in 1861, remained in ruins for decades. Many of the leading families who returned to the city took in boarders or found other means to support their households. Some freedmen remained with their former owners, but the staff working on townhouse properties was greatly reduced from antebellum levels.[38]

Freedmen helped forge a new order by taking steps to "redefine their roles as workers." Former slaves were now citizens; they made their own decisions about where to live and work. One consequence of emancipation was that Charleston once again had a black majority, due to in-migration of rural freedmen. Urban freedmen deserted their former residences and owners as a way of exercising their new freedom. Powers suggests that the desertion of domestic servants was particularly common. He describes the case of Quash, who left the Porcher family to sell fish on the street. Although Reconstruction extended political rights to disenfranchised men, it did not radically alter economic and social stratification. The occupations of newly freed men and women were similar to those practiced during slavery.[39]

The emancipation of enslaved laborers, along with the credit system of international markets, spelled the end of profitable rice production in South Carolina. In 1867 some 90 percent of the plantations on the Cooper River were idle. Planters swore allegiance to the Union and returned to their cotton and rice plantations. They contracted with freedmen for labor but were unable to realize antebellum returns. Freedmen worked for low wages but refused to do the most dangerous and miserable tasks, those that involved winter work in cold water digging and maintaining ditches and banks. The mechanized rice production successful in Arkansas and Louisiana was not practical in Carolina. The lowcountry produced a significant portion of the nation's rice crop in the 1880s but could not do so in the next decade. The last Santee River plantation to produce rice was David Doar's Harrietta in 1927.[40]

The postbellum economy did diversify. Although many planters continued to grow cotton and rice, some tried new crops. Phosphate rock, abundant in the area and long considered a nuisance by lowcountry farmers, became known as a source of fertilizer for improving exhausted fields. The lowcountry's phosphate replaced depleted sources of South American guano. By 1874 six companies mined and processed the rock. Phosphate production was a victim of the 1893 hurricane, which destroyed boats, dredges, and machinery. The lowcountry enterprises were replaced by mines in Florida.

Lumbering was an important late-nineteenth-century industry. Hayden Smith notes that "forest growth returned to abandoned cotton fields. Inland rice fields returned to cypress and hardwood communities." Lumber companies built causeways, railroads, and logging camps to extract hardwoods from the former rice fields. The resulting devastation of the southern forests prompted expansion of the National Forest System in the 1930s.[41]

African Americans worked in these and other extractive industries. The phosphate industry was staffed primarily by freedmen, who resisted efforts by factory owners to impose strict work rules. Shepherd McKinley suggests that freed people developed work patterns derived from the task system. They continued to raise subsistence crops and support urban markets with produce, game, and fish, forming what McKinley calls "a shadowy but vibrant economic community." Some freedmen in the lowcountry bought land, often in pine forests adjacent to prime rice land.[42]

Gradual changes to the urban landscape received impetus from a series of disasters, offsetting economic and social gains. The densely settled city, tightly packed with wooden buildings, was a prime target for wind-driven fires. Natural disasters befell the lowcountry with alarming frequency. Hurricanes struck between Savannah and North Carolina in 1893, 1894, 1899, 1906, 1910, and 1911. These storms destroyed fragile rice dikes up and down the coast. The 1893 hurricane alone killed over 1,000 people on the sea islands south of Charleston and destroyed rice fields and phosphate dredges with equal ferocity. Hurricanes were familiar to weary lowcountry residents, but the earthquake of 1886, the most powerful to strike the East Coast of North America, was a new and terrifying event. Nearly 2,000 buildings were damaged, most of them on the filled, or "made," land on the peninsula's former creeks.[43]

During the late nineteenth century, demands for civic improvements increased, most notably for a waterborne sewage system. By 1896 the City Sewerage Commission initiated a program of separate sanitary sewers, and removal of stormwater by means of a tidal drain system. This system was used until the 1960s. The 1799 Middleton-Pinckney House was refitted as a pumping station and reservoir for the artesian water system. Lack of funds, rather than lack of interest, kept Charleston's civic leaders from moving ahead on such water projects. The economic depression that waned in the 1880s returned in the early 1900s. The city did not recover until after World War II.[44]

The widespread poverty of the era inadvertently preserved much of the city's architectural heritage. Buildings slowly decayed through the decades of economic depression, fires, and storms, and the earthquake. Appreciation for the city's history and architecture was fostered by the Charleston Renaissance, a cultural and artistic movement of the early twentieth century. Indeed, the city's first archaeological investigation (of the Granville Bastion by Albert Simons and Samuel Lapham) was conducted during this period. As historic buildings were restored, however, many African American and poorer residents left for the areas above Calhoun and Line Streets; the racially integrated neighborhoods that had characterized the city for decades disappeared from the lower peninsula.[45]

Two new threats to the city's historic architecture attracted the attention of Charlestonians in the 1920s: the proliferation of gasoline filling stations, built to service the growing number of automobiles, and the dismantling of homes for their historic interior appointments. In 1920 Susan Pringle Frost, a suffragist and the first female real estate agent in the city, founded the Society for the Preservation of Old Dwellings (later the Preservation Society of Charleston). This formalized the city's preservation efforts.

The zoning ordinance of 1931 gave the City the authority to protect historic architecture. Historic Charleston Foundation, founded in 1947, preserved numerous buildings by purchasing them and imposing protective easements. Preservation of the city's historic buildings became the catalyst for a thriving tourism industry, even as gentrification of formerly diverse neighborhoods continued up the peninsula. The city remains at the forefront of a complex and evolving preservation movement, one that has embraced urban archaeology.[46]

"Made Land" and the Urban Environment

The "natural" landscape of Charleston is the result of human interactions with the lowcountry environment over centuries. Transformation of the terrain, plants, and animals to suit the needs of the growing urban center began almost immediately and increased when the Grand Modell's grid of streets and lots was imposed onto a very irregular, marshy terrain. Over time, the peninsula's creeks and marshes were diverted and filled to create land deemed more usable, more desirable, and certainly more regular. Dell Upton suggests that early Americans thought of such regulated space as essential to human society.[47]

Accommodating the growing urban population involved landscape changes on individual properties and at the municipal level. Bernard Herman describes two phenomena: intensification and regulation. Intensification is reflected in increased functional demands on limited urban lands. Individual buildings, complexes of buildings, and entire urban lots evolved to fit the needs of a growing population. Intensification involves subdivision of lots, addition of new structures or additions to existing structures, and repeated utilization of urban land. This constant reorganization of space stimulates regulation. Regulations may impose community standards, such as those involving fire and sanitation. They also require individuals and households to modify their properties and behaviors to meet them.[48]

City maps from 1739, 1788, 1852, and 1872 show a startling amount of new land. In the early decades most settlement was between Vanderhorst and Daniel Creeks, natural barriers providing safety to the city. Later, these creeks, and other low, marshy areas, were viewed as impediments to the city's growth and the flow of goods and people. Routes following the edges of the peninsula required bridges to cross intersecting creeks and marshes.

Much of this low-lying, boggy city was drained and filled to create new land and improve transportation. The resulting "made land" reduced the peninsula's natural relief. King Street, originally a ridge of high land running up the peninsula, is hardly recognizable as such today. The first made land was created in the broad marshy area along the west side of the peninsula. Next, creeks were filled to become streets. Vanderhorst Creek became Water Street. Daniel Creek was transformed into Market Street and the Centre Market by the early nineteenth century. Daniel Cannon's mill pond on the west side of Calhoun Street disappeared. The last, largest development of new land occurred when Murray Boulevard was built along the southwest edge of the peninsula. Low areas on individual lots were filled, too. Much of the city's archaeological record consists of this early landfill.

Plant remains from archaeological sites document the decrease in marshes and lowlands as these small moist pockets were drained or filled. They show dramatic deforestation of the Charleston peninsula during the second half of the eighteenth century. Both pine and hardwood trees disappear from the urban landscape, replaced by weedy species that colonize open spaces.

Buildings are the most familiar above-ground features, but other devices altered the peninsular environment as well. Walls and fences restricted the flow of breezes, animals, and humans. Enclosure of lots and yards with wood and, later, brick fences blocked and channeled physical movement and altered visual access. Charleston's low relief meant that cellars were above-ground and wells were shallow. Poor-quality water was a constant problem, particularly when urban density forced wells and cisterns ever closer to privies and accumulating trash. By the nineteenth century, rainwater collected in cisterns was a common alternative to well water.

Shaping the City

From its earliest days, the Carolina colony was an evolving landscape, land modified for human occupation. It was shared space, serving a growing community of people, plants, and animals. Many of the processes by which the natural landscape of the peninsula became the cultural landscape of today's Charleston were intentional, such as clearing lots, filling creeks, and constructing imposing buildings. Some were unintentional consequences of these actions, such as poor drainage, deforestation, refuse accumulation, congested lots and streets, and new habitat for vermin. Efforts to manage drainage, transportation, sanitation, public health, and potable water can be seen in the archaeological record.

II

THE CITY AND COAST

The Eighteenth Century

5

SETTLEMENT

On May 23, 1674, Lord Anthony Ashley Cooper sent instructions for beginning his Carolina plantation to his agent, Andrew Percivall. Ashley's ship, the Edisto, was to "sail with all possible speed to Bermudas" to acquire "Indian corn for six months and other necessaries fit for the plantation of Carolina, as hogs, poultry, potatoes, orange trees &c." Percivall was "to inquire about the price of cattle and what number to be had fit to be transported." He was then to learn if it was better to "get cattle from Maryland, for he is not without further order to trade either to New York or Virginia." Percivall was to take some grown cattle for milk from Bermuda. We know from further correspondence that Percivall eventually did acquire "300 or 400" cattle. Where did he find the stock? And was it from multiple sources? Our research on cattle in the Charleston area suggests intriguing, and complicated, possibilities.[1]

Our story does not begin in the historic district of Charleston, but several miles upstream on the Ashley River. There British colonists established Charles Town in 1670, on the recommendation of the cacique of Kiawah. The colonists considered the location to be highly defensible, because it was surrounded on three sides by marsh and connected to the mainland by a narrow land bridge. It was here, during the first decades of the colony, that the primary provisioning strategies used in the Carolina lowcountry and the lowcountry cuisine were forged.

Two archaeological sites from this period, the Miller and Le Sade components, are associated with Charles Town itself. Soon after the location was selected for Charles Town, colonists erected a protective log palisade around nine acres. Settlements quickly extended beyond that barrier. Although the colony's leaders emphasized the town proper, most of the settlers lived some distance from town, where they engaged in farming, herding, and trade with local Native Americans. In 1672 Spanish spy Antonio Cumunas reported a few lodgings inside the palisade, housing as many as 20 families, and a village of some 90 houses outside the enclosure. After Charles Town was moved to its present location, the old town became part of the Le Sade plantation.[2]

The third archaeological site from this period is St. Giles Kussoe, the Carolina plantation of Anthony Ashley Cooper, the first Earl of Shaftesbury and one of the colony's eight Lords Proprietors. Although Lord Ashley never visited the Carolinas, he was the most active of the colony's proprietors, envisioning a colony for "planting and trade." Lord Ashley arranged financing for the settlement, recruited settlers, and supplied three ships. With his physician and friend John Locke, he drafted the Fundamental Constitution of Carolina. All three sites bear Lord Ashley's imprint.

The Miller Site at Charles Town

Although Charles Town was moved to the peninsula in 1680, some settlers remained near the original site. By 1694 the original Charles Town location was granted to James Le Sade and became known as Old Town Plantation. The Le Sade family owned the property until 1732. The site is now part of Charles Towne Landing State Historic Site.

The 1670s fortifications and a single structure, interpreted as a storehouse, were located by archaeological survey, testing, and excavations in the 1960s and in 2001. Little evidence has been found of buildings inside the palisade, except for the storehouse. Work just outside of the palisade, however, recovered an important array of early domestic artifacts and animal remains.

This locus is known as the Miller site, after John Miller, the first person to excavate at Charles Town. Miller worked there in 1967–68 under the auspices of the South Carolina Tricentennial Commission. While searching for the north palisade wall, Miller uncovered the remains of a structure he interpreted as a tavern. He suggested the structure was occupied in the 1690s by James Le Sade but might have an earlier component. Years later, as part of his own research at Charles Town, Stanley South concurred. Shovel testing in 2005 by Parks archaeologists recovered additional artifacts from the 1670s period. The Miller site yielded an unusually rich artifact assemblage compared to other areas of Charles Town.

This encouraged Department of Parks, Recreation and Tourism archaeologists David Jones, Cicek Beeby, Rebecca Shepherd, and Andrew Agha, assisted by a College of Charleston field school, to initiate a testing program in 2009. Their work located trenches excavated by Miller, and an intact floor made of tabby, an oyster shell, sand, lime, and water mixture. Agha later isolated deposits from the 1670s beneath the 1690s Le Sade features. Fine-screening recovered many small objects, such as seed beads and lead shot. Large pit features produced additional domestic artifacts and animal remains, including those of Old World rats.

Lord Ashley's St. Giles Kussoe

Although some colonists remained near Charles Town, others ventured beyond the town to establish farms and other enterprises along major low-country rivers. The extent of early settlement is reflected in Lord Ashley's complaint that the colonists had taken up all the best land on the river and "left me not a tolerable Place to plant." Late-seventeenth-century maps show the banks of these rivers dotted with settlements, particularly along the Ashley River. A survey by Stanley South and Michael Hartley in 1979 found many of these sites by cross-referencing historic maps with modern topographical maps and reports of areas where clusters of seventeenth-century artifacts occurred.[3]

The 1695 Mortier map highlights a homestead labeled "the Lord Ashley" near the headwaters of the Ashley River. The site is on private property and protected from development by the owner. With the owner's permission, South and Hartley recovered seventeenth-century artifacts from the site. Years later Historic Charleston Foundation obtained funds for a small archaeological study of the Ashley River, and Katherine Pemberton suggested this site as an excellent candidate. The property owner again granted access, and Brockington and Associates tested the property in 2009. Additional documentary research and the artifacts recovered demonstrated that this was Lord Ashley's St. Giles Kussoe settlement and trading post.

Lord Ashley sent his agent, Andrew Percivall, to establish a plantation on the Ashley River in 1674. He instructed Percivall to take up the land, build a defensive fortification, house and quarters, and settle servants there. Percivall was instructed to import hundreds of cattle and place them in the care of both indentured servants and African slaves. Lord Ashley also dispatched goods to begin the Indian trade under the direction of Henry Woodward. Woodward, the most knowledgeable trader of the period, was instructed to "setle a Trade with the Indians for Furs and other Commodities." When Woodward arrived at St. Giles Kussoe, he found the Westo

Figure 5.1. Brick foundation at St. Giles Kussoe, excavated in 2011. (Collections of The Charleston Museum, Charleston, South Carolina.)

waiting for him. Formerly known as the Erie, the Westo were refugees from Virginia. They possessed firearms and intimidated local Indian groups. The Lords Proprietors held a monopoly on trade with the Westo until 1680.[4]

Lord Ashley's death in 1683 brought an end to St. Giles Kussoe. Percivall, implicated in fraudulent dealings, took up another property farther up the Ashley River. St. Giles Kussoe was abandoned, and four defensive guns were moved to Dorchester, an early colonial town located along an Indian trading path.

The 2009 survey of St. Giles Kussoe found seventeenth-century artifacts clustered on a grassy knoll above the river swamp. As is all too common in fieldwork, researchers found evidence of a brick foundation on the last

Friday of the season. A call for volunteers brought area archaeologists and historians to the site for a weekend of additional work. The large crew excavated along the brickwork to expose a chimney corner and the northeast corner of a building. This is the earliest British brick construction known in the lowcountry.

Bolstered by this discovery, Pemberton and Historic Charleston Foundation approached MeadWestvaco (MWV) for support to continue the excavations. MWV Foundation funded two field schools in 2011 and 2013 under Agha's direction. Students encountered posts and mud sills from additional buildings, as well as Native American, African, and European ceramics, tobacco pipes, and glass bottles. Employing the same fine-screening technique used at the Miller site, students also recovered small beads, lead shot, and animal remains.

Jon Marcoux of Salve Regina University joined the research team in 2012, conducting a magnetometer survey of the knoll at the heart of Lord

Figure 5.2. Lead-glazed earthenware cream pan fragments from the moat at St. Giles Kussoe, excavated in 2013. (Collections of The Charleston Museum, Charleston, South Carolina.)

Ashley's settlement. The remote sensing survey revealed an L-shaped anomaly across the site, strong evidence for the moat and palisade surrounding the compound. Using the magnetometer survey as a guide, students located three sections of the moat and the four corners of the brick structure at the top of the knoll.

Oyster shell and mortar are very rare at St. Giles Kussoe. Shell and mortar contain calcium carbonate, and their presence is critical for preserving animal remains. Mortar was found with the brick foundation and in a small pit outside of the moat, accompanied by animal remains in relatively good condition. Otherwise, preservation of faunal specimens was poor. The surviving materials, however, show that Charles Town's settlers set the stage for the provisioning strategies that flourished in Charleston in subsequent centuries.

Materials of the Early Settlers

Materials recovered from these sites highlight the broad reach of the colonial provisioning strategy. British ceramics dominate the European artifacts recovered from the sites, but German, Caribbean, and Native American ceramics are present, as is glass from Venice and porcelain from China. They underscore the multiple sources of goods accessible to colonists even at this early date.

The British ceramics are predominantly utilitarian vessels used for preparing and storing food. Lead-glazed earthenwares were abundant. Large, shallow earthenware cream pans were a common vessel form in Britain and other British colonies, and several were recovered from the St. Giles Kussoe moat. These are particularly interesting in light of Lord Ashley's interest in "grown cattle for milk." Two earthenwares from North Devon are hallmarks of the seventeenth century. One of these, a gravel-tempered, green lead-glazed ware, is the most common, and is found as cream pans, jars, and bowls. Sgraffito slipware, also from Devon, has a similar paste. It is more varied in form, but most fragments are from pitchers and bowls.[5]

Two finds in particular show that the Carolina colony was not isolated from popular developments in British ceramics. Slipwares made by Staffordshire potters were relatively new in the late seventeenth century. Although uncommon, slipware fragments were present in the St. Giles Kussoe assemblage. These fragments have the detailed, carefully combed decoration typical of the period. Brown and yellow combed slipware bowls and cups were intended for poor-to-middling kitchens, dining tables, and

Figure 5.3. Examples of seventeenth-century ceramics from St. Giles Kussoe and the Heyward-Washington House. Clockwise from top: Staffordshire combed and trailed slipware; brown salt-glazed stoneware; North Devon gravel-tempered ware; and North Devon sgraffito slipware. (Collections of The Charleston Museum, Charleston, South Carolina.)

taverns. Relief molded bowls also were present in the assemblage. Manganese Mottled ware was produced in the 1670s and was present in very small amounts. A bowl recovered from the storehouse at Charles Town demonstrates that this ware was among the 1670s imports to the colony. Tankards and open bowls were decorated with a manganese-based glaze that produces a brown, speckled surface.

Tin-enameled wares are the only table ceramics found at late-seventeenth-century lowcountry sites. These were the most common ceramic type in the St. Giles Kussoe assemblage, constituting between a quarter and a half of the European wares. Almost all of the tin-enameled wares from St. Giles Kussoe appear to be British delftware, characterized by chalky, opaque glaze over a soft yellowish body. Delftwares are often pale blue, with no decoration, but some vessels have hand-painted decoration. Almost all have a tin-enamel finish on both sides of the vessel. Several examples of lead-backed tin-enameled ware, typical of the seventeenth century elsewhere in British North America, were recovered from the Miller site, but this finish is extremely rare in the lowcountry.

The British mercantile system was not yet formalized, and seventeenth-century sites are characterized by artifacts of diverse origin. British colonial sites of this period contain Spanish, French, Dutch, and Native American wares. Spanish Olive Jars were widely used in the Americas for five centuries, and a surprising number of Spanish tin-glazed earthenwares, known collectively as majolicas, were present in the Miller assemblage. In addition, French lead-glazed wares were represented in the Miller and St. Giles Kussoe assemblages.[6]

The only other table or teaware recovered was Chinese porcelain. Ceramics scholars suggest that porcelain exported from the Orient was expensive and relatively rare in the seventeenth century. Sites in the Chesapeake Bay region, for example, contain virtually no Chinese porcelain during this period, yet porcelain tea bowls were recovered from the relatively small Miller and St. Giles Kussoe excavations.[7]

European trade with China began in 1516 and grew after 1573, when Spain controlled the Philippines and supported the Manila galleon trade. Oriental goods were shipped to Pacific ports in Mexico, carried overland to Veracruz, and then sent to Spain on the plate fleets. Kathleen Deagan notes that a good amount of porcelain stayed in Spain's American colonies. Chinese porcelain was present in small but consistent quantities in St. Augustine during the sixteenth and seventeenth centuries. It is possible that porcelain reached Carolina through Spanish trade. This is but one of several lines of evidence pointing to the British colony's unauthorized and undocumented exchange of goods with Spanish colonies in Florida and the Caribbean.[8]

The Miller and St. Giles Kussoe sites produced a number of distinctive stonewares from the Germanic region. Collections from both sites contain Rhenish stoneware. Jugs with reeded necks and bulbous bodies were embellished with sprig molding, combed lines, and cobalt and manganese enamel. St. Giles Kussoe yielded a brown salt-glazed stoneware vessel in the same form. Many of the brown salt-glazed stoneware vessels from the two sites, though, are British. These include fragments from large jugs and bottles, as well as smaller drinking vessels and tavern wares such as those produced by Dwight Fulham in England beginning in 1671.[9]

The most intriguing and enigmatic non-British ceramics are humble redwares. Michael Stoner's study of artifacts from the Charles Town storehouse identified lead-glazed wares produced not in Britain but in Barbados. Stoner is familiar with the long tradition of pottery production in Barbados through his own excavations at kiln and domestic sites on that island. Stoner identified Barbadian redwares from physical attributes; brown and green lead-glazed exteriors, a soft paste, and clay with a fine, smooth, well-mixed texture and a grey core. Petrographic analysis by Michael Smith identified the Barbadian wares through the presence of potassium feldspar, a volcanic ash found in Barbadian clays. Though Barbados is not an actively volcanic island, all of the windward islands of the Caribbean are volcanic in origin.[10]

Stoner's identification of Barbadian pottery prompted a search through other lowcountry assemblages curated at The Charleston Museum and elsewhere. St. Giles Kussoe produced a number of soft, lead-glazed redwares. George Calfas analyzed some of these redwares using X-ray fluorescence (XRF) and scanning electron microscopy (SEM). This analysis showed clear differences in the elemental composition of clays used to produce this pottery. St. Giles Kussoe wares cluster with those from Barbados. No doubt research will continue to explore this connection between Carolina and British Caribbean colonies.

Tobacco pipes and olive green glass bottles form a large percentage of the early materials. St. Giles Kussoe produced an assemblage of pipes made from soft, yellowish clay, distinct from the hard, white ball clay used in later British pipes. The St. Giles pipes bear further study, but likely they are British. The olive green glass bottle bases are from the squat "onion bottles" characteristic of the period.

Seemingly out of character with the "frontier" nature of these early sites are fragments of elaborate wine glasses. The few table glass fragments recovered are Venetian-style vessels instead of the simpler forms with drawn stems popular after 1690. Venetian glassmakers worked in Britain by 1571 and influenced the style of British table glass into the 1670s. Venetian drinking glasses were a status item; the term "Venetian" refers to the elegant style as well as to the place of manufacture.[11]

Other aspects of late-seventeenth-century material culture are more in keeping with the frontier setting of these early sites. Lead shot of all sizes, gunflints, flint debitage, and gun hardware form a relatively large percentage of the artifacts recovered. Sections of sprue (scrap from pouring lead into bullet molds), attached shot, and lead scraps all demonstrate that shot was molded on-site at St. Giles Kussoe. Gunflints and flint debitage were also common.

Trade with Native Americans is reflected in the number and variety of glass beads recovered from both sites, including small seed beads and larger beads in a number of shapes and colors. Archaeologists studying Native American sites in the Southeast occupied between 1607 and 1783, most notably Marcoux, have developed a chronology for these glass beads. Beads from St. Giles Kussoe cluster in the 1650–1720 period. The most common glass beads are known as cornaline d'aleppo. These have an opaque red outer core and a dark green-to-black transparent inner core. They are present in a range of sizes, in tubular and spherical shapes. The St. Giles Kussoe assemblage includes numerous blue, turquoise, white, and clear beads.[12]

The presence of both Native Americans and Africans is reflected in the pottery recovered from these sites. Native American pottery dominates the St. Giles Kussoe assemblage. Some of this was made by local groups; other wares came from more distant communities, possibly the Savannahs living along the middle section of the Savannah River. The Miller and St. Giles Kussoe sites also produced the earliest examples of colono ware recovered so far. This type is largely attributed to African American potters and is more common in eighteenth-century collections.[13]

Feeding the New Colony

European settlers quickly observed that most European farming techniques were unproductive in the Carolina lowcountry. They modified familiar husbandry strategies and foodways to include methods and resources better suited to the colonial setting. They identified novel combinations of commodities to support local and international trade. They also developed a strategy for feeding the colony that merged local resources with introduced crops and animals that did flourish in the lowcountry. This new pattern is evident in the Miller and Le Sade collections from Charles Town and in that from St. Giles Kussoe. The broad form of this new strategy persisted with only subtle changes throughout Charleston's history.

Little is known about Native American animal use in the Carolina lowcountry prior to colonization, but in Georgia and Florida animal remains recovered from early colonial sites are very similar to those in Native American deposits. This may be so for a number of reasons. Perhaps colonists adopted the successful strategies they saw their Native American neighbors using. More likely, Native Americans provided many of these resources through trade, as tithes or tributes, or unwillingly as colonists requisitioned what they wanted. Some Native Americans were slaves or domestic servants in colonists' households, and others married colonists of European or African descent. Native cooks in such households may have preferred to use familiar ingredients in familiar cookwares. Native American foodways combined a suite of well-adapted cultivated plants with local wild plants and animals.[14]

The emerging colonial strategy might also reflect African influences instead of Native American ones, particularly in Carolina, where Africans were such a large part of the early population. Africans, however, were also "strangers in a strange land" and had to learn productive techniques just as did European colonists. Local Native American foods might be prepared, served, and consumed in a European or an African style, however.[15]

Although much of the emerging lowcountry cuisine was indigenous, it remained European in other ways. Colonists continued to use introduced domestic animals, but the emphasis was on pigs and, especially, cattle. These animals were better suited to the lowcountry than were sheep and goats. Although Native Americans did eventually incorporate Eurasian livestock into their economies, this was limited in the early decades.[16]

Animal use at Charles Town and St. Giles Kussoe combined 21 local, noncommensal wild animals with four domestic ones. Wild animals contribute half of the individuals though less than a tenth of the meat at these early sites. A quarter of the animals used were aquatic turtles and fishes. Wild terrestrial mammals are primarily opossums, rabbits, raccoons, and woodrats. Considering the number of native mice and introduced Old World rats in these collections, the presence of a cat among the commensal animals is not unexpected.

Three-quarters of the meat consumed was beef. The dominance of cattle and beef persisted into the late nineteenth century at both rural sites and urban Charleston sites. The early settlers at this British colony used higher quantities of domestic meats, particularly beef, than did settlers in Spanish Florida during the early decades of that colony. The use of beef at early Carolina settlements may reflect lessons learned about cattle from Spanish Florida and in Virginia and Maryland. By the time Charles Town was settled, free-range cattle, the progeny of animals from Spanish settlements abandoned decades earlier, likely were well adapted to local conditions. The early habit of combining beef with local wild meats persists into the twenty-first century.

Although these three Carolina collections share the broad outlines of what became the lowcountry cuisine, they also show variations on that pattern. Given the proximity of Charles Town to the coast, it is not surprising that the Miller and Le Sade collections contain four estuarine fish individuals. The Miller collection also contains the remains of a sea turtle, and the Le Sade collection those of a diamondback terrapin. More surprising is that the St. Giles Kussoe collection also contains the remains of an estuarine fish though it was much farther from the coast. A fossil shark tooth recovered from St. Giles Kussoe may be from the fossil-rich Carolina coast or from phosphate deposits on the coastal plain.

Deer are present only in the St. Giles Kussoe collection. We have pondered the absence of deer at the Miller site and currently have no explanation. Preservation at the site is good, so it seems unlikely to be due to preservation bias. The most recently excavated samples from the Miller site have not yet been analyzed, and we wondered if they held the missing deer. Our curiosity was so great that Agha brought the new samples to the Southeastern Archaeological Conference for a quick perusal. A late-night meeting in a hotel room verified that these bags too contain no deer. Perhaps access to terrestrial wild resources was limited at Charles Town, for unknown reasons.

The more striking difference between the Miller and St. Giles Kussoe collections, however, is in livestock. Despite the large cattle herd at St. Giles Kussoe, beef contributed less than half of the estimated meat consumed there. This is a much lower quantity than estimated for the Miller site collection, which was dominated by beef. Pork contributed a much higher percentage of the meat in the St. Giles Kussoe collection than in the Miller collection, in which pork was rare. Most of the cattle specimens recovered from both sites are teeth and skull fragments, which may be evidence of poor bone preservation. Or perhaps cattle were slaughtered in large numbers at St. Giles Kussoe, but their remains were discarded outside of the excavated area. The difference also may reflect an early provisioning system in which live cattle were trailed from St. Giles Kussoe to other locations for sale and slaughter.[17]

Early Cattle in Carolina

Beef production was important in the early Carolina economy. Cattle thrived in the pinewoods, canebrakes, and marshes of the lowcountry. Lord Ashley's 1674 directive to acquire hundreds of animals reflects his confidence in this venture; cattle and cattle products were already successful lowcountry exports by this time. Live cattle, preserved meats, and tanned hides were shipped from cowpens to Charleston, and later to Savannah, and thence to other markets. The Carolina colony shipped four tons of salt meat to Barbados in 1680.

Most cattle received little or no supplemental feed or shelter. They largely were managed under an open-range system. Lowcountry winters are generally mild, and forage is available throughout the year. The relative ease of raising cattle was described by Thomas Nairne in his promotional pamphlet of 1710: "South Carolina abounds with black Cattle, to a Degree much beyond any other British Colony; which is chiefly owning to the Mildness of the Winter, whereby the Planters are freed from the Trouble of providing for them, suffering them to feed all Winter in the Woods." Much of the coast experiences natural fires that foster improved grazing for cattle; favorable pastures sometimes were maintained and expanded through intentionally set fires. Coastal cattle foraged in "hard feeding marshes" on cordgrasses, saltgrasses, and Spanish moss. Switchcane in swampy areas was a favorite food. Fires and large herds of grazing cattle likely contributed to significant landscape changes, particularly as cattle replaced Native Americans who were displaced by colonists.[18]

John Otto describes an annual cycle in which fields were burned in the winter to improve forage; cattle were rounded up for slaughter in the fall and the meat salted for sale in the West Indies. Some animals were kept near settlements by providing them modest food and shelter. The cycle included some milk production; calves and nursing females in particular might be penned or staked to keep them from running wild. Nairne wrote: "Our Cows graze in the Forests, and the Calves being separated from them and kept in Pastures, fenced in, they return home at night to suckle them. They are first milk'd then shut up in a Fold all Night milk'd again in the Morning, and then turned out into the woods." In the early decades many animals had no brands or other marks of ownership. Wild cattle often were considered pests or vermin. It was the responsibility of farmers to fence their crops to keep cattle out, rather than the responsibility of ranchers to fence cattle in.[19]

Cattle hands could be Africans, Europeans, or Native Americans skilled as cattle hunters or herders. From the earliest settlement, enslaved Africans tended herds with little supervision. Peter Wood notes that an inventory of a James Island property in 1692 lists "in sight and by account appeareth 134 head of Cattle and one negro man." Lord Ashley purchased 17 Africans from Sir Peter Colleton in 1677, likely to work the hundreds head of cattle at St. Giles Kussoe.[20]

Little is known about early cattle themselves other than that they flourished and cattle from Spanish Florida were described as larger than Carolina animals. Mart Stewart suggests that the hardy Florida Scrub had emerged by the second quarter of the seventeenth century. Though small, this criollo breed is heat-tolerant, long-lived, resistant to parasites and diseases, and productive on low-quality forage. Stewart further suggests that both Spanish cattle and Carolina "black cattle" adapted successfully to the southeastern environment. By the early eighteenth century, large numbers roamed the region, and Georgia settlers in the 1730s found the land full of feral cattle. The diverse origins of colonists and raids between Spanish and British colonies likely ensured that cattle lineages were mixed.[21]

Early cattle centers in South Carolina are referred to as cowpens. Early cowpens were common between the Edisto and Savannah Rivers, and in neighboring areas of North Carolina and Georgia. Georgia cowpens were well established by the late eighteenth century, especially between the Ogeechee and Savannah Rivers. In the Carolinas, cowpens might encompass 100 to 500 acres with clusters of corrals, outbuildings, living quarters, and gardens. The herds might have 1,000 to 6,000 head, suggesting that overgrazing occurred even if the acreage and herd sizes were exaggerated by colonial promoters.[22]

The cattle industry experienced a marked decline in the 1700s, a decline clearly visible in the mid-eighteenth-century Charleston archaeological record. Epidemics in 1742 and 1743 killed many cattle. The decline was sudden and large, characteristic of a new disease in a virgin population. Georgia cattle were implicated in the spread of the disease, which was said to have originated in Spanish cattle. One of the diseases involved, "Spanish staggers," may be babesiosis (also known as Texas or Southern fever), caused by a tickborne parasite. Babesiosis is characterized by massive organ damage. Animals with acquired immunity have a low-grade infection and are carriers of the disease but must be reinfected to sustain immunity. The free-range animal-husbandry practices common in the lowcountry permitted infected animals to mix with healthy ones. Restrictions on the movement of cattle from Carolina pinewoods in the 1700s may have been intended to control this disease.[23]

Figure 5.4. (*Top*) Florida Scrub cattle on the James Durrance estate, 1971; (*bottom*) *A Spring Day* by M. B. Paine, taken near Charleston in 1920. The cattle in these photos exhibit the mottled coloration and lean appearance described in Spanish accounts; the Florida Scrub exhibits horns like those recovered in Charleston. (Scrub cattle from *World Cattle, vol. III*, by John E. Rouse, copyright © 1973 University of Oklahoma Press. Reproduced with permission. All Rights reserved. *Spring Day* from Collections of The Charleston Museum, Charleston, South Carolina.)

Lessons from Early Sites

These early sites offer enticing glimpses into colonial life in the lowcountry. Colonists were instructed to find and develop commercially viable products, and these collections show that they had every intention of doing so. The presence of the latest British ceramics and of Chinese porcelain and other goods likely obtained from Spanish traders indicates that external ties between Carolina and global markets were important from the first years of the colony. Colonists also found that the Indian trade and cattle ranching had economic potential. Very quickly, settlers modified their traditional economic, husbandry, and dietary practices to emphasize ones that offered greater chances of success. They also altered the landscape as deer were overhunted, Native American farms were abandoned, additional lands were cleared or burned, and cattle grazed freely. These early sites contain many of the significant elements that came to characterize Charleston and other lowcountry sites.

6

RAIDING AND TRADING

In 1706 Spaniards from St. Augustine launched a seaward invasion of Charleston. A French frigate and four Spanish sloops entered the harbor. The invaders hoped to find the town's residents weakened from an epidemic of yellow fever. But a new brick seawall greeted the invaders. "When the fleet came in view of the fortifications, they suddenly bore up and came to anchor." The governor "summarily dismissed the demand for surrender." The Spanish launched a few ineffective skirmishes and limped home. Katherine Saunders Pemberton notes that the inhabitants of Charleston must have been pleased. But they remained on guard; a year later the Commons House warned of "ffinishing our ffortifications wch under God hath been our security and will be a ffuture terror to our Enemies and deter them from giving us any more such visits."[1]

Charleston's early years were shaped by distrust, alarms, attacks, sieges, competition, and trade, primarily with Spanish Florida. Spain had long claimed the same lands and trade alliances now claimed by Britain. The city was only 75 miles from Parris Island, where Spanish Florida's original capital, Santa Elena, had been. Charles II of Spain made tensions worse in 1693 when he proclaimed sanctuary and freedom for Africans fleeing enslavement in the Carolinas if they converted to Catholicism. Competition for the Indian trade and insecure sea routes further complicated the uneasy relationship between the two colonies. The Spanish presence also created opportunities for Native Americans, both as individuals and as groups, to play British, Spanish, and, eventually, French interests against each other for economic and political advantage. Alliances among Native Americans, and between colonists and Native Americans, changed regularly. Pirates of all nationalities—or none—harassed shipping lanes and coastal communities along the Atlantic seaboard, in the Gulf of Mexico, and in the

Caribbean. The late seventeenth century witnessed raids and threatened raids among all of these groups. Massive fortifications dominated the Charleston and St. Augustine waterfronts. Away from the watchful eye of the Spanish crown and the Lords Proprietors, however, colonists engaged the "enemy" in trade.

Colonists quickly spread throughout much of the lowcountry, claiming the best lands. They established a lively trade in deerskins, furs, lumber, naval stores, Indian slaves, cattle, and agricultural products. Much of this bounty was shipped to Caribbean markets.[2]

Colonists found that Charleston's original location was difficult to defend against Spanish attacks and was a poor place from which to engage in maritime trade. Security was essential for access to inland deer herds, grazing lands, and forest products. The intercoastal trade in provisions and access to international markets were vital to Carolina's success and needed to be protected. In 1680 the city was moved downstream, to the confluence of the Ashley and Cooper Rivers. The new location was not only more defensible but "ideally cituated for trade."[3]

Charleston's prosperity also demanded that the Spanish threat be removed. The outbreak of Queen Anne's War in 1702 presented an opportunity for Carolina governor James B. Moore to take action. He besieged St. Augustine by sea and by land. Residents of St. Augustine, including Africans who had fled Carolina, were forewarned by Spanish soldiers and Guale Indians fleeing missions north of the town. Townspeople barricaded themselves in St. Augustine's Castillo de San Marcos. Moore and his men occupied the town, but they were unable to capture the Castillo. When ships from Cuba appeared on the shoreline, Moore abandoned his siege and ships, returning to Carolina by land.[4]

Moore sought to restore his reputation two years later, in 1704, with a ruthless raid on Spanish Florida's Apalachee Province. Carolinians and their Native American allies devastated the missions, killing and torturing scores of people. They returned to Carolina with nearly 1,000 Indian slaves and other plunder, including cattle on the hoof. The destruction of the Apalachee missions effectively gave control of the greater Southeast to British traders. Spain retaliated in 1706, invading Charleston Harbor while the city again languished under a yellow fever epidemic. Charleston was prepared this time, by virtue of its new fortifications.

Today's city emerged after Charles Town was relocated to its present location. The harbor was the key to the colony's success. From this setting, colonists could link their interior trade networks and plantations with an expanded overseas market. The city became the social and intellectual center of a late-eighteenth- and early-nineteenth-century plantation-based economy. In the seventeenth century, however, settlers were justifiably fearful of their location "in the very chap of the Spaniard."[5]

The Walled City

Despite the open settlement proposed with the Grand Modell, Charleston became a walled city. Construction of the town's protective wall began in 1694 when the colonial government ratified the first of many statutes authorizing construction of a brick "wharf wall" or "curtain line" after several years of watching the town's waterfront erode. Construction of a brick seawall began in 1696 and continued for a decade. A "fortress" was commissioned for the southeast corner of the town, now known as Granville Bastion. In 1699 a brick "half moon" was built at the eastern end of Broad Street, now known as Half Moon Battery. Both Granville Bastion and Half Moon Battery replaced earlier wooden forts.[6]

A plan to enclose the entire town within a system of entrenchments, flankers, parapets, sally ports, a gate, and drawbridges was ratified in 1703. British masons and African slaves laid approximately seven million bricks along the east side of the bay (now East Bay Street) between 1696 and 1708, creating a solid defensive line from Granville Bastion to Craven Bastion. The seaward curtain line also included the Half Moon Battery and three redans projecting into the harbor. The seawall was brick, but the three landward walls were built of earth and wood. Four additional bastions, a ravelin guarding the town gate at Broad and Meeting streets, and eight redans were included in the new works. A brick powder magazine built in 1712 against the northern wall completed security plans for the city.

When construction ended, Charleston was a walled city. But the city quickly expanded beyond the wall. The redans, ravelin, and bastions eventually became part of the archaeological record. No trace of the original city wall is visible aboveground, challenging us to imagine the early Charleston landscape with the walls that defined it. Protecting this largely undocumented aspect of Charleston's heritage from construction projects and erosion also is challenging.

The exact location of the wall was generally unknown until Granville Bastion was exposed in 1925 during renovation of the Missroon House. Albert Simons and Samuel Lapham made photographs, notes, and a sketch map at the time, but they did not conduct formal excavations, and they retained no artifacts. Those brave enough to flatten themselves into a 15-inch crawl space may view Granville Bastion in the basement of the nineteenth-century Missroon House, now Historic Charleston Foundation headquarters.

Following work on Granville Bastion, no further archaeological work was conducted on Charleston's defenses, or elsewhere in the city, until 1965, when a small portion of the Half Moon Battery was exposed by John Miller. That portion is still visible to the public in the basement of the Exchange Building, which was built over the battery. Otherwise, the exact footprint of the wall is largely unknown.[7]

South Adger's Wharf: The Redan at Tradd Street

Three sites are associated with this protective wall: the redan at Tradd Street (now known as South Adger's Wharf), the Half Moon Battery (now the Exchange Building), and the Powder Magazine. In 2005 Charleston mayor Joseph P. Riley Jr. appointed a Walled City Task Force, charging it with developing a plan to interpret and protect the wall. Two years later Nicholas Butler discovered a 1785 plan of "a Water Lot and Wharf, the property of Mrs. Rebecca Motte," drawn by Charleston's premier surveyor, Joseph Purcell. Butler's discovery prompted the first controlled archaeological excavation of the city wall.

The detailed 1785 plat of Mrs. Motte's wharf shows the curtain line along East Bay Street and the 1750s Lower Market in front of a demolished redan. The plan also shows a series of waterfront buildings along the north side of the street and plots of land purchased by the Commissioners of the Markets. The portion of the wall shown in the 1785 plat is now underneath a historic cobblestone street known as South Adger's Wharf. That very spot was temporarily paved in asphalt in 2007 to protect it from damage by a municipal drainage project. At the urging of Task Force co-chairs Katherine Pemberton and Peter McGee, the City of Charleston and Mayor Riley agreed to fund an archaeological project before the cobblestones were restored to their historic position.

The Task Force assembled a team to locate and document the redan. Archaeologists from The Charleston Museum and Brockington and Associates were joined by historians, preservationists, docents, students, volunteers, and skilled crews from the City of Charleston Parks Department and Charleston Water Systems. The dig began on a blustery January day with a backhoe trench across South Adger's Wharf. The trench revealed an intact, layered archaeological site, but no redan. A second trench, perpendicular to the first, uncovered a massive brick drain from the 1850s and several recent service lines.

Eric Poplin caught a glimpse of bright-white lime mortar and soft, red brick, both characteristic of early-eighteenth-century fortifications. Screeners busily sifted the soil, layer by layer, recovering artifacts spanning the eighteenth century. This work eventually revealed about 20 feet of the redan's north flank. The wall was intact and lay about a foot below the present ground surface. When the wall was demolished in 1784, apparently the parapet was simply pushed into the mudflat in front of the wall, and the foundation was left standing. The area was filled and then paved to enhance access to what was, by that time, the Lower Market.

These were promising findings, so the Task Force petitioned the City to continue excavations the next year, following the footprint of the redan southward into a nearby city-owned parking lot. The second phase of fieldwork, conducted by the same crew plus field school students from the College of Charleston, exposed the point of the redan and a large expanse of its south face. This time we excavated below the water table to expose the redan's foundation and learn about the construction and maintenance of the wall.

Figure 6.1. A portion of the redan exposed at South Adger's Wharf in 2009. (Collections of The Charleston Museum, Charleston, South Carolina.)

The design and construction of the redan match descriptions in seventeenth- and eighteenth-century manuals. The surviving brick face was 102 inches high, resting on a cribbing of two-foot-high cypress piles. A line of larger pilings driven vertically into the marsh five feet from the brick created a moat. The cypress, and occasionally cedar, pilings were seven feet long, sharply pointed at the bottom and rounded at the top.[8]

The fill was markedly different inside and outside the pilings. The area between the redan and the posts was filled with large ballast stones, while the mud outside the moat contained brick, mortar, and shell rubble. Artifacts were much more common outside the moat, particularly green bottle glass, ceramics, and pipes. Food debris such as peach pits and fish vertebrae accumulated in the mudflats. Shells from peanuts, a South American domesticate, were preserved in the waterlogged deposits.

Casual and continuous filling and silt accumulation outside the seawall at South Adger's Wharf produced a complex stratified archaeological site. Multiple layers of refuse contained materials dating from the very early eighteenth century, as well as from the later eighteenth, nineteenth, and twentieth centuries, including refuse from the Lower Market (see chapter 9).

Much of the animal debris outside of the seawall was discarded from nearby residences and waterfront businesses before municipal refuse collection began in Charleston. This debris included remains of pigs, cows, and chickens, as well as opossums, turkeys, sea turtles, freshwater turtles, and six different kinds of local fishes, among other animals. Beef was the dominant meat, in proportions very similar to that at other sites in the city during this period. The moat collection, however, is most memorable for the high percentage of rats that died, and probably lived, there. A quarter of the individuals in the moat collection are Old World rats. This suggests that the Charleston waterfront provided more than a place for boats to dock and merchants to conduct business. The area beneath the docks and buildings, full of accumulating refuse, provided ideal habitat for rats, much as such places do today.

This dig presented an excellent opportunity for neighbors and tourists to share in the process of discovery and interpretation. Docents from Historic Charleston Foundation greeted visitors to the highly visible excavations on a busy street. Soon, Charleston tour guides were describing the dig to their clients. The tours were updated often, thanks to a blog maintained by Butler. Many visitors expressed disappointment when excavation units were

refilled and no longer visible to the public. With the support of private do-
nations and a Public Outreach Grant from the Southeastern Archaeological
Conference, the Task Force placed two wayside exhibits and a section of the
retrieved parapet in front of the city-owned parking lot near the excavated
area. The City paved the footprint of the redan in brick to distinguish it
from the surrounding historic cobblestone pavement. A trip down East Bay
Street always finds someone at the exhibit.

Half Moon Battery

The Half Moon Battery and its associated guardhouse were constructed in
1699 at the foot of Broad Street, where they dominated the harbor. Eventually, in 1771, the Exchange Building was built on top of the battery. The
battery was located by John Miller during his 1965 excavations in the basement. Working in an area approximately 7.5 × 28 feet between the eastern
wall of the Exchange and the front of the battery, Miller exposed the face of
the battery and reached its base. The Half Moon Battery was sloped (bat-
tered) in a manner similar to Granville Bastion, and its foundation was
intact underneath multiple layers of fill. The exposed face extended eight
feet from its base to the surviving top portion, just below the Exchange
basement floor.

Miller found two parallel rows of vertical posts in front of the battery,
with planks against the inside of the inner row. He interpreted this as a
coffer dam to hold back seawater during repair of the battery in 1752. We
revisited photos of Miller's dig during the South Adger's Wharf project and
were struck by the carefully carved tops of the pilings. They seem too well
finished for a temporary construction. It is possible that they were part of
a breakwater, like the row of pilings located five feet from the face of the
redan at South Adger's Wharf.

Miller died shortly after completing the Half Moon Battery excavation
and did not write up his findings. The artifacts he recovered remained
unanalyzed and were divided between The Charleston Museum and the
Rebecca Motte Chapter of the Daughters of the American Revolution,
owners of the Exchange Building. They languished there until Elaine Herold transferred the materials to the Museum and analyzed Miller's finds.

The American Bicentennial commemoration in 1976 prompted renovation of the Exchange Building and a renewed interest in archaeology.
Herold excavated test units and monitored construction trenches as stair

Figure 6.2. Barrel fragments recovered by Elaine Herold from a mid-eighteenth-century layer of naval stores in front of the Exchange Building in 1979. The spilled naval stores preserved many organic artifacts. This layer likely represents debris in the storm surge during the hurricane of 1752. (Photo by Sean Money, Collections of The Charleston Museum, Charleston, South Carolina.)

towers were installed on the east side of the building in 1979. She recorded several layers of fill deposited before the Exchange was built. The lowest layer is one of the most interesting and unusual in the city. Dark grey to black soil was cemented together with pine pitch. The deposit had a strong petroleum-like smell when first exposed. The pitch contained well-preserved wood, grass, cloth, and leather fragments, including barrel staves and bands, shingles, wood scraps, wood shavings, and wood trimmings. Herold recognized these as barrels filled with naval stores. The artifacts recovered date to the middle of the eighteenth century. Herold thought they might be associated with the 1752 hurricane.

We returned to the basement of the Exchange for a small mitigation project in 1988 and recovered animal bones from an area in front of the Half Moon Battery. None of these were from the 1710s–1750s, but a small sample was recovered from the 1750s–1790s, when the Half Moon Battery was still standing, as well as from the 1820s–1850s when the Exchange Building stood on top of it.

The Exchange Building animal remains provided our first snapshot of public health and the urban environment. Little was known about animal use in Charleston when we analyzed these specimens, but the small sample proved prophetic. The 1750–1790 collection contained no commensal animals at all—no rats, dogs, cats, horses, or snakes; but two-thirds of the meat represented was beef. By the 1820s–1850s, Old World rats constituted a quarter of the individuals, accompanied by a cat. In the 1980s we interpreted the emphasis on cattle and the absence of rats in the 1750–1790 collection as biases related to site formation processes, such as preservation, and to the analytical bias associated with the small Exchange sample. The dominance of beef and the increase in rodents are now understood to be fundamental aspects of life in the city. Here, too, was our first evidence that public buildings looked like private homes in other ways. The mere presence of animal remains in the guardhouse should have been an adequate clue that people lived at public sites such as this, or at least ate meals at such sites, and that these meals included pork, beef, duck, and chicken. Beef was evidently the preferred meat in the guardhouse, as it was throughout the city. The pattern of animal use sketched in the 1750–1790 Exchange materials persisted within the city into the late nineteenth century.

In hindsight, we see that even small assemblages from secondary deposits, such those from the Half Moon Battery and Exchange Building, offer accurate perspectives on life in the city unavailable from written sources. This is contrary to what most archaeologists believed in the 1980s. It required work at the Powder Magazine in the 1990s to drive home the truth of these surprises.

The Powder Magazine

The Powder Magazine, constructed in 1712, is the city's oldest standing structure. The fortified town needed a place to store munitions, a place that was within the wall and close—but not too close—to the rest of the town. In 1703 the Assembly directed that a "country magazen" be built for proper storage of powder and arms, within the "intrenchment" on the lands of three indifferent freeholders.[9]

The Powder Magazine was built on the sparsely occupied northern edge of the walled city, inside the wall but isolated from the most densely developed sections of the early town. The northern portion of the wall ran from the intersection of Cumberland and Meeting Streets to Craven Bastion, which is now under the U.S. Customs House on Market and East Bay Streets. The Powder Magazine today sits at an odd angle along Cumberland Street, because Cumberland is part of an urban street grid imposed long after the Powder Magazine was built.

The Powder Magazine was the first preserved historic building in Charleston. The low brick structure was used as a magazine intermittently until 1820. After that time it was used as a wine cellar, livery stable, print shop, and blacksmith shop. A proposal to demolish the building stimulated the South Carolina Chapter of the National Society of Colonial Dames of America to purchase the property in 1902. The Colonial Dames renovated the structure and subsequently used it as their headquarters and a museum.

Lowcountry humidity took a heavy toll on the building. Historic Charleston Foundation leased the property from the Colonial Dames in

Figure 6.3. Excavations in the yard of the 1712 Powder Magazine in 1993. (Collections of The Charleston Museum, Charleston, South Carolina.)

1993 and directed extensive research and renovation. The project included archaeological study to reveal details about the construction and evolution of the building. An early-twentieth-century tile floor was removed, and a block of five-foot squares excavated in the exposed sand floor. Excavations in the north yard of the magazine exposed remnants of a wall and a series of pits filled with eighteenth-century debris. Features and fill both inside and outside the building contained nineteenth- and twentieth-century materials. Unexpectedly, we also documented daily life in the early-eighteenth-century town.

We expected to recover primarily arms-related artifacts, considering the purpose of the building. Post stains for powder racks and a few military artifacts were found: a silver scabbard tip, two gunflints, and a link of decorative chain. We also encountered large and varied quantities of domestic refuse, including imported ceramics, wine bottles, pharmaceutical bottles, tobacco pipes in large numbers, colono ware, and great quantities of animal remains. These domestic artifacts came from mid-eighteenth-century features located outside the structure and from the sand floor inside the building.

We began work at the site with the assumption that this military site would be relatively clean, that any food debris would be from rations, and that no one lived at the site other than guards on duty. The wide range of animals present, the types of pig and cow bones recovered, and the relative absence of sawed bones all suggested otherwise. In addition to remains of cows and pigs, we recovered rabbits, raccoons, deer, ducks, chickens, turkeys, common pigeons, freshwater turtles, sea turtles, sharks, rays, freshwater fishes, and estuarine fishes. Some of the domestic animals likely were slaughtered on the property; we recovered specimens from all parts of the carcass, including teeth and phalanges (toe bones). Sawed bones were expected because sawing is more often associated with commercial butchery, such as one would expect of military rations. Instead, we found low percentages of sawed bones and high percentages of hacked, cut, and burned specimens, what one might expect if butchering, cooking, and trash disposal took place on the site. The cut specimens probably are the result of on-site food preparation, and the burned specimens likely originated from on-site trash disposal. The remains of a fetal or newborn pig in the 1750–1820 materials are further evidence that animals were raised on the property. The only commensal animals in the 1710–1750 deposits are two rats, out of 30 individuals. The Powder Magazine animal remains are very similar to those recovered from eighteenth-century residential sites.

We initially thought it unlikely that soldiers stationed at the Powder Magazine would raise and butcher their own livestock, but the animal remains and material culture testify to a strong domestic component and to on-site butchery. We considered the possibility that the 1820 Powder Magazine materials might be refuse from surrounding residences tossed onto the property. This seems unlikely, however, because ceramic fragments recovered from inside and outside of the magazine cross-mend, indicating that refuse originated on the property and remained there after it was discarded.

Did some Charleston sites serve as residences as well as public facilities? The Powder Magazine appears to be such a multifunction structure. The artifacts recovered are typical of eighteenth-century domestic refuse. Butler recently uncovered documentary evidence that the gunner stationed at nearby Craven Bastion lived at that site with his family and slaves. In times of crisis, sentries, gunners, and even prisoners lived within the bastion. It is likely that this arrangement prevailed at the Powder Magazine as well.

Materials of the Early Town

The Half Moon Battery, the redan, and the Powder Magazine were primarily defensive, but the artifacts recovered from them suggest commercial and domestic functions, too (appendix 4). Zone 10, excavated in front of the redan at South Adger's Wharf, produced a representative sample of materials used in the city at the beginning of the eighteenth century. This zone was the original intertidal mudflat in front of the brick seawall in 1703. Though the mudflat accumulated casual refuse throughout the first half of the eighteenth century, here we discuss only the early-eighteenth-century deposit, as a sample of the early colonial period.

The archaeological record of this waterfront deposit reflects contributions to this urban society by people from a variety of backgrounds. The recovery of Native American pottery, though limited, shows that Native Americans played a role in urban life, even as their numbers diminished and many moved away from the Atlantic seaboard. The amount of colono ware increases as African Americans became the majority of urban residents. Interactions among Native American, African, British, Caribbean, French, and Spanish traditions are reflected by the presence of a variety of ceramics.

Olive green glass from wine bottles was the most common waterfront discard. Ceramics were less common. The waterfront deposit contained few small, personal household items, such as clothing, furnishings, and personal possessions. Artifacts associated with storing and shipping goods, such as barrel straps, were more abundant.

Clay pipes, from plain stem fragments to distinctive bowls, were discarded in the mudflats. Clay tobacco pipes are relatively rare in Charleston, particularly when compared to the tobacco-producing colonies of Virginia, Maryland, and even North Carolina, where both locally produced and imported pipes supplied colonists "besotted" by tobacco.[10]

Several imported ceramic types were recovered from the mudflat, particularly examples of delftware, a soft-bodied earthenware with an opaque tin-enamel glaze. Delftware table and teawares were often painted in blue, or a palette of colors, and included bowls, cups, and serving vessels. We also found small ointment pots, squat bulbous containers with a cylindrical foot and everted rim. All of the examples in Zone 10 were undecorated, with a bluish tin glaze. We also recovered taller, cylindrical gallipots. These have flat bases, straight sides, and everted rims; they once held medicines. The South Adger's Wharf gallipots were decorated with blue horizontal stripes. A small amount of Chinese porcelain also was recovered. Most porcelain fragments were decorated in blue, but a few pieces were Imari porcelain, embellished with red and gold enamel over a blue-painted underglaze decoration.

Staffordshire slipware was the most common ceramic type on the waterfront, and our sample included early-style press-molded and relief-decorated vessels. The majority were open dishes, featuring glazed interiors with a variety of trailed and combed slip decorations, unglazed exteriors, and coggled (pie crust) rims. These were widely used kitchen and cooking wares. Small cups and drinking pots, decorated with a series of dark dots around the rim and combed-and-trailed decoration around the center of the body, also were common; we recognized small fragments of cups from glaze on both sides.

Black-glazed Buckley earthenwares, lead-glazed redwares, and stonewares stored food and beverages and served as kitchen wares. Utilitarian stonewares, particularly brown salt-glazed stoneware and Rhenish stoneware, filled the waterfront. North Devon gravel-tempered ware, North Devon sgraffito slipware, Manganese Mottled ware, and slip-coated wares, types typical of the late seventeenth century, were less common.

Colono ware is South Carolina's contribution to the ceramic world and is found on most lowcountry sites. This low-fired, unglazed earthenware can have European, African, and Native American characteristics. Colono ware initially was attributed to Native American potters by Ivor Nöel Hume and

Figure 6.4. Basic forms of colono ware: a globular jar and open bowl. (Photo by Sean Money, Collections of The Charleston Museum, Charleston, South Carolina.)

Stanley South, who called it Colono Indian ware. By the late 1970s Ronald Anthony, Lesley Drucker, Patrick Garrow, Thomas Wheaton, and Leland Ferguson proposed that African Americans might be the primary producers and users of the ware, because they recovered the pottery on plantation sites.[11]

By the early 1980s researchers could define colono ware varieties based on paste, finish, and overall composition. Colono ware likely was made by people of both African and Native American descent from the late seventeenth century into the early nineteenth century. Colono ware is also recovered from households occupied by Europeans and evidently was included among the kitchen wares used on plantations. It is unclear if enslaved African Americans used these wares to prepare their own food, food for the master's table, or both. Ferguson suggests that colono wares also were used to prepare traditional medicines.[12]

Most colono ware is found at sites occupied by African Americans, such as slave villages or the kitchens of planters' complexes. Evidence for Native American influence and manufacture has emerged more recently, at sites with a strong historic Native American presence such as St. Giles Kussoe. Although scholars define characteristics that distinguish African from Native American wares, many argue that colono ware is a product of creolization, the mixing of cultures. Colono ware from the waterfront includes some examples that are similar in style to those from St. Giles Kussoe, and likely the product of Native American potters.[13]

Zone 10 also produced Spanish ceramics, particularly the ubiquitous storage vessels known as Olive Jars. The amphora-shaped olive jars were produced for five centuries with only modest changes in form and size. They were used to transport and store liquids of all kinds. These heavy vessels are solidly built with a buff to pinkish mineral-tempered clay body and a white slipped exterior. The interior is often glazed green.

Trade with Spanish Florida

Spanish Florida was a constant source of concern in Charleston. The struggle for dominance resulted in four intercolonial wars between 1689 and 1763. Colonial governments erected costly fortifications at both Charleston and St. Augustine. The proximity of St. Augustine to Charleston also

Figure 6.5. Example of a Spanish storage jar. Several Spanish and Spanish Caribbean ceramics, including Olive Jars and Spanish storage jars, were recovered from Atlantic Wharf in 1983. (Photo by Rick Rhodes, Collections of The Charleston Museum, Charleston, South Carolina.)

presented opportunities for trade and exchange, if only in the guise of seiz-ing one another's vessels. Archaeological evidence suggests British and Spanish colonists capitalized on the proximity of the towns, the political situation of Spanish Florida, and the relative isolation of St. Augustine to engage in illicit and lucrative trade, beginning in the late seventeenth cen-tury. Archaeologists find British goods in St. Augustine by the late 1600s, and these increased steadily during the 1700s. A flourishing illicit trade is well documented for the period after 1713, but archaeological evidence suggests this trade began shortly after Charleston was founded. It declined only during periods when wars between Britain and Spain spilled over into the colonies.

Spanish Florida was governed under a mercantilist philosophy: colonies should produce raw materials for the mother country and receive manu-factured goods in return. Colonial self-sufficiency was discouraged, and dependence on manufactured goods from Spain was encouraged. St. Au-gustine's primary mission was to serve as a military and coast guard station. Much of the population relied upon an annual allotment of funds and sup-plies known as the *situado*. The *situado* was notoriously unreliable; years went by without delivery of the annual stipend. Colonists turned to illicit trade to supply the city. Merchants in Charleston and Savannah officially supplied the St. Augustine *situado* after 1750.[14]

Charleston's unsanctioned trade with St. Augustine, interrupted dur-ing Queen Anne's War, resumed in the 1710s and flourished in the 1730s. Charleston merchants offered St. Augustine products that were superior to those from Spain and relatively inexpensive. Ships from Charleston, and a smaller number of vessels from New York, Virginia, and Georgia brought St. Augustine beef, port, butter, cheese, rum, spirits, and "European goods" such as ceramics, glassware, clothing items, and other material necessi-ties. In exchange, Charleston received oranges and other tropical fruits, and payment in Spanish silver and gold coinage. Coinage, or specie, was rare in Carolina, and Spanish silver was highly valued. Spanish coins are nearly as common as British halfpennies on Charleston sites. Many of these Spanish coins were altered into charms or medallions, but others were evidently just specie. Charleston sites also contain small but consistent numbers of Spanish, as well as French, ceramics. Chinese porcelain, Spanish Olive Jars, Muscovy ducks, and guinea pigs may be additional evidence of this trade.[15]

The landward walls of Charleston were demolished gradually in the 1730s as the city expanded, despite intermittent hostilities between Charleston and St. Augustine. The brick seawall, though, remained intact through the

American Revolution. Charleston's port grew as new docks and wharves, known as bridges, were built. An ongoing struggle between those wanting to maintain the curtain line to secure the waterfront and those wanting to breach the curtain line for easier access to wharves reflects the changing attitude of the city. A 1736 law allowed the parapet to be opened on East Bay Street "for all Bridges that extended twenty Feet beyond Low Water Mark." The openings could be "Convenient for . . . communication of said bridges with the said Bay Street." The 1739 map of the city shows eight such wharves. The brickwork was demolished to ground level in 1784; the land was subdivided, and new structures were built over the old seawall. Charleston had expanded beyond the wall long before that.[16]

Charleston and St. Augustine Follow Different Paths

Moore's raids changed the outlook and development of both St. Augustine and Charleston. They gave Carolina a more secure hold on the Indian trade and bolstered Charleston's growth. After Moore's raids, Charlestonians quickly ventured beyond the town walls. Hides, forest products, game, livestock, and other materials flowed from local farms and the Carolina backcountry into Charleston, fueling the city's rise as a commercial center. Moore's audacity somewhat embodies the broader British colonial attitude described by Walter Edgar: "Everyone in Carolina was here to

Figure 6.6. Charleston's focus on commerce is embodied in a delftware punch bowl declaring "Success to Trade," recovered from the interior of the Exchange Building in 1965. (Photo by Sean Money, Collections of The Charleston Museum, Charleston, South Carolina.)

make money." Commerce and the quality of life in Charleston overshad-owed concerns for defense by the mid-eighteenth century. Colonists in St. Augustine, however, became more defensive. Carl Halbirt notes that the ever-expanding British settlements created "an environment of fear and uncertainty" in Spanish Florida. Spain's response was to build additional defensive structures and establish peripheral buffer communities.[17]

These contrasting attitudes played out in animal use at the two towns, despite sharing a similar bountiful coast. The percentages of terrestrial and aquatic animals in the archaeological record starkly portray the differ-ences. In Charleston between 1710 and 1750, terrestrial animals contribute 61 percent of individuals, while reptiles and fishes constitute 28 percent of the individuals (appendix 5). Preferences are reversed in St. Augustine; in the 1700–1763 assemblage, terrestrial animals account for 28 percent of the individuals, whereas reptiles and fishes contribute 67 percent of the indi-viduals. Local, estuarine-based fishing was clearly important in both cities, but more so in St. Augustine. It is possible that the dominance of fish at St. Augustine reflects the growing Native American population in the city. Many Native Americans who sought refuge in St. Augustine followed their long-standing practice of relying on fish, and this may have influenced the availability and use of fish in the Spanish town.[18]

One of the chief differences between St. Augustine and Charleston is the archaeological evidence for mullets. They contribute 2 percent of the indi-viduals in the 1710–1750 Charleston assemblage, compared to 26 percent of the individuals in the 1700–1763 St. Augustine assemblage. Cast nets are usually used to catch mullets, because these vegetarian animals rarely take a hook. The abundance of mullets in St. Augustine suggests frequent use of such nets. Mullets may have been more frequently consumed in Charleston than the animal remains suggest. Cast net weights are regularly recovered from Carolina lowcountry archaeological sites, and an early engraving of Charleston includes a group of fishermen with a fish net in the foreground.

Figure 6.7. Cast net weights from Stono Plantation, Dill Sanctuary on James Island, excavated by Ron Anthony in 1992–2000. (Photo by Sean Money, Collections of The Charleston Museum, Charleston, South Carolina.)

Figure 6.8. In this detail of the 1739 *Prospect* by Bishop Roberts, men in the foreground fish with a scoop net. (Collections of The Charleston Museum, Charleston, South Carolina.)

While St. Augustinians found the sea a reliable source of food, Charlestonians relied upon the bounty of both land and sea, raising cattle, pigs, and chickens as well as hunting in swamps, fields, and forests. The Charleston hunting tradition was so extensive that commercial hunters probably supplied Charleston with game on a regular basis, with some sold in markets, by street vendors, and in other outlets. Most of the commercial hunters and fishers were enslaved African Americans. Hunting at St. Augustine is usually interpreted as primarily, though not exclusively, an individual activity, one in which few people engaged. Not only did Charlestonians feel free to fully utilize the resources of the lowcountry, both close to the city as well as farther afield, but other aspects of the animal remains testify to the rapid growth of the colony, even during the relatively brief 1710–1750 period. And, as the town grew, so too did the amount of trash.

Lowcountry Cattle

Fortified Charleston supported a crowded settlement within the walls. The streets and yards were filled with livestock as well as people. Residents complained about penning and slaughtering animals in town, noting that the "air was infected" and that "dung and entrails of beasts were everywhere."

The Assembly appointed a town scavenger by 1710 and prohibited keeping and butchering livestock in the city. These efforts were not successful; the city was evidently filled with animal remains. Similar statutes were issued repeatedly. A 1744 grand jury presentment decried "disregard of proclamation in having drove, and still driving distempered cattle through other peoples' plantations, pastures, stocks, and lands, and even down to the Quarter House where several have died lately; and people who have killed sick cattle and sold them at market; and people who have left their dead cattle unburied on the lands and marshes." Lisa O'Steen analyzed the faunal remains from Charleston Judicial Center, adjacent to the town gates; she describes colonial Charleston as a community of farmsteads on urban lots, a city filled with roaming pigs, cattle, sheep, and goats, some dying and lying unburied on the edge of town.[19]

Beef production was important in the early economy and made possible because cattle were both numerous and healthy. British colonists took advantage of cattle left behind by late-sixteenth- and early-seventeenth-century Spanish outposts along the Atlantic coast. Carolinians also raided deep into Spanish Florida, likely ensuring that the Carolina cattle lineage was mixed. Spanish accounts declared that most Carolina cattle were from the missions and ranches of Spanish Florida. According to Alonso de Leturiondo's *Memorial to the King of Spain* (written in 1700), the British "have sought to carry off cattle from Florida because their own are so scrawny that their bulls and cows are not much different than the one-year-old calves of Florida." After his raids on Spanish Florida, Moore returned to Carolina with Native American slaves and "all that could be collected, including cows and horses." Cattle taken to the Carolinas after such raids joined feral and semiferal cattle, escapees from earlier Spanish settlements.[20]

British appetite for Spanish cattle did not end with Moore's raid. Four years after Spanish missions and ranches were destroyed, Thomas Nairne wrote to "your Lordship" that the Neck of Florida was ideal for settlement, as "the country is full of catle and horses which before the war belonged to ye Spaniard and Apalachia Indians but are now all wild."[21]

These animals were largely unimproved, pre-breeds; breeds as we know them today are a recent phenomenon. It is likely that early improved cattle did not reach the Atlantic seaboard until the very late 1700s. The only improved breed animals imported in large numbers prior to the 1860s were shorthorns, sometimes known as Durhams. None of the early cattle were the humped zebus, animals that are recent introductions.[22]

Figure 6.9. A view of Ingleside Plantation, located north of Charleston near Goose Creek, ca. 1880s. Note the small size of the ox. (Collections of The Charleston Museum, Charleston, South Carolina.)

Determining where these early animals were from is difficult; it is unlikely that they had a single origin. Colonists originated from many different parts of Europe, as well as Africa, the Americas, and Asia, and sailed from many different ports. Carolina colonists also had at least trading ties with both British and non-British partners. Spanish cattle originally came to the Americas from the Iberian peninsula or northern Africa. This is supported by mitochondrial DNA in three cow teeth deposited between 1565 and 1600 in St. Augustine and by studies of European cattle. Cattle in Spanish Florida, however, were probably the progeny of free-range Spanish herds in the Caribbean rather than imported from Iberian herds. Some Carolina cattle probably were from the British Isles or northern Europe, and others from British colonies in Bermuda, the Caribbean, or elsewhere on the Atlantic seaboard. Lord Ashley's order for cattle from Bermuda or from Maryland for St. Giles Kussoe is an example of this diversity of sources. Ashley and other early Carolina settlers also had interests in Barbados, and some cattle could have originated on that island. Barbados was originally claimed by Spain, raising the possibility that "British Caribbean" cattle had Spanish lineages instead of British or northern European ones. The thriving cattle industry in the early lowcountry indicates that cattle had long since adapted to the lowcountry, whatever their origins.[23]

Measurements of cattle bones from Spanish Florida and Charleston archaeological sites indicate that Spanish animals were larger than those of
Charleston and that at least some Carolina cattle were from Spanish terri-
tories, as the Spanish colonists claimed they were. The small animal shown
in figure 6.9 may be characteristic of Carolina animals. This conclusion is
based largely on evidence from Puerto Real, an early Spanish town occupied between 1503 and 1579 on the northern coast of Hispaniola in what is
now Haiti. Cattle bones from Puerto Real are quite large compared to those
from Florida, Charleston, and Annapolis, Maryland.[24]

Spanish cattle at Puerto Real were abundant and free-ranging. They were
also very large, approaching the size of aurochs, the large wild ancestor of
modern cattle, which reached over 2,000 pounds. Before the twentieth century, domestic cattle were much smaller than aurochs, so the large size of
the Puerto Real cattle is unexpected. Their large size is probably due to the
extensive fertile grasslands, mild climate, long growing season, and lack of
competitors, predators, and diseases on Hispaniola, conditions also found
on other Caribbean islands in the sixteenth century.

If the large size of the Puerto Real cattle can be generalized to other
sixteenth-century Caribbean islands, such as Cuba, the cattle of Florida
probably were large as well, at least initially. Florida cattle, however, were
prey to diseases shared with deer, predators such as wolves, and limited
nutritional pasturage. Thus, their body size was relatively small compared
to the animals on Hispaniola. In recent years unimproved Florida cattle,
known as criollos or scrub cows, weighed about 450 pounds when grazing
on palmetto lands, and 650 pounds when grazing on prairie.[25]

Anecdotal evidence suggests that cattle in British colonies along the Atlantic seaboard were small, even by comparison with their British counterparts. Peter Kalm, who visited Pennsylvania, New York, and New Jersey
between 1747 and 1751, wrote that livestock, including sheep, goats, pigs,
and cows,

> degenerate here and gradually become smaller. . . . The cows, horses,
> sheep and hogs are all larger in Britain, though those which are
> brought over here are of the same breed. But the first generation de-
> creases a little in bulk and the third and fourth is the same size as
> the cattle already common here. The climate, the soil and the food
> together contributed towards producing this change.

Not everyone agreed with this description, and a certain amount of national and/or colonial pride probably hampered objective reporting.[26]

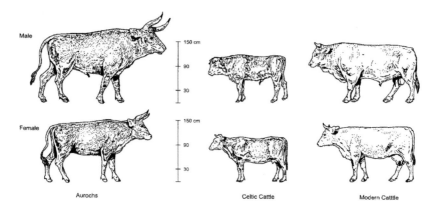

Figure 6.10. Artist's reconstruction of the aurochs or wild ox (*Bos primigenius*), Celtic, and modern domestic cattle (*B. taurus.*) (From S.J.M. Davis, *The Archaeology of Animals*, p. 135, originally produced by the late Joachim Boessneck. © 1987 by Yale University Press. Drawn by Evelyn Davis. Reproduced by permission of Simon J. M. Davis, Yale University Press, and Taylor & Francis Books, United Kingdom.)

Charleston cattle show their diverse origins by not conforming to a breed standard. Some of the best evidence for this is from horn cores. Horn itself is extremely rare, but horn is supported by an underlying bony core. Bony horn cores are seldom recovered from Charleston or Spanish Florida archaeological sites, but when they are found, they tell us a great deal about early cattle.

A most fortunate opportunity to study horn cores began with a Friday afternoon telephone call in 1988. Construction workers at the Visitor Reception and Transportation Center (VRTC) called The Charleston Museum to report that a deep backhoe excavation had encountered a waterlogged deposit full of horns. We rushed to the site and encountered a muddy pile of bones and horn cores. Wooden crates, or retaining walls, were visible in the backhoe cut. Faced with a short window of opportunity, we took photographs, collected a small sample, and sent it to the Georgia Museum of Natural History. As the zooarchaeological staff sorted through the sample, excitement grew; a range of animals and breeds, not a single breed, was represented. The horn cores appeared to be debris from a slaughter yard, horn-working industry, or tannery. They were discarded into the creek that once bisected the block and now runs under the Visitor Center. But the site was reburied before we realized the significance of the deposit.

Horn cores rescued hastily from the mud included those from short-horned and medium-horned males, females, and oxen (castrated males)

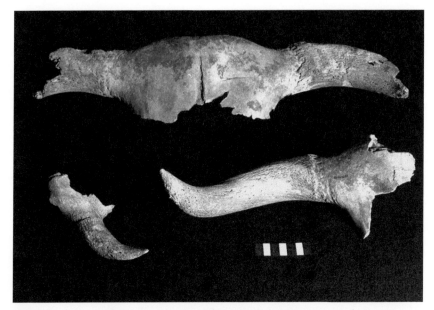

Figure 6.11. Range of horn cores recovered from the Visitor Reception and Transportation Center in 1988. (Photo by Robert Mann, Collections of The Charleston Museum, Charleston, South Carolina.)

that were between two and ten years of age at death. One of the horn cores from a medium-horned female is almost identical to a horn core from a Spanish mission. None were from the long-horned cattle often associated with Spanish cattle in North America. Although long-horned cattle were popular in Britain in the seventeenth and early eighteenth centuries, the Longhorn breed was not developed until the late eighteenth or early nineteenth century.[27]

The range of different sizes and shapes is what we would expect if animals were drawn from several different lineages. These horns probably were from animals that originated in many regions; likely some were from Spanish cattle and others from various locations. It is unlikely that many were from northern Europe, given the proximity of Spanish animals and the early success of lowcountry cowpens. Chinese porcelains, Spanish Olive Jars, and Florida oranges were not the only goods exchanged by raiding and trading between the Spanish and British colonies.[28]

Two Fortified Cities: Conflict and Commerce

Charleston was the only British walled city built in North America. Perceived threats from French, Spanish, and Native Americans stimulated the citizens of Charleston to fortify 60 acres of high ground with earthen embankments, bastions, and a substantial brick seawall by 1711. For similar reasons Spanish authorities began construction of the Castillo de San Marcos in 1672, the only extant seventeenth-century masonry fortress in the United States.

Very quickly, however, Charleston's defensive walls were breached and then destroyed to accommodate the growth of the city, first westward across the peninsula and then onto the vulnerable waterfront. Colonists explored and exploited the hinterland to provision the city and to participate in global commerce. The growth that followed Moore's raid did not end until the 1850s, when Charleston's political and psychological commitment to plantation agriculture and slavery marginalized the city's economy.

7

SUPPLYING THE EARLY CITY

In 1831 John James Audubon described the most common method for procuring wild turkeys. Turkeys were captured in pens made with a lattice of young trees. The trapper dug a tunnel under one side of the pen and laid a trail of corn into the trap. "No sooner has a Turkey discovered the train of corn, than it communicates the circumstances to the flock by a cluck, when all of them come up, and searching for the grains scattered about, at length come upon the trench, which they follow, squeezing themselves one after the other through the passage under the bridge. . . . I have heard of eighteen Turkeys having been caught in this manner at a single visit to the trap."[1]

Supplies reached the early city from two sources. One of these was outlying communities that arose along the fluid and permeable frontier. This brought an influx of products from the interior. These early towns began as nucleated settlements, but most settlers took advantage of the generous land grant system. Small farms and plantations soon dotted the frontier. Beginning in the 1690s, exports of naval stores, deerskins, beef, and rice brought economic stability to Carolina, and the city's population grew. Rice cultivation in particular relied upon the knowledge and skills of the growing number of Africans imported as enslaved laborers.[2]

The other source of supplies was coastal and maritime trade. Charleston entered the mainstream of the global mercantile economy in 1729, after royal rule replaced the inefficient proprietary government. Profitable economic ventures led to the development of additional plantations and to expanded support services in the town. Artisans, craftspeople, merchants, and professionals swelled Charleston's population. The city's economic expansion was matched by its physical expansion in the 1730s. Commercial and residential activities took place on the same property, regardless of whether the building was a humble row house or an elegant Georgian edifice.[3]

Sites of the Early Eighteenth Century

Early-eighteenth-century sites are found both inside and outside of the wall, illustrating the rapid expansion of the city beyond its protection. Six sites date to the 1710–1750 period; three of these were within the city wall, and three were close but outside it. Four sites with 1740–1760 deposits are even farther from the wall's protection.

Three of these sites, two public and one residential, illustrate the buildings, artifacts, and activities of the early eighteenth century. All of these properties are deeply stratified, multipurpose sites used in some way throughout most of Charleston's history. The Beef Market illustrates commercial activities within the city. Dock Street Theatre represents intellectual and cultural interests in the growing port town. Residential life is exemplified by one of The Charleston Museum's historic house museums. Thomas Heyward's house was built in 1772, but at least two earlier homes and businesses had occupied the lot previously.

Two additional sites highlight the colony's connections to the interior lowcountry and the goods that poured into the city from towns such as Dorchester and Willtown, as well as outlying plantations. One of these is James Stobo's rice plantation, occupied by the planter's family and the enslaved Africans and Native Americans who worked there. The other rural site, the Cowpens, was Mary Musgrove's trading post and cattle operation on the Savannah River.

The Charleston Beef Market

Charleston's first market lies beneath the massive foundations of City Hall. This location was a civic square on the Grand Modell and was designated as market square by the colonial Assembly in 1692. The market's location, just inside the city gate, provided ready access to products coming into town from outlying farms and ranches. Many different products were sold here until the market burned.

The character of the market changed over the decades. Numerous complaints suggest this was a poorly regulated, informal, open area for many years before a large brick market building was constructed in 1739, accompanied by strict regulations for its management. The structure evidently fronted on Broad Street, close to the intersection with Meeting Street. It was deemed unfit by 1760. A "neat building, supported by brick arches and surmounted by a belfry" was constructed behind the 1739 structure, and the name was changed to Upper Market or Beef Market. The new name distinguished the Beef Market from the Lower Market, built on Tradd Street in 1750, and the Fish Market, built on Queen Street in 1770. Fire destroyed the Beef Market in 1796, and it was not rebuilt. A new Centre Market was constructed on Market Street, and all of the colonial markets were closed. For sake of simplicity, the entire market on Market Square is referred to as the Beef Market, regardless of which stage in the market's operation is actually under discussion.[4]

The Beef Market did not reflect the role of the neighborhood by the time it burned. It was described in 1774 as a "low, dirty looking market for beef," a structure "whose character does not match that of the other three." As so often happens in urban settings, demolition after the fire brought new construction more in keeping with the character of the intersection. A massive new building replaced the old market in 1800. Originally built as a bank, the building became Charleston's City Hall in 1818. City Hall anchors one of the "four corners of law," a local idiom referring to the public buildings that now occupy the intersection of Meeting and Broad streets. City Hall represents local law, the historic State House (now the county courthouse) represented state law, the post office and courthouse represent federal law, and St. Michael's Episcopal Church represents God's law.[5]

In 1984, with a small grant from the University of Georgia, we excavated a single 5×10-foot unit in Washington Square Park, adjacent to City Hall, hoping to find remnants of the market. The unit revealed undisturbed deposits from the entire market period, as well as materials extending into the 1830s. The soils were so filled with artifacts and animal remains that this small unit took four people working an entire week to excavate. The unit produced an important commercial collection, one that differed substantially from domestic deposits. We planned to return to the site as soon as possible, but it was 20 years before another opportunity came our way.

That opportunity came with the renovation of Charleston's City Hall in 2004. Faced with an aging building, the City's renovation plan combined modern technology with a late-nineteenth-century decor. Evans and Schmidt Architects, well aware of the location's archaeological significance, contacted The Charleston Museum about returning to the site for mitigation and salvage. Excavation was limited to the structure's footprint, so we

Figure 7.1. The authors screen soil from the Beef Market excavations in Washington Park, 1984. Note the shell and bone concentrated in the screen. (Photo by Michael Trinkley, Collections of The Charleston Museum, Charleston, South Carolina.)

would be working in the basement, a warren of small rooms and thick brick walls. Monitoring exterior construction trenches eventually linked the archaeological evidence recovered from underneath City Hall with the materials recovered earlier from Washington Square Park.

The 1984 work in the park found undisturbed stratigraphy and rich, unique archaeological deposits. But blueprints for City Hall suggested that little of the market would be intact beneath a multiroom structure with massive foundations. We feared the market layers would be jumbled, but perhaps the 1800 building could have, should have, sealed any surviving eighteenth-century deposits, protecting them from post-1800 disturbances, even if the colonial deposits were mixed. The site was likely to yield significant data either way, and we planned an ambitious excavation project.

Excavating inside a public building while people conducted the City's business upstairs presented some logistical considerations. Horizontal control was challenging, as the walls made it impossible to establish a visual plane for a unified grid, the usual way archaeologists maintain control over the spatial and temporal contexts of the materials they recover. Each of the four interior rooms had only one door, a narrow, angled opening from the central hallway. No line of sight could be established from one room

Figure 7.2. Excavating the Beef Market in the basement of City Hall in 2004. (Collections of The Charleston Museum, Charleston, South Carolina.)

to another, and it was difficult to determine how excavation units in each room related to those in other rooms. Units were mapped in relationship to walls and corners, features that clearly were permanent. There was likewise no visual plane for vertical control, and the ceiling prohibited full extension of the stadia rod.

Managing the dirt removed from each unit was another issue. Archaeologists refer to this dirt as backdirt. Typically backdirt is removed from units and taken a few feet away to sifters to recover materials. Since the sifted dirt is replaced in the squares at the end of a project, it is prudent to screen near the unit. Some of the excavation units under City Hall were nearly three feet deep, producing a lot of backdirt. The rooms were small. Placement of squares measuring 5 × 5 feet had to allow space for the screen in each room, as well as for the people doing the screening, and for the ever-growing backdirt piles.

Soil color is a basic characteristic archaeologists use to maintain control over their excavations. A change in soil color often is the first clue that something different occurred at the site in the past. Good lighting is essential to "reading the soil," and fluorescent lighting affects the visible colors as well as the quality of color photographs. The lack of natural light made interpreting and photographing soils difficult. Neither the film types nor the special filters on both 35 mm and digital cameras corrected the color spectrum completely. Another challenge to photography was getting high enough above the excavation unit to have a full view. A position on the ladder far enough above the square to frame it entirely put the photographer's head, and camera, above the drop ceiling.

There were advantages to digging inside City Hall, however. The light fixtures were still functional; all we had to do at the beginning of the day was flip the switch. The air conditioning also worked. The field crew was not exposed to sunburn, cold weather, storms, or biting insects. The site and the field equipment were secure from erosion, vandalism, and liability injuries. Lack of ventilation can be a problem under buildings, because soils are often dry and dusty. This was not the case in City Hall's basement, because the soils had been sealed for decades by a concrete floor. Both temperature and humidity were relatively stable inside the basement, so soils maintained optimum moisture levels during and after excavation. Exposed profiles did not dry, erode, or grow mold, mushrooms, or ferns, as is often the case on long-term projects. There were no snakes or frogs in the units to greet us each morning.

Much to our surprise, the massive foundations of City Hall disturbed only a narrow strip of soil around the walls, what had been the original builder's trench. The archaeological record was pristine, with easily defined layers: the "layer cake" described by Nicholas Honerkamp in 1984. The ground surface in the basement was two feet beneath the present-day surface of Washington Square Park, so the upper levels of the market (Zones 1 thru 4) were gone, and the layers began with Zone 5 and extended through Zone 11, averaging three feet of accumulated soil. These layers were deposited between the 1690s and the 1790s and were essentially undisturbed.[6]

The deepest deposits (Zones 10 and 11) were associated with initial use of the block as Market Square, between about 1692 and 1730. At the time, the market was simply an open area. These early soils were very dark sandy loam, apparently pasture or stall muck. The black dirt of the early market was filled with large fragments of bones, teeth, and other debris. The underlying zone appeared to be naturally sterile subsoil stained by cultural activity and organic remains. Throughout the city, and just outside the footprint of the market, natural subsoil is a tan to yellow sand, and we found yellow subsoil along the exterior of City Hall, close to the market site. The heart of Market Square evidently absorbed enough organic matter to permanently stain the soil. The renovation project later exposed a portion of the 1739 market's foundation in the Broad Street sidewalk in front of City Hall, through no evidence of that building was found in the basement.

Early market activities evidently spilled out beyond this single quadrant of the central square. During their work at the Charleston County Courthouse (the Statehouse building) across Meeting Street from City Hall, J. W. Joseph and Rita Elliott of New South Associates uncovered midden deposits from the first half of the eighteenth century. These materials were highly trampled. Shell, pipe stems, pottery, and glass were common, but animal remains were the dominant artifacts. Joseph and Elliott recovered cow teeth and bones from the head as well as bones from the lower legs. Accumulations of these types of elements often are interpreted as debris from on-site butchering. Joseph suggested this reflects informal market activities and butchery of animals brought to market on the hoof.[7]

Foresight and careful planning by restoration architect Joseph Schmidt and accommodations by the City of Charleston allowed archaeological research to proceed at a deliberate pace without impacting the demolition and remodeling activities. We expected the site beneath City Hall to be compromised by nineteenth-century construction. Instead, the opposite was true. The massive footprint of the 1800 building had preserved the site. The many layers of colonial occupation, filled with market debris, were undisturbed except for the relatively narrow trenches from the building's construction. The market site possesses a physical and material signature that is very different from that of contemporary residential sites. Moreover, the remarkable preservation of the site is an important lesson for future archaeological research in Charleston and other urban settings.

Dock Street Theatre

Merchants and planters prospered during the 1730s, and some used their new wealth to support the arts. Musicals and plays presented in taverns and long rooms were so popular that a theater was constructed at the corner of Church and Queen (formerly Dock) Streets in 1736. This was the second colonial theater built in the United States, and it continues to be a significant city landmark and an active performance hall. The original theater burned in 1754.[8]

A 1930s renovation of the property was extensive, so when additional renovation was planned in 2008, we assumed that no intact archaeological evidence of the original structure would be found. The 2008 renovation plan therefore did not include archaeological study. Workers excavating

Figure 7.3. Foundation of the privy discovered during construction of an elevator shaft at Dock Street Theatre, 2008. (Collections of The Charleston Museum, Charleston, South Carolina.)

an elevator shaft in the northwest corner of the courtyard, however, encountered a brick foundation beneath a concrete floor and three feet of sterile sand. Archaeologists called to the site placed a shovel cut inside the foundation to test the fill. The shovel cut revealed very organic soil, filled with tiny bones and seeds. We carefully slid the blade out of the feature and told the architects that we would be back to sample this important deposit. The unexpected discovery of this feature in the theater complex enabled us to explore public dimensions of civic entertainment and socializing by the city's elite.

Fieldwork by The Charleston Museum and Eric Poplin of Brockington and Associates revealed a shallow foundation constructed in a haphazard fashion. The size of the foundation (6 × 8 feet) and its location suggested a single-story structure, such as a privy. Only the bottom course of bricks and the deepest fill were intact by 2008. The feature contained three layers of organic soil, 1.8 feet deep. The soil held only a few ceramic and glass artifacts, but these were large and readily identifiable as types from the second quarter of the eighteenth century. This confirmed the association of the privy with the early colonial theater. The deposit included animal remains, pollen, charcoal, wood cinders, and plaster, as well as ceramic and glass artifacts, suggesting that food service and consumption was part of theater life.

Palynologist John Jones found well-preserved pollen in the highly organic soil. Some pollen is from popular shade or landscape trees, likely ornamentals growing in the city at the time. Pollen grains from weedy vegetation also were present. Much of the pollen was from flowering plants, likely used in floral arrangements and decorations, particularly carnations, lilies, and honeysuckles. Pollen grains from plant groups that include broccoli, goosefoot, dill, caraway, buckwheat, beans, maize, and cereals were well represented. Some of the pollen probably was from plants growing near the theater, and not pollen from foods, though some pollen from the brassica family (e.g., broccoli, cauliflower, turnips) might have been ingested.

The plants highlight the global reach of the lowcountry cuisine. The brassicas, for example, were largely domesticated in Europe, buckwheat was originally domesticated in China, and both beans and maize were domesticated in the Americas. The combination of Eurasian crops with American ones illustrates what Alfred Crosby called "the Columbian Exchange," in which plants, animals, and pathogens were transferred in both directions across the Pacific and Atlantic Oceans and between the Southern and Northern Hemispheres.[9]

The animal remains are similar to those in other Charleston collections, with one exception. The Dock Street collection contains an unusually large number of bird bones. Twenty-nine of the 72 chicken specimens are small bones from the end of the wing. This high number is largely due to the fine-screen recovery used in Zone 2, which recovered 29 bones that are so small they would rarely be recovered in a larger-meshed screen. In life, these bones are involved in flight and support primary flight feathers. The same feathers were historically favored for quill pens or for quills in general. Flight feathers were also used as bobbins, paintbrushes, arrow fletching, and picks for musical instruments. The latter use best fits the profile of a theater, and these bones may be evidence of quills used as plectra for harpsichords.

The harpsichord is a horizontal stringed instrument, similar in appearance to a piano. The strings are plucked, not struck, and each string has a separate plectrum. The harpsichord was considered somewhat portable and was transported from a musician's home to rehearsal and performance. Musicians usually maintained their own instruments, and replacing plectra was a regular part of the servicing. Crow quills were most commonly used;

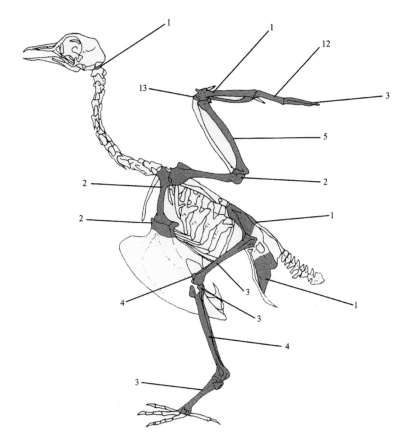

Figure 7.4. Diagram showing chicken bones recovered during fine-screen recovery at the Dock Street Theatre privy. (Used by courtesy of the Georgia Museum of Natural History, Collections of The Charleston Museum, Charleston, South Carolina.)

chicken quills lack the necessary stiffness. Perhaps that is why so many were discarded in the privy. The chicken bones indicate pen production or the maintenance of musical instruments. Both are activities likely to occur at a theater. Though the specimens do not exactly match the prescribed materials for either task, the fact that this cluster of chicken bones is unique among the numerous Charleston assemblages suggests they reflect events specific to the theater.

The Heyward-Washington House in the Early Eighteenth Century

Archaeological excavations in the 1970s by Elaine Herold at the Heyward-Washington House highlight the complex, multifunctional histories of Charleston's townhouses. Grand Modell lot 72 was granted by 1680. Several different people owned the site, only some of whom are known by name. The archaeological and documentary records become clearer after 1730, when gunsmith John Milner lived and worked there. Thomas Heyward's townhouse was the last of at least three houses on the property. In the late nineteenth century, the site was a boardinghouse and a bakery. The Charleston Museum acquired the property for a historic house museum in 1929. Despite the site's complex history, it is interpreted as an elite residence because of its association with Heyward, who signed the Declaration of Independence.[10]

Beginning in 1974, Herold and volunteers excavated in the present-day work yard between the kitchen, stable, and rear of the main house, the basement of the kitchen, the privy, the driveway, and selected areas in the basement of the main house, dividing the available yard into five-foot squares. Materials were recovered by screening the soil through ½-inch mesh screens, in contrast to the combination of ¼-inch mesh screens and fine-screening used subsequently in Charleston. Herold encountered a lot cluttered with houses, sheds, wells, and pits from multiple occupants and a material assemblage unparalleled in quantity and variety. Artifacts include early colonial ceramics, a large and varied assemblage of colono wares, and Native American pottery. The privy yielded a trove of materials associated with Heyward's occupation. Artifacts from the kitchen cellar were associated with the boarders who lived on the property in the nineteenth century.

The three-story brick townhouse has an imposing presence today. Arrayed behind the house is a seamless and orderly flow of brick service buildings: a two-story kitchen/laundry with servants' quarters, a single-story stable and carriage house, and a neat brick privy. A formal garden is laid out beyond the paved work yard, with a discrete rear access to the alley behind. This layout suggests a single, planned development. The layout followed that of the previous property owner, with the kitchen constructed on a previous foundation.

John Milner Sr. lived with his wife and five children in a small wooden house (24 × 18 feet). Behind his home he operated a gunsmithing business "at the sign of the Pine Tree." A well lined with barrels, a three-sided post and frame structure that enclosed a furnace and forge, and other features crowded onto the lot. Just outside of the frame structure was another large well with a square, wood-lined shaft. This second well, Feature 65, was filled with artifacts.[11]

Two artifacts from the well demonstrate the complex network of people and trade that prevailed in the early eighteenth century. A well-made bowl with a smoothed interior and curvilinear-stamped exterior was finished with a red film on the wide brim. This vessel was probably produced by Yamasee Indians during the first quarter of the eighteenth century. The Yamasee lived in 10 towns south of Charleston until the war of 1715. The second vessel was an incised jar with a narrow neck and wide shoulders. This shell-tempered vessel matches those recovered from Fusihatchee, a lower Creek town excavated by Craig Sheldon, and from Ocmulgee, described by Carol Mason. This latter vessel was likely made between 1710 and 1730. How and why either vessel came to the gunsmith's well is unknown, but their presence reminds us that Native Americans, both local and those from farther away, were significant players in Charleston life.[12]

The elder Milner's home and business burned in Charleston's monumental 1740 fire. Herold's excavations encountered a scatter of gun parts, flints, coal, cinders, and ash. This same ash layer was found inside the stable building when that structure was excavated by Zierden in 2002. The 1740

Figure 7.5. Shell-tempered incised jar, likely Creek, recovered from the yard of the Heyward-Washington House in 1976 and identified by Jon Marcoux. (Photo by Terry Richardson, Collections of The Charleston Museum, Charleston, South Carolina.)

Figure 7.6. Excavations in the stable at the Heyward-Washington House in 2002. (Collections of The Charleston Museum, Charleston, South Carolina.)

ash layer enables us to distinguish between Milner Sr.'s 1730s use of the property and that of John Milner Jr. in the 1750s.

Milner Sr. and his son evidently continued their gunsmithing business after the fire, working together until the older Milner's death in 1749. At the time of his death, Milner Sr. owned 11 slaves, at least three of whom were skilled smiths. Milner Jr. inherited the property and constructed a brick house along the northern property line in addition to the present-day kitchen and stable buildings. The house measured 18 feet along the street and extended into the lot an unknown distance. As with the elder Milner's 1730 wooden house, a portion of Milner Jr.'s brick house was preserved in the Heyward's basement. The younger Milner also built two wells and paved the area around the service buildings. Milner Jr. lost the property in 1768 to meet his debts, and the property was purchased from the provost marshal by Heyward in 1772.[13]

The Early Urban Landscape

The Milner structures illustrate Bernard Herman's interpretation of early-eighteenth-century Charleston's landscape as "in keeping with . . . a transatlantic British tradition of provincial ports and market towns, linking paired housing, row housing, and single dwellings that combined commerce and residence." In this transatlantic tradition, the younger Milner built in the new single-house style, but he worked in the cellar of his house and likely operated a shop on the ground floor.[14]

New South Associates archaeologists J. W. Joseph and Theresa Hamby uncovered further evidence of early-eighteenth-century lot use at the Charleston Judicial Center site in 1998. Excavating an entire city block gave them a perspective of the city not offered by the more limited excavations typically possible in Charleston. The block was occupied during the first decades of the eighteenth century, when it was close to Market Square but outside the city gate. Joseph and Hamby concluded that the early urban landscape had evolved to fit the needs of the ever-growing colonial population, but that growth did not conform to a single lot plan or house form.

The earliest buildings at the Judicial Center were modest houses fronting directly on the street. Building styles and materials ranged "from African earth-walled structures to European half-timbered dwellings to low-country tabby structures to Caribbean buildings of Bermuda stone." Most intriguing was a house of earthfast construction, consisting of clay walls supported by posts set in trenches. Earthfast construction is found on plantation sites but is very rare in the city. The placement of the building on the lot and the size of the building are similar to Milner's 1730s house, though the gunsmith's home was set on brick piers.[15]

Joseph's study of land use and lot organization offered further surprises. He found an array of features (e.g., root cellars, storage pits, wells, privies) and small structures immediately behind houses that fronted on Broad Street, but no features or structures in the rear yards. He argues that more than half of the space on these lots was used to produce crops, raise livestock, and conduct other farming activities. Milner's use of what became the Heyward property is very similar: a modest house located at the front of the lot with a work yard and smithy immediately behind it and likely open space beyond.

A change in lot organization occurred in the mid-eighteenth century, coinciding with the city's economic growth and landscape-altering disasters. The fire of 1740 and the hurricane of 1752 gave people the opportunity to rebuild using newer building styles. The new work yards generally were smaller, were located toward the center of the lot, and contained fewer pit features. Joseph suggests that fenced rear yards may reflect security concerns, though some space continued to be devoted to gardens.[16]

The Stono Rebellion

On Sunday, September 9, 1739, about 20 Angolan slaves under the leadership of Jemmy attacked a store on the Stono River south of Charleston. They then moved from plantation to plantation as the ranks of the rebels swelled. Although the immediate unrest was quelled the same day, Peter Wood argues that the rebellion continued throughout the lowcountry for some time. The following year the Negro Act was passed by the Assembly. This served as the core of South Carolina's slave code for more than a century.[17]

Wood suggests that the Stono Rebellion was the climax of two decades of change and adjustment in lowcountry slave society. The early polyglot labor force of indentured white servants, Spanish prisoners of war, and Indian and African slaves disappeared, as Africans came to dominate the workforce. Fears that the African majority might join in an armed uprising led to increasingly harsh restrictions, especially after 1738, when Spanish Florida established the town and fort of Gracia Real de Santa Teresa de Mose near St. Augustine for the growing population of former slaves converting to Catholicism.[18]

The Stono Rebellion reverberated throughout the Carolina colony. The intent of the perpetrators and the chain of events are unclear. The consequences are very clear, however: stricter slave codes and increased restrictions on the activities and movement of enslaved Africans. Charleston's fenced yards may reflect those concerns, but the consequences of the uprising are also evident at James Stobo's planation south of Charleston, close to the center of the uprising.

James Stobo's Plantation

New towns and plantations developed along the rapidly expanding frontier. Willtown was founded in 1690 on the Edisto (Pon Pon) River during the first wave of frontier settlements. The inland swamps near Willtown were suitable for growing rice, and settlers took up those lands quickly. Slavers brought growing numbers of Africans to the lowcountry to produce this labor-intensive commodity. By the end of the colonial period, Willtown was a center of inland rice plantations operated by enslaved Africans and Native Americans, linked to the larger shipping and mercantile economy through Charleston.

In 1997 Hugh Lane invited The Charleston Museum to look for Willtown on his property. Evidence for the town along the banks of the Edisto was tenuous, but an uprooted oak about a mile from the riverfront revealed an impressive assemblage of colonial artifacts. We dug there instead. Suzanne Linder, tracing the history of the tract, learned that many Willtown residents established rice plantations around the small frontier town, hoping to cash in on the new crop. What we discovered was James Stobo's plantation.

The property was first granted in 1710 and evidently experienced two building episodes before Stobo acquired it in 1741. Stobo built a grand three-bay manor house with an enclosed central courtyard. James Stobo left Willtown abruptly in 1767 but continued to own and operate the plantation until his death in 1781. Stobo stocked his house with the finest goods. The layout suggests that the balance of power was tenuous, at least from Stobo's perspective; the house resembled a palisaded or fortified compound. The site also showed that the plantation itself was fragile, eventually falling victim to natural disasters and economic forces.

The property was home to people of European, African, and Native American heritage, all living together but on unequal terms. Artifacts recovered from Stobo's house include some fine objects, ones that are not normally discarded and are usually interpreted as evidence of abandonment. These apparently abandoned objects included furniture hardware, curtain rings, a brass sword handle, a silver cane tip engraved with Stobo's initials, and a barrel brand bearing Stobo's name. Some ceramic and glass objects were broken after they were discarded, instead of the more usual sequence in which objects are discarded after breaking. Objects recovered farther from the main house were more typical of items tossed away when they could no longer be used.

The African and Native American presence and interactions between the two groups are documented by colono ware recovered from the site. Ron Anthony discovered a higher-than-expected percentage of colono ware made in the Native American style in addition to African-made colono ware. Trade with Indians may explain some of these materials, but several Willtown-area planters listed Indians among their slaves. Ira Berlin's study

Figure 7.7. Artifacts from James Stobo's plantation associated with enslaved residents. Top to bottom: colono ware marble marked with an *X*, blue beads, quartz crystals, finger ring with crucifixion scene. (Photo by Sean Money, Collections of The Charleston Museum, Charleston, South Carolina.)

of colonial slavery suggests that some descendants of Native American slaves remained in the Willtown area in the eighteenth century, though they were no longer listed as Indian.[19]

Although some of the enslaved laborers were Native Americans, most were Africans. The Stobo courtyard yielded a quartz crystal and a colono ware sphere, or marble, with cosmographic markings. Leland Ferguson suggests that the incised "X" or cross found on some lowcountry colono ware may be a religious cosmogram for the Bakongo people. The Kongo cosmogram has a variety of ritual meanings in Africa. The blue glass beads and cowrie shell recovered from Stobo also may have belonged to African residents.[20]

The most dramatic evidence for cultural interaction is also the smallest: a brass finger ring with a glass setting. The glass setting bears an image of the crucifixion, with a robed Christ on the cross and two kneeling figures, possibly Mary and Mary Magdalene. The ring most likely did not belong to James Stobo, a strident Dissenter. Nor did it belong to neighboring Anglicans. The ring may have belonged to Christianized Indians, possibly Catholics originally from Apalachee Province in Spanish Florida. Perhaps the ring belonged to African residents. John Thornton and Ira Berlin report that some Africans in early-eighteenth-century Carolina were devout Catholics, originating in the African kingdom of Kongo. Leaders of the Stono Rebellion, usually identified as "twenty Angolans," included

Catholics. Thornton suggests this fueled their desire to rebel and reach freedom in Spanish Florida. It is also possible that the ring changed hands many times before being discarded, lost, or hidden at Stobo's plantation. By whatever path it reached the site, the ring symbolizes the meeting of peoples, beliefs, and iconography in colonial Carolina.[21]

Some animal remains offer another tantalizing insight into the cultural complexity of the site. Jennifer Webber and Daniel Weinand analyzed the faunal remains at the University of Georgia laboratory. They report that three cattle bones found with a concentration of Native American pottery in the yard show very unusual hack marks. These bones appear to have been repeatedly and forcefully hacked in a random manner, suggesting the butcher was unfamiliar with the animal or the tool.

Other aspects of the Stobo animal remains reveal similarities and differences in the use of animals by residents of the city and those living in the countryside. People at Stobo used large quantities of turtles and alligators, which may have been abundant in rice fields and ditches. The collection also contains the remains of four European domestic rabbits, which have not been found in Charleston itself. Domestic rabbits were introduced to this hemisphere from Europe, and their presence at Stobo clearly shows a European connection.

Mary Musgrove's Trading Post and Cowpen

Beef sold in the city and shipped out of Charleston Harbor likely originated in cowpens and plantations in the lowcountry, as well as from animals raised within the city itself. One supplier was Mary Musgrove, who operated a trading post and cowpen on the Savannah River between 1732 and 1751. Musgrove was a Creek Indian woman who parlayed her multicultural heritage into a thriving cattle and deerskin trade. The Cowpens (later known as Grange Plantation) reminds us that Native Americans, singly and in groups, were very much part of the lowcountry landscape throughout the colonial period. Native Americans regularly traveled from Indian lands to Charleston, and all points between. The Native American pottery recovered from the Heyward-Washington House and Stobo Plantation is material evidence of this interaction.

Mary, or Coosaponakeesa, was the daughter of a Creek woman and a British trader. Multilingual, literate, and Christian, Mary was educated at the Pon Pon community near Willtown and maintained a presence there as an adult. She is best known for her role as interpreter and negotiator

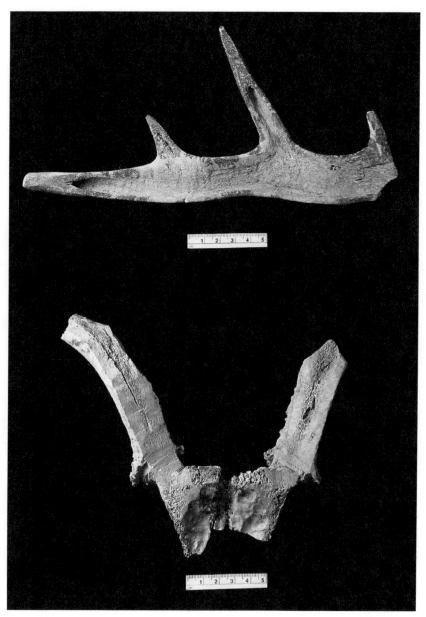

Figure 7.8. Deer antlers from Mary Musgrove's trading post and cowpen, 2003. The antlers were modified to serve as hunting disguises. Note that saws were used to produce these specimens. (Photograph by Chad O. Braley, used by permission of Southeastern Archeological Services, Inc., and Georgia Ports Authority.)

for James Oglethorpe's Georgia colony, south of the Savannah River. She married three times, claimed ownership of three Georgia sea islands, and died in 1765 on one of those islands. At the time of her death, she was the wealthiest woman in colonial Georgia. She and her husbands were heavily involved in both the deerskin trade and the cattle industry, as well as in colonial politics.

Mary and her first husband, John Musgrove, also a trader of British and Native American descent, received rights to land located on the Savannah River. They built a house, a trading post, and cowpens there. At one time or another, Indian slaves, Spaniards, Salzburger cowkeepers, dairymaids, missionaries, insurgent colonists, and Yamacraw, Creek, and Yuchi chiefs and hunters visited or lived at the site. Cattle and deerskins from the Cowpens made their way to the Charleston market, where the Musgroves were represented by Samuel Eveleigh.[22]

The site was discovered during an expansion of the Georgia Ports Authority and was excavated in 2002–2003 by Chad O. Braley of Southeastern Archeological Services. Two cellars at the site produced a collection of animal remains that showed the strong association between the Native American trade and the production of beef, dairy products, hides, and tallow at the site. Bones from foxes, bears, raccoons, otters, skunks, mountain lions, and bobcats indicate that more than deerskins were brought to the Cowpens for trade. Both freshwater and estuarine fishes are present in the collection, further evidence of the wide area from which the trading post drew. The dominant animal remains from the Cowpens, however, are from cattle and deer.

The recovery of both dairy pans and deer antler decoys (stalking heads) testifies to the cultural melding that occurred in the Carolinas. Native Americans made deer antler decoys from "the head of a buck, the back part of the horns being scraped and hollow for the lightness of carriage." The Cowpens specimens conform in every detail to these descriptions. The use of a metal saw to produce some of the decoys suggests they were manufactured at the site, either for trade or for local use.[23]

Artifacts of the Early Eighteenth Century

Artifacts related to the lowcountry cuisine dominate early-eighteenth-century archaeological assemblages. Over half of all artifacts are ceramic or glass vessels. The proportions of wares used in food preparation compared to those used for serving and consuming food and beverages at stylish tables changed in favor of table wares as Charlestonians became more affluent later in the century.

Early-eighteenth-century assemblages are dominated by British delft table wares, combed and trailed slipwares from the Staffordshire region, and lead-glazed utilitarian earthenwares. They also contain locally made colono wares. Coarse earthenwares include North Devon wares, Buckley earthenware, and a wide variety of lead-glazed redwares from Britain. Early-eighteenth-century sites also contain small quantities of Chinese porcelain as well as French and Spanish earthenwares.

Table wares of stoneware were new, and their presence in Charleston shows the ability of citizens to purchase the newest goods. The earliest stoneware type is slip-dipped white salt-glazed stoneware, which was developed in 1715 and manufactured until 1775. Slip-dipped stoneware features a grey body and thick white glaze. Less common is the contemporary Nottingham stoneware, a thin vessel featuring a grey paste, lustrous brown glaze, and bands of rouletted decorations. Many of these vessels are dining and teawares, reflecting the growing importance of manner and display during formal meals.

After 1740, lowcountry dining tables displayed several new ceramic types, as ceramic assemblages became larger and more diverse. This reflects both the availability of imported manufactured goods and the ability to afford them. Molded white salt-glazed stoneware, in a variety of forms and styles, largely replaces slip-dipped stoneware. Nottingham stoneware is more common than previously. Delicate new teawares, such as Astbury ware, Agate ware, and Jackfield ware, are present in small but consistent amounts. Chinese porcelain also is more common. Despite the growing popularity of new, more durable wares, delftware table ware was still used, even in late-eighteenth-century table service.

Nearly half of early-eighteenth-century ceramics are utilitarian food preparation vessels, but only a quarter of the ceramics are utilitarian wares in the second half of the century. Utilitarian stonewares increase in frequency, while lead-glazed earthenwares become less abundant. Staffordshire combed and trailed slipwares become a cornerstone of kitchens, accounting for nearly a quarter of all ceramics in the mid-eighteenth century. Staffordshire slipwares are augmented by red-bodied earthenwares produced in the mid-Atlantic colonies. Products from the port of Philadelphia include slip-decorated redware bowls, redware pans with trailed slip decoration, and lead-glazed vessels in a number of forms ranging from cooking pots to pitchers.

A small but significant number of French and Spanish ceramics are recovered from this time period in Charleston. French green-glazed coarse earthenware, a utilitarian ware with a dull green lead glaze, was common in Charleston during the mid-eighteenth century. Bonnie Gums and Gregory Waselkov recovered this ware at Old Mobile, the first French colony on the Gulf of Mexico. The distinctive Spanish Olive Jar persisted as part of the Charleston kitchen into the late eighteenth century. The most notable evidence of ethnic diversity in Charleston is colono ware. The popularity of this locally made ware peaked in the mid-eighteenth century, when a tenth of the ceramics were of this type.[24]

Charleston artifact collections are broadly similar due to general patterns of manufacture, trade, and style. We distinguish site-specific activities by quantifying the materials at each site, and measuring proportions of various types and groups of materials. Another measure of site activity is the volume of discarded artifacts. To standardize this measure, against the amount of excavation at each site, we calculate the number or weight of artifacts for each artifact category divided by the cubic feet of excavated soil. Soil volume is measured by the depth of the deposit and the dimensions of the excavated area. Bone weight is measured in the same way.

The artifact assemblage from the Beef Market illustrates these measures and how they are used to discern differences among the Charleston sites. The density of artifacts at the Beef Market is unusually high, but the range of artifacts is limited when compared to other sites. Personal possessions and furniture-related items are very rare at the Beef Market. Artifacts associated with clothing are only slightly more common. Architectural items also are relatively rare, even after market buildings were present. On the other hand, the percentage of weaponry-related objects is high at the market compared to other Charleston sites; there are large quantities of British flint debitage, perhaps associated with gunflints or small flake tools. Ceramics, bottle glass, and tobacco pipes dominate the market artifacts.

The range of kitchen wares from the Beef Market is narrower and stylistically more conservative than elsewhere in the city. Kitchen wares resemble assemblages found at British taverns elsewhere in North America. An unusually large number of inexpensive drinking vessels, such as drinking pots, tankards, and canns, are present at the market, but expensive teawares are less common. The market contains Manganese Mottled ware, slip-coated ware, slip-dipped white salt-glazed stoneware, British brown stoneware, and Staffordshire combed and trailed slipware tankards and drinking cups. Utilitarian cookwares are common; most of these are lead-glazed earthenwares. North Devon gravel-tempered ware and Buckley earthenware pots and pans are present as well. Stoneware storage vessels include jugs and pots of brown salt-glazed stoneware. Pots or butter pots are a recurrent vessel form at the market.[25]

Glass was also recovered from the market. Green glass bottles are particularly common, with shapes ranging from the squat forms of the early eighteenth century to the taller bottles of the later eighteenth century. There is aqua glass from small pharmaceutical bottles. The most unexpected find was a relatively large quantity of table glass, particularly elaborate wine goblets. Goblet fragments large enough to identify are from styles popular between 1700 and 1760.

Despite the popularity of colono ware in the mid-eighteenth century, we were surprised to find a smaller quantity of colono ware at the market than at contemporary Charleston sites. We expected that colono wares were sold at the market, or at least were used there, because documents suggest that African American men were the principal fishers and that black women dominated the market itself. In addition, plantation slaves and their gardens were major suppliers of produce and poultry. But if these vendors, or others, were using or selling colono ware pots at the market, these vessels did not remain on-site.[26]

The combination of tobacco pipes, drinking glasses, some table ware, and cooking vessels reveals the market was a public setting for social activities beyond simple commercial transactions. Similarities between the market assemblage and colonial tavern assemblages suggest the market was a vibrant public area, one used as a gathering space, where residents might visit and converse, and perhaps share refreshment, as well as buy and sell wares. Of course, all of these activities were secondary to the purchase of foods and other provisions.

Using the Bountiful Coast

The extent to which Charlestonians took advantage of the bountiful coast is shown by the observation that the collection of animals identified in Charleston includes the remains of 119 different types (taxa) of non-commensal wild animals and eight domestic animals. Zooarchaeologists quantify collections such as these by estimating the Minimum Number of Individuals needed to explain the materials in each collection. Almost half of the individuals in the Charleston cuisine were wild, and half were domestic. But the primary source of meat was beef. The combination of an array of wild animal taxa with beef was shared by people of all economic and social strata and persisted into the late nineteenth century.[27]

Many of the non-commensal wild animals are aquatic. These include turtles, alligators, and fishes. Almost half of the turtle individuals are sea turtles and diamondback terrapins, which may be evidence of commercial turtling. Charleston merchant Henry Laurens shipped sea turtles, live in a bed of purslane, to London for sale and as gifts to friends and business associates. Remains of a 60-pound green sea turtle were recovered from a late-eighteenth-century well in London, and sea turtles also have been recovered from other contemporary sites in that city, though we do not know if these were specifically from Charleston. Most of the Charleston fishes are common in local estuaries, especially sea catfishes, sea basses, sheepsheads, seatrouts, Atlantic croakers, black drums, red drums, mullets, and flounders. Freshwater fishes and fishes from beyond the local estuaries are rare. Charlestonians also ate crabs, Atlantic ribbed mussels, oysters, quahogs, and periwinkles, though these have not been studied formally.[28]

Wild mammals and birds are somewhat less abundant in the Charleston assemblage. Although over half of the wild mammal individuals are deer, other mammals also were consumed, including opossums, rabbits, squirrels, beavers, muskrats, minks, raccoons, and black bears. Some of these animals also provided grease, bone for tools and ornaments, hides, and furs. Feathers may have been less commonly used, as wild birds are rare. Although many birds are water fowl such as wood ducks, mallards, and diving ducks, or shore birds such as herons and rails, over half of the wild bird individuals are turkeys and Canada geese. These are interpreted as wild birds instead of domestic ones because wild turkeys and Canada geese were, and still are, common in the lowcountry. Passenger pigeons are present in two nineteenth-century collections, represented by only four specimens.

Hunting provided sport as well as food, but trapping was likely the preferred method for acquiring many of the animals gracing lowcountry tables, from the formal dining rooms of planters to the cramped rooms of servants. Turkeys trapped in the manner described by Audubon could be pinioned, fed, and kept in the yard until needed. Snares were set to capture nighttime raiders of gardens and poultry houses. Many of the turtles could be captured in rice fields or along the banks of streams. Traps could be left unattended and the animals collected at convenient times, providing a meal at the end of the workday or a live animal for dinner another day. Weirs, nets, and set or trot lines landed fish of all kinds.

All of the domestic animals are introduced from elsewhere, with the possible exception of dogs. Chickens are by far the most common of the three domestic birds. Muscovy ducks are tangible evidence of direct or indirect ties between Spanish America and British colonies. Although rare, they have been recovered from four sites. Common pigeons are present in deposits from every time period. Pigeons in Powder Magazine deposits from the 1710–1750 period may be evidence that they were used in the city's defense, but pigeons often are recovered from townhouses and likely represent animals raised for food, recreation, and sale.

Domestic mammals constitute a quarter of the individuals in Charleston. These are primarily pigs and cattle but include some sheep and/or goats. Contrary to the notion that the South was a "kingdom of pork," beef was far more common in the Charleston diet than was pork. Beef constituted three-quarters of the meat, and pork a tenth. The dominance of cattle and beef over pigs and pork persists from 1710 until the 1900s, though beef's popularity declined over the centuries as the use of pork increased.

The prominence of cattle over hogs in the archaeological record may reflect provisioning decisions and food preservation methods. Prior to refrigeration, meat had to be quickly consumed, preserved, sold, or bartered. The most common method of preserving meat was to cure it with salt or by smoking. Pork lends itself to curing more readily than does beef, because pork's high fat content keeps the meat from hardening. Mutton was rarely cured. There were several other ways to preserve meats, such as potting.[29]

Rural and Urban Contrasts and Connections, 1710–1750

The broad pattern of animal use just summarized ignores differences over time and between rural and urban locations. Animal use at Stobo and the Cowpens was considerably different from non-market locations in Charleston in the 1710s–1750s. Two factors guided animal use at rural sites, compared to those in the city: location and economic interests.

Cattle ranching and the hide trade influenced the types of animals used at the Cowpens compared to Stobo and Charleston, though beef was the dominant meat at both rural and urban locations. Cattle are far more abundant than pigs in the Cowpens collection, reflecting the Cowpens' role in the cattle industry. The use of domestic birds at Stobo and the Cowpens is about half that in Charleston at this same time, suggesting some difficulty in raising chickens, particularly in keeping them safe from predators. Sheep and goats are very rare everywhere, but somewhat more common within the city than outside it.

Some of these differences are likely due to the presence of Native American hunters at the Cowpens. Wild mammals are much more abundant in the Cowpens collection compared to collections from Stobo and Charleston at the same time; venison accounts for a quarter of the meat estimated for the Cowpens collection. Deer are much more abundant in the Cowpens collection than in either the Stobo or Charleston collections. At least eight of the wild mammals in the Cowpens collection are commonly associated with the fur and hide trade; of this list, only bears, raccoons, and deer are present in the Stobo collection also.

Animal use in Charleston was different from that at rural locations in several ways. Charlestonians enjoyed greater access to domestic meat and to a broader array of domestic meats, including greater use of chickens. If turkeys and Canada geese are counted as domestic species, the contrast between rural and urban diets is even more pronounced. A pig, cow, or goat could be slaughtered any day in Charleston with a reasonable expectation that its fresh meat could be used or sold before it spoiled. On the other hand, the amount of beef estimated for Stobo is very similar to the amount of beef consumed within Charleston. Beef is less abundant in the Cowpens collection; perhaps cattle were too valuable as a marketable commodity to slaughter and consume locally, or maybe venison was the preferred meat at this Native American trading post.

Old World rats were more abundant in locations where food was stored, regardless of whether that location was rural or urban. A quarter of the Stobo individuals are commensal animals, and a quarter of those commensal animals are rats. Commensal animals are rare in the Cowpens collection, but a third of those commensal animals are rats. By way of contrast, two-thirds of the commensal individuals in the non-market Charleston assemblage are rats.

These differences reflect the resources available in rural and urban locations as well as the economic activities at each location. Hunting and cattle herding were major activities at the Cowpens, with regional economic potential. Maintaining untended traps at Stobo was facilitated by its proximity to rice ditches and ponds, but livestock was a less important aspect of the rice plantation's income and could be slaughtered for local use.

The Growing City

During the early decades of the eighteenth century, the urban landscape was already a crowded one and had expanded beyond the city wall. Farming, manufacturing, and commercial enterprises pressed against the confining protective wall, as did livestock, trash, and commensal animals. Some of the accumulating debris was used to fill low-lying areas, enlarging the urban area. Charlestonians drew upon cowpens and plantations for local goods and commodities for overseas trade. Overseas trade was not one-way; the city received in return plants and animals native to other parts of the world, as well as elements of cuisine such as elegant ceramics and glassware. Goods from Europe and Asia joined locally made colono ware in Charleston kitchens. In some ways, site function influenced the types of materials recovered during excavation, but in other ways distinctions between residential and commercial sites were not pronounced. This applies equally to urban Charleston and to rural locations such as Stobo and the Cowpens. As at other colonial sites on the Atlantic seaboard and the northern Gulf of Mexico, colonists routinely combined indigenous wild animals with introduced domestic ones. These combinations represent transformations in the use of animals as raw materials, as commodities, as food, and in cuisines. Some of these new patterns of animal use persist in regional cuisines today.

III

City Life

8

TOWNHOUSE LIFE

Describing his visit to Charleston in 1773, Josiah Quincy wrote: "Dined with considerable company at Miles Brewton, Esqr's, a gentleman of very large fortune, a most superb house. The grandest hall I ever beheld, azure blue stain window curtains, a rich blue paper with gilt, mashee borders, most elegant pictures, excessive grand and costly looking glasses &c. At Mr. Brewton's side board was very magnificent plate." Unfortunately, Quincy does not describe the foods served. Perhaps his meal was ho-hum. That is unlikely, but setting and accoutrements, as well as manners, were the measure of a socially successful event, and Quincy describes what he considered important.

But there is another detail that catches our attention: "A very fine bird kept familiarly playing over the room, under our chairs and the table, picking up the crumbs &c and perching on the windows, side board, and chairs. Vastly Pretty." What was this "very fine" bird? A colorful local species, such as a cardinal or painted bunting? A native songbird that flew in through the open window? Or something more exotic, perhaps, a tropical bird such as a macaw or parrot, brought to Charleston as a pet? Such a species was recovered at Thomas Heyward's house; this faunal specimen has confounded zooarchaeologists for years.[1]

Townhouses, such as Miles Brewton's, present facades of gracious living. Behind the facades, however, the properties were shared space, with people of varied backgrounds and status living and working in a confined area, a space shared with animals. Excavations at townhouses are defined by the surviving buildings, but they encounter evidence of numerous activities, from conspicuous consumption and refined dining to the gritty chores and daily lives of slaves and servants toiling in kitchens and crowded work yards. Concepts such as urban landscape, foodways, cuisine, and provisioning apply equally to master, indigent relatives, guests, and slaves on these properties.

Charleston was one of the largest and wealthiest cities in North America by the mid-eighteenth century; the economic heyday persisted another seven decades. Britain's financial success extended to South Carolina, attracting factors, merchants, and craftsmen to the city. Charleston's economy expanded, and many of its citizens grew wealthy. Planters and merchants prospered, purchasing goods deemed appropriate to their elevated station in life. Personal wealth in the form of furniture, silver, tableware, clothing, jewelry, and paintings from Europe and Asia poured into the city. Imported goods were matched by finery produced locally, particularly by cabinetmakers, silversmiths, and their slaves.[2]

Rising personal wealth created a building boom in the city. Planters and merchants built imposing new townhouses, sometimes replacing more modest structures on the same lot. Others renovated and enlarged existing townhouses. Many townhouse properties, large and small, included pleasure gardens. Such changes reflect a general shift in architectural style that began in the third quarter of the eighteenth century. The large townhouses built by these merchants and planters survive today largely as house museums and private homes.

Charlestonians also commissioned imposing new public buildings. The natural disasters that devastated the colonial town made way for larger structures built in new styles. St. Michael's Episcopal Church was built in 1751 at Meeting and Broad Streets, and the State House rose on the opposite corner. The Exchange Building, completed in 1771, covered the Half Moon Battery and guardhouse that once protected the city.[3]

Archaeological assemblages from this period also are the most robust. The archaeological artifacts of this affluent period are principally ceramics for the merchant-planters' dinner tables and tea tables, along with embellishments for clothing and furniture. The quantity and variety of artifacts are higher in this period; so too are the numbers of archaeological features and deposits. The work yards of Charleston's townhouses were used for gardening, tending livestock, and discarding trash; they simply contained more debris than work yards in previous decades.

Most of the archaeological samples for Charleston for this period are from townhouses occupied by the city's social elite. These include historic house museums operated by The Charleston Museum and Historic Charleston Foundation. Sites such as the Heyward-Washington House stable, the Russell House, and the Rutledge House combine archaeological study with public interpretation and structural restoration. Some privately owned townhouses also incorporated archaeological study into restoration and preservation projects. These sites produced the largest and richest assemblages of material culture and animal remains; they provide much of what we know about the Charleston landscape as well. This chapter focuses on the gentry's townhouses and on domestic life at those urban compounds. We revisit these sites, more modest home sites, and commercial sites in later chapters.

The Miles Brewton House

The house built by merchant and slave trader Miles Brewton is one of the most celebrated in Charleston. Printed on postcards, touted in tours, and studied by scholars, it is one of the finest examples of Georgian architecture in the country. The house remains a private residence, in the same family for successive generations. Each made changes to the property, leaving imprints in the archaeological record.

The large lot was unimproved until Brewton, grown wealthy from trade, built a grand townhouse there in 1769. He and his family were lost at sea in 1775, and the property was inherited by his sister, Rebecca Brewton Motte. She maintained the house throughout the Revolutionary War and Charleston's two-year British occupation. Her daughter's family, the William Alstons, expanded the house and added to the inventory of outbuildings during their 1791–1839 tenure.[4] The family's fortunes waned thereafter. William Alston's youngest daughter, Mary Motte Alston, and her husband, William Bull Pringle, sold the back half of the Brewton lot and garden in 1857. This portion of the property was subdivided into lots facing Legare Street. The Civil War exacerbated Pringle's financial situation.[5]

In 1987 the owners embarked on a full restoration that included archaeological research and mitigation. Tommy Graham, Joe Opperman, and Charles Phillips coordinated archaeological investigations with architectural questions. A second archaeological phase, in 1989, focused on mitigating the impact of service trenches across the yard. Archaeologists, instead of backhoes, excavated portions of these trenches.

The Brewton property is large by Charleston standards. The rear garden wall is 185 feet from the street, and there is 100 feet of street frontage. The main house centers on the street front. The entrance features a columned portico, approached through a large wrought iron gate. The fence and its gate are original to the house, but the *chevaux-de-frise* (a spiked defensive

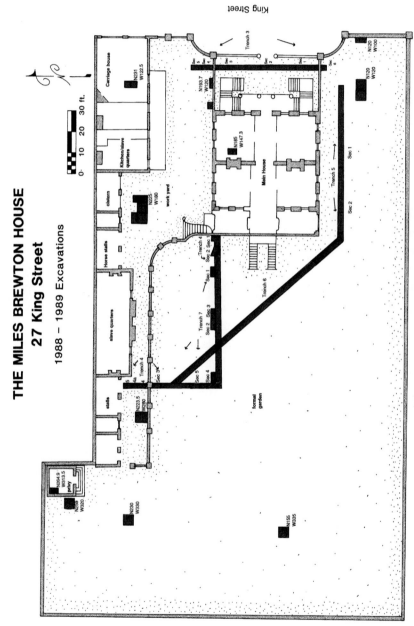

Figure 8.1. Plan of the Miles Brewton House and lot showing the 1988–1989 excavation units. (Collections of The Charleston Museum, Charleston, South Carolina.)

railing) topped the gate in 1822 after the Denmark Vesey insurrection. Walls extend from the front corners of the house to the sidewalk, separating and barricading the front entrance from the side yards. The front gate takes pedestrians to the portico, but nowhere else, leaving visitors clearly visible from the street and the yard but unable to proceed. The remainder of the lot is surrounded by brick walls. Outbuildings and the service yard align along the northern property line. A 1770s kitchen and carriage house front on King Street. Small gates access the service yard between the main house and carriage house; these are the only entrances to the walled compound.

The kitchen/carriage house was altered in the 1830s, when William Alston constructed a row of new buildings behind it. This series begins with two horse stalls and a tack room. The easternmost horse stall later was converted to a cistern. Next in line is a large structure built as servant quarters. This is followed by additional horse stalls and another tack room. The work yard is separated from the formal garden by brick coping and a wood picket fence anchored to the northwest corner of the house. Just beyond the fenced area, in a corner behind the last stable, is a large building of yellow brick also original to the house. This enigmatic building, altered over the years, has been interpreted as the privy. The remainder of the back yard, as well as the south side yard, contained formal gardens. The present-day spacious Brewton garden was twice as large before the Pringles' 1857 sale.

Brewton was 34 years old and married for six years when construction began on the grand house. Brewton also invested in furnishings and accoutrements appropriate to its scale. In 1771 rice planter Peter Manigault wrote his London agent, "I stand in need of some plate and furniture of which I enclose you a list. . . . I suppose you will think either my wife or myself very extravagant. I should almost think so myself if I had not seen Brewton's." The house became the center for entertainment and opulent display it was designed to be. The blue color scheme described by Josiah Quincy during his dinner at the house carried over to the Chinese porcelain plates used for dining, found by archaeologists as fragments discarded in the formal garden. Delicately mold-blown tumblers and goblets were recovered along with the porcelain.[6]

It was the work yard that provided the most valuable information on foods served in that elegant room. Some animal remains recovered from the work yard remind us that not all animal remains are food. Among the curios is a premaxilla from a queen triggerfish recovered from a Motte-Alston deposit (1775–1830). The premaxilla is a small cranial bone that forms part of the upper jaw, and in triggerfishes it has a unique shape.

This fish is associated with reefs along the continental shelf edge of North America or in the Caribbean. The bone may be a souvenir from Caribbean travels or a curio brought to amuse. It may also be from a salted fish imported from the Caribbean. Whatever the case, it reflects the broad reach of Charlestonians' interests. A fossilized great white shark tooth is more clearly a curio collected by someone during the Pringle-Frost (1840s–1880) occupation of the house. The tooth may be from the beach or Frank Frost's phosphate pits.

Thomas Heyward's House

John Milner Jr. sold his Church Street property in 1768 to satisfy heavy debts. Thomas Heyward razed the single house built by Milner and constructed a three-story brick double house in 1772. He also rebuilt Milner's kitchen and stable buildings. Heyward developed a formal garden toward the rear of the lot and added a brick privy.

Thomas Heyward was a prominent lawyer and plantation owner, known nationally for signing the Declaration of Independence. He served on several revolutionary committees and was paroled as a prisoner of war. He and other Charleston prisoners were transferred to St. Augustine for part of the Revolution. During the British occupation, Mrs. Heyward and her sister, Mrs. George Abbot Hall, remained at the Church Street property. Thomas Heyward returned to his home and to public life after the Revolution but eventually retired to his plantations, left in ruins by the war. The townhouse was occupied by his aunt, Rebecca Jameson, and rented to President George Washington during his 1791 southern tour. The property is known today as the Heyward-Washington House to commemorate this event.

Heyward offered the house for sale in 1792, describing it as having "12 rooms with a fireplace in each, a cellar and loft; a kitchen for cooking and washing with a cellar below and five rooms for servants above; a carriage house and stables, all of brick surrounded by brick walls." The house sold to another prominent Charlestonian, John F. Grimke, who owned the house until 1818. The large Grimke family eventually included two daughters, Angelina and Sarah, who resisted their father's strong will and were staunch abolitionists in the years leading up to the Civil War.

Archaeological excavations in the privy vault, yard, basement, and kitchen cellar by Elaine Herold in the 1970s and in the stable by Martha Zierden in 2002 encountered a large number of deposits associated with the Heyward and Grimke occupations. Levels 8–10 of the privy contained

Figure 8.2. Elaine Herold directs excavations beneath the kitchen of the Heyward-Washington House in 1976. (Collections of The Charleston Museum, Charleston, South Carolina.)

many pieces of ceramics and glassware that once graced the Heyward table. Excavations in the stable and in the basement of the main house also produced late-eighteenth- and early-nineteenth-century artifacts, while the kitchen cellar yielded materials discarded throughout the nineteenth century. Fewer artifacts were recovered from the yard, because it was paved with bricks during Heyward's occupation.

The neat brick stable and carriage house, locus of archaeological excavations in 2002, evidently supported more animals than just horses. Ten rats, two dogs, a cat, and a horse constitute a third of the individuals in the 1750–1820 stable; three-quarters of the commensal individuals are rats. By comparison, the Atlantic Wharf collection, interpreted as a communal dump, contains 20 rat individuals. Rats may have been common in stables, where warmth, shelter, and food were readily available. Associated with the large number of rats, a quarter of the modified animal bones are gnawed by rodents. The only evidence that the structure was a stable is a horse, represented by a single toe bone. Two cock spurs attest to the death of a couple of roosters, and the collection also contains the remains of a common pigeon. None of these are complete skeletons; perhaps bits and pieces of bone discarded or buried elsewhere on the property were brought into the stable by scavenging animals.

John Rutledge's House

Archaeology at the John Rutledge House began when Mrs. Arthur Parker, a trustee of The Charleston Museum and descendant of John Rutledge, learned that the house was slated for development. The site was far from pristine. The house was empty and in disrepair. The kitchen interior was gutted, and a large cistern had been removed. The rear half of the lot was subdivided and sold in the twentieth century, likely resulting in the loss of some outbuildings and a portion of the work yard. Mrs. Parker and Mrs. Frederick Bunting funded a small archaeological project, facilitated by architects Will Evans and Joe Schmidt. Artifacts from the excavation are on permanent display in the public room of what is presently the John Rutledge House Inn.

The Rutledge House is an imposing structure, built in 1763 and radically altered in the 1850s by owner Thomas N. Gadsden. The house narrowly missed destruction in the 1861 fire; the buildings on the adjoining property, St. Andrews Society Hall and Saint Finbar's Cathedral, burned in that conflagration.

John Rutledge and his second wife, Elizabeth Grimke, built the stately townhouse that stands there today and shared the property with 20 of his mother's slaves. Rutledge's political career began in 1761, when he was elected to the Commons House of Assembly, and he remained a political figure through the Revolution. Much of Rutledge's personal fortune was lost. He died intestate in 1800, and the home was sold.

Wealthy planter John McPherson owned the property until 1838. McPherson is credited with improving the stock of racehorses in the lowcountry. His holdings included plantation lands and 200 bondsmen with a variety of skills. His runaway groom, Ned, was evidently well known "in Charleston and throughout every part of this state, as a keeper of horses . . . a hair dresser and compleat butcher." Ned evidently was also skilled in eluding his owner, as McPherson's ad suggests "he will endeavor to pass as a free man, and to those who know him as if engaged on my business. . . . There is every reason to suppose he has a forged pass."[7]

As with many of the townhouse projects, archaeology at the Rutledge House was designed to answer questions about the architectural evolution of the house and daily life on the property. Five units were excavated in a two-week period. Units 1 and 3 near the kitchen produced a sizable assemblage of materials from the 1730s through the early twentieth century; however, the majority of proveniences and most of the artifacts were associated

Figure 8.3. Soil profile at the John Rutledge House, 1988. The narrow pit in the center of the eighteenth-century zones was filled with musket balls stashed under clam shells. (Collections of The Charleston Museum, Charleston, South Carolina.)

with the Rutledge and McPherson ownerships (1760–1820). Debris from their occupations accumulated in deep zones before the area was paved with brick in the 1850s. The most interesting deposit was a pit of loose sand containing a number of clam shells covering clusters of musket balls. This cache of ammunition could be associated with the Revolution or, given its location near the kitchen/quarters building, Rutledge's resident slaves.

These two units contained strong evidence for on-site butchering: 109 of the 120 cow specimens recovered from 1760–1820 deposits are from Units 1 and 3. Forty-nine of the cow specimens from these two units are from the wrist (carpals) and the ankle or hock (tarsals). The wrist and hock are not associated with purchases of meaty portions; they are typically interpreted as butchery waste. They may be used as flavoring in stews or in other dishes, but their abundance in these two deposits, and the cluster of such bones, suggest that at least six cows were butchered nearby.

The William Gibbes House

The William Gibbes House was one of the first townhouses excavated in Charleston. William Gibbes, a merchant and factor, purchased a large plot of land on South Bay Street, where he constructed a wharf in partnership with Robert McKenzie, Edward Blake, and George Kincaid. His wharf was one of the few on the Ashley River and was "suitable for off-loading lumber and naval stores" transported from Ashley River plantations. Gibbes also offered free wharfage in exchange for off-loaded ballast. He built his town-house across the street from his wharf in 1772.[8]

Gibbes' ardent support of the American cause during the Revolution cost the merchant his home; British forces sequestered his estate and used his house as a hospital. Gibbes was imprisoned and sent to St. Augustine along with 67 other patriots, including Thomas Heyward. After the Revolution he reclaimed his Charleston property and his Johns Island planta-tion. His petition to the British government for compensation lists posses-sions used by the invading forces, including "70 head of cattle, 60 of sheep, horses and other work animals" as well as "linen, dishes, wine, sugar, coffee, and other provisions." Gibbes lost "21 Negroes, carried or enticed away, three of which have returned to me," as well as "Toney, a very valuable boat hand, patron of a schooner and a good coasting pilot . . . Ned a good boat hand . . . Richmond and Cooper still in town with them." He also asked for compensation for two of his largest stores on the South Bay wharf, "pulled down and with a great deal of other lumber which was used in the building of public works." Gibbes continued his business ventures, but his success was short-lived. He died in 1789, and executors of his estate sold the house in 1794. The property was owned by a series of residents until 1984, when the house was purchased by Historic Charleston Foundation and resold with protective covenants.[9]

Historic Charleston Foundation's protective easement on the property includes the grounds, and they required archaeology within the footprint of a planned swimming pool. Excavations were conducted for a week in the 24×24-foot area of the pool near the center of the rear yard. Three five-foot-square units revealed four zones, the lowest associated with Gibbes' occupation. The units were full of wood charcoal and coal; Gibbes' use of coal is an indication of his wealth, as well as of the rising cost of firewood in the late eighteenth century.

Archaeological proveniences from the Gibbes excavations date from the late eighteenth century through the mid-nineteenth century. Meat con-sumption in the Gibbes household focused almost exclusively on domes-tic animals. The swimming pool footprint contained the remains of two pigs, three cows, and three sheep/goats. Beef provided most of the meat. The types of cattle bones recovered are similar to what would be found if portions from all parts of the cow carcass were used: half of the specimens are from the head and lower body, and half are from the meaty upper body.

The Nathaniel Russell House

Nathaniel Russell, a merchant from Rhode Island, arrived in Charleston in 1765 and gradually transferred his business interests to South Carolina. He participated in trade of all sorts, including the slave trade. The Russell family lived near the wharves on East Bay Street for 20 years after his marriage in 1788. Like many of his social peers, Russell moved away from the busy waterfront and onto a large, showy lot in 1808. The house features a tripart plan with a rectangular, an elliptical, and a square room on each floor. Carved wood, plaster, and applied composition ornaments abound, reaching their apex in the second-story elliptical drawing room. Wrought iron balconies inscribed with Russell's initials brought visitors outside. There they could view the formal garden on the south half of the lot. The main house and service buildings fill the northern property boundary. The kitchen and quarters building was followed by a stable and a carriage structure, both two stories, and an attached single-story privy.

Today the Russell House is a historic house museum owned and operated by Historic Charleston Foundation and is the focus of several archaeological studies. Fred Andrus monitored the installation of an air-conditioning system in 1990, following Hurricane Hugo. Andrus recovered an impressive amount of material and demonstrated that intact deposits were present at the site. Historic Charleston Foundation, with a grant from the Getty Foundation, sponsored additional archaeological testing in 1994 and 1995 as part of a historic structure analysis. In consultation with architectural historians Willie Graham and Orlando Ridout, and architect Glenn Keyes, we excavated adjacent to the main house, kitchen, and pantry to document the evolution of the house and grounds. The excavations revealed formal garden features and areas of refuse disposal. Excavations in the front entryway between 2003 and 2006, funded by the Ceres Foundation, revealed garden features from the first decades of the nineteenth century.

Excavations produced deposits and artifacts dating before and after the Russell family's ownership of the property (1808–1857). Units near the southern property line (Price's Alley, a filled creek) revealed materials from colonial-era residents. Excavations near the house produced materials likely owned by the Russell family while they still lived on East Bay Street. As in the Gibbes collection, cattle specimens recovered from the Russell

Figure 8.4. The Nathaniel Russell House kitchen in 1995. The soil deposits beneath the kitchen, filled with coal, animal remains, and porcelain fragments, were accessed through the arched opening visible on the left. (Collections of The Charleston Museum, Charleston, South Carolina.)

property are present in proportions similar to what we would expect if all parts of the cow carcass were discarded on the property.

The most amazing finds were from the kitchen crawl space: three feet of coal, soil, and animal remains. Enameled Chinese porcelain and sprigged whiteware from beneath the kitchen building indicate this material accumulated between 1820 and 1850. Also in this kitchen crawl space were 836 animal bones and teeth, 305 from cattle, over half of which are from the lower body. Many of the specimens under the kitchen are characteristic of primary butchery. Given the nature of the cramped, trash-filled deposit, it is surprising that the remains of only one rat were recovered.

Charleston's Domestic Architecture

The excavated residential properties feature two principal house styles, double-pile houses and the narrower style known as the single house. The Charleston single house is a local form that emerged in the mid-1700s. It replaced a more diverse range of pan-Atlantic building styles and dominated the city's architecture for the next 150 years. The single house is one room wide and two rooms deep on each floor, with a central hall and stair, and a side piazza, or porch. The narrow end typically fronts the street. The piazza usually is located on the long axis of the house, facing south or west. The opposite (back) wall features chimneys and relatively few windows. One enters the house from the street through an entry that opens onto the piazza, rather than into the house proper. The main door is located in the center of the long axis, bringing the visitor into the central hall and stairway. Within the house, the "best room" was located on the second floor, removed from the noise and debris of the public street. The first floor was more public, often housing a business.

Many scholars suggest the single-house style reflects British tradition adapted to tropical Africa and West Indies. Bernard Herman instead attributes the single house to the pervasive ideology of Atlantic mercantilism and the plantation system, calling these "urban plantation houses" with a highly stratified and processional use of space. He proposes the house must be considered with the dependencies and other features of the lot, to understand the spaces between buildings and links among them. Herman notes that the organization of the single-house property displayed "a functional shift from predominantly social to predominantly utilitarian" from front to back. Unlike the more common row houses, or paired dwellings of earlier periods, Herman suggests the single house actually squandered urban space.[10]

The double house of the late eighteenth century, as its name implies, featured a four-square plan with a central hall. By its very nature, a double house required a larger, more expensive lot. Double houses displayed a more elaborate version of the room use found in single houses. A well-appointed room, designed for entertaining, often filled the entire second-floor front space. The first floor remained the most public, and the upper, rear chambers the most private.[11]

Work yards of the double house lots included above-ground structures such as kitchens, slave quarters, stables, carriage houses, livestock sheds, and privies, as well as below-ground features often found only through archaeology: wells, cisterns, and drainage systems. Activity areas around, between, and beneath these structures filled much of what free space remained in the lot. Livestock management, gardening, storage, and other activities were incorporated into these buildings or housed in additional structures. The support structures were usually aligned along one or more side walls behind the main house. On larger properties, the work yard was separated from formal gardens, and gardens often fill the majority of the lot.

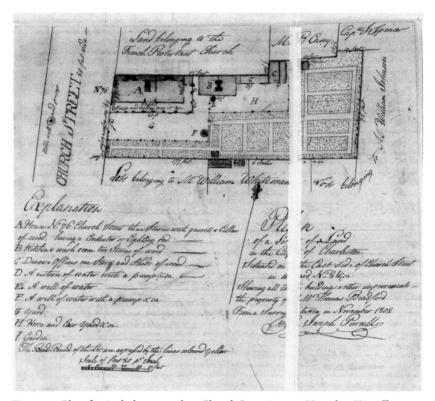

Figure 8.5. Plat of a single-house yard on Church Street in 1802. Note that *H* is a "horse & cow yard." (Historic Document Collection, Book I-6, p. 39, Property of the Charleston County Register Mesne Conveyance Office, Charleston, South Carolina. Used by permission.)

More modest single-house lots offered an abbreviated version of this arrangement, crammed into a smaller space. A single service building often served many functions. Fewer, if any, slaves resided on the second floor. Privies in the rear corner might be shared with a neighbor; eventually, small sheds filled the remaining spaces.

Archaeologists consistently encounter specialized and intensively used work yards on both single-house and double-house lots. Excavation reveals aspects of the urban landscape most clearly on large lots with a segregated work yard. The townhouses in our study each had four to six separate outbuildings. A dominant brick structure housed the kitchen and washing rooms on the first floor, and living quarters for slaves on the second and third floors. The next-largest structures often housed carriages, horses, or both. These were usually single-story, of either brick or wood. Tack rooms and stables were combined in a single building on two sites and segregated into separate structures on at least two others. Privies, singly or in pairs, were present at all sites; most were of brick. Some yards contained storage sheds, often in between the better buildings. Most townhouse lots featured a pleasure garden, a kitchen garden, or both, usually separated from the work yard by a fence.

Townhouse owners periodically enlarged or remodeled their homes to make them more fashionable. William Alston made numerous changes to the Brewton House in the early nineteenth century. The Russell family added rooms as the family grew. Many townhouse owners added pantries and other features in the early nineteenth century, connecting adjacent buildings. Outbuildings were also remodeled. Large pits filled with architectural debris, such as half-bricks, broken roof slates, and excess mortar, provide evidence for these changes. Recovery of nails and similar hardware provides additional evidence of repair or remodeling.

Material Culture and Consumer Choice

Maurie McInnis notes that townhouses were "the most permanent statement of established lineage" and that wealthy Charlestonians of the nineteenth century tended to remodel existing houses rather than construct new ones. As the concept of refinement and gentility took hold in the early eighteenth century, the first object acquired by the rising gentry was a new house. Within these houses, well-crafted and well-appointed interiors became a "carefully orchestrated processional space." These spaces and the objects in them legitimized and reinforced the control exerted by wealthy white men over those with less legal, social, and economic standing.[12]

"Gentility" was the visible expression of good social position, proclaimed through possession and use of proper accoutrements from European markets. The latest designs in carpets, mahogany furniture, drapes and coverings, tableware, fine fabrics, candlesticks, buckles and buttons, hats, and other material objects signified social position. Charlestonians had a particular affinity for British styles and goods. As gentility trickled down to the middle class, the demand for "refined" objects created an unprecedented mass market for individual items. Import statistics suggest that from 1700 until 1775 South Carolina's dry-goods imports multiplied twentyfold.[13]

The archaeological record contains only those accoutrements that were discarded, lost, hidden, destroyed, or abandoned and were able to survive decades or centuries of what archaeologists call post-depositional processes.

The imported goods and exotic foodstuffs that dominate advertisements in the *South Carolina Gazette* rarely find their way into the archaeological record. Likewise, the goods and services touted by local craftsmen are rare. These include portraiture, silver ornaments, clocks, cabinetry, luxurious dresses, draperies, and china painted with "gentlemen's coats of arms." Nonetheless, excavations at townhouses have recovered some of these objects, enabling us to consider what they meant to their owners, guests, and others in the city.[14]

Many artifacts are associated with taking tea. Tea, coffee, and chocolate revolutionized mid-seventeenth-century drinking and socializing habits in Britain. Queen Catherine's use of tea and Chinese porcelain in the 1660s made both the height of fashion. Falling prices and increased availability made tea drinking accessible to the socially aspiring in the eighteenth century. Tea manners were considered good measures of one's refinement, but not all who drank tea did so genteelly, or with the proper service.[15]

Tea etiquette required a retinue of new, specialized material items, beginning with the tea table. Centered on the tea table was the teapot, preferably silver or porcelain. The equipage included a cream pot, sugar bowl and tongs, cups, saucers, and teaspoons. There might be a stand for the urn or pot, a slop bowl, a canister, a strainer, a spoon tray, and plates for breads or cakes. Although we have not found all of these items in the ground, we do find innumerable fragments of teacups and saucers, with occasional fragments of teapots, cream pots, and sugar bowls. Some are in sets.

Assemblages with large quantities of Chinese porcelain dinner and teaware, elaborately decorated drinking glasses, and British creamware are the archaeological signature of late-eighteenth-century townhouse ownership. The Rutledge House produced porcelains with both underglazed and overglazed decorations, as well as creamwares in new styles. The small Gibbes House assemblage included elaborate wine glasses and creamware with a beaded border.

Chinese porcelain and elaborate table glass filled the soil layers in the Brewton garden. The porcelains were blue-on-white underglazed wares; over a dozen plates in a number of patterns could be reassembled from the excavated fragments. The same excavation units yielded a nested set of octagonal delftware platters, decorated in blue. Glassware included tankards, tumblers, and finger bowls in a molded diamond pattern. There were goblets with drawn enamel-twist or faceted stems, jelly glasses, and decanters. The assemblage also contained porcelain and white salt-glazed stoneware teawares. The somewhat more mundane creamwares included a pattern of hand-painted dinner wares, possibly a special order for the family.

Additional examples of Brewton's tablewares were excavated a decade later from the Simmons-Edwards House. This lot bordered the large Brewton garden. Brewton's servants, or perhaps occupying British soldiers, discarded refuse in a swampy area between the two properties. The eighteenth-century trash deposits contained English and Chinese porcelain teawares, elaborate creamwares, and a variety of colono wares, including globular jars and large bowls. One feature contained a green wine bottle with a seal that read "MBrewton." A second feature contained a small teaspoon handle engraved "M*B." This trash clearly originated in Mr. Brewton's household.

The most significant ceramic development of the eighteenth century was the gradual perfection of thin, hard-fired refined earthenwares dipped in a clear glaze by potters of the Staffordshire region. The resulting wares were durable, attractive, and inexpensive. They spread rapidly throughout the colonial world. The original cream-bodied ware, by Thomas Whieldon, featured clouded or swirled underglaze designs. Whieldon-type wares were a principal product of local potter John Bartlam, who operated his pottery in Cain Hoy after 1765 until he moved to the Camden area in 1774.[16]

British potter Josiah Wedgwood ultimately perfected creamwares and marketed them successfully; they are the most common refined earthenware in late-eighteenth-century Charleston deposits. They came in expensive, highly decorated sets, which appealed to the Charleston gentry, but also in relatively plain and affordable patterns. The Russell assemblage produced two fragments of a thin, very fine creamware saucer with a scallop motif, part of an elaborate Leeds creamware centerpiece.[17]

Creamwares decorated with enameling over the glaze were found at many townhouse sites. Some enameling is British in origin, but others could have been painted in Charleston. Mr. Lessley, a local artisan, advertised in 1770 that he "also paints on china and the cream colored ware Gentlemen's Coats of Arms, or any patterns they might choose." The Brewton's creamware featured a straight rim decorated with black spheres filled in yellow enamel. The Russell's royal-pattern creamware was decorated with a brown and black swag. The decorated creamware and fragments of elaborate Chinese porcelain from Mrs. Russell's dining room were mixed in layer upon layer of coal dust and cattle bones beneath the kitchen building.[18]

The privy at the Heyward-Washington House contained the most complete assemblage of the ceramics that define townhouse life. Levels 8–10

Figure 8.6. Examples of locally decorated and produced ceramics. Creamwares with overglaze enamel decoration, possibly painted by local artisans, from the (*left*) Miles Brewton and (*right*) Nathaniel Russell Houses; (*center*) clouded or Whieldon-type wares produced by John Bartlam at his Cain Hoy factory in 1765. (Photo by Sean Money, Collections of The Charleston Museum, Charleston, South Carolina.)

yielded a seemingly complete set of feather-edged creamware, including at least nine plates and ten soup bowls. Serving pieces included a teapot lid with finial in the design of a lily, an elegant sauce boat, a small mustard pot, and a sprig-decorated tureen lid. On a visit to The Charleston Museum, John Bivins, Brad Rauschenberg, and Stanley South attributed an equally elaborate tankard, with sprigged decoration and a lighter color, to John Bartlam, suggesting a local source for some of the Heywards' decorative items.[19]

Two sets of porcelain teaware, likely owned and used together, were discarded together. A panel-decorated Imari set features tall, narrow cups with handles. This style, likely for chocolate, is relatively rare in Charleston. The second porcelain tea set features tea bowls without handles in two sizes, decorated in delicate florals with a dart border. The Imari ware may predate the second teaware set by a decade or two, but their simultaneous discard into the privy suggests they were used at the same time.

The lower levels of the Heywards' privy also produced a well-made colono ware bowl and other fragments of colono ware pottery. A complete colono ware plate in European form features a smooth rim impressed with a design likely made from the edge of a cockleshell. The most unusual, and perhaps most significant, artifacts were two charred fragments of a coiled basket. These were retrieved from the lowest level of the privy, where their charred condition and the privy's persistent dampness permitted these perishable fragments to survive. The coiled basket was made of rush, sewn with palmetto strips, and represents the earliest known example of the low-country sea grass basket tradition.[20]

The recovery of colono ware and basketry with porcelain teaware and wine glasses from the same privy pit reinforces our argument that the record of African American residents in the city cannot be separated from that of wealthy European Americans. The artifact assemblages reflect the physical and social mixing of unequal groups. Only a few artifact types can be ascribed with some certainty to enslaved residents. These include Spanish coins pierced and worn as charms, quartz crystals, certain glass beads, and possibly cowrie shells; all held spiritual meaning. Possessing these important symbols provided a sense of empowerment or control, as they were believed to bring good luck and protect the wearer. But these artifacts are far more rare than the ubiquitous colono ware pottery.[21]

Figure 8.7. Coiled basket fragments from a late-eighteenth-century deposit at the Heyward-Washington House, identified by Dale Rosengarten. (Photo by Sean Money, Collections of The Charleston Museum, Charleston, South Carolina.)

Colono wares are a significant part of late-eighteenth-century Charleston deposits, though they are less numerous than on lowcountry plantation sites. They are a fifth of all ceramics in the second quarter of the century, and still 5 percent by the turn of the nineteenth century. Brian Crane, J. W. Joseph, and Nicole Isenbarger suggest that most colono wares in Charleston were made by enslaved African Americans on plantations for the urban market.[22]

But probably not all colono ware of this period came from African American potters. At least some is likely the product of Catawba Indian potters. Beginning in the late eighteenth century, this Native American group developed pottery production centers and established a regular trade with settlers. Catawba potters also traveled between New Town (near present-day Rock Hill, South Carolina) and Charleston, bringing wares for sale or making pottery on-site. Santee River plantation owner Philip Porcher recalled that "the Catawba Indians . . . traveled down from the upcountry to Charleston, making clay ware along the way. They would camp until a section was supplied, then move on, till finally Charleston was reached."[23]

Among the thousands of colono ware fragments recovered in Charleston are those distinguished by relatively thin, highly fired bodies and very smooth, mica-flecked surfaces. The most recognizable characteristic is red and black painted designs, ranging from simple dots and dashes on bowl rims to floral and sunburst patterns. These wares were first classified as River Burnished by archaeologist Leland Ferguson. Ferguson noted in 1989 that he was confident that the wares were the product of Catawba potters, but he resisted attaching a name to the pottery variety. Ron Anthony and Joseph agreed with Ferguson. Carl Steen carried this argument further, proposing that most colono wares were produced by anonymous "settlement Indians" living in small enclaves throughout the lowcountry. Then, in 2003, Brett Riggs, Stephen Davis, and Mark Plane of the University of North Carolina found the locations of Catawba Old Town and Catawba New Town. Both sites, but particularly New Town (occupied from the 1780s through the 1820s), produced large and impressive assemblages of pottery with clear evidence of local production for an external market. The wares recovered at New Town match those found in Charleston. Our most impressive example of Catawba-made River Burnished ware is from a privy vault excavated in the 1970s. The nearly complete pitcher copies forms found in creamware and other British refined earthenwares. The recovery of this vessel with European and American ceramics reflects the role of local wares in the urban kitchen.[24]

Archaeologists view an artifact bearing the owner's name as the holy grail, a rare find that links inference with documented occupants. The most common inscribed artifacts from the colonial period are sealed wine bottles. Again, the Heyward-Washington privy produced our largest collection, all identical and belonging to "G. A. Hall 1768." George Abbott Hall was the brother-in-law of Thomas Heyward; the men's wives were sisters. Mrs. Hall lived on the property with Mrs. Heyward during the British occupation of the town during the Revolution.

Sometimes, personalized artifacts take researchers on unexpected journeys. Sealed wine bottles evidently traveled with their patrons. Although the Simmons-Edwards property produced a bottle monogrammed for "MBrewton," Brewton's own property did not. The only wine seal recovered from the Brewton House, from the basement hallway, in fact, was emblazoned "C Pinckney." This is the seal of Charles Pinckney, owner of Snee Farm plantation in Mt. Pleasant. Excavations at Snee Farm, now a National Park Service property, produced an identical seal, with the same incorrect spelling of his name, as well as two others monogrammed for Mr. Pinckney in a different font and with a different spelling.

Perhaps Mr. Pinckney sent a bottle of wine to Brewton as a gift. David Hancock suggests that gifts of wine were common in the eighteenth century, drawing on the "social and pleasurable connotations of wine and drinking." The personalized bottles prized by gentlemen of the late eighteenth century provide graphic evidence of the movement and transfer of material items, before they became archaeological material culture. The gentlemen's bottles were likely filled with wines from the Atlantic island of Madeira, ideally situated for the transatlantic trade. Their hardihood and heat resistance made Madeiras a staple at British plantations. Charlestonians often stored their Madeira in the warm attics of their townhouses. Perhaps Mr. Pinckney was part of the "considerable company" that dined with Miles Brewton as described by Quincy.[25]

Although we have no archaeological evidence of the fine bird described at Brewton's dinner, the Heyward-Washington townhouse deposit does contain exotic animals. In 1980 Bruce Manzano studied some of the animal remains recovered by Herold. He identified both a guinea pig and a parrot in early-nineteenth-century layers of the privy fill. Although guinea pigs are consumed throughout the South American Andes, this particular guinea pig was probably a pet. The parrot specimens have been more difficult to identify. They have been examined by a number of specialists, including Manzano, Nicolas Laracuente, Daniel Thomas, Dan Ksepka, and

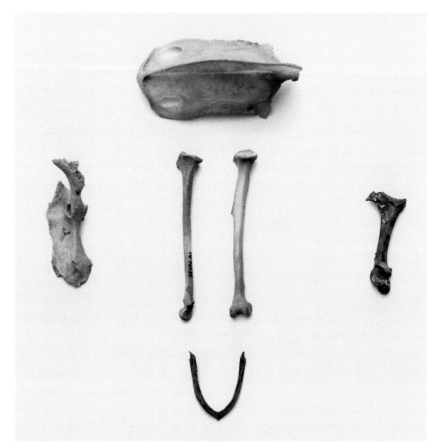

Figure 8.8. Parrot bones from an early-nineteenth-century deposit at the Heyward-Washington House, identified by Bruce Manzano. (Photo by Sean Money, Collections of The Charleston Museum, Charleston, South Carolina.)

the authors, with uncertain results. We considered the possibility that the bird was a Carolina parakeet, but comparison with images of a skeleton from this extinct species in the Smithsonian's collections confirms that the Heyward-Washington bird is too large. Given Charleston's role in overseas trade, this bird is likely one of the large parrots from tropical America or Africa.

Although the Heyward-Washington parrot remains unidentified, the search for a comparable specimen led us to a 1789 portrait of six-year-old Ann Proctor in the collections of the Hammond-Harwood House in Annapolis, Maryland. This painting, by Charles Willson Peale, features young Miss Proctor with two favorite possessions. A doll is cradled in her arms, and a rose-ringed parakeet perches saucily on the back of the chair. Ksepka,

Dwight Williams, and Laurie Reitsema identified the parakeet; the long tail and large bill are evidently classic markers of this bird. Rose-ringed parakeets have a particularly broad range, including western and sub-Saharan Africa, and are popular pets. Keeping birds and other unusual animals has a long tradition; exotic, rare animals often are symbols of status. Elisabeth Garrett notes that birds, monkeys, and other faraway imports were popular pets in early North American homes, and birdsong enlivened both

Figure 8.9. Portrait of Miss Ann Proctor, painted by Charles Willson Peale in 1789. Miss Proctor is shown with her doll and a pet rose-ringed parakeet. (Collections of the Hammond-Harwood House Association, Annapolis, Maryland.)

the sitting room and the kitchen. Some pet birds were from far-off places, testimony to the travels of ships and sailors, and the purchasing power of wealthy customers. Parrots were particularly common. Garrett suggests that Quincy's comment about Brewton's "very fine" bird indicates it was an unusual one. The guinea pig and parrot from the Heyward-Washington House provide evidence for the widespread trade network of the city and the eclectic interests of the city's residents.[26]

Garrett also found references to songbirds such as: "a cardinal in a nice new cage above the desk and a beloved mockingbird." A portrait of Ann Proctor's sister painted the same year shows Mary Proctor holding a cardinal. As early as 1700, John Lawson extolled the virtues of some lowcountry birds as caged pets. Lawson recounts that "the red birds . . . sing very prettily, when taken old, and put in a Cage." Several merchants advertised cages for sale. In 1785 Grant and Simons advertised a range of items for sale on the *Caroline*, lying at Gadsden's Wharf. These included "elegant Parrot Cages, and Red Bird ditto." William Bartram reported seeing "a cage full of rice birds" at a gentleman's door in Charleston. It is possible that some of the songbirds recovered from townhouses, such as the cardinal and other songbirds found in nineteenth-century deposits at the Brewton House, were captive pets. It is equally likely that they were accidental inclusions or victims of the work yard cat.[27]

The Townhouse Work Yard

Exotic pets, Chinese porcelain, and elaborate furnishings were part of the formal facade of Charleston townhouse life. Beyond that formal facade, the work yard was the center of daily life. The "yard" was the acknowledged domain of the enslaved residents, who occupied the small rooms on the second story of the kitchen building or perhaps an attic room in the main house. Slaves cleaned and dusted the house, made and tended fires, emptied chamber pots, and polished silver. Seamstresses made and mended clothes and linens, while others washed the clothes, prepared meals, made baskets, minded the children, and tended the animals. Many of these activities took place in the work yard.[28]

The work yard was an active place. We found archaeological evidence of informal hearths. Such fires might be used to cook food, provide warmth, or support leisure time. Open fires may be work-related, for heating wash water or scalding pig carcasses. It is likely that livestock, including pigs, cattle, sheep, goats, ducks, chickens, and common pigeons all lived in yards,

Figure 8.10. Soil profile from the work yard of the Miles Brewton House. The deepest, dark deposit is an outdoor hearth (Feature 11). Mixed soils (Zone 4) reflect construction in the work yard. Overlying refuse-filled zones and small pits were deposited in the late eighteenth and early nineteenth centuries. The work yard was paved with brick by the 1830s, reducing the accumulation of soil and debris. (Collections of The Charleston Museum, Charleston, South Carolina.)

along with dogs, cats, and draft animals. Songbirds, snakes, rats, frogs, and toads joined the menagerie. Opossums, rabbits, squirrels, and raccoons likely took advantage of the debris, finding food in the gardens, storerooms, and back edges of each lot. These traditional ingredients in lowcountry cuisine may have been captured in the act of raiding the garden or trash pit. The types of bones and teeth recovered show that pigs and cattle were butchered in portions of some yards. The refuse deposited in yards, either deliberately in trash pits or secondarily as fill dirt, was concentrated in particular areas associated with specific activities. Concentrations of fish bones and scales in the silt of brick-lined drains, such as that found at the Brewton House, show that fish were cleaned in these yards, perhaps near drains such as these.

The work yard was where refuse accumulated, a critical problem of urban life and the one most visible in the archaeological record. The Brewton work yard provides a graphic and complex example of the cultural and non-cultural processes transforming work-yard activities into archaeological deposits. Soil and accumulated refuse in the courtyard immediately behind the kitchen was nearly four feet deep. The lowest level contained an outdoor hearth and a concentration of refuse dating to the mid-eighteenth century. These mid-eighteenth-century zone deposits were impacted by a construction trench for a brick yard drain, installed in the late eighteenth century, and a complex series of extensions to this drainage network added in the early nineteenth century. The next-higher zone contained some domestic artifacts and large brick fragments in a matrix of mixed sand, reflecting construction of the outbuildings. The overlying layers of midden accumulated in a series of sheet deposits and small trash pits. These layers contained charcoal flecks, animal bone, and domestic artifacts of all types. Many of the bones were gnawed by rodents or dogs. This suggests that some trash was exposed to scavengers after being casually discarded and only later was buried beneath the accumulating debris.

Units elsewhere in the Brewton work yard likewise exhibited a dizzying array of sheet-midden deposits, crosscut by large features. Three units near the rear tack room contained an extension of the yard drain and features such as a cistern and fence posts. These features were embedded in multiple layers of refuse-laden soil. Cinders suggest this was a favored dumping spot for fireplace sweepings. Dispersed zones and concentrated refuse piles were capped with brick in the 1830s and 1840s.

The stratigraphy of the Brewton work yard contrasts with that of the formal garden, just on the other side of the fence but socially a world away. Soil deposits in the garden were less than two feet deep, encountered as broad, relatively undisturbed layers. A deliberate deposit of bone and artifacts, likely intended to promote drainage, was capped by late-eighteenth-century planting beds that were largely devoid of artifacts. Above these features were soil beds and paths of finely crushed shell associated with a second, mid-nineteenth-century garden. The thin layer of topsoil that accumulated after the garden was abandoned in the twentieth century contained little cultural material.

The yard at the Rutledge House is less well defined, but archaeological deposits conform to a pattern found at most townhouse sites. Refuse was concentrated near outbuildings, instead of scattered about the yard or clustered in far corners. Units near the kitchen contained over four feet of refuse in four zones. A century of accumulated material was paved over in the 1830s, and only six inches of refuse accumulated thereafter. Excavations in the middle yard area revealed less than three feet of accumulated dirt, and fewer artifacts. Artifacts from the yard are similar to those near the kitchen, but there are fewer of them, and they are more fragmentary.

The Charleston elite were defined, in part, by ownership of and coresidence with people of different social and ethnic affiliations. The pattern of refuse disposal described here changed during the nineteenth century, as we discuss in a later chapter. Here it is important to note that the work yard contains the refuse of all townhouse residents, not just the enslaved workers living above the kitchen or the elite family dining in elegant company. This archaeological reflection of the living patterns of urban residents makes it difficult to study the material possessions of the two social groups separately.

Provisioning the City: Body Parts

The debris in Charleston's work yards is filled with animal bones and teeth, particularly those of cows and pigs. This refuse produced a number of surprises, which led to our interest in the ways the city was provisioned. Three questions related to provisioning are considered. Do the types of cow and pig bones recovered reflect the socioeconomic status of the site's owner or residents? Was all of the meat consumed in the city purchased from commercial vendors, such as butcher shops and markets, or was some meat obtained from butchery on-site? Can we distinguish among private residences, nonresidential locations, and markets?

To answer these interconnected questions, we must convert fragments of animal bones into cuts of meat. Each pig or cow bone is classified into one of three standard skeletal portions: the head (including teeth), the upper body (vertebrae, ribs, upper forequarters, and upper hindquarters), and the lower body (lower leg bones, feet). The number of bones in each portion in a modern, intact animal establishes a standard for the number of bones that would be present if the entire skeleton or only parts of the skeleton were represented in the archaeological sample. Thus, an animal burial might have all of the bones normally found in all three skeletal portions, and a steak would be represented only by a few bones from the upper body. By comparing the number of archaeological specimens with the number of specimens in each undisturbed skeletal portion, we may observe an overabundance or under-abundance of specific portions of the carcass. This, in turn, might reflect consumer choices and provisioning strategies. The closer the archaeological count in all three carcass portions is to the standard, the more likely it is that the animal was slaughtered on-site or nearby, or was a burial. Pets are often skeletally complete, while butchery waste might consist only of bones from the head or lower body.[29]

Skeletal portions are linked to the status of the consumer by the price of cuts of meat from each part of the carcass. This association is based on the assumption that affluent people could afford expensive cuts of meat, and less affluent people purchased lower-quality meats or received them as rations. "Value" is based on the quality of meat, fat, flavor, tenderness, and quantity of meat associated with each cut. Tender, juicy, flavorful, meaty portions of the carcass are thought to be more desirable and often cost more than tough, dry portions that contain less meat. Value also includes social concepts unrelated to nutrition, such as fashions in food preparation, dining customs, and attitudes toward animals. Some wealthy people, of course, pinch their pennies, and some less affluent people live beyond their means.[30]

The first clue that this association was anything but simple came in the form of a "cut" of meat found in Charleston sites, one which we refer to as the Charleston cut. This portion consists of the elbow, a joint formed by the distal humerus and the proximal radius and ulna. This cut is found at several sites in Charleston and occasionally all three pieces are found together, as in the case of the Charleston Place example, where the three bones were hacked and sawed across the joint when it was clearly still articulated. This cut is not part of a standard unit of meat familiar to today's shoppers and is not readily linked to records of commercial prices in Charleston.

Further, records for the price of specific cuts of meat in Charleston are rare, especially for the early decades. To trace provisioning we need a single consistent measure, one that can be applied to the archaeological materials. To do this, carcass portions are classified in terms of value based on the amount of meat typically associated with each. This permits us to classify the archaeological fragments in terms of high-quality, "meaty" cuts and low-quality, less "meaty" cuts. Bones from the upper body are interpreted as evidence of high-valued cuts, and bones from the head and lower body are interpreted as low-quality cuts. If the only source of meat at upper-status sites was a butcher shop or market, and the affluent household purchased only high-quality cuts of meat, those deposits should be dominated by specimens from the upper body. Sites occupied by lower- or middle-status households might have many specimens from the head and lower body but few specimens from the upper body.

To our surprise, the types of pig and cattle bones recovered do not reflect the socioeconomic status of the site's residents. In hindsight, this should have been obvious. Elements from both high-value and low-value cuts are present at all townhouse sites, because people with very different social

Figure 8.11. Three articulated cattle bones forming
the "Charleston cut." The
distal humerus, proximal
radius, and proximal ulna
fragments form part of the
elbow. The specimens were
recovered from Charleston
Place in 1980. (Photo by
Sean Money, Collections of
The Charleston Museum,
Charleston, South Caro-
lina.)

status and ethnic backgrounds lived there. Preferred cuts of meat might
grace the elite dining table, while less desirable cuts were used by the enslaved staff. The material culture recovered from Charleston's townhouses
demonstrates that garbage from both meals was deposited in the same
places, along with the cooking pots, tableware, and serving platters used
by these distinct social groups. The residue of meat consumed by people
of many different social ranks was commingled by the time it reached the
trash heap, whether that trash heap was beneath the kitchen, in a vacant
lot, or in a creek at the back of the property. It is difficult, if not impossible,
to separate the meats consumed by one group from those consumed by
another on the same property.

A second surprise was that commercial outlets, such as markets, were
not the exclusive, or even the primary, sources of meat in the city. All sites
yield clusters of bones from all three skeletal portions of entire carcasses, a
classic signature of on-site butchery. This pattern is not restricted to townhouse sites. Sites throughout the city yield pig and cattle bones from the
entire skeleton regardless of social rank; there is no clear distinction between "meaty" or "non-meaty" portions. Often bones from the less meaty
portions are more abundant than are bones from the more meaty portions,
regardless of who lived at the site.

Beef and pork probably were purchased by some or all of the occupants
of these sites, but many urban residents had direct access to sources of

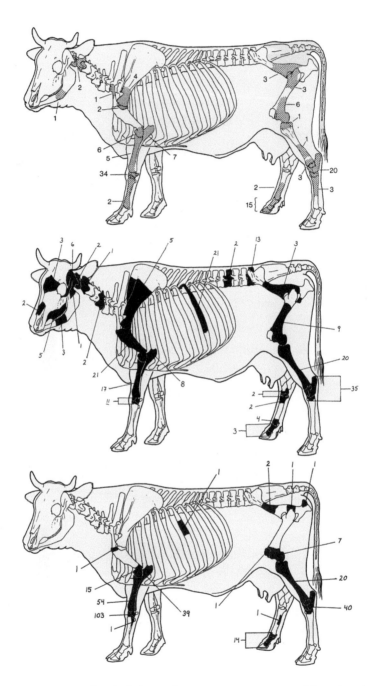

Figure 8.12. Diagrams of cattle skeletons showing specimens recovered from the John Rutledge House and Nathaniel Russell yard and kitchen cellar. Teeth, some cranial elements, and a hyoid bone are not illustrated. (Used by courtesy of the Georgia Museum of Natural History, Collections of The Charleston Museum, Charleston, South Carolina.)

production. Meat purchased from commercial sources could be augmented with meat from animals butchered on the property or otherwise obtained outside of the commercial provisioning network. Elite households could receive meats from their plantations; others had access to animals raised within the city. Although lower-status households might be expected to own fewer animals and to butcher them less frequently than the multistatus residents of townhouses, both could acquire at least some meat on the hoof, mixing the slaughtering debris of these animals with waste from meats purchased from commercial outlets.

It seems likely that in the days before mechanized, refrigerated transportation, live animals were brought to a point of slaughter that was as close as possible to the distribution point and that, after slaughter, the meat was quickly dispersed within the household and shared with relatives, friends, and neighbors. Recipients of this meat would be expected to reciprocate in the not-too-distant future. Some animals slaughtered on the property may have been raised there, and others may have been raised elsewhere and brought to the site specifically for slaughter. Home slaughter dilutes the relationship between the prices per pound of meat and the cultural values such prices reflect.

A third ingredient in the provisioning of the city is the function of the site in question. We have materials from residential sites, markets, and public sites. At the beginning of our work in Charleston, we assumed public spaces such as Dock Street Theatre, Half Moon Battery, and the Powder Magazine had little or no residential function. Skeletal elements recovered from these public sites, however, are very similar to those recovered from sites we think of as residences. We now argue that all sites had a residential component, perhaps guards or custodians and their families. Further, a variety of commercial activities took place on properties that we originally thought were exclusively residential sites, including townhouses.

Modern food taboos are revealed in the expectation that units of meat should be associated with household status. Our study forces archaeologists to confront their assumptions about what constitutes a "valued" portion, reconsidering recent food preferences and prejudices. Many people in the United States today value cuts of meat from the upper part of the carcass, and not from the head or the lower legs. Pork chops, pork loin, ham, bacon, and spare ribs may be the only portions of the hog considered edible, though portions that some might deem undesirable on other occasions are eaten on ritual occasions. The link between hog jowls, pig feet, and New Year's celebrations is a particularly strong one. It is clear from recipes and illustrations that many parts of pig and cow carcasses could be present on the tables of elegant colonial households. The expectation that higher-status households might purchase only portions that today are considered valuable may bias interpretations of archaeological collections.[31]

In Charleston many animal remains reflect processes that transcend status, ethnicity, and value. What eventually became rubbish on many sites likely was discarded by more than one social and economic group, obtained through multiple avenues, and conformed to standards of value that may no longer be in vogue.

Late-nineteenth-century data do hint at a widening gap between production and consumption locations, as city residents became concerned about crowding, sanitation, and health. City leaders were more successful in regulating the urban animal population, distancing the city from its rural heritage. Pig and cow specimens differ in the 1850–1900 deposits, when raising livestock within the city was on the wane. The percentages of specimens from the head and lower body portions of pig and cow skeletons generally are lower in the city's 1850–1900 deposits than in earlier ones, with specimens from the upper body forming a higher proportion of specimens in most assemblages.[32]

Provisioning the City: Bone Modifications

The portions of carcasses are one aspect of butchery; the tools used to disassemble carcasses are another. We have recovered only one such instrument, a cleaver from the Beef Market. Tools used in butchery are primarily understood from the modifications or marks they leave on bones.

Modifications are broadly classified as hack marks, saw marks, clean-cuts, and cuts. Hack marks are deep, wide, and often irregular. They are evidence that a large chopping tool, such as a cleaver or machete, was used to dismember the carcass. Cuts are small incisions across the surface of specimens, made by small tools like knives, as meat was removed from bones. Cuts may also result from attempts to disarticulate the carcass at joints. The presence of parallel striations on the cross-section of a bone is evidence that the specimen was sawed, presumably before the meat was cooked. Specimens with flat, even surfaces across the bone are called "clean-cut" and also are interpreted as evidence of sawing, though they lack the characteristic striations. Broadly speaking, hacking is associated with dismembering the carcass into major units (primary butchery), and cuts are associated with smaller portions (secondary butchery).[33]

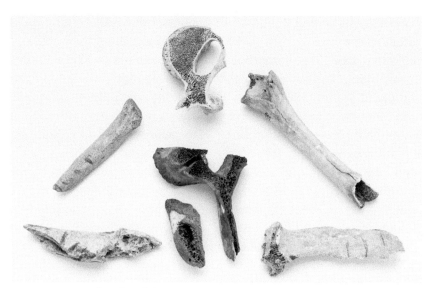

Figure 8.13. Examples of modifications to cattle bones: hacking, cutting, and sawing. (Photo by Sean Money, Collections of The Charleston Museum, Charleston, South Carolina.)

Butchery marks suggest that more secondary cuts were sold from the Lower Market than from the Beef Market. Hack marks are characteristic of commercial butchers, who remove large portions of pork and beef from carcasses to sell to customers. Hack marks are abundant on Beef Market specimens, reflected most dramatically in the dense layer of small, hacked bone fragments in Zone 6 from the 1760s market. Hack marks are also common on modified bones in the Lower Market collection, though the 1750s–1820s Beef Market collection contains a higher percentage of hacked specimens than does the Lower Market collection. Sawed specimens, often considered markers of commercially produced meats and of secondary butchery, are rare in all market collections, though somewhat more abundant in the Lower Market collection than in the Beef Market collection. Beef Market bones are rarely cut, but a quarter of the modified bones from the Lower Market are cut. Likewise, few of the market bones are burned. This suggests that secondary butchery was not common at either market but was somewhat more common at the Lower Market, and that burning was not a common trash disposal method at either location.

Primary and secondary butchery modifications are not restricted to the markets. Hack marks are found on a third or fewer of the modified specimens recovered from non-market locations, though the presence of hacking on non-market specimens suggests that some primary butchering took place at such sites and was common at some of them. The percentage of hacked specimens in non-market collections is much lower than in market collections, though the percentage of hacked specimens declines over time in both market and non-market collections. By the late 1800s only a tenth of the modified specimens from non-market sites are hacked.

In contrast, cut marks and sawed specimens generally are more common in non-market collections. A quarter of the modifications on non-market specimens between 1710 into the 1850s are cut marks; a frequency that is similar to that found in the Lower Market collection, but much higher than that found in the Beef Market collection. By the end of the nineteenth century, however, fewer of the modified specimens are cut, and sawing is found on almost half of the modified specimens. The fivefold increase in the percentage of sawed specimens in non-market collections over time is a substantial line of evidence for a growing reliance on commercial meat purchases by the end of the nineteenth century, though this is not evident in the materials from the Beef or Lower markets because these markets had long since been closed.

Burned specimens are much more abundant in non-market collections than in market ones, suggesting that households tried to control their trash, and vermin, by burning the rubbish. Burning persisted as a waste disposal method into the late 1800s, though slightly less than a quarter of the modified specimens in deposits between 1820 and 1900 are burned.

Both the growing role of market-purchased meats and the persistence of home butchery are evident in specimens from residential and public sites occupied after 1820. Perhaps the most obvious change is that by 1850 both the Beef Market and the Lower Market were closed.

Provisioning the City: Using Young Animals

The age of the livestock slaughtered for consumption is another aspect of the city's provisioning strategy. We often assume that colonial livestock were rare and precious, particularly in the early days. Colonists were admonished not to slaughter young animals, in order to permit them to reach breeding age to allow herds to grow. The abundance of cattle at the Miller site, St. Giles Kussoe, Stobo Plantation, and the Cowpens suggests that cattle flourished in the colony and that this conservative husbandry strategy was unnecessary. Further evidence for this is found in the slaughter ages of pigs and cattle in Charleston.

Many of the animals died young, even during the early decades of the city's history. Nearly half of the pig individuals in the 1690–1750 Beef Market assemblage were juveniles (under 18 months of age) or subadults (under 24–36 months of age) when they were slaughtered. Two-thirds of pig individuals at non-market residential and public locations during this same time period were slaughtered before reaching adulthood. Two-thirds of the cow individuals in the early Beef Market assemblage were slaughtered before reaching adulthood, and over half of the cow individuals in non-market residential and public sites were slaughtered at an early age. Two-thirds of the pigs and over half of the cattle slaughtered in the 1750–1820 period were probably under 24–36 months of age at death. This same preference for meat from young animals persisted into the late 1800s. At the end of the nineteenth century, three-quarters of the pigs and over half of the cows were slaughtered as young animals.

Charleston's residents could afford to raise animals primarily for food, and they routinely slaughtered young, tender animals. Stock was raised specifically for food, and animals were slaughtered at an optimal age for weight gain. The young age of pigs and cattle indicates that conserving breeding stock was unnecessary and that the city could be provisioned with young animals. The preference for young, tender meat is reflected in a list of animals sold in the Lower Market: "Beeves 547; Calves, 2907; Sheep, 1994; Lambs, 1501; Large Hogs, 791; Small Hogs and Shoats, 4053."[34]

Urban Density

Our study of townhouse sites finds evidence of the elegant lifestyle enjoyed by Charlestonians grown wealthy through plantation ownership and business arrangements. Archaeology provides a clearer picture of the myriad tasks necessary to maintain the owners' elegant lifestyles. Although our excavations recover only a portion of the material trappings purchased and used by these wealthy city residents, the artifacts illustrate that townhouse residents had access to the latest goods from Europe and the Orient. Yet they continued to use locally made pottery for everyday kitchen activities. We also see that the refuse of wealthy urban residents was mixed with that of the laboring men and women who lived and worked on the same property.

Archaeological evidence is an important source of information for animals living in the city, and on the ways products from these animals were acquired and distributed throughout town. Cows and pigs supplied most of the meat consumed by city residents, and most of the information about provisioning. Analysis of the pig and cow bones suggests that live animals occupied work-yard space until they were butchered and that they were butchered at an optimal age. The bountiful woods, marshes, and pastures of the lowcountry allowed these animals to flourish.

9

THE COMMERCIAL CITY

James Wilson's apprehension turned to despair as the tremendous fire approaching from the southwest reached his seed store on King Street. Although firefighters scurried about, shouting orders, there was little they or other shocked citizens could do to stop the fury of the flames. By the next morning, April 28, 1838, nearly 700 acres of the city lay in ruins. Wilson and his neighbors began the arduous task of cleaning and rebuilding. Needing a convenient spot to dispose of much of his refuse, Wilson hauled loads of damaged merchandise to an abandoned well in his back yard. Nearly 150 years later, archaeologists excavating the Charleston Place site found evidence of Wilson's loss from the tragic fire.[1]

If townhouse lots were busy places, then properties in the city's commercial core were even more so. While wealthy planters and merchants had large residential compounds, many lower and middling class city dwellers lived in cramped quarters, often above shops or other enterprises. These crowded domestic, craft, and commercial spaces left little room for refuse disposal and other mundane affairs of daily life. Such sites are physical manifestations of a teeming, increasingly crowded urban environment.

But the archaeological assemblages are also selective, reflecting principally the residential aspects of these multipurpose properties, with just occasional evidence of their commercial or public functions. We recovered merchandise from Wilson's seed store only because of a disaster—what archaeologists call abandonment. When Wilson discarded the flowerpots after his building and its contents were damaged, the well in the back yard was a convenient place to dispose of the unusual refuse.

Wilson's seed store was located on the northwest corner of the block now occupied by the Charleston Place hotel and retail complex. The block was the City of Charleston's centerpiece for urban revitalization in the 1980s. It was the first federally mandated archaeological investigation and the largest of the mixed commercial and residential properties investigated in the city by archaeologists. The Charleston Place project demonstrated that archaeological sites in the middle of cities are deep, complex, and highly varied in quantity and types of deposits. Sites such as Charleston Place are physical manifestations of the pace and scale of urban life.

Many, perhaps even most, Charleston properties housed businesses and residences in the same structure, particularly during the late eighteenth and early nineteenth centuries. The first floor was public space; the floors above were private quarters for those who owned or rented the space below. Other Charleston sites were public facilities, such as taverns, markets, or theaters. Some, such as tanneries, ropewalks, and sugar houses, were used for craft production or other industries. But even these public buildings served as dwellings, either long- or short-term. The public sites contributed to our study of lowcountry cuisine, because they contained a dizzying array of wild and domestic foods sold by markets, shops, and street vendors, served in public settings, and otherwise obtained by the site's occupant(s). They also contained vessels used to serve this food and drink, and the remains of animals living in the city, both wanted and unwanted.

Commercial and Residential Life

The location of commercial and industrial activities changed as Charleston grew. The eighteenth-century port was a pedestrian city. Merchants needed to be near the waterfront for convenience and ease of transportation. The congested areas near the docks contained most of the shops, offices, and warehouses. Merchants and craftsmen lined East Bay Street and the three principal east–west streets, Broad, Tradd, and Elliott Streets, which carried traffic from the docks westward across the peninsula. Broad Street initially terminated at Meeting Street, in the civic square and market. Growth in the commercial sector was accommodated by subdividing lots and building into the center of blocks.[2]

King Street was the major route into town, following the ridge of highest land along the center of the peninsula. Down this road came wagons from the interior, carrying plantation produce and deerskins from Indian traders, as well as cattle on the hoof. Wagons returned to the interior bearing imported goods and provisions for the Indian trade and plantations.

To cater to the backcountry trade, merchants built stores and wagon yards along a two-mile stretch of King Street.[3]

Charleston was incorporated in 1783, and the city limits were moved four blocks north, from Beaufain Street to Boundary Street (now Calhoun Street). The area north of Boundary Street, known as the Neck, gradually filled with residences, industries, and businesses. The transportation orientation of the city changed from its earlier east–west axis to a north–south axis, as traffic along King Street increased in importance. The Charleston Place block was on this major thoroughfare. The new Centre Market, built by 1807 on the filled Vanderhorst Creek bed one block east of Charleston Place, replaced the three colonial markets and became the hub of the nineteenth-century retail and residential district. The Neck itself was annexed in 1849.

King and Meeting Streets were transformed into bustling retail centers. Nineteenth-century businesses became more specialized, with merchants pursuing either retail or wholesale trade. The city remained pedestrian, however, and the business district continued to be compact. As late as 1875, Arthur Mazyck described King Street as containing "about two miles of small stores, with here and there a really fine store. One could live in any part of the city and still be within walking distance of shops and tradespeople."[4]

Meeting and King Streets

Urban renewal projects in the 1970s and 1980s concentrated on the commercial core defined by the Meeting and King corridor. Our research was designed to identify the processes that formed the urban archaeological site, to define the temporal parameters of site use, and to study site functions reflected in the artifacts. Occupants of these sites had diverse backgrounds and means, with successful merchants living next to low-income laborers. The deposits reflect primarily the domestic activities at each site.

The limited samples obtained from these small projects could not be associated with specific residents with any certainty. Many of the residents were anonymous renters. This required us to query the activities of undocumented groups of people representing broad time periods, rather than single individuals, families, or events. Archaeologists working at prehistoric sites almost always work from this perspective, but it was a novel experience for historic site archaeologists accustomed to documentation.

Knowing who owned each Charleston lot did not capture the full range of activities and people at residential sites and was even less helpful at these mixed domestic-commercial lots. Had we ignored these mixed sites, however, we would have known very little about Charleston's evolving urban landscape. Exploring the nineteenth-century deposits helped us interpret the eighteenth-century public sites we excavated years later.[5]

Charleston Place

Charleston Place taught us these lessons well and laid the groundwork for our study of the urban landscape. The block was occupied from the late eighteenth century to the late twentieth century, with deposits from all time periods. It was the heart of the city's commercial district in the nineteenth century. In this chapter we focus on the site's earliest occupations, when the area was used intensively by many domestic and commercial establishments, including a stable. The Charleston Place animal remains are from the mid-nineteenth century, and these are considered in a later chapter.

The block-wide site encompassed dozens of individual properties, many of them used in a variety of ways over two centuries. Initial excavations were conducted in 1980 by Nicholas Honerkamp of the University of Tennessee–Chattanooga (UTC). UTC archaeologists dug 15 large units to varying depths, their location guided by documents and maps and a series of research questions. UTC's controlled excavations were followed by monitoring and salvage excavations by The Charleston Museum. With heavy equipment looming in the background, the Museum's team moved quickly. Only the largest features were identified and excavated. Large features, such as privy vaults, often are filled under special conditions, such as abandonment, that do not reflect the daily rhythm of normal urban life. The shallow zones and small features that were missed undoubtedly contained equally important information associated with daily discard. Fortunately, we could compare the results of the monitoring project to Honerkamp's excavations, which did capture more routine aspects of life in this area.

The block now bounded by Meeting, Market, King, and Hasell Streets was occupied gradually as the city expanded up the peninsula. By 1700 all of the lots were granted to settlers, but 30 years passed before the block was developed. By 1739 a few modest structures fronted King and Meeting Streets. What later became Market Street was a broad expanse of marsh. By the end of the eighteenth century, some structures lined King Street, and houses appeared along the newer streets, Hasell and Market.

Figure 9.1. View of the Meeting Street corridor in 1980, facing north. Charleston Place is the empty lot in the foreground. (Photo by Preservation Consultants, Courtesy of Historic Charleston Foundation.)

In the nineteenth century, Charleston Place bustled with commercial activity. Merchants built multistory structures along the front of their lots, plying their wares from shops on the ground floor and living in the rooms above. The Waverly, a large hotel on King Street, brought a steady flow of visitors to the block. As land increased in value, property owners subdivided their already narrow lots in a linear fashion, as street frontage was the desired, but expensive, commodity. By the close of the nineteenth century, lots averaged 30 feet wide but over 200 feet deep. Buildings covered 80 percent of the block. Larger, more substantial brick buildings gradually replaced smaller structures and outbuildings. The transition from wood to brick was complete here, due to fires in 1835 and 1838, which destroyed major portions of the block and made way for new, more substantial buildings.

Excavations at Charleston Place produced a large collection of material. UTC's controlled testing excavated 105 features, over 12,000 artifacts, and 412 pounds of bone. During the monitoring phase, archaeologists encountered 63 features and recovered 252 cubic feet of artifacts, bones, seeds, and soil samples. Although most of the deposits and artifacts reflect the domestic affairs of residents in the upper floors, a few features contain artifacts from the ground-floor retail and commercial establishments. Most of these deposits are produced by abandonment, such as Wilson's flowerpots, rather than daily discard. A wood-lined privy pit on the lot next door to Wilson's seed store, abandoned at the same time, was filled with burned household trash and dry goods associated with merchants William Calder and James Moffett. Farther down the block, a privy behind a grand hotel was abandoned in the 1850s. This deposit included unusually large numbers of inkwells, toothbrushes, and toilet wares, as well as heavy tumblers, goblets, and dinner china used in the hotel's dining room.

Horses normally are very rare in Charleston archaeological collections. (We use the term *horse* for convenience, though it is often impossible to determine whether the specimen is from a horse or a mule.) Only 12 "horse" individuals have been identified in the entire Charleston assemblage. Six of these are from Charleston Place, and four of them are from a single Charleston Place feature (Feature 145). Over half of the 63 horse specimens (38 of the elements) are teeth. Feature 145 was a rectangular pit filled in the mid-eighteenth century. It contained an almost complete, but disarticulated, horse skeleton and 16 horse canines. Feature 145 may have been a root cellar originally; but eventually it was used to dispose of a dead horse and teeth from other individuals.

Horses can have up to four canine, or wolf, teeth. Stallions and geldings normally have a full set of four canines. Only a few females have canine teeth, and those that do normally have one or two that are partially erupted. Canine teeth often are extracted to accommodate bits, and this may have been a routine procedure. It is possible that one of the nearby businesses was a stable or a knacker's yard where gelatin or glue was made.

Horse bones and teeth are normally rare in the archaeological record, but other objects reinforce that horses were common in Charleston. Snaffle

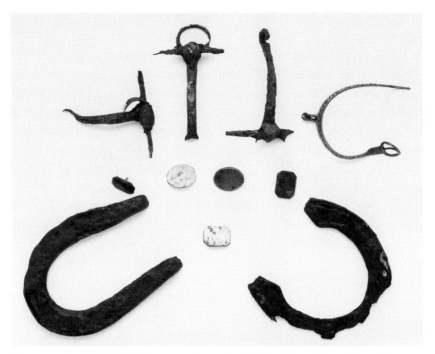

Figure 9.2. Snaffle bits (*top*), decorative bosses (*middle*), and horseshoes (*bottom*) recovered from various sites in Charleston. (Photo by Sean Money, Collections of The Charleston Museum, Charleston, South Carolina.)

bits and saddle hardware are found at sites throughout the city. Four harness and saddlery shops were located in the Charleston Place block in the late nineteenth century, and several pieces of horse equipment were recovered from Charleston Place. The Powder Magazine, which was a stable in the mid-nineteenth century, yielded two horseshoes and a stirrup. William Hieronymous, a mid-nineteenth-century owner of a house on Society Street, operated Hieronymous and O'Brien Livery Stable on Church Street, though no horse equipment was recovered from his Society Street home. Many of the townhouse sites contained horseshoes and snaffle bits associated with horses likely kept in the work yards and stables. Decorative bosses, or small brass ornaments fitted with pointed tabs to affix to leather, are common finds as well.

The First Trident Site

The First Trident site is a few blocks south of Charleston Place, at the corner of Cumberland and Meeting Streets. A new bank/office building, proposed for the site in 1983, impacted two of the original lots and provided the opportunity to dig here.

When first occupied, the location was a finger of high land adjacent to a marshy creek outside the city wall. In the early 1700s the periphery attracted artisans who could not afford real estate in the city core, needed more space, or engaged in activities considered offensive or dangerous by residents of the town. The First Trident site evidently fell into the latter category. Numerous leather scraps were recovered from moist deposits near the water table, suggesting that residents engaged in tanning or leatherworking. The percentage of cattle elements from the head and lower body is much higher than for any other site in this time period, including the Beef Market and the Lower Market (South Adger's Wharf). Evidently waste bone accumulated here.

By the late eighteenth century, the creek bed was filled, and the property was used for other commercial and domestic activities. The lots changed hands often during the nineteenth century and apparently were used largely as rental properties. John Kennedy kept a billiards saloon on this corner in the 1860s. The mill and machine business of Cameron and Barkley burned on this lot in the fire of 1861. Nineteenth-century artifacts recovered from two excavation units, however, are largely domestic and suggest a resident of at least modest means. Cattle bones from these later deposits are similar to those found at residential sites; in fact, they are very similar to those recovered from the Motte-Alston occupation at the Brewton House.

East Bay Street

Charleston is dominated by water. The city plan and its economic trajectory rose from its waterfront location. Charleston's dependence on shipping and maritime mercantile business for the prosperity enjoyed by some low-country families led to a preference for property on or near the wharves. Mercantile and craft activities, and workers employed in those industries, clustered along East Bay Street (or "on the Bay") in the late eighteenth and early nineteenth centuries.

Two mixed-use properties near the waterfront characterize this hive of activity. Lodge Alley is a narrow block-long thoroughfare running from East Bay Street to State Street. The alley featured a Masonic lodge, but women operated boarding houses there, too. Small, dank, and close to the fish market, Lodge Alley was seldom the choice of those who could afford to live elsewhere. Tradesmen, craftsmen, and shopkeepers were often forced by ruinous rents to house both their families and businesses in crowded tenements along such passages.[6]

The *South Carolina Gazette* reveals some of the residents and activities on or near Lodge Alley. Alexander Alexander advertised a school there in the mid-eighteenth century. Elinor Bolton flaunted herself as a "pastry cook from London, late housekeeper." Mary-Brown Packwood did "clear starching, lace mending, and dressed silk stockings." She also had two rooms to let, ready furnished, with use of a kitchen and cellar. Some female residents were listed as seamstresses. Although there is no proof of this for Charleston, many women listed as seamstresses in other cities worked in brothels. Mariners, ship carpenters, coopers, and riggers also resided in Lodge Alley during the late eighteenth century. Residents of nearby State Street enjoyed slightly higher status. City directories for 1790 list teachers, carpenters, bakers, shopkeepers, fishermen, seamstresses, bricklayers, mariners, and tide waiters along that street.[7]

When warehouses on East Bay Street were renovated for a hotel complex in 1983, archaeologists had the opportunity to excavate in Lodge Alley and State Street. Open ground was scarce, and test units were placed wherever space was available. December excavation in the narrow alley reminded us that this was never a pleasant place to live. The passage was cold, damp, and dark, receiving direct sunlight for only a few midday hours. The roadway evidently rutted easily and needed constant maintenance; the excavation revealed multiple layers of sand surfaces filled with small, trampled debris, likely from the buildings fronting the thoroughfare. Test units behind 38 State Street, adjacent to the alley, produced an intact deposit of wares from an assayer or metalsmith, burned in a hot fire. Clay and graphite crucibles in a range of sizes, melted glass decanters, and slate pencils filled the unit. Lodge Alley is our archaeological standard for a mixed-use, lower-status site. Despite this, the animal remains include much the same fare found at other sites: deer, turkeys, sea turtles, diamondback terrapins, and fishes.

Down the street, at the corner of East Bay and Unity Alley, developers renovated a maze of late-colonial buildings to house an upscale restaurant, one that mirrored an earlier use of the property. Two hundred years earlier, in 1770, Edward McCrady purchased what had been a rental property and operated a successful tavern there. Ten years later, McCrady purchased a tract behind his tavern and built a long room over a kitchen. The tavern was connected to the kitchen and long room by a piazza and open arcade. The tavern, long room, and kitchen covered the property almost entirely. A storeroom, a well with pump, and a small yard paved in brick completed

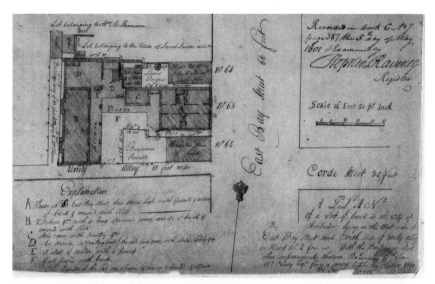

Figure 9.3. Plat of McCrady's Tavern and Long Room in 1801, following the death of pro-
prietor Edward McCrady. (Historic Document Collection, Book C-7, p. 387, Property of
the Charleston County Register Mesne Conveyance Office, Charleston, South Carolina.
Used by permission.)

the labyrinthine complex. Taverns served meals and offered lodging, but
long rooms were rented for special, festive occasions and served as banquet
halls, conference rooms, ballrooms, and theaters. McCrady's Long Room
was the scene of concerts, caucuses, and plays, often attended by Charleston's political and social leaders. President George Washington was enter-
tained by the Society of the Cincinnati with "a very sumptuous dinner" at
McCrady's Long Room during his 1791 southern tour.[8]

Test excavations within the arcade and paved work yard produced a rich
archaeological assemblage. The most remarkable discovery came from a pit
uncovered during construction. This feature was filled with wine goblets in
a variety of styles, as well as bone-handled cutlery and animal bones. This
small project prompted the first study of animal remains in the city. The
McCrady's Tavern and Long Room period (1750s–1820s) is one of the very
few Charleston deposits to contain Muscovy ducks and sea turtles (but no
diamondback terrapins). The menu also included shark. Two deer skull
fragments suggest either trophy skulls or a recipe that featured deer heads
much like some recipes featured calves heads. The remains of two suckling
pigs and two calves also were recovered. Perhaps McCrady's menu featured
presentations of small pigs, as well as dishes made from the heads and feet

of calves. Botanical analysis by Michael Trinkley identified peaches; pine was the dominant fuel wood.

The Wharves

Although sites on the west side of East Bay Street can sometimes be associated with specific residents and activities, sites on the east side of the street are anonymous. The harbor side gradually filled with refuse, building rubble, and soil accumulating along the early waterfront and wharves, producing filled or "made land." Excavations at Atlantic Wharf, the Exchange Building, and South Adger's Wharf reveal deep deposits of soil and rubble filled with discarded artifacts from nearby properties, as well as from activities on the wharves.

Historical archaeologists first encountered such "made land" when they began to study large urban centers on the eastern Atlantic coast. These secondary deposits contained rich material assemblages, but they could not be connected to specific individuals or activities. As a result, some scholars suggested that excavation and analysis of filled land should be avoided. Archaeologists traditionally build their interpretation on primary deposits, thought to indicate the original use of the materials in the original location of use. The contents of secondary, or fill, deposits, no longer where they were originally used, are considered "disturbed" and thus incapable of providing reliable information.

As they gained experience with secondary deposits, urban archaeologists realized that filled land and "disturbed" deposits are important aspects of urban behavior. The land modifications reflected in fill are artifacts of the evolving urban landscape. The urban landscape, like urban life, is, by its nature, mixed. The challenge was to develop analytic techniques and research questions appropriate to such deposits, questions that did not require knowing exactly who lived at these sites and what they did there. This required working within a broader framework of association between site history and artifacts.[9]

Excavations at three waterfront sites over three decades have produced materials that add greatly to our archaeological knowledge of Charleston's evolution. Much of the material at these sites was generated by activities on the waterfront itself. The mud banks under and between the wharves likely received a considerable amount of casual debris from ships, waterfront workers, and the adjacent wharves. As the city became more crowded, and trash disposal a more urgent problem, the waterfront was an attractive and

Figure 9.4. Fragments of slate recovered from the Exchange Building and a nearby plantation show tallies in groups of five. (Photo by Sean Money, Collections of The Charleston Museum, Charleston, South Carolina.)

readily accessible alternative to the neighbor's yard. This debris was from unknown sources, tossed there by unknown people, but representative of life in the city nonetheless. Some artifacts, such as slate fragments etched with tallies, were discards from waterfront activities.

The first project on "made land" was at Atlantic Wharf in 1983. This site is now about a quarter mile from the waterfront and supports a parking garage; but in the eighteenth century it was a wharf at the water's edge and a dump. A layer of late-eighteenth-century fill lies just above today's mean high tide. Timbers encountered were those of a crib-style wharf. Both the fill and the timbers lay beneath deep layers of twentieth-century fill. The late colonial layer contained numerous Spanish ceramics, including types not found elsewhere in the city. These included several pieces of El Morro ware, manufactured in the Spanish Caribbean, Spanish Olive Jars and majolicas, and unglazed greyware. The site also yielded a retinue of English wares typical of those used throughout the city. The fill also included a parrotfish bone. Parrotfishes live in tropical waters, where they feed on coral reefs. Some of their cranial bones are adapted to this feeding behavior and appear strange by comparison with those of the local drums and sea catfishes Charlestonians knew well. This specimen might have been a sailor's curio or good luck charm.

The most remarkable aspect of the work at Atlantic Wharf reinforces the image of a crowded, dirty, refuse-strewn waterfront swarming with vermin. The wharf deposit contained a tremendous number of rats and a large number of burned bones. Over 2,800 animal specimens were recovered, and 307 of these were from Norway and black rats. A third of the individuals in this deposit were rats, the highest percentage of any Charleston collection. Over half of the modified bones were burned, but only two rat bones were burned. Perhaps a smoldering fire was sustained in a casual attempt to control the accumulating refuse and the vermin attracted to it. Rats apparently were adept at avoiding the flames. The layers of debris encountered in the basement of the Exchange Building had similar characteristics.

So, too, did South Adger's Wharf. The artifacts found in the deep layers of soil in front of the brick fortifications suggested casual disposal from wharves and other waterfront activities, nearby residences, shops, taverns, and other businesses for over a half century. The lowest level at South Adger's Wharf contained discarded wine bottles, tobacco pipes, and fish bones. A bottle seal with the name Laurens likely belonged to wharf owner John Laurens. As at Atlantic Wharf, the mudflat beneath the wharves teemed with rats (a quarter of the individuals). Fire apparently was not used to control trash and vermin here, perhaps due to its central location. Almost none of the specimens from the mudflat were burned. The high frequency of rats at both Atlantic Wharf and South Adger's Wharf suggests that Charleston's harbor was generally used for trash disposal and was prime habitat for rats.

South Adger's Wharf was later filled to accommodate the Lower Market and other waterfront businesses. The frequency of rats dropped at the wharf when the Lower Market began operation, suggesting either that the Lower Market was intentionally kept clean of trash and debris (unlikely, given the constant complaints about the market), or that the hustle and openness of the market did not provide ideal rat habitat. The low numbers of rats associated with the Lower Market mirrors similarly low numbers of rats at the Beef Market.

Figure 9.5. Mouth plate fragment from a parrotfish, recovered from Atlantic Wharf in 1983. (Photo by Sean Money, Collections of The Charleston Museum, Charleston, South Carolina.)

0   cm   1

The Beef Market and the Lower Market

Two sites provide data from Charleston's markets in the late eighteenth century. The dig at City Hall recorded the clutter and accumulated debris at the relatively undisturbed Beef Market. The Lower Market site was, by comparison, a much more open and complex archaeological site.

In 1760 a new structure was completed at Charleston's original market square to replace the more modest 1739 building. The market received a new name, the Beef Market (see chapter 7 for a discussion of the earlier market). Our excavations encountered much of the footprint of the 1760 market, as well as layers of debris deposited between 1760 and 1796. The 45×105-foot foundation was well preserved, though construction of City Hall evidently removed the building's floor. A hard-packed sand surface (Zone 7) may be an original, unpaved market surface or foundation for paving. Zone 7 was covered by water-washed sand filled with small fragments of hacked bone (Zone 6). Soil stains near the foundations were evidence of wooden posts placed in carefully dug holes. Such posts may have supported hooks and pegs for displaying meats and other products. The walls likely had a series of arched openings. The description of the structure as "low" suggests a single-story building. The southern facade featured a four-foot projection spanning the central third of the structure. A central brick well and a large brick drain were integral parts of the 1760 market and likely were used for daily cleaning.

Despite the name, the market offered a broad range of products and had done so since its inception in 1692. The market continued in operation until it was destroyed by the 1796 fire. A 1794 coin embedded in a deep ash layer provided archaeological corroboration of that event. After this third market burned, it was not rebuilt. The central location of the Beef Market, once advantageous for a market, now hampered the ability of butchers to slaughter on-site, or nearby, and to dispose of the waste easily. Evidently in response to recurring problems, a 1783 issue of the *South Carolina Weekly Gazette* reminded readers that butchering cattle "within the city limits" was prohibited.[10]

As seen in the last chapter, the only butchering tool recovered in Charleston was found at the Beef Market. The cleaver in question is from the market but was not recovered during either the 1984 dig in Washington Park or the 2004 dig inside City Hall. Instead, it was pulled from a 1985 sidewalk repair on the Meeting Street side of City Hall. Our first hint of this discovery came on the local evening news. Broadcasters reported that "bones

Figure 9.6. Cleaver recovered from the western side of Washington Park, near the Beef Market, in 1985. (Collections of The Charleston Museum, Charleston, South Carolina.)

and a possible murder weapon" were found in the hole in the sidewalk and were being studied by the Charleston County coroner. We knew immediately that these were likely beef bones, rather than human bones. Moreover, the cleaver was a rare and important find. We were on the phone with the coroner's office the next morning. After identification, the City donated the materials to the Museum.

Two new markets were constructed in Charleston in the late colonial period. The Lower Market, on Tradd Street, opened in 1750, and the Fish Market opened in 1770 on Queen Street. The Lower Market was built directly in front of the old redan and later expanded over the foundations of the demolished fortification. This market was well situated for receiving the day's catch or provisions brought from plantations by boat. Its waterfront location also meant that waste could be easily discarded into the mudflats below. Study of the Lower Market occurred in conjunction with the City Wall project described in chapter 6; archaeologists have not yet worked at the Fish Market.

References to the Lower Market in local newspapers indicate that it was a center of activity during the final quarter of the eighteenth century. Access to the Lower Market by vendors and customers, however, was hampered by what remained of the old curtain line and redan of the city wall. The brick redan was razed to ground level in 1785, and the Lower Market was enlarged. A new shed built on the south side of the market was reserved for "those persons who come first to market with butter, poultry, wild fowl, or vegetables." The Commissioners of the Markets also addressed other issues plaguing the Lower Market. They recommended the market "be immediately paved, as in its present situation it is extremely offensive." There were complaints about "the very great number of dogs which are suffered to go at large through the streets, particularly those which crowd each market-place." Evidently, dogs were not the only disorderly market attendants; the Commissioner resolved that "all persons who bring poultry or vegetables to the Lower Market, be placed in two lines running west from the market to the street." Those arriving first would be ushered into the shed on the south side.[11]

The waterfront market was still too small to accommodate Charleston's growing needs, and expansion of the wharves after the Revolutionary War made the area too congested for a public facility there. To consolidate the city's market activities on the new Market Street, the three colonial markets were all closed in 1799. They were replaced by Centre Market, which became the hub of nineteenth-century activities.

The opportunity to study the Lower Market was a secondary aspect of the City Wall project. The area available for excavation did not include the 1750 market building, but it did cover the area west of that building and beneath the market expansion. The fill over the old redan revealed that the expanded market square was paved with a single layer of narrow bricks on a base of orange clay. The paving covered layers of refuse-filled sand. The superimposed layers, Zones 3 through 9, were deposited between 1770 and 1800 and contained 35,000 artifacts, including a large collection of animal remains. The brick paving at the base of Zone 3 provided corroborating archaeological evidence of documented events.

The animal debris from the Lower Market differs from the Beef Market assemblage in many respects. Similar animal products were sold in both markets, but in different proportions. One of the more inexplicable differences is in the quantity of fish. Over a third of the individuals recovered from the Beef Market deposits were fish, while a tenth of the individuals in the Lower Market collection are fish. Both markets sold similar fish taxa from local waters, but what the Lower Market appears to have sold in abundance was beef.

Provisioning the Market

Carolinians in the eighteenth century drove cattle to market on the hoof and then fattened them on grazing lands close to market. Slaughter pens and houses were likely located on the edge of town. In 1791 a Charleston butcher advertised "pasturage at the new race grounds" at Hampton Park and well outside of the city limits at that time. Legislation was passed repeatedly to keep such facilities outside the town, but they continued to operate within the city. A grievance filed in 1764 complained of two men "having Slaughter pens and killing cattle, in and about Ansonborough; to the great annoyance of the neighborhood, by the filth and stench of their pens, and to the endangering the lives of passengers passing and re-passing on the public road."[12]

Ansonborough was inside the city limits at that time. A 1783 ordinance banned killing cattle within the city limits, which by then extended to Calhoun Street. Butchering cattle just outside the city limits probably explains the creek filled with horn cores and other butchering waste at the Visitor Reception and Transportation Center, one block north of Calhoun.[13]

The slaves who lived and worked on local plantations were the primary producers of vegetables, fruits, and small meats sold in the city. Plantation slaves were customarily allotted quarter-acre garden plots for their own use. This relationship is underscored by a 1786 ordinance reserving six stalls at the Lower Market for "the use of the planters that bring or send their own stock to market." Such arrangements were stipulated again in legislation for the new Centre Market in 1807, providing "for the use of planters bringing

Figure 9.7. Horn cores discovered at the Visitor Reception and Transportation Center site in 1988. (Collections of The Charleston Museum, Charleston, South Carolina.)

or sending meat of their own stock or raising to market, there shall be reserved six stalls in the Centre Market."[14]

Slaves from both the city and the countryside made up a large portion of the markets' vendors. These hucksters peddled a variety of items for their own benefit and that of their enslavers. Slaves also provisioned the planters and bartered with their owners on plantations. Maurie McInnis notes that most planters encouraged these enterprises. Bondsmen and women from the countryside sold their own eggs, chickens, and garden produce, as well as cakes and other baked goods. Vendors provided vegetables and fruits that later were characterized as "truck farming."[15]

The entrepreneurship of enslaved Africans was a common complaint of white townspeople. In 1772 "Stranger" commented on black women around the Lower Market, "who are seated there from morn 'til night, and buy and sell on their accounts . . . These women have such a connection with and influence on, the country Negroes who come to market, that they generally find means to obtain whatever they choose, in preference to any white person." Philip Morgan suggests that slaves from nearby James Island were important links in the lowcountry marketing system. He cites several documents that refer to James Island slaves working the Charleston markets, surmising that "an identifiable group of island peddlers had emerged by the late colonial period." Island residents grew vegetables such as watermelons, muskmelons, tomatoes, okra, peanuts, Irish potatoes, green peas, beans, squash, cabbages, turnips, and sweet potatoes for the Charleston market. Even after the Lower Market closed in 1799, the wharf at the foot of Tradd Street served as the arrival point for James Island hucksters and their wares well into the twentieth century.[16]

Slaves also may have sold colono ware. Beginning in 1993, Brian Crane suggested the colono wares in the city were acquired through trade. Nicole Isenbarger and J. W. Joseph have identified subtypes, principally the burnished wares classified as Lesesne, as market wares. Thus far there is no direct evidence for the manufacture of colono ware in the city. Crane conducted a detailed sourcing study using colono wares from Stono Plantation on nearby James Island and from the Heyward-Washington House. Half of the plantation wares clustered in a uniform group, suggesting manufacture in a single place. The other half displayed much more variability, indicating multiple sources. The urban colono wares did not form a uniform cluster, suggesting they are from many different sources and obtained through trade. It is likely that most of the colono wares recovered in Charleston were made on nearby plantations and sold in Charleston by African Americans.[17]

Many of the goods sold by African Americans in the Charleston market arrived by boat. Both Joseph and Chris Espenshade suggest the large number of intact colono ware ceramics recovered from area streams may be the result of accidents that occurred as pottery was transported by water to Charleston. African American dominance of the waterways was noted by many travelers and cited as an opportunity for subterfuge. An advertisement for runaway slaves in the *South Carolina Gazette* reports that two men were "seen three or four times in the lower market" and were traveling by canoe.[18]

Morgan notes that Charleston's urban markets created opportunities for enslaved men. Some butchers were slaves. John Jackson's 1790 advertisement for a runaway slave named Peter notes he "is well known in Charleston, having for upwards of four years attended a butcher's stall in the lower market." Likewise, most of the fishing for the urban market was done by African American men. The fishermen's catch was sold by women in the market and men who peddled in the residential areas. As a result of this monopoly, slave hucksters readily manipulated supplies and prices for the Charleston market.[19]

Provisioning the City

African Americans evidently brought a good deal of wild game to the Charleston markets, in addition to produce, poultry, and seafood. The assemblages from the Beef and Lower Markets show that numerous wild animals were sold along with domestic meats. The 1750s–1820s Beef Market collection contains the remains of 20 non-commensal animals, and the contemporary Lower Market collection contains the remains of 28. Collections from non-market residential and public sites, in comparison, contain 69 different types of non-commensal animals in the same time period. Though neither market specialized in a single type of meat, a wide range of meats were obtained by householders from sources other than these two markets. The non-market avenues for provisioning are as diverse as the city itself. In some cases provisions were obtained through households' or individuals' rural connections (e.g., gifts among kin); by individual efforts within a household to fish, trap, or hunt; from animals raised within the city or nearby; and from people selling outside the official markets.

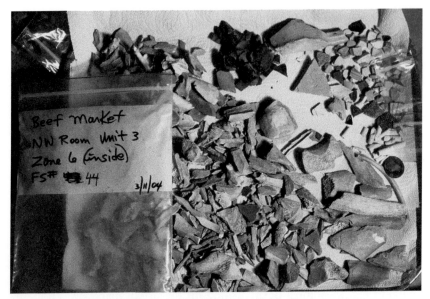

Figure 9.8. A typical assemblage of artifacts from a Charleston provenience. This tray is from the 2004 excavations at the Beef Market; note the quantity of bone fragments relative to other artifact groups. (Collections of The Charleston Museum, Charleston, South Carolina.)

Non-market deposits in the late eighteenth century contain twice as many different types of fishes as do either of the market collections. Although it is possible that customers removed all of the fishy evidence from markets when they purchased fish, it seems equally plausible that fish was caught by members of each household, perhaps by enslaved staff, or purchased directly from fishermen or their wives.

Over time the products sold at the Beef Market changed. Pork and beef were always the largest volume of sales, but the quantity of beef gradually declined as the number of small animals increased. These small animals contributed little to the quantity of meat sold but contributed greatly to the variety of meats available, and to the sights and sounds of the market. Evidently complaints about livestock, particularly of cattle and cattle products, did mean that meat from large animals was sold less frequently from the Beef Market. Perhaps beef largely was sold from the Lower Market just before the Beef Market closed. Three-quarters of the meat sold from the Lower Market in the 1750s–1820s period was beef.

Despite complaints about conditions at both markets, few rats are found at either site. The frequency of rats increases at the Beef Market as the eighteenth century progresses, as it did throughout the city. The Lower Market, contemporaneous with the Beef Market in the 1750s–1820s period, has a similar proportion of rats. Despite the observation that rats are more abundant in markets in the 1750s–1820s markets than previously, rats were more abundant at non-market contexts in every time period. Archaeology tells us that the markets actually were cleaner than other locations within Charleston. Perhaps markets did not supply rats with the ideal food and habitats needed for them to thrive, or they were kept at bay by market predators such as cats or small boys.

The increase in small animals seen in the archaeological record may be an accommodation to and a consequence of the congested urban environment as keeping cows and other large animals in the growing city became impractical. The decline in cattle at residential sites is particularly pronounced by the end of the nineteenth century; but sheep and goats are less common as well. It is likely that the decision to reduce the presence of these animals was based less on smell and more on management issues, such as tractability, feeding requirements, and waste management.

As keeping large animals became less feasible, and slaughtering animals within the city less acceptable, vendors and householders turned to animals they could raise inside the city limits. Both pigs and chickens can be fed kitchen waste in back yard pens and coops. Keeping pigs in the city may have been discouraged, because gardens and accumulating trash are equally attractive to them. Nonetheless, they persisted as a small but consistent component of the urban scene. Chickens became more abundant. Chickens, as well as ducks, geese, and pigeons, are more suitable to small back yards. The increase in poultry would be even more pronounced if Canada geese and turkeys are counted as domestic birds.

Life in the Commercial City

Excavations at Charleston Place, especially the debris discarded after the 1838 fire, reminds us of the many events, some benign and others tragic, that occur frequently in cities. People may maintain an elegant facade, but they rarely bother to make their trash conform to social standards. So it is in the archaeological record that we see the full picture of life in the city. Particularly, we see the consequences of large numbers of people crowding onto a low-lying, damp peninsula, raising families, gardens, and livestock there, and otherwise engaging in the business of life. It is only through the archaeological record that we see the extent and ramifications of people merging their domestic lives with public and commercial activities in the same places. We may not know exactly who lived or worked at each site, but we can see evidence of the daily lives of people living beyond the affluent townhouses. The archaeological projects of the 1980s remind us that the pace of life we see along the King Street corridor today is not new. Neither is the problem of what to do with the trash.

Plate 1. Houses along the Charleston Battery in 1992. (Historic American Buildings Survey photograph, Library of Congress.)

Plate 2. Aerial view of a portion of the Santee River in 2006, showing Hampton Creek. Dikes from former rice fields are visible in the river delta. (Courtesy USDA Forest Service.)

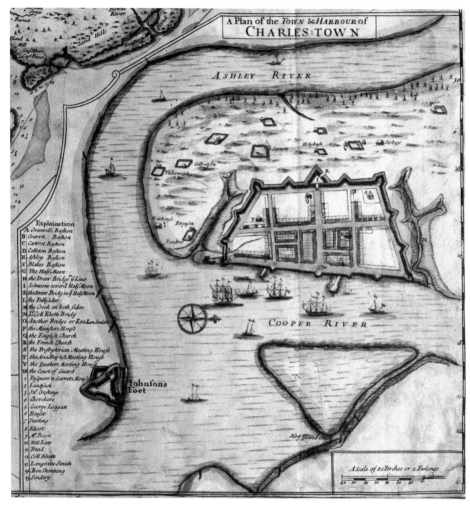

Plate 3. Inset of the Edward Crisp map of 1711, showing Charleston as a walled city. (Library of Congress.)

Plate 4. Earthenwares commonly used in the eighteenth century: Staffordshire combed and trailed slipware, Manganese Mottled ware, slip-coated ware. From the Heyward-Washington House. (Photo by Sean Money, Collections of The Charleston Museum, Charleston, South Carolina.)

Plate 5. A group of Florida Scrub, or Cracker, cattle. The breed descended from animals introduced to St. Augustine by the Spaniards. They are adapted to the low-quality forage shown in this image, typical of the grasslands and swamps of the lowcountry. From the heritage livestock program at the Florida Agricultural Museum, Palm Coast, Florida. (Photo by Olga Maria Caballero, at the Florida Agricultural Museum.)

Plate 6. A harpsichord, ca. 1686, in the drawing room of the Heyward-Washington House. (Collections of The Charleston Museum, Charleston, South Carolina.)

Plate 7. Sealed bottles inscribed "G. A. Hall 1768" recovered from the privy at the Heyward-Washington House. (Photo by Sean Money, Collections of The Charleston Museum, Charleston, South Carolina.)

Plate 8. Chinese porcelain teawares, drinking glasses, and creamware tablewares, from the Heyward-Washington House, on exhibit at The Charleston Museum. (Collections of The Charleston Museum, Charleston, South Carolina.)

Plate 9. Colono wares in European forms: (*left*) a plate decorated with impressed lines; (*center*) a pitcher painted in red and black; and (*right*) a plate painted along the rim. The pitcher is likely the product of Catawba potters. (Photo by Sean Money, Collections of The Charleston Museum, Charleston, South Carolina.)

Plate 10. Drinking glasses and bone-handled cutlery from McCrady's Tavern and Long Room. (Photo by Sean Money, Collections of The Charleston Museum, Charleston, South Carolina.)

Plate 11. Soil profile from South Adger's Wharf, showing fill deposits associated with the Lower Market, excavated in 2009. The single layer of brick is evidence of the 1789 paving of the market site. Soils below the paving were deposited between 1785 and 1789. (Collections of The Charleston Museum, Charleston, South Carolina.)

Plate 12. *Charleston Square* by Charles J. Hamilton, 1862. The painting portrays a vibrant street, filled with vendors and shoppers. Buzzards circle the market, growing more numerous near the waterfront. (Colonial Williamsburg Foundation, Museum Purchase.)

IV

THE NINETEENTH CENTURY

10

THE CROWDED CITY

"Last night I was at the handsomest ball I have ever seen—given by Mrs. Aiken—Miss Lowndes that was—they live near Boundary Street in a house he has added to and furnished very handsomely—two floors were entirely thrown open—the orchestra from the theatre played for dancers—and the supper table was covered with a rich service of silver—lights in profusion and a crowded handsomely dressed assembly." So wrote Frances Kinloch Middleton in 1839, describing a party at the newly renovated home of William and Harriet Aiken, a large edifice in Charleston Neck. The Aiken home evidently set the bar for entertaining in the antebellum city.

Nearly two decades later, J. B. Grimball hosted a dinner for William Aiken. Eager to please this scion of Charleston society, he recorded the menu in his diary:

> *1st course—Calf's Head Soup, and Vegetables*
> *2nd course—Broiled Bass and Fried Whiting*
> *3rd course—Saddle of Mutton, Ham, Roast Turkey, Oysters*
> *Dessert—Ice Cream 4 quarts, 1 dozen apples, 1 dozen bananas, and groundnuts*

This meal of the 1850s is likely typical of the elegant dinners served by Charleston high society, for archaeology shows that townhouse residents made regular use of wild foods to enhance and augment the domestic meats. The Aiken-Rhett House has some of the latest examples of such seemingly exotic fare as beaver, diamondback terrapin, and chicken turtle.[1]

The already cramped work yards of townhouses, commercial lots, and middle-class residences grew more congested by the 1820s–1850s. The large slave population in the crowded city prompted changes to the layout and traffic flow of residential properties. We see these modifications in townhouses built in the early nineteenth century and in older houses remodeled during the antebellum period. Alterations are evident aboveground and in archaeological excavations.

Disasters and civic improvement prompted other changes. Archaeology reveals alterations designed to reduce accumulating debris and to improve sanitation. The rear lots of some properties were still filled with bottles, dishes, and other debris, though other lots were frustratingly free of artifacts. Kitchens were renovated. Charleston residents still included wild foods in their diets and cuisine, but they used smaller animals and purchased more meat than they had previously. Novel food preparation styles were adopted, too.

Civic Improvements

Planting offered ample opportunities for amassing great fortunes. Some residents prospered during the antebellum nineteenth century with profits from rice and Sea Island cotton. This growing wealth was used to build new houses along the edges of the city: south to the Battery, north beyond the city boundary at Calhoun Street, and westward toward the Ashley River. Residences and workplaces were more frequently separated from each other.[2]

American cities were industrializing, and at first Charleston kept pace with the rest of the country. During the early years of the nineteenth century, new enterprises, including two railroads, were located on the Neck, the burgeoning suburbs between Calhoun and Line streets. The Neck quickly transformed from the "country" and a favored location for many planters' townhouses, into the center of Charleston's industrial zone. Charleston's economy remained dependent on the plantation system, though, and commercial growth slowed after the nationwide depression of 1819. Charleston's population growth also slowed during this time, and the city's rank fell from fourth in the nation in 1775 to twenty-second in 1860.[3]

Civic improvements and new buildings offered little protection from fires, which ravaged the city with frightening regularity. The major fires of the eighteenth century were followed by equally devastating ones in 1835, 1838, and 1861. These conflagrations gutted large sections of the city.

Wooden buildings were particularly vulnerable to fires, and legislation to limit wood construction was passed after each disaster. Enforcement invariably lapsed, however, and the opportunities these fires offered for rebuilding met with mixed success. Recurring fires led to a paranoia concerning arson that inevitably focused on the slave population.[4]

Slavery was synonymous with labor, even in the city. Owners routinely "hired out" enslaved artisans to others. Slaves also were allowed to hire out their own time and keep part of the earnings. Some had permission to "live out," away from the master's compound. The Neck, which was beyond the city limits and the purview of city police, was a favored location for these slaves. The purported Denmark Vesey slave rebellion in 1822 brought vague fears of an uprising by the enslaved majority to a fevered pitch among white residents. Despite their fear of the African American population, many Charleston residents continued to rely on the enslaved for food and services.[5]

Ansonborough

Ansonborough was the first suburban development of the expanding colonial city. By the early nineteenth century, Ansonborough was filled with small lots and modest houses occupied by merchants and skilled craftspeople. The area also became home to a disproportionate number of Charleston's poor Irish workers, who crowded into slum areas north of Market Street and along the waterfront. They were joined by free and enslaved Blacks, who constituted a third of the neighborhood's population.

Much of Ansonborough was rebuilt in brick after a devastating fire in 1838. The house built by stable owner William Hieronymous was the third on that property. Juliana Dupre's brick house, built in 1850, incorporated portions of an original house destroyed in the 1838 fire.[6]

The condition of Ansonborough homes declined dramatically in the early twentieth century. In response, Historic Charleston Foundation initiated the first preservation revolving fund project. The Foundation purchased houses, renovated them, and sold them with covenants to protect their historic character. Now fully restored, the Hieronymous-Roper and Juliana Dupre houses reflect Charleston's "long-standing commitment to historic preservation standards and the city's traditional appearance."[7]

Archaeological studies in Ansonborough were conducted in the late 1980s. A single test unit was excavated at the Juliana Dupre House during renovations to that structure. Somewhat more extensive work was conducted at the Hieronymous-Roper House, where plans to construct a swimming pool in the rear yard triggered archaeological testing. The lot measures 45 × 127 feet and contains a three-story brick single house. Behind the house, a single outbuilding housed functions usually divided among several structures on larger townhouse properties. Alterations to the buildings and lot hampered interpretation of the property, but excavations revealed trash pits filled in the nineteenth century.

The Kohne-Leslie House is one of the larger surviving Ansonborough structures. Built in 1846 by Eliza Neufville Kohne, it replaced a two-story wooden structure that burned in 1838. Mrs. Kohne willed the property to her nephew in 1852. She also attempted to leave an annuity to her freed slave, Emma Harbeaux, but Mrs. Kohne's family blocked the bequest. Later, African American entrepreneur Charles C. Leslie purchased the property and retired from his fish marketing business. Curiously, no fish were recovered from deposits associated with Mr. Leslie's ownership. Changes to the property and garden in 1992 prompted Historic Charleston Foundation to request archaeological testing.[8]

The Simmons-Edwards House

The Simmons-Edwards House is a neoclassical building of national significance. Planter Francis Simmons constructed the house in 1801. Beaufort planter George Edwards purchased the property in 1816 and added many elegant features, including the famous towering brick columns surmounted by marble carvings known locally as "pineapples." Wrought iron panels on the fencing feature Edwards' initials.

A brick single house of three stories dominates the double lot. Behind the house, a two-and-a-half-story kitchen/slave quarters and a large carriage house fill the northern lot line. Later infill connects the main house and kitchen. A small brick privy is tucked behind the carriage house. The lot is surrounded by brick walls of various styles; the front wall features brick columns supporting the stone finials. An internal wall parallel to the main house separates the formal garden from the work yard.

Architect Glenn Keyes and landscape historian C. Allan Brown coordinated a large archaeological project as part of the private restoration. The primary goal was to locate the pleasure garden. Archaeology proceeded in five phases, beginning with limited testing. The discovery of possible garden features prompted a block excavation to expose the northern half of a formal garden, and the results facilitated restoration of the garden's footprint. This was the first archaeological study of the contents and evolution of a historic formal garden in Charleston. We also excavated in the less formal middle and rear gardens to define features there, and in the work yard to mitigate damage from construction and installation of an underground geothermal system.

An unexpected discovery at the Simmons-Edwards House is germane to our broader study of the evolving city landscape. The house fronts on Legare Street but shares a boundary with the rear of the Miles Brewton House, which fronts on King Street. Although William Bull Pringle sold the back part of the Brewton lot in 1857, the two properties continued to share a small common boundary. Aspects of the Brewton work yard excavated in 1989 were fully understood only after excavations at the Simmons-Edwards House a decade later.

Figure 10.1. Features encountered at the Simmons-Edwards House include a well filled with late-eighteenth-century refuse from the adjoining Miles Brewton House and an early-nineteenth-century foundation for the garden fence. (Collections of The Charleston Museum, Charleston, South Carolina.)

The Aiken-Rhett House

The 1818 Aiken-Rhett House, a historic house museum owned by Historic Charleston Foundation, is located on the Neck in Wraggborough. All of the service buildings are intact, and it has original paint finishes, wallpaper, and lighting fixtures, making it a site of national significance. Limited archaeological testing was conducted there in 1985 by The Charleston Museum to determine the presence and integrity of archaeological resources. This was our first opportunity to study the features and strata of a nineteenth-century residential property. Grants from the Maybank estate and the Joanna Foundation enabled Historic Charleston Foundation to prepare a historic structures analysis report. Architectural historians Willie Graham, Orlando Ridout, and Carl Lounsbury conducted the research and coordinated additional archaeological investigations in 2001–2002.

John Wragg created the neighborhood of Wraggborough in 1801 from 79 acres that he had inherited. John Robinson, a wealthy factor, purchased lots on Elizabeth Street and Judith Street in 1817, building dwellings on both. The house on Elizabeth Street included four rooms on each floor, "all well finished, cypress and cedar piazzas and fences, and large cellars and store rooms under the dwelling." Financial difficulties led Robinson to sell that property, which was purchased by William Aiken Sr. in 1827.[9]

Following his father's death in 1831, William Aiken Jr. inherited the property. He and his bride, Harriet Lowndes, began an ambitious renovation of the house. These renovations included "enlarging the house, modernizing its layout, and updating the interior finishes." Improvements extended to the service buildings and the rear yard. The two-story kitchen was doubled in size, and a second story was added to the stable. Gothic revival detailing was added to all of the outbuildings, and privies and garden buildings were constructed in the yard. The rear yard was likely a pleasure garden accessed through a well-ordered work yard. Aiken's financial, political, and social successes engendered another round of renovations and expansions in the 1850s. He redecorated with gas light fixtures, wallpapers, and carpets, and added an art gallery wing in 1857 to display items acquired during a year-long European tour.[10]

Among the improvements to the kitchen was a stew stove. This, and copper sauce pans, were the equipment of French cuisine embraced by wealthy Americans in the early nineteenth century. William Aiken's stew stove is a waist-high platform of red brick with multiple openings, or "stew holes," fitted with iron grills. They functioned much like burners on a modern stove,

Figure 10.2. Archaeologists excavating near the garden folly in the rear yard of the Aiken-Rhett House. The garden building later served as a cowshed. (Collections of The Charleston Museum, Charleston, South Carolina.)

Figure 10.3. The 1830s stew stove in the kitchen of the Aiken-Rhett House. (Collections of The Charleston Museum, photo courtesy of Historic Charleston Foundation.)

Figure 10.4. Cattle bone retrieved from the Aiken-Rhett stew stove in 2013. (Photo by Sean Money, Collections of The Charleston Museum, Charleston, South Carolina.)

allowing for greater temperature control and fuel efficiency. Aiken's was clearly the "latest rage," added during the 1830s renovations and improved with an iron top in 1858.[11]

House administrator Valerie Perry was cleaning and documenting the stew stove in 2013 when she discovered a remnant pocket of ash. In the ash were three preserved bones. Perry immediately recognized the significance of this find, and the bones were shipped to the University of Georgia. They are all cow bones, representing portions from the neck (axis), the lower foreleg (ulna), and the upper hindquarter (innominate). All three were carefully sawed in a most unusual manner.

The Nathaniel Russell House

Nathaniel and Sarah Russell moved into their new grand townhouse on Meeting Street in 1808. Their home, and their garden, immediately became the focus of much admiration and discussion. In 1819 British visitor William Faux "called on the venerable Nathaniel Russell, Esq., residing in a splendid mansion, surrounded by a wilderness of flowers, and bowers of myrtles, oranges and lemons, smothered with fruit and flowers . . . living in a nest of roses . . . I saw and ate ripe figs, pears, apples, and plums, the rich productions of this generous climate." Russell's garden was evidently tended by locally famous gardener Philip Noisette, who came to Charleston from Santo Domingo in the early 1800s. Noisette lived on Russell's eight-acre farm a few miles up Meeting Street. This farm was a source of fruits, vegetables, and livestock for the townhouse.[12]

Russell died in 1820, but his widow, their children, and grandchildren remained in the mansion until 1857. Although the Russell family partici-pated in the rounds of parties, balls, and teas that characterized Charles-ton's social season, they were known for their austere, pious lifestyle. Mrs. Russell died in 1832, and ownership of the house passed to daughter Sarah Russell Dehon. By then a widow, she lived in the house with her daughter, also named Sarah, and son-in-law, the Reverend Paul Trapier, and their 12 children. Reverend Trapier resigned from St. Michael's Episcopal Church to establish Calvary Church as a place of worship for African American slaves; he performed numerous weddings for slaves at the Russell House.

Although Sarah Russell Dehon was known among her peers for her good deeds, the inventory of her property at her death itemizes elaborate furnishings, including 355 ounces of silver; cutlery; teawares and serving pieces of "Blue India China"; plates; glassware; gold and white dessert ware; and bonds and bank shares. Test excavations adjacent to the main house, outbuildings, and garden in the 1990s and in the front yard in 2003 recov-ered examples of many of these.[13]

The Denmark Vesey Insurrection

The purported 1822 uprising masterminded by freed slave Denmark Vesey shook the city. The plot is unclear, and some scholars question whether a rebellion was in the works at all. Far more clear were the results of the hys-teria. In the immediate aftermath of the conspiracy, 35 of the 131 accused were executed, including Vesey and four of his principal associates, Gullah Jack, Monday Gell, Ned Bennett, and Peter Poyas.[14]

An additional convicted conspirator was blacksmith Tom Russell, be-longing to Sarah Russell. Tom Russell kept a blacksmith shop on East Bay Street and was reportedly Gullah Jack's "armourer." Mrs. Russell submitted testimony through attorney James Gray that "Gullah Jack was constantly with Tom at breakfast, dinner, and supper, and that she cautioned Tom not to have so much to do with Jack or he would be taken up."[15]

Long-term consequences of the rebellion included persecution of free persons of color, expansion of the police department, and additional restrictions on various "privileges" such as education, religion, and manumission of slaves. Physical changes to the city and to townhouse compounds also reflect this heightened fear.

Physical Transformation of the Lots

The concept that land is not "natural" but modified for human occupation and use underlies the archaeological study of Charleston. The urban landscape is a shared space, evolving to serve a community. The same landscape was viewed in different ways by the various groups who used it. Townhouse lots, large and small, changed as the nineteenth century progressed, reflecting social, political, and physical needs of town residents. One example of this is a formerly swampy tract between the Miles Brewton and Simmons-Edwards houses.[16]

Our investigation of filling and improvement of both sites began with recovery of refuse clearly belonging to Miles Brewton from large pits in the back yard of the adjacent Simmons-Edwards lot. Initially, the contents of three features deposited in the 1780s were attributed to undocumented previous occupants of what eventually became the Simmons-Edwards property. But a bottle marked "MBrewton" and a silver tea spoon handle engraved "M*B" gave us irrefutable evidence that some trash recovered from the Simmons-Edwards property originated on the Brewton property. The bottle clearly did not belong there. Clean-up of the Brewton property in 1780 by occupying British officers is recorded in documents. But who discarded Brewton's trash on the neighboring lot? This question led us to reexamine some puzzling features in the Brewton work yard, excavated a decade earlier, as well as soil strata from the rear of the Simmons-Edwards yard. What did the backs of these properties look like, and how did this facilitate movement of Brewton's refuse?

Physical characteristics of Zone 4 at the rear of the Simmons-Edwards property suggest that an area between the lots was swamp in the eighteenth century, an interpretation supported by period maps. This same swampy soil was excavated as Zone 5 on the Brewton property. The nature of the damp, low-lying area between the Miles Brewton and Simmons-Edwards properties is particularly well documented by the analysis of pollen from Zone 5 and Feature 11 on the Brewton property by Karl Reinhard of the University of Nebraska. Reinhard interpreted the pollen in the Brewton

Zone 5 as evidence of the precolonial environment. Zone 5 accumulated slowly, a wooded environment with limited evidence for herbaceous plants and grasses. The dense pollen profile reflects the dominance of arboreal pollen, especially from hardwood trees. Much of the pollen in Zone 5 was from oak. Zone 5 also contained pollen from hazel, a tree that disappeared from the city in the 1700s (revived only in the 1860s).[17]

Feature 11 was an outdoor hearth built on top of Zone 5 and therefore more recent than Zone 5. The quantity of pollen from hardwood trees in Feature 11 was lower than in Zone 5, and the quantity of pollen from herbaceous plants and grasses was higher. The environment by that time was more open and disturbed, with fewer trees. Both Zone 5 and Feature 11 contained similar quantities of pollen from mesic plants, those adapted to wet environments. In Zone 5, however, mesic pollen was largely from alder and willow, and mesic pollen in Feature 11 was largely from herbaceous plants.

The pollen profile from the overlying Zone 4 at Brewton, deposited in the 1770s, indicates that the environment had changed considerably. Though still damp, it was highly disturbed. There were some hardwoods, especially willows, but herbaceous and mesic plants were more abundant. The loss of hardwood trees and increase in herbaceous plants continued into the 1860s.

The pollen evidence for vegetation changed our interpretation of the Charleston landscape. We have described both the Brewton and Simmons-Edwards properties as highly ordered and well maintained. By the second quarter of the nineteenth century, this order included a brick wall between the two properties. In the eighteenth century, however, the Georgian emphasis on symmetry and order seems to have ended somewhere between the work yard gate and the edge of the garden, leaving the back part of the property swampy and unorganized. Although no longer wooded, it was uncontrolled in what Bernard Herman has termed "a progression of decreasing order and increasing dirtiness." If the boundary was marked, it was not yet barricaded. This unimproved and possibly unfenced area evidently provided the pathway for refuse disposal on an adjoining lot; perhaps the path was well used for other unrecorded activities.[18]

The filling sequence noted on the Brewton and the neighboring Simmons-Edwards property is not unique. The general pollen profile for Charleston documents an overall decline in hardwoods in the city and an increase in herbaceous, disturbance plants as the eighteenth century progressed. Studies elsewhere in the city, particularly at the Rutledge House, show a decrease in the number of hardwoods by the end of the eighteenth century, an increase in plants that colonize open, or disturbed, habitats, and eventually a decrease in mesic pollen. Although some of these changes reflect clearing lots for construction of residences and other structures, and efforts to control drainage, much of the widespread deforestation of the area was likely for lumber and firewood. The price of firewood steadily increased throughout the eighteenth century. Michael Trinkley documents heavy use of pine for firewood, as well as increasing amounts of coal during the eighteenth century.[19]

Segregation and Segmentation

The marshy, unimproved area between the Brewton and Simmons-Edwards properties was probably used for refuse disposal because it was close and unclaimed. Even more interesting than the movement of refuse to this marshy space is the agency of that movement. Those responsible for discarding the trash were likely household slaves. Both Herman and Theodore Rosengarten discuss the "seen but unseen" aspects of behavior and survival of the urban slave population, what Rosengarten calls the "parallel worlds" of black and white Charlestonians. Herman suggests that such "marginal" spaces defined a locus of "political and economic agency" for the people who lived and worked there, seemingly under the careful scrutiny of their masters. These marginal spaces included markets, streets, wharves, and waterways, as well as the work yards and back lots of domestic compounds. Some marginal spaces were created during the reorganization of work yards in the early nineteenth century.[20]

Much of this reorganization took the form of structural responses to growing fear of the Black population. Open walls and wood fences surrounding properties were rebuilt in brick, yards were subdivided with additional walls and fences, and exterior windows were sealed. Both Herman and Maurie McInnis suggest that domestic spaces became more segmented and isolated. From the 1780s onward, living quarters, kitchens, and washhouses were carefully defined spaces. The new organization restricted access to and flow within the domain of the enslaved residents, even as it also provided better finishes for the quarters.[21]

The Brewton House provides the most graphic example of this reorganization. Archaeological evidence shows gradual changes to fences and boundaries, both within the compound and along the property lines. It was during the 1988 fieldwork that Herman suggested the brick walls enclosing the front entry might be nineteenth-century additions to the eighteenth-century layout. He challenged archaeologists to dig adjacent to these walls to determine their date of construction. Excavation along the northern wall revealed an intact builder's trench, filled after 1820. A second excavation unit along the northern wall was less conclusive. Excavation along the front brick wall revealed a posthole from an earlier, less formal wooden fence. A seam in the brick courses suggests the wall was originally three feet high and was raised later to eight feet.[22]

Internal segregation of the urban compound appears to have been an equally incremental process (see figure 8.1). The row of outbuildings along Brewton's northern property line is separated from the large formal garden by a low brick wall surmounted by wooden pickets. Artifacts from the builder's trench tell us this interior wall also was built in the 1820s. Beneath the brick foundation, excavation revealed well-defined posthole stains. Creamware from within the posthole features indicates that they were dug after 1770 but before the brick foundation was constructed in 1820. This suggests that the present-day low brick wall replaced an earlier, less formal, and less restricting post fence. Other nineteenth-century townhouse properties feature comparable internal fencing and segregation of the work

Figure 10.5. *View from Mr. Fraser's City Residence*, from untitled sketchbook by Charles Fraser, 1796–1805. The image captures a relatively open urban landscape, prior to construction of brick property walls. (Image Courtesy Gibbes Museum of Art/Carolina Art Association.)

yard from the pleasure gardens. The Simmons-Edwards House has a similar network of walls subdividing the property. Post-and-rail and low picket fences are now uncommon in the city, but their existence, and the more open urbanscape associated with them, are captured in Charles Fraser's watercolors, particularly in the *View from Mr. Fraser's City Residence, 1796*. Mr. Fraser's residence was just a few houses north of the Brewton property.[23]

Other changes were made to the Brewton compound in the early nineteenth century. A new two-story quarters and stable complex was added, likely to house the additional slaves and horses William Alston brought to the property. A few years later, under William Bull Pringle's ownership, the original kitchen/carriage house received an updated Gothic facade. The second-story windows facing the adjoining property were closed. These were the windows of the slaves' quarters.

More than half the yards at all townhouse lots were devoted to formal gardens. On some properties, work yards were confined to one side of the property, as at the Brewton, Russell, and Simmons-Edwards houses. On other properties, outbuildings were arranged along both sides of the lots, creating courtyards, as at the Aiken-Rhett and Heyward-Washington houses. In the latter cases, visitors traversed work yards to enter the gardens. Paint and other finishes in the Aiken-Rhett outbuildings suggest they were decorated to show them off to guests.

African Americans constituted the majority of those living on townhouse properties, including those that are now historic house museums. One of the frustrations of townhouse sites is that the rubbish of enslaver and slave is likely mixed in most primary contexts and certainly in all of the secondary ones. This is the material manifestation of townhouse life. Further, the privileged and the underclass used many of the same mundane objects, ascribing to them different meanings that are difficult to decipher from archaeological data alone.[24]

Few artifacts are clearly associated with African American residents. The most significant, and distinctive, objects of urban slavery are slave badges. These brass tags were city licenses purchased by slave owners, permitting them to hire out their slaves to others on a long- or short-term basis. The owner was required to renew these licenses annually, and a license was to be on the person of the hired-out slave. Many antebellum cities had such laws, though Charleston is evidently the only one that issued badges made of a durable material. Laws requiring tickets or badges appeared in statutes as early as 1712. The earliest known brass badges date to 1800, and the latest date to 1864. Badges specify the year of issue and a particular skill.

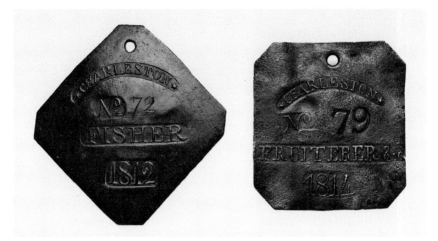

Figure 10.6. Copper slave badges, for "Fisher" and "Fruiterer." (Photo by Sean Money, Collections of The Charleston Museum, Charleston, South Carolina.)

The most common and least expensive badges were for a generic "servant." Those for "mechanic" and "porter" were the next most common. In 1783 unskilled-laborer badges were available for five shillings; those for "carpenter, bricklayer, fisherman, blacksmith . . . gold or silversmith" cost 20 shillings. Badges for "butchers" were the most costly: 40 shillings. Three years later, when fees were reconfigured in American currency, day-laborer badges commanded $2.00, while huckster or vendor badges were $6.00.[25]

Table Wares

We have limited our discussion to unique artifact types, such as slave badges, and relatively complete individual artifacts because they assist us in dating archaeological deposits and reveal the meaning of the other materials found with them. These individual artifacts tell us about past peoples and their affairs. In truth, however, the thousands of small, less identifiable fragments actually say much more about life in the city. The study of such ordinary artifact types, groups, and assemblages is a key tool used by archaeologists to interpret sites and to compare behaviors through time and space (appendix 4). It is these commonplace materials, and their quantification, that guide all of the presentations in this volume.

Most of these mundane materials were associated with food preparation, display, consumption, and storage, the physical manifestations of cuisine. Kitchen and dining-related materials dominate artifact assemblages. The nineteenth century witnessed the expansion of industrialization and mass production of such items. This resulted in an overall increase in frequency and uniformity of kitchen and table wares.

Refined earthenwares developed in the late eighteenth century and mass produced in the British factories of Staffordshire are frequently used to date and compare archaeological deposits, because they are very common. Staffordshire Potter Josiah Wedgwood continued to experiment with ways to produce a whiter ware and achieved what he termed "pearl white" in 1780, the beginning of an era in which the previously popular creamware was replaced by "pearlware." Pearlwares constitute a fifth of all Charleston ceramics in the 1780s, and the still-popular creamwares contribute a quarter.[26]

Many pearlwares are teawares: inexpensive cups, saucers, teapots, and sugar bowls. Some townhouse sites produced vessels with elaborate shapes, including delicately scalloped and fluted teacups, cruets, and leaf-shaped dishes. As the nineteenth century progressed, the delicate designs on these wares gradually became bolder.

Shell-edged pearlware is perhaps the most readily recognizable historic ceramic. The plates, soup bowls, and platters feature rims molded in a feathery design and painted in blue or green. Beginning in 1795, transfer or bat printing produced more detailed designs. This development coincided with a significant reduction in porcelains imported from Canton after 1793, which created a large market for a replacement ware. Transfer-printed wares were the most expensive pearlwares and came in a variety of forms, including plates and bowls of all sizes, teacups and coffee cups with or without handles, mugs, and saucers. The list of service pieces was equally lengthy, including platters, sauce boats, tureens, and teawares. Annular ware, or "dipped ware," was the least expensive pearlware, usually limited to bowls, mugs, jugs, or chamber pots. By the mid-century, refined earthenwares were heavy and largely undecorated, with paneled or octagonal forms. It is often very difficult to date whiteware, though careful inspection reveals clues to the age and manufacture of specific pieces.

Sets of refined earthenwares and porcelains fit the prescription for fine dining, presentation of meals, and genteel manners. Late-eighteenth-century tables groaned with carefully presented dishes, served in two courses, plus a separate dessert. The courses were served in paired dishes, arranged symmetrically on the table. Special serving vessels such as sauce boats and castor sets were featured. Desserts were served in stemmed glasses, custard cups, or cream pots. Fruits, jellies, and ices were presented on elaborate epergnes in the table's center.

The early nineteenth century marked a change in table settings and serving habits. Formal dining still required a retinue of plates, and serving vessels held an equally large and varied menu. Knives, forks, and glasses for each course were placed on the table prior to the meal. Floral arrangements and decorative fruit centerpieces replaced the serving dishes in the table center. Servants brought out the dishes, which were staged on the sideboard, rather than placed on the table. Barbara Carson recounts meals served in the nation's capital during this period. There were several courses, each with the same number of dishes. Meats and vegetables were served together, then puddings and pies. A course might include a "remove," a platter of meat taken away during the course and replaced with another. Meats often outnumbered vegetables.[27]

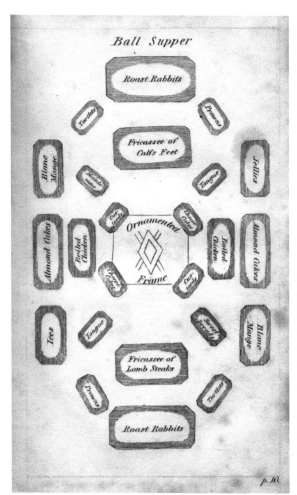

Figure 10.7. Diagram for a "Ball Supper," showing a balanced array of dishes, including "tongue" and "Fricassee of Calfs Feet." From *Family Cookery, Combining Elegance and Economy*, by R. House, 1800. (Courtesy of Winterthur Library, Printed Book and Periodical Collection.)

A Rich and Varied Diet

The wide range of animals recovered from Charleston townhouses likely reflects such fine dining fashions and the necessity for a large and varied presentation. The menu for a dinner party of 20 was described by a visitor to Charleston in 1832:

> I dined with a large party this day in a very handsome house of some antiquity. . . . Twenty persons sat down to dinner at about half-past four o'clock. We had a most abundant feast, of which I mention the particulars merely to show the style of such a dinner here. It was attended by an upper servant and three servants in livery, all of course slaves. The table was covered with turtle soup, fish, venison, boiled mutton, roast turkey, boiled turkey, a ham, two boiled salted tongues, two tame ducks, two wild ducks, some dressed dishes, boiled rice, hominie, potatoes, cauliflower, salad, &c. The whole dinner was at once placed on the table before we sat down. When it was removed, a complete course of pastry and puddings succeeded, and then a most excellent dessert of oranges, shaddocks, bananas, and a variety of West India fruits, with iced cream in profusion. The liquids consisted of champagne, Madeira, sherry, port, claret, porter, lemonade, Etc.[28]

Although a single sumptuous meal such as the one described by this clearly impressed visitor does not equate to a regular diet, our studies indicate that city residents, particularly wealthy ones, did enjoy a rich and varied diet. This richness was not confined to the early days of the colony; it persisted into the nineteenth century. Surviving nineteenth-century menus like the one above, and cookbooks, highlight the range of wild foods served and describe preparations for many dishes using unusual animals. Recipes for turtles, pigeons, and calf's head in Harriott Pinckney Horry's 1770 recipe book may appear exotic to some but were common on elegant tables at the time. These dishes continued to be enjoyed into the twentieth century. The South Carolina Institute in 1870 awarded prizes for "cured Pigs' tongues, cured Pigs' feet, sausages, pickled Beef tongues, smoked Beef tongues, best fresh, salted or dried tongues." Prizes were also given for venison hams, as well as pork hams. The authors of *Two Hundred Years of Charleston Cooking* note the lack of recipes for wild game but argue that consumption of game was common nonetheless, as the archaeological record attests.[29]

Perhaps no wild animal better illustrates the richness and creativity of the nineteenth-century lowcountry diet than the rice bird, or bobolink.

These small songbirds were the scourge of rice planters, arriving just as the crop ripened, descending on the fields in voracious droves. Planter and slave, men and boys, shot the birds with abandon, and many of them became dinner. The most likely method for preparing these small morsels was in a pie or pilau with rice. Recipes abound for squab (pigeons) prepared in this manner, and most state that a variety of small game birds could be prepared in the same way.

A startling recipe for bobolink offered by Eliza Perroneau Mathewes in the mid-nineteenth century was reprinted by Karen Hess in her *Carolina Rice Kitchen*. It is worth quoting in its entirety:

Rice Birds

Select the fattest birds, remove the entrails, bake them whole or split them up the back and broil. Permit no sacrilegious hand to remove the head, for the base of the brain of the rice bird is the most succulent portion. Or the birds may be placed in either shape in a round bottom pot with a small lump of butter, pepper and salt, and cook over a quick fire. Use no fork in eating. Take the neck of the bird in the left hand and his little right leg in the right hand. Tear away the right leg and eat all but the extreme end of the bone. Hold the bill of the bird in one hand and crush your teeth through the back of the head, and thank Providence that you are permitted to live. Take the remaining left leg in your right hand and place in your mouth the entire body of the bird, and then munch the sweetest morsel that ever brought gustatory delight. All that remains is the front portion of the head and the tiny bits of bone that formed the ends of the legs. To leave more is to betray your unappreciativeness of the gifts of the gods.[30]

This style of dining would leave little or no archaeological evidence. By comparison, the twenty-first-century menu is sadly depauperate.

One of the chief characteristics of the Charleston menu is its richness; by this we mean the number of different taxa, rather than individuals, found in the city's archaeological record (appendix 6). The remains of 155 different taxa are found in the Charleston archaeological record. Of these taxa, 28 are interpreted as commensal animals, animals that were not part of the menu. The remaining 127 taxa are considered part of the lowcountry menu because either they are eaten today or we have written evidence that they were consumed in the lowcountry in the past. Charleston assemblages contain the remains of 62 fish taxa. Only three taxa, however, are present in every Charleston collection, regardless of time period, site function, or who lived there. These are pigs, cows, and chickens. A second tier of common taxa includes deer, sheep or goats, Canada geese, turkeys, and diamond-back terrapins.

People living at townhouse sites consumed a far greater variety of meats than anyone else in the city, regardless of time period. The number of taxa in Charleston's archaeological record increases over time, until a late-nineteenth-century decline. The number of taxa recovered from markets and non-townhouse sites is generally lower than the number of taxa found at townhouses. The richness of the market and non-townhouse assemblages declines over time, while that of townhouse assemblages increases until the end of the nineteenth century. Richness at all types of sites declined in the postbellum 1850–1900 period, though townhouse collections continue to contain more taxa than do those from other types of sites. Only in the nineteenth century do we have information about middle-class households. Those households had a richer array of meat sources than did people interpreted as the urban poor living at public sites, though the choices were fewer than at townhouse sites.

The decline in the number of taxa in townhouse assemblages at the end of the nineteenth century likely has several explanations. The first might be financial constraints placed on these households by the national depression in the early nineteenth century, and later by the aftermath of the Civil War. In addition to reduced incomes, repeated fires, and the 1886 earthquake, the loss of the enslaved staff undoubtedly meant these households set less elaborate tables and used rare meats less often. This reduced access to exotic foods was joined by the increase in commercial sources of food, including meats. By the postbellum period, it is possible that most foods were purchased from shops and that very little was acquired by the household itself, resulting in a citywide homogenization of the types of animals used. Finally, the archaeological record may reflect more diligent efforts to remove trash from in-town properties.

Another way to look at these differences in animal use is to consider to what extent different social groups used rare animals. A collection that contains many different types of animals likely includes some animals that are rare, unusual, or seldom used. Such prestige foods are typically luxuries that are costly to acquire and may require additional effort. Prestige foods generally may be limited to households with more resources. The less costly menu is usually based on low-risk resources with moderate yields: foods that are local, are affordable in terms of time, effort, and money, and are normally reliable. Obtaining rare foods fosters dietary diversity, one generally afforded by elite members of the community. Diversity in this sense considers not only the number of different animals used at a site (the collection's richness) but also which animals are abundant, common, occasional, or rare. An affluent household might have a collection of animals that was more diverse than a less affluent household's; the affluent household would have many more taxa, and the rare animals would be used frequently. A less affluent household might not only use fewer animals but would focus on just one or two of these.[31]

Measured this way, townhouse assemblages are generally more diverse than other types of sites in every time period; they contain more different types of animals, some of which are rarely used elsewhere. There is one exception to this generalization, though. Collections from public sites occupied during the 1710–1750 period, such as the Dock Street Theatre and Powder Magazine, are richer and more diverse than those from contemporaneous sites such as the Heyward-Washington and Rutledge houses. This is one reason we argue that at least some "public" sites should be interpreted as residences.

The richness and diversity of assemblages in the late nineteenth century clearly reflect economic disparity. Despite the limited means of some townhouse property owners, assemblages from these sites are far more diverse than are those from middle- and low-income residential sites and public/residential sites such as the Powder Magazine. At the end of the nineteenth century, both the public and middle- to lower-income residential assemblages have the same low diversity, though the middle/lower-income assemblage contains more taxa than does that from public sites. Although the middle-income households used many more different types of animals than did the lower-income households, in terms of individuals a single animal (the chicken) dominated both non-elite groups. In terms of meat, it was beef.

The above discussion focuses on the number of different animals in these assemblages. Another aspect of diet, however, is the amount of meat each of these animals might contribute to that diet. During all time periods, diversity of meat sources is very low, due to the dominance of beef. This is one of the interesting features of human diets even today. Although most of our meals consist of only a few items that dominate each meal, we value a rich, diverse diet, drawing upon many other sources of food to accompany the old standby. Charlestonians apparently ate a great deal of beef but also killed a chicken from time to time, ate fish, and enjoyed turtle soup. They varied their diet with sufficient frequency for that variety to be reflected in an archaeological record dominated by beef. Throughout the archaeological sequence, however, people living at townhouse sites enjoyed a wider variety of foods as supplements to their beef than did people at other locations.

The Work Yard in the Nineteenth Century

Reorganization of space on townhouse properties, construction of specialized service buildings, separation of work yards and pleasure gardens, and definition of specific areas for refuse were conscious attempts by influential urban residents to create a landscape reflecting their social values and physical needs. These values and needs changed during the nineteenth century. These changes are most visible in efforts to improve sanitation and control disease in the increasingly crowded city.[32]

Refuse disposal on private properties reached a critical point in the early 1800s. Many daily activities, including food preparation, livestock maintenance, cleaning, and laundering took place in outbuildings, work yards, and public areas. Animals were raised and butchered within the city, their waste discarded nearby. Charleston grew over the centuries upon a vast accumulation of ceramics, glass, building debris, and animal refuse. Privies throughout the city were used as general waste disposal locations, as well as natural traps into which unwary animals might fall. As just one example, the early-nineteenth-century Brewton privy contained the remains of four rats, a cardinal, a dog, and two frogs or toads. The accumulating garbage at sites such as Atlantic Wharf and Lodge Alley was a threat both to public health and to refined sensibilities. It was necessary to do something.

Some early-nineteenth-century townhouse owners responded to the accumulating refuse by paving it over. Paved work yards were found at the Brewton and Rutledge houses. Before the Brewton work yard was paved, soil and trash accumulated around outbuildings. The first effort to control this debris was to cover it with irregular lenses of tabby mortar. The mortar and soil were later paved with brick and bluestone. Ceramics embedded in the paving layers indicate that the mortar was laid down after 1800; the brick and stone pavers were added between 1830 and 1840. Only a half foot of soil and artifacts accumulated during the next 150 years. Artifact density is low for the post-paving period, as most, though not all, refuse was discarded elsewhere.

The central courtyards at the Aiken-Rhett and Heyward-Washington houses exhibit multiple layers of paving. Elaine Herold uncovered three

Figure 10.8. Brick drain in the work yard of the Miles Brewton House. (Collections of The Charleston Museum, Charleston, South Carolina.)

superimposed brick surfaces near the Heyward-Washington kitchen. A mortar bed for an earlier paving and six inches of fill sand lie beneath the current (1850s) brick courtyard of the Aiken-Rhett House. Interestingly, both yards have poor drainage today, so filling and repaving may have been early efforts to solve this problem. The two yards also were equipped with brick drains in the nineteenth century.

No evidence of paving was found at the Russell House, and only a small area was paved at the Simmons-Edwards House. The test units at the Russell site were dispersed, so that any paved area may simply have been missed, if there was one. Artifact density, however, was low at these two early-nineteenth-century properties, compared to that at Brewton. It may be that people at Brewton needed to find a way to control trash more urgently than did those at Russell and Simmons-Edwards. People at Russell and Simmons-Edwards may have had much of their refuse hauled away, making it unnecessary to pave their work yards to control accumulating debris.

Paving occasionally took novel forms. In 2009 Eric Poplin of Brockington and Associates tested an area of swimming pool construction at the Sanders House. This test exposed a small section of structural floor, paved with cow toes (phalanges). Yes, really! Recognizing both the novelty and significance of this paving, after photography and mapping Poplin collected a second sample for The Charleston Museum, analyzed at the Georgia Museum of Natural History.

This sample from a single 1×1-meter test unit yielded one fragment of a cow humerus, 7 carpals and tarsals, 44 long bones from the forefoot and hindfoot (metapodials), and 596 toe bones (phalanges), estimated to be from 36 individual cows. Twenty-seven individuals were subadults or older at death, two were subadults or younger, and seven were juveniles. Only eight of the cow specimens were cut, and none showed evidence of wear or other modification.

The property owners agreed to additional work to expose a larger area. This work exposed the edges of the bone deposits and their relation to the larger structure. Most of the floor was paved in brick, but the brick paving was interrupted by two 0.7-meter-wide linear areas consisting primarily of phalanges. The bones had no particular orientation, and there was no other refuse that might suggest waste from on-site butchery or carcass processing. The bone accumulation appears to be deliberate, using bone brought from elsewhere specifically for this purpose. The deposit may have been inside a single-story building. The recovery of flat glass fragments suggests there were windows. A nearby brick well may be associated with the structure. Poplin proposed that the building could be either a garden folly or a dairy.[33]

Deposits such as this are not unknown in Britain. Bones, horn cores, and teeth were used in floors, to line pits, in field drains, as foundations for roads, and to fill other architectural, agricultural, and industrial needs. They might also be used to decorate buildings, walls, and pavements. Philip Armitage and others describe the use of bones as paving for floors on late-seventeenth- and early-eighteenth-century British sites. Often referred to as "knuckle bone floors," many of these creations were ornamental, the designs formed by horse, deer, cow, or sheep metapodials, the distal ends of which have a distinctive rounded appearance. When laid with the distal

Figure 10.9. Analysis of cattle bones from the bone paving on the Sanders lot, Zooarchaeology Laboratory, Georgia Museum of Natural History, 2009. (Used by courtesy of the Georgia Museum of Natural History.)

end protruding above the ground surface, they form an attractive pattern and a durable walking surface. Generally, they were laid in gravel, clay, or mortar. These were particularly popular as decorative elements in the floors of follies on country estates. Teeth and other bones were occasionally used as decorative devices as well, as were phalanges. Unfortunately, the distinctive nature of these "floors" generally is unrecognized until it is too late to do a thorough in situ study or to preserve them.[34]

The Sanders House example consists almost entirely of phalanges that were not laid in mortar and did not appear to have been originally laid on end or in a design. Nor were they worn, as would be expected if they were a pavement. The phalanges might have formed a foundation for an overlying covering or to facilitate drainage in a low-lying area. If the structure was a garden folly or a dairy, the strips of bone would facilitate drainage while making good use of the city's accumulating butchery waste. The nineteenth-century Sanders House feature represents an unusual, but practical, use of Charleston's excess animal remains, solving two problems at once.

Widespread improvements were made to water management by drains, wells, and cisterns. Drainage systems are significant vehicles for more sanitary yards. In this way, as with the city's overall architecture, Charleston followed British designs. Dan Cruikshank and Neil Burton's study of

Georgian-period British cities found that many of the better houses had some type of drain by the early nineteenth century.[35]

Household drain systems were uncovered at most of Charleston's townhouses. Drains on low-lying lots clearly channeled stormwater runoff, but those built on higher lots suggest other functions. A well-built 1780s drain in the Brewton yard was expanded in the 1800s (based on pearlware in the builder's trench). The addition was poorly constructed; artifacts from the mid-nineteenth century in collapsed portions of the drain suggest that periodic repairs were required. Nathaniel Russell included a large, vaulted brick drain in the driveway of the house he built in 1808. He later added a small drain in the garden. A modest drain system at Simmons-Edwards appears to be contemporaneous with the house and outbuildings. The accumulation of small artifacts, particularly lost items, and animal remains suggests drains were used for the disposal of debris that could be washed away with wastewater. The Brewton drain, for example, contains 2,587 animal bones and teeth; 2,207 of these are fish bones and scales. It is little wonder that drains clogged from time to time. Larger municipal drain systems were constructed in Charleston and other cities around the middle of the nineteenth century.

Wells were the principal source of water, including drinking water, in seventeenth- and eighteenth-century Charleston. Wells were relatively easy to dig in Charleston's sandy soils and did not have to be deep. Due to the city's low elevation, potable water is found 10 to 12 feet below surface. Early wells were lined with wood planks or barrels, but later well shafts were brick. Because of their open tops, these shallow wells were frequently contaminated; rats and kittens fell in, and foul substances seeped in from the sides. A badly decayed human tooth was recovered from the 1750s–1820s well at the Simmons-Edwards House, along with over 7,000 bones and teeth of other animals. Contaminated wells often were abandoned and new ones built nearby. Other contaminated wells, particularly public ones, remained open as a source of water for fighting Charleston's frequent fires. Many properties, such as the Heyward-Washington House, had several active wells at the same time, often close to the kitchen.

The aboveground cistern in the front set of horse stalls at the Brewton House is the most visible example of an alternative source of potable water. Cisterns collect rainwater from roofs via gutter systems. They were first constructed in Charleston in the early nineteenth century and were a standard feature by the 1850s. Cisterns were rectangular or circular vaults, often with stucco interiors. They were designed to be free of contamination.

When encountered archaeologically, cisterns are empty or filled with clean sand. Unlike wells, they usually contain no cultural materials. All of the townhouses have at least one cistern; the Aiken-Rhett House has several.[36]

Urban Density

Disasters, civic improvements, and concerns about public health and safety changed Charleston during the antebellum period. Fires, crowding, and a sense of insecurity among the white population prompted remodeling of urban properties. Fences became sturdier, built more for security than for display or livestock control.

Residents drew upon overseas sources for the newest fashions in dinner and teaware but continued to feature the local coastal bounty at fashionable meals. Novel food preparation styles were adopted. The cuisine established in the 1600s persisted into the 1800s, but the menu changed. Charleston residents used smaller animals and purchased more meat than they had previously. They continued to include wild foods in their diets, a hallmark of the lowcountry cuisine.

As the nineteenth century advanced, Charlestonians became increasingly concerned with public health and sanitation, concerns that are clearly seen in the archaeological record. Trash disposal continued to be a problem in some areas, but other households took measures to control the accumulation on their own properties, improve drainage, and secure safe drinking water. They began to focus their concerns on poor sanitation and other problems associated with the increasingly populous urban environment.

11

LANDSCAPE CHANGES

In 1851 the South Carolina Society for the Improvement of Domestic Poultry held its first annual exhibition in Hatch's Hall on Hasell Street. A report of the executive committee, issued the next year, pronounced it a rousing success. "Although we were prepared to witness a fine spectacle in collecting together the favored specimens from the Poultry yards of our citizen fanciers, yet this Exhibition far surpassed the expectations of the most sanguine." The exhibition featured ducks, geese, white and wild turkeys, pheasants, and dozens of varieties of "domestic Fowls," or chickens.

A favorite of the show was the "Cochin Chinas," the "very best Birds in the Exhibition, and they excited the admiration of all who beheld them." Moreover, the contributions, with the exception of three grown Birds, "were raised in the City." It is likely that "the City" produced far more back-yard fowl than the prize-winning Cochins of "Messrs. Hugh Wilson, Sr., A. C. Phin, J. Michel, A. Elfe, and E. S. Horry."[1]

The mood was darker a decade later. The 1861 fire dealt a harsh blow to the Charleston landscape. The Civil War and its aftermath had an even greater impact on the plantation economy that supported the city. Many residents struggled to rebuild and put their properties in working order, though the plantations produced little or no income. The townhouses of formerly wealthy Charlestonians were converted to businesses and boardinghouses. The late-nineteenth-century city became even more crowded. Archaeological sites reveal the resulting lack of maintenance. They also reflect a growing centralization of services and supply as citizens increasingly shopped at commercial markets for their foods. At the same time, they continued to draw upon the wild bounty long relished in the lowcountry.[2]

Archaeological sites of this period clearly show an increase in municipal services and efforts to improve public health. Sites at the end of the nineteenth century contain fewer artifacts as off-site refuse disposal became more common. Despite growing awareness of connections between sanitation and health, however, many animals continued to live in the city.

A New Order

Photos of Charleston after the Civil War show the lower city in ruins. Although Union shells did damage the city, most of the destruction shown in those photos was caused by the fire. On December 11, 1861, winter winds fed an accidental fire near a sash-and-blind factory at East Bay and Hasell Streets. The fire spread to the factory and to Cameron's Foundry next door. Rising winds carried the flames southwest until they reached the Ashley River. Nothing was left in their path.

This "Great Fire" burned over 540 acres and was the most damaging of all of Charleston's fires. It left a long diagonal scar across the peninsula. For years, the burnt district lay in ruins, its "charred timbers, . . . crumbling walls, broken pillars, and fallen spires symbolic of a ravaged civilization." The area recovered so slowly that "30 years later small dairy herds still were pastured among the chimney stumps and cellar-holes." By 1870 the "ruins" were a tourist attraction. *A Visitor's Guide to Charleston*, published that year by the South Carolina Institute, suggested "a cold, raw, damp, misty, cloudy, gusty day is the time of all times to see them in perfection," and a visitor should "by all means select it for a tour among the ruins."[3]

The profitable venture of phosphate mining and the election of progressive Mayor William Ashmead Courtenay in the 1880s initiated a period of civic improvements. Mayor Courtenay and other civic leaders cleaned up and organized everything from dusty streets to the urban poor. The City of Charleston installed streetcars, a gas works, and an electric lighting plant. A salaried fire department replaced volunteer companies. Streets were paved, stray dogs were rounded up, and the turkey vultures that kept the market clean were shot. The City appointed a board of health to tackle the most vexing problems: the lack of running water and the large number of privy vaults. It was decades, though, before a municipal sewer system was installed. The late-nineteenth-century city continued to be crowded, and many large compounds, some of which were now rental properties, featured rambling arrangements of outbuildings.

Figure 11.1. *Bird's Eye View of the City of Charleston, South Carolina*, printed in 1872 by C. Drie. The path of the "Great Fire" is evident as a line of relatively open lots. (Library of Congress.)

Natural events thwarted progressive efforts. On August 31, 1886, the disaster-weary city was struck with a new calamity: the largest earthquake to hit the East Coast in centuries. There were warning tremors during the summer and for many years prior, but no one expected a quake of this magnitude. The quake centered on a fault line north of Charleston, and was felt as far away as Chicago, Illinois, and Detroit, Michigan. Rebuilding took years. The aftermath of the earthquake is still visible in the form of decorative metal discs affixed to buildings. These discs anchor tie-rods that run through structures, literally holding them together.[4]

All over the city, white Charlestonians moved back to their homes, patched them up, and adapted to postwar life. Some took in boarders. Others turned their homes into businesses; the widow of Governor R.F.W. Allston operated a girls' school at the Russell House. Refurbishing, re-building, and new appointments were postponed, and many townhouses suffered from neglect. Ironically, buildings avoided demolition in the late nineteenth century because of Charleston's poor economy; many were saved in the twentieth century as the threat of demolition and decay gave rise to the historic preservation movement.

Late Nineteenth-Century Sites

Viewing late nineteenth-century Charleston through the lens of archaeology requires us to revisit the townhouses. Some properties were transferred to new owners, and others remained in family hands. In either case, many were used in new ways. The Aiken-Rhett, Brewton, Russell, and Simmons-Edwards houses all exhibit post–Civil War changes. Archaeological deposits reflect ongoing site maintenance, or lack of it.

The saga of Brewton House summarized by Richard Côté illustrates the all-too-common condition of planter families in the postbellum period. In 1865 the Pringles lived upstate as refugees; the Union Army occupying the city used their townhouse as its headquarters. The Pringles regained possession of their Santee River plantation and their townhouse in October of that year but were heavily in debt. William Bull Pringle entered into labor contracts with his former slaves. He and son-in-law Frank Frost stayed in the nearly empty plantation house and struggled to plant a crop, but their efforts were unsuccessful. They borrowed funds each year to prepare for the next year's crop. By 1871 the Pringle family was forced to sell their plantation.[5]

The family retained the King Street house but lived there in reduced circumstances, purchasing little more than necessities. Instead of having 34 enslaved workers, Mary Pringle hired three house servants. She was shocked in 1871 when her "beloved personal servant," Cretia, demanded improved work conditions and moved out of the servant yard to live with her son. Every space capable of generating income was used. The ground floor was rented out, as was the coach house, now refitted as a store. Homeless relatives moved into the first floor of the house, and the Pringle family lived on the second floor. Mary and her daughters made and sold marmalade and floral arrangements. Mary considered a business selling terrapins. Only son Julius, who had married a Louisiana cotton planter's daughter, carried his prewar fortune into the late nineteenth century. His periodic gifts of money kept the family's creditors at bay.

Valued at half a million dollars in the 1850s, the Pringle estate was worth 89 dollars when probated in 1895. Unwed daughter Susan Pringle lived in the house until 1917. Her sister Rebecca and Rebecca's husband, Frank Frost, joined Susan after Frost abandoned rice planting in 1876. Three unmarried daughters of Frank and Rebecca Pringle Frost offered to buy the house from the other heirs in 1918, with loans from the DuPont family. The

Figure 11.2. The 1840s Jackson House, in 2001. (Collections of The Charleston Museum, Charleston, South Carolina.)

Frost sisters continued to rent out rooms; income from rents, tours, and gardening maintained the home. Susan Pringle Frost became Charleston's first female real estate agent, a pioneer in women's suffrage, and, in 1920, founder of the Society for the Preservation of Old Dwellings, now the Preservation Society of Charleston.[6]

Excavations at several smaller properties provide contrasts to the town-houses of Charleston's elite. A simple wood structure on Nassau Street housed the Jacksons, free persons of color, in the nineteenth century. This single house was constructed in 1840, with rooms added in the 1850s. The cramped lot included a smaller two-story residential unit, constructed after 1872. The property was restored by Historic Charleston Foundation in 1990. Excavations recovered late-nineteenth-century refuse from an open well beneath the 1850s addition, and a privy pit filled during the postbellum period. This is one of the few sites excavated in the city clearly associated with African Americans.

Limited testing was conducted in 1988 at the property renovated for the city's Visitor Reception and Transportation Center (VRTC). The excavation produced household refuse from the mid-to-late nineteenth century, though the block was occupied earlier. The two blocks bounded by Meeting, John, King, and Mary Streets in Wraggborough were subdivided in

1801 from lands owned by the Wragg family. Prior to the Civil War, King Street ran through a mixture of commercial and residential properties. These blocks display the integrated residential pattern typical of the city at that time. Wealthy merchant and planter William Aiken Sr., father of William Aiken Jr., built his imposing home here in 1811, but next door were two modest houses owned by free persons of color. Middle-class artisans, such as bricklayer John Brady, and professional men, such as W. J. Laval, J. H. Honour, and Edwin Prince, bought lots in the same block. Businesses included a shoe factory, dry goods stores, tailor shops, pharmacies, and groceries. Tradespeople lived here, including tailors, cabinetmakers, shoe-makers, and bakers. The prevalence of rental properties along King and Meeting Streets indicates a substantial number of low- to middle-class oc-cupants. The South Carolina Railroad terminal, freight depot, and cotton yard made the two blocks along King Street a hub of activity; goods and people were constantly in transit.

By the twentieth century, the railroad terminal was empty and the Meet-ing Street block converted to establishments such as a meat factory and an auto dealership. Only a few houses remained among the commercial buildings. Much of the archaeological record of the Visitor Center site was highly disturbed, but intact residential deposits were recovered from a sin-gle lot on the block, occupied by the Tupper family. This middle-class resi-dential property featured a single house and two service structures. Refuse retrieved from trash pits indicates that on-site trash disposal continued into the late 1800s.

The area available for excavation along President Street on Charleston's west side was similar to the Visitor Center: occupied during the nineteenth century and highly disturbed in the twentieth century. The President Street block was a low, marshy tract owned by Daniel Cannon in the late colo-nial period. Cannon was a prosperous house carpenter and mechanic who operated lumber mills on the Ashley River. By 1853 the property had been subdivided into nine lots. The earliest building on the property was a small residence built on a point of high land overlooking Cannon's extensive mill ponds. The ponds were gradually filled, creating more real estate. Mod-est residences filled the block during the nineteenth and early twentieth centuries.

When the Medical University of South Carolina planned construction of the Institute of Psychiatry on the property, Bob Raynor developed an innovative project that combined recreation therapy for inpatients with ar-chaeological study by The Charleston Museum. Excavation of two units in the block located an area of high, undisturbed land and a portion of former marsh that was filled with soil and debris in the late nineteenth century. Refuse recovered from these units cannot be ascribed to a particular household but likely was from neighborhood activities.

The largest archaeological collection from the late nineteenth century is from Charleston Place, one of the first sites excavated in the city. The Charleston Place block is located in the city's nineteenth- and twentieth-century commercial district. Although many retail and craft enterprises contributed to the archaeological deposits, the bulk of the materials were from residential activities. Most of the deposits from the postbellum period are large pits, wells, and privy vaults that were filled with refuse when these features were abandoned.

Postbellum Artifacts

Mass production made many goods more available and more affordable than they had been previously. Clothing and personal items increased in quantity and variety in the late nineteenth century, and many of these became part of the archaeological record. Toys are a hallmark of this era. Porcelain doll parts and miniature tea sets are regularly recovered from yard deposits. White clay marbles, sometimes painted with stripes, swirls, and floral designs, and glass marbles decorated with latticino filigree, a treatment developed in 1880, were lost in corners of the yards. Slate pencils were lost or discarded; they were particularly common at the Russell House, reflecting its use as a girls' school.

Architectural debris also characterizes postbellum deposits, reflecting the continual construction, maintenance, and demolition common to sites occupied over decades or even centuries. Over time, the archaeological record contains more nails, hardware, rubble, plaster, and broken window glass. Wire nails, invented in 1850, are characteristic of construction and carpentry after 1880.

Postbellum deposits are filled with everyday whitewares, bottles, bottle glass, and tin cans. Machine-made brown, clear, and light green bottles held a wide range of liquids. Archaeological assemblages still include dark green wine and ale bottles, but small aqua bottles for patent medicines are more common. Soda water bottles are telling artifacts of urban life; these heavy bottles in blue, green, and clear glass, developed in the 1880s, are the precursors to today's bottled water.

Figure 11.3. Late-nineteenth-century soda water bottles and bone toothbrushes from Charleston Place. (Photo by Sean Money, Collections of The Charleston Museum, Charleston, South Carolina.)

The privy assemblage from the Jackson House provides the only artifacts from an African American household for this period. Assuming the privy fill reflects an average range of materials used by people living there, it appears that the residents paid particular attention to dress and appearance. Dressy artifacts include a gold collar stud, a hat pin, and black glass buttons. Everyday garments are represented by 4-hole bone and white porcelain (prosser) buttons. Hair combs and toothbrushes reflect personal hygiene and attention to appearance. The Jackson household's kitchen and table wares are types associated with everyday informal table settings. There are tumblers, but no goblets. Glass containers for beverages and condiments suggest many foods were purchased.

Municipal Services

Charleston in the eighteenth century was congested, its organization chaotic, and its sanitation inadequate. It was not so different from other colonial towns. By 1860, however, most American cities had improved their appearance and expanded municipal services. The ideal modern city was efficient, attractive, orderly, clean, and healthy. It provided basic services such as firefighting, police protection, potable water, lighting, trash removal, and sewage management. No longer were individual property owners expected to control these challenges. Cities centralized to provide these services, and Charleston's municipal government expanded accordingly.

Fires and attempts to prevent them punctuate Charleston's history. Crowded streets lined with wooden buildings made some parts of the city particularly vulnerable. Despite legislation to end wood construction, enacted after each disaster, enforcement invariably lapsed. Fires struck year after year.

Streets in colonial and antebellum Charleston were bare earth. Dusty in dry weather and muddy in wet, they were a nuisance and health hazard. Some streets were paved with wooden planks or crushed shell. Residents urged the City to build sidewalks, and some wooden walkways were in place by the 1850s. Several important thoroughfares were paved with granite Belgian block from upstate quarries in the mid-nineteenth century. Streetlights illuminated some Charleston streets by the 1830s, first lit by oil, and later by gas.[7] Electric lights were installed above Calhoun Street in 1884; the streets below Calhoun continued to be lit by gas because residents there preferred the older style.[8]

Stagnant water and sanitation were ongoing concerns. Epidemics of typhoid, typhus, cholera, and the dread yellow fever periodically scourged Charleston. Transmission of these diseases was attributed to "bad air" and "stagnant water" rather than to vectors such as fleas, ticks, and mosquitoes. Disturbing the dirt streets during warm weather was declared a health hazard. Charlestonians first tried to rid the city of standing water by filling low areas, such as the First Trident creek, Price's Alley along the Russell garden, and the boundary between the Brewton and Simmons-Edwards houses. City maps indicate that filling was an early and continual activity, a boon for archaeologists in later centuries. Apparently, any kind of refuse could be used to fill these areas: ballast, building rubble, industrial by-products, sawdust, and domestic garbage. By the mid-nineteenth century, however, the City restricted the types of materials that could be used as fill.

The second approach to stagnant water was construction of tidal drains. The drainage system built in 1806 was augmented and expanded over the years. These "old drains," presumably made of wood, were intended to lower "subsoil water" and to carry off "rainfall and those liquids commonly called sewage." Such drains rely on a regular flow of rainwater to keep them clean, but the rains "did not come with the regularity demanded." The ensuing backup aggravated the unhealthy situation by producing a "series of detached ponds." In 1822 Dr. Samuel Prioleau attributed "The Stranger's Fever" to these conditions. A number of low-lying lots were outfitted with "yard drains" such as those at the Aiken-Rhett, Brewton, Russell, and Simmons-Edwards houses.[9]

Shallow, open wells provided water to the city for most of its history. The growing concentration of buildings and people meant that wells and privies were increasingly close to one another, contaminating the water supply. By the mid-nineteenth century, citizens regularly constructed cisterns to collect and store rainwater. The few public wells were primarily sources of water to fight fires. Attempts to tap deep freshwater aquifers began early in the 1800s, but these artesian wells did not supply water until the late nineteenth century. A municipal water system was developed in the 1880s.[10]

The most persistent health problem plaguing Charleston into the twentieth century was the "privy question," referring to the disposal of human waste. Privies and their below-ground vaults had been standard urban features since the colonial period. Surface runoff was an obvious evil, but the absorption of impure liquid into the soil was a greater health hazard. Running-water sewerage systems were developed in American cities in the 1880s, but Charleston's slow implementation of a municipal sewerage system prompted annual complaints from the board of health. Year after year, the board harangued the City, commenting, "These horrible vaults are nasty and obnoxious in the extreme." The lower city below Calhoun Street was serviced by 1905, and a few hundred additional properties were connected each year thereafter.[11]

Charleston also had problems with garbage disposal. The creeks and marshes that laced the city had long been dumping grounds for refuse, offal, and night soil. Ordinances designed to curtail discarding garbage in streets were first enacted in the 1760s. Frequent amendments to these ordinances indicate townspeople were largely unsuccessful in controlling this practice. Human scavengers hauled garbage to designated locations; an ordinance of 1806 directed that slaves be hired for this task. The abattoir on the banks of Gadsden's Creek, on the west side of the peninsula, was known as "Butcher Town." Free-ranging chickens, hogs, dogs, cats, rats, buzzards, gulls, and other scavengers likely were attracted to this refuse, providing an important community service.

A less well-known health hazard was associated with the livestock kept within the city. Horses, hogs, cows, goats, and poultry were common urban dwellers. Charleston's cow population escalated after the Civil War. Cows were smelly and attracted flies, a city official noted in 1905. Like his predecessors 30 years earlier, the health officer regretted having to point out this health hazard, "for some of my best friends are keepers of cows." In 1912 the board of health mandated that dairies be moved beyond the city limits.[12]

Urban livestock compounded problems caused by poor trash and water management. Animal manure, urine, and bedding likely accumulated along with other garbage and held significant potential for spreading diseases. People share parasites with their pets and livestock, and other parasites are shared among domestic animals. Many are spread through fecal contamination and contaminated water.[13]

Archaeological Evidence

New municipal services were good for public health, but as a result late-nineteenth-century sites usually contain few of the materials archaeologists study. Garbage collection meant that trash was no longer discarded in the yard. Nineteenth-century features often contain few of the artifacts archaeologists use for dating deposits and reconstructing the sequence of activities at each site. The numerous privy vaults that were abandoned and filled when homes were connected to waterborne sewerage are an exception to this rule.[14]

Urban lots exhibit aspects of late-nineteenth-century city life. New buildings, often less substantial than the earlier structures, were added to lots. Both main houses and outbuildings gained additional residents, as homeowners took in boarders or rented outbuildings to strangers. The Heyward-Washington property, converted to a bakery by the Fuseler family, was filled with sheds and other buildings, covering the former garden. New structures were built in the rear of the Russell House lot.

Other properties were poorly maintained, and this is often reflected in the archaeological record. The brick-paved cellar under the Brewton kitchen filled with debris. An 1863 coin recovered from the top of the brick floor, beneath 18 inches of soil, suggests this debris accumulated after the Civil War. Such evidence of poor housekeeping may reflect the staff reduction from nearly three dozen slaves to three free servants. The kitchen cellar at the Heyward-Washington House also filled with animal remains and other debris after the primary entry was sealed and covered with a pantry/cistern in the second quarter of the nineteenth century. The privy and wood storage sheds behind the Russell House were abandoned. The original privy was replaced with a new, poorly constructed structure in the rear corner of the lot. Small brick piers indicate that other outbuildings were added in the late nineteenth century, though these are now gone.

Although the garden structures behind the Aiken-Rhett House were eventually abandoned, the archaeological record suggests there was a significant amount of activity in the rear yard during the late nineteenth century. The eastern garden building fell during the 1886 earthquake, and the western one was used as a cowshed in the twentieth century. This led to a long-standing description of the yard as "simply a working yard." Research by architectural historians, however, indicates the yard was an antebellum garden that was used for other purposes after the Civil War. The reuse of one of the original garden buildings as a cowshed supports our interpretation that cows were present on the property and in the city into the twentieth century, as does the description of dairy herds in the burned district after the 1861 fire. In addition to the changes in garden buildings, a new driveway surface was laid down the center of the yard. An avenue of magnolias replaced an earlier garden fence and trellis, and the northwest quadrant of the yard and the front yard were replanted.

Formal gardens on other properties were maintained, in design if not in their antebellum elegance. The gardens at the Brewton, Russell, and Simmons-Edwards houses survived the Civil War. Historic photos suggest the Brewton and Russell gardens were tremendously overgrown in the late nineteenth century, reflecting a lack of funds and personnel to maintain them. Some townhouse garden areas were converted to lawns. These were simpler to maintain and provided a play area for children, a concept that grew in importance in the Victorian era.

Centre Market

Foods in the nineteenth-century city were likely obtained from the Centre Market. This new, consolidated market was built on lands given to the City in 1788 by the Pinckney family, with a clause stipulating that the family could reclaim the property if the City ceased to use it as a public market. The complex still functions as the Charleston Market, drawing thousands of visitors each year.[15]

Centre Market was built gradually, between 1790 and 1806, on a filled creek that had been the northern boundary of the walled city. The new market eventually stretched from Meeting Street to the waterfront. An impressive Market Hall, constructed on the western end in 1837, features a frieze with ornamental ox skulls (bucrania) and rams' heads, signifying the presence of a meat market. The single-story market stalls were raised a foot above street level at that time.[16]

A description of Centre Market in 1883 stated that: "meats, vegetables, and fish are sold in separate parts of the market. The stalls are arranged on each side, with a broad walk between. The whole arrangement is quite convenient, and well adapted to a Southern climate." Isabella Leland reported that the beef section featured "some 112 stalls, as well as three sections for vegetables, a fish market, and storerooms." Some decades earlier, the *Southern Agriculturalist* gave the following account of animals brought to the Centre Market for sale in the last quarter of 1836: "Beeves, 3081; Calves 583; Hogs; 2718; Sheep, 1275; Lambs, 115; Goats, 18; Wagons with Poultry, Bacon &c. 260 and Venison, Game, &c." Prizes offered by the South Carolina Institute in 1870 included those for venison hams, as well as beef and pork, suggesting wild game was still available in the city.[17]

Charleston Square, painted by Charles Hamilton in 1865, captures the vibrancy of daily life at the market. Market Hall dominates the image. Streets in the foreground bustle with hucksters, draymen, and townspeople of all sorts. African American vendors dominate the streetscape. Wagons and baskets are loaded with provisions. More tellingly, buzzards (vultures)

Figure 11.4. Buzzards (turkey vultures) at the Charleston Market, ca. 1900. (Collections of The Charleston Museum, Charleston, South Carolina.)

circle the stalls behind Market Hall, their numbers increasing nearer the waterfront. The colorful image is a reminder that avian scavengers were integral to the market's function. The buzzards are not the artist's fancy, for they are found in late-nineteenth-century photographs and in the Duke of Saxe-Weimar's 1826 description of his visit to Charleston.[18]

Because they helped clean the city, buzzards were protected by city ordinance and described in flowery detail as the "Charleston eagle." The 1870 South Carolina Institute guide describes them as

> a melancholy bird. . . . The headquarters are in Market street, in the neighborhood of the butchers' temple, and there, of a fine morning, he may be seen in all his glory, flying, flapping, moping, standing, fighting, stealing. . . . He has been known to steal meat from a market-basket, and to make frequent raids upon the butchers' stalls, and yet these trespasses were committed with impunity, the law protecting his life by a penalty of five dollars.[19]

Only one buzzard has been identified in Charleston's archaeological record, from an early-nineteenth-century deposit at the Brewton House. Gulls and terns also are scavengers that would contribute to keeping the market clean. A gull and two terns were found in the antebellum Simmons-Edwards collection, and a gull was found in the postbellum Jackson House collection.

Fish

Charleston offers an archaeological record of fishing that begins in the 1690s and extends into the late nineteenth century. We were surprised to find so little fish in Charleston's archaeological deposits. The survival of fish remains may be sensitive to context and degradation in the heavily impacted urban soils. Still, it is curious that two visitors to the city mention the scarcity of fish. Before describing the buzzards, the Duke of Saxe-Weimar commented: "Fish were not presented in so great a variety as I expected. Of shell-fish, I saw oysters only, which are roasted in the shell at market, and consumed by the negroes with great avidity."[20]

Some 50 years earlier, "A visitor in 1774" likewise reported a shortage of fish:

> The town in general is very ill-supplied with fish, which is not owing to a real scarcity for there are plenty to be caught if there were but proper people to seek after them, but as that is not the case they are

scarce and dear; however that is pretty well made up for by having plenty of fine turtle one half the year from 4d to 8d per pound.[21]

Charleston is a coastal city with a long-standing maritime heritage and an active fishing tradition. Most of the fishing for both homes and markets was done by African American men, an activity that began in the eighteenth century. The ability to fish in the antebellum period was rooted in the personal time afforded by the task system. Before the Civil War, free Black men served as boatmen and fishermen, roles monopolized by slaves until masters, fearful of defections, curtailed these occupations. D. E. Huger Smith recollected in the late nineteenth century, "They had followed this occupation from generation to generation, running out in their open boats until out of sight of land." Smith recalled, "From sunrise to sunset in every kind of weather, the men would fish beyond the bar, sometimes 40 miles out. Several hundred black men engaged regularly in boat fisheries with a fleet of as many as fifty vessels."[22]

We see evidence of the mosquito fleet in the 1850–1900 archaeological record. About a fifth of the fish individuals in the city's postbellum assemblage are sea basses, locally known as blackfish. Blackfishes were popular throughout Charleston's history but were slightly more frequently used in the late nineteenth century than in previous periods. This increase may be due to African American entrepreneur Charles C. Leslie, who controlled much of the postbellum fish market. Smith captures the direct connection between fishermen and table, noting, "Many old gentlemen would time their dinner if possible to suit the tide, and the wharf where they landed would be crowded with servants and hucksters, through whom the fish might reach the kitchens."[23]

Travelers' disappointment in the amount of fish available in markets aside, fish was a significant part of the Charleston cuisine. All but four of the Charleston collections contain at least one of the 62 fish species found in the city's archaeological record. A core group of fishes is found at most, if not all, sites during all time periods. This group includes sharks, hardhead and gafftopsail catfishes, sea basses, sheepsheads, weakfishes, Atlantic croakers, black and red drums, mullets, and flounders. A quarter of the fish individuals in the late-nineteenth-century archaeological assemblage are drums, primarily seatrouts, croakers, and black drums, with a few kingfishes and red fishes; a tenth of the fish in postbellum deposits are sea catfishes. All of these fishes could be captured within the harbor, in local tidal creeks, or around nearby sea islands. Marine resources were supplemented

Figure 11.5. Fishermen of Charleston's mosquito fleet, early twentieth century. (Collections of The Charleston Museum, Charleston, South Carolina.)

with freshwater fishes, mainly freshwater catfishes and sunfishes. This fishery used relatively simple gear and, prior to emancipation, could be exploited by enslaved Africans when they were not otherwise employed.

The list of fish in the archaeological record is considerably different from that documented for the retail market, so the market was evidently not the only source of fish. Of the 38 fish taxa represented in the Charleston 1820–1850 assemblage, for example, only five are present in the contemporaneous market assemblage. Some fish may have been taken by householders fishing for themselves. More likely, fish were sold directly from boats or by hawkers. Although some hucksters set up at or near the market, others walked the streets with baskets or carts. When Samuel Kelly visited Charleston in 1780, he noted that blackfishes were caught with hook and line by slaves in canoes working the fishing ground south of the Charleston bar.[24]

Sometimes fishing was an assigned task. In 1853 Beaufort planter Thomas Chaplin "sent Robert out fishing." Fishing for sport was an activity that sometimes united planter and skilled slave with a single goal, as described by Chaplin in the 1840s.[25]

Groupers, snappers, and grunts may not be from local waters. Such non-local fishes are not present in the 1710–1750 assemblage. They are present only in townhouse collections during the 1750–1820 period, with the exception of the Atlantic Wharf parrotfish. Thereafter, non-local fishes are found in collections from all non-market locations, though in very limited numbers; non-local fishes are absent from the market collections.

Consistently, at least a quarter of the noncommensal individuals present are fish in all time periods in non-market contexts. The number of fish species (richness) and their dietary contribution (measured as biomass) actually increases over time. The highest number of fish taxa is associated with townhouses during the 1820s–1850s, though non-market assemblages contain more fish taxa than do market assemblages. Either people obtained fish outside of the markets, or they purchased whole fish at the markets and removed most of the fishy evidence from the market scene altogether. It is likely that fish, whole and filleted, not only were purchased from markets but also obtained from vendors selling outside of the markets, and hooked by household residents.

Townhouse assemblages are the most diverse: they contain more kinds of fishes compared to other types of sites. Using rare, and perhaps more costly, fish may be a marker of high status. Further, the diversity of fishes in modest-status residential assemblages is higher than in public and lower-status assemblages after the 1820s. None of Charleston's diversity values are particularly high, due to the dominance of a few fish taxa in each time period: sea catfishes, sea basses, and flounders in 1710–50; sea catfishes and sea basses after 1750. This suggests that fishing gear and the habitats exploited changed little over the decades and that the fishery itself remained healthy.

Livestock Maintenance and Sanitation

Keeping animals, including cattle, on urban properties was common and persisted in some form into the twentieth century. The character of animal husbandry did change as the link between sanitation and health was recognized, and as the problems caused by raising animals in the city grew. A large part of yard maintenance involved keeping chickens and pigs out of the garden, cats out of the well, and rats out of the pantry. The archaeological record, and to a lesser extent the documentary record, suggests the work yard was filled with animals raised for milk, eggs, and feathers but

Figure 11.6. Children pulled by goat cart, December 29, 1905. (Collections of The Charleston Museum, Charleston, South Carolina.)

ultimately destined for the dinner table. These were joined by work animals, pets, and scavengers.

Over time, the types of animals changed in favor of smaller animals. Cattle continued to be present in the city, but their numbers declined. Pigs remain more or less unchanged, sheep or goats decline somewhat, and chickens increase considerably. The preference for pigs and chickens may be related not only to their smaller size but also to their willingness to eat table scraps and scavenge on their own. They served first as garbage disposals and, eventually, as dinner. Slaughter of some animals on residential properties apparently persisted. The bedding, feed, and refuse from domestic animals attracted other, less desirable, animals.

Mid-nineteenth-century plats show a variety of back buildings, including pigeon houses, poultry houses, cow houses, and, most telling, slaughterhouses. Gina Haney quotes prominent planter Ralph Izard, who in 1816 reported, "I have a cow yard fenced off & a division made for poultry & a fence running across the lot meeting these, give us a tolerably sized garden

Figure 11.7. An early-twentieth-century Charleston back yard. The small yard of bare earth features pens for a variety of fowl. (Collections of The Charleston Museum, Charleston, South Carolina.)

& square secured from intrusion for drying clothes." A South Carolina Institute committee noted that many of the prized fowl of 1851 were "bred in the city." The 1870s Adger family correspondence reports that numerous birds were kept at the Simmons-Edwards House: "Everything looks very well at our house—chickens, ducks, turkeys & dogs all answering quite blithely to roll-call," Andrew Adger noted in 1873. A year earlier Adger listed "one turkey, two hens, and five chickens" on the property.[26]

Commensal Animals

The remains of commensal animals offer another perspective on the city's growing sanitation problem. Between Charleston's founding years and the end of the nineteenth century, the percentage of rodents, dogs, cats, small birds, snakes, frogs, and toads in the archaeological record doubles. The steady increase in commensal animals over time and abundant animal remains found in drains, wells, privies, trash pits, and work yards show the extent of the sanitation problem.

The number of commensals varies by lot size. In the 1850–1900 period, over a third of the individuals recovered from the small Jackson House property are commensal, while less than a fifth of the individuals from the larger townhouse properties are commensal. This may indicate that crowding was a more significant issue on small properties or that efforts to control vermin at townhouses were successful. Masons John and Peter Horlbeck were contracted to build a brick wall in the city to "keep out the rats." This was unlikely to provide significant control, but something had to be done.[27]

Rats and their predators, cats and dogs, are the most abundant commensal animals in every time period, but by the latter part of the nineteenth century, most of the commensal individuals are Norway and black rats. Although there is no clear pattern in terms of status or site function, collections from dumps, neglected corners, and wells tend to contain more rodents. Rats constitute a third of the individuals in the Atlantic Wharf collection, for example. Wells appear to have been natural traps for a variety of animals; the well at the Jackson House contained the remains of 43 rats.

Figure 11.8. Bones from Norway and black rats recovered from Atlantic Wharf in 1983. (Photo by Sean Money, Collections of The Charleston Museum, Charleston, South Carolina.)

There were fewer rats where there was more human activity or where edibles were limited. Although the Beef and Lower Markets were littered with tasty refuse, the market assemblages contain comparatively few rats. Perhaps the open-air nature of markets and high level of activity discouraged these scavengers. It also appears that efforts to control rats in such public spaces were more vigorous and more successful than elsewhere in the city.

Compared to markets, residential properties had the larger rat problem. The otherwise elegant Heyward-Washington household, for example, shared the property with a host of rats, particularly inside its stable, where a quarter of the individuals were rats in the 1750–1820 period. The increase in rats during the nineteenth century may be related to the amount of waste discarded on residential properties, the quantity of foods stored there, and the quality of the storage facilities. Clearly, removing some of the trash was important.

Dogs and cats are always rare but increase through time. Cats show the greater increase. This may be evidence of efforts to control the growing rat problem, but it may also reflect limited space in the increasingly crowded city. With less space available on many properties, dogs and cats were buried closer to the house, the area most likely to be studied archaeologically. Some of these animals may have been well-loved pets, but not all were. The construction ditch for Brewton's vaulted drain contained two kitten bones, and Brewton's privy contained a dog bone. The remains of a dog were mixed with tin cans and other refuse in a large pit at the Hieronymous-Roper House. Only four of the 36 cats recovered from Charleston were from the markets; three of those four were from the Lower Market.

Charlestonians were ambivalent about dogs, considering them both friend and foe. Dogs performed many services in the public milieu, but they were subject to numerous regulations and eventually were licensed. Beginning in 1798, dogs had to be muzzled, collared, and secured. Those being moved through town had to be leashed. Both slave and free African Americans could keep a dog only if the animal's collar bore the name of a "reputable white person." Butchers' dogs had to be secured to carts and were banned from the market. The City Marshall used his canines "in catching or taking up hogs or goats about town." Free-ranging dogs, however, continued to be a problem in late-nineteenth-century Charleston, as in most American cities.[28]

Horses and/or mules do not appear to have been part of the lowcountry cuisine. Their remains are absent from the earliest deposits, and the remains of only 12 individuals have been identified in collections from later periods. These low numbers are one of the reasons they are considered commensal animals; they are not found in deposits containing food refuse. The horse buried at Charleston Place is particularly significant, because this single example comes from a site on the edge of town, and not a residential property in the heart of the city. On the other hand, the work yard at the Simmons-Edwards House yielded a complete horse cannon bone, suggesting that horses were sometimes buried on residential lots, even in the 1820s–1850s. Horses undoubtedly made important contributions to the sights, sounds, and smells of Charleston, but recovering them archaeologically may require excavating commercial stables or places where by-products were rendered.

Charleston is an interesting case, because many of the wild mammals identified in the archaeological record are indigenous animals that likely stayed in place as Charleston grew around them or were attracted into the urban environment, what Maciej Luniak calls a "free ecological niche" where food was plentiful and predators few. Ecological, demographic, and behavioral plasticity were the main requirements for taking advantage of this opportunity. Some animals moved into the city because they were attracted to the resources, protection, and habitats found there. Others were introduced by people for various reasons. These attributes not only apply to animals referred to here as commensal but also describe many of the animals classified in this study as wild members of the lowcountry cuisine, especially opossums, rabbits, squirrels, and raccoons.[29]

Postbellum Changes

The post–Civil War years were difficult ones for all residents of Charleston, regardless of race or status. Elegant townhouses were converted to businesses and boardinghouses. Lots were subdivided, back lots were rented out, and some were abandoned. The urban middle class, however, was growing, as can be seen in the many smaller homes built in the city. Although citizens increasingly drew upon commercial sources for household goods and foods, they continued to enjoy the local wild resources long relished by Charlestonians.

Growing awareness of links between poor sanitation, bad drainage, accumulating debris, and disease led to efforts to clean up the city. But the habits of keeping livestock in the city and discarding trash casually were hard to abandon. Many animals continued to live and die in Charleston.

Mixed with the ornamental gardens and fine buildings on townhouse lots were kitchen gardens, stables, cattle pens, pigsties, dovecotes, chicken coops, and dog pens. Livestock, work animals, pets, assorted fowl, and numerous unwanted or unremarked visitors were part of the urban landscape into the twentieth century. Vermin made the dark corners and unimproved areas their home, eating food supplies and refuse with equal vigor. Although much of this was hidden behind buildings and fences, the odors and sounds of livestock, their slaughter, and the discard of rubbish must have been common.

The impact of animals on the urban environment was considerable. Moreover, it was long-lasting. Archaeological deposits recovered in Charleston, as in other cities, reflect long-term refuse disposal. Eventually, it was no longer possible to discard debris all over lots, or even in trash pits, drains, wells, and privies. Public water supply, sewage projects, and garbage collection were driven by necessity. The good health enjoyed by urban residents today may owe as much to improved public services as to improved medical care. Archaeological and zooarchaeological study provides ample evidence of the formidable problems of daily life faced by Charleston residents.

12

ARCHAEOLOGY IN THE CITY, ARCHAEOLOGY OF THE CITY

We didn't set out to study cattle. We began our study of Charleston with a general interest in all of the artifacts, the garbage of the community. We focused on those that are familiar: the ceramic, glass, metal, and stone objects most frequently studied by archaeologists. Charleston sites are filled with broken cooking pots and plates. We found delicate stemmed glassware. We searched the screens for small buttons, thimbles, and beads. We explored buildings and foundations. Our imagined vision of the past read like a stroll down Meeting Street in the colonial period, peering into shop windows and examining the wares available for sale.

When preservation conditions are right, archaeologists also recover plant and animal remains. Soon, screens filled with bone changed our vision of Charleston. Instead of peering into shop windows along the street front, we were glancing down alleys and narrow streets, over fences and behind buildings, catching glimpses of kitchens and cook fires, and of animals penned and tethered in the yard, or wandering the streets. With analysis of the animal bones, we were peering directly into the stew pot.

The artifacts we recovered show us that Charleston was on a bountiful coast and that Charlestonians took advantage of that bounty. Three decades of carefully controlled archaeological excavation and analysis tell a story of Charleston through three broad queries. Archaeological sites and animal remains recovered from them document modifications to the land through human activities over time. Lists of animals and materials used to store, cook, and serve food tell about the foodways and cuisines of the lowcountry. Environmental and material discoveries provide a backdrop for the production, distribution, and consumption of goods and services linking the city with its rural neighbors and global markets.

Our studies began with a broad view of the evolving urban environment. Material culture, architecture, and landscape outline the trajectory of Charleston's development as a dwelling place for a diverse population. Using a landscape approach, we linked social, behavioral, ideological, and natural elements to form the Charleston story. Of particular significance for this perspective is the concept that land is not "natural" but "modified for human occupation and use. The urban environment is a shared space, evolving to serve a community." The same landscape was viewed in different ways by the diverse groups who used it. This community includes the plants and animals that lived there. The city is buildings and open spaces, but those spaces are filled with people, as well as plants and animals, even today.[1]

From this broad view of the urban landscape, we focused more tightly on details of life in the city. We learned about foodways and cuisine from the animal bones we recovered, and how this is unique to the lowcountry. Charlestonians could have taken another path, as people in Spanish St. Augustine had done in a very similar environment. Charlestonians made choices. These choices extend not only to the animals used but to the cuisine that featured these animals. Our consideration of urban cuisine includes all of the artifacts we recover, not just the animal remains, so we discussed objects ranging from fragments of bottle glass to elegant porcelain platters to entire houses. The urban environment can be understood only in reference to the greater lowcountry, so environmental data, historical documentation, and selected rural archaeological sites assisted in developing our understanding of Charleston.

Provisioning the city was an important part of lowcountry life. Charleston's trade networks, both inland and overseas, contributed to the evolving landscape. Animals, wild and domestic, were transported to markets and distributed to consumers. Excavation of the markets was one stop on this journey from field to table. Equally important were the other sites that illustrate social connections contributing to the city as a site.

These topics kept bringing us back to cattle. The study of cattle became a journey of unexpected discoveries. Slow and steady analysis of bones, site by site, led us first to acknowledge the dominance of beef. From there, we noted the overall size of the cattle. This led us to consider the sources and characteristics of early animals. From here the journey took us to St. Augustine, where we learned about the relative size of Spanish cattle. British and Spanish cattle were different, and animals from Spanish colonies were significantly larger. To our surprise, Charleston cattle were in the middle.

We revisited documents from James Moore's raids and noted that cattle were among the plunder brought to Carolina.

We focused on the journeys that may have brought Spanish cattle to Carolina, contributing to hybrid stock. Following our study of Moore's raids of St. Augustine and Apalachee, we connected Charleston with the fortuitous discovery and analysis of Mary Musgrove's Cowpens in Georgia. Both sites, beyond the boundaries of Charleston and even Carolina, illustrated the routes and mechanisms that brought cattle to market in Charleston. Detailed study of cattle remains showed connections among otherwise disparate sites; just as The Cowpens is linked to the Beef Market and to the nearby Charleston Judicial Center, James Island planters and their slaves are linked to the Lower Market. Our envisioned city tour added wagon yards on upper King Street and cattle driven on hoof down this thoroughfare, then across to the city gate at Meeting and Broad Streets. Imaginary wagons carried freshly slaughtered portions, followed by dogs.

Our journey with cattle also took us to the back lots and cellars of Charleston townhouses. The carcass portions found at these sites demonstrate that markets were not the only, and not even the principal, source of beef in the city. Time and time again we found evidence of on-site butchery, changing our interpretation from possibly to probably to absolutely. McCrady's Long Room, the Exchange Building, and the Heyward-Washington House—all locales used to entertain President Washington in 1791—are connected by a web of food production and food presentation. We struggled to separate fine dining from everyday meals, and cattle embody this conundrum. Were cow skull bones recovered from the work yards at the Aiken-Rhett, Heyward-Washington, Miles Brewton, and Simmons-Edwards houses butchery waste or table scraps? If they were table scraps, whose table had they graced? Were elegantly presented calves' heads served at fancy dinners in those mansions? More often than not, we found few differences in the beef consumed by those dining on the second floor of the Brewton and Nathaniel Russell houses and those preparing meals in the shadows of Lodge Alley or the Powder Magazine.

If cattle are the star of our show, then dozens of animals play supporting roles. Cattle were joined in the yard by pigs, goats, and chickens. Provisions came from the market and from townhouse work yards. Some came from Spanish America, at least indirectly. And they came from the woods and coastal waters of the lowcountry. If we are to complete our imaginary tour of Charleston and its resident animals, we must travel by wagon through pine forests, by canoe along rivers and creeks, and by horseback through swamps. We spy snares in the gardens adjoining cabins, and baskets beneath logs in the rice fields. A ride through the swamp may bring us in contact with deer and turkey, but we are just as likely to encounter a cow, ears notched with the mark of the owner. Back in town, we find these animals for sale in markets on Broad Street and on the Bay (East Bay Street).

As we journeyed with cows, so too did we journey with rats. We found plenty of rats in the crowded, industrialized city of the late nineteenth century, but we also found them in the earliest Charles Town deposits. Rats stepped off the boats with the first European settlers. They poured off of transatlantic ships onto the wharves, where they thrived. As with cattle, we were surprised by where we found rats and where we did not. We found that they settled into the dark corners of otherwise elegant properties, subsisting on grains and other refuse in the stables and back lots of the elite townhouses. They avoided the busy, crowded markets, despite the likelihood of plenty of food. If cows were a measure of trade connections and provisioning routes, rats were measures of landscape evolution and maintenance, or lack of it. We found them in the seemingly unkempt Powder Magazine.

The Powder Magazine

Throughout this volume, we told the story of Charleston by drawing from many sites, scattered across the peninsula and beyond. Here we return to a single site, one that embodies the topics that are the focus of this volume. Archaeology in the oldest public building in Charleston revealed many aspects of city life. And the site produced animal bones, pollen, and cultural materials that drew together all of our discoveries about life in Charleston.

This site strengthened our suspicion that people lived anywhere and everywhere. There are no discernible archaeological differences between residential and commercial functions, or public functions. Seemingly secure and removed from the heart of the settlement, the 1712 Powder Magazine was built to store arms and other munitions. The recovered artifacts, or lack thereof, in the earliest layers suggest that armaments were not stored here. Noticeably absent from the deposits were gunflints, shot, or almost any other evidence of armaments. European ceramics, colono wares, wine bottles, pharmaceutical bottles, tobacco pipes in large numbers, and great quantities of animal remains filled the three pits and the soil layer in the building's interior.

The site offered other surprises or confirmed suspicions developed during the study of other collections. This untidy site does not conform to the fastidious, safety-conscious behavior expected at magazines. But it is typical of Charleston. This was a dark, dank, but substantial building; one probably used as a residence for sentries and perhaps their families. At the very least, a range of domestic activities took place there. Although buttons could have been lost from military clothing, scissors and straight pins suggest clothing repair. Perhaps the trash was the sentry's daily discard, scattered and lost among the barrels and racks of powder stored in the building, thereby explaining the untrampled condition of the materials. The presence of the domestic artifacts, however, is undeniable. The interpretation as domestic debris is supported by the characteristics of the animal remains; in fact, the domestic interpretation originated in the zoo-archaeology laboratory.

The animal remains closely resemble those from other Charleston sites. It appears that most people throughout the city used many of the same animals, with few obvious status or ethnic differences. Many of these animals were the common suite of lowcountry wild animals. Here, as elsewhere, animals were raised on the property, and beef was the preferred meat. We found no solid evidence of rations at the Powder Magazine, but we did find evidence of on-site butchery combined with some use of market purchases. Even in the earliest deposits, the Powder Magazine was clearly an urban site and not a rural one. Commensal species, particularly rats, were present at the Powder Magazine, and a large portion of the mammal bones recovered were gnawed by rodents. Cross mends and vessel matches from interior and exterior proveniences indicate all of this refuse originated from activities on the site and not from elsewhere.

The magazine was a dilapidated and underutilized structure through the nineteenth century but remained standing as much of Charleston's earlier architecture was replaced by massive buildings, both private and public. The pollen and parasite records of the nineteenth-century building suggest a neglected space with a weedy exterior. Animal- and human-borne parasites reflect an unkempt, unsanitary interior. The only known well for the Powder Magazine straddles the property line to the west and was shared with a neighbor. These unsanitary conditions were only a little worse than those generally found throughout the town, for Charleston had long struggled with the health problems attending a growing and overcrowded city.

It was Gabriel Manigault's 1897 proposal to demolish the building that

Figure 12.1. The Powder Magazine and surrounding properties in 1900. (Collections of The Charleston Museum, Charleston, South Carolina.)

stimulated the first effort in Charleston to preserve a historic structure, an effort that began in 1902, received a boost in 1993, and continues today. The Powder Magazine occupies an evolving symbolic role in Charleston, from protector, to anonymous commercial space, all-but-abandoned "problem," romanticized symbol of past glories, and a piece of revised history. It is no accident of the urban landscape that this squat building survives, sitting at an odd angle among parking garages and lofty church spires. It reflects Charleston's changing role from frontier settlement to commercial center, economically struggling city, and reinvigorated tourist destination.

Answers to Our Questions

So what have we learned from our digs at the Powder Magazine and elsewhere? How does this project fit into 30 years of excavations, archival research, and laboratory analyses? How has this story emerged from untold hours of conversation with scholars of history, architecture, archaeology, biology, landscape, material culture, and museum studies?

We first learned that, despite significant land use change, construction, and demolition, the archaeological record of Charleston is largely intact. Large buildings, layers of fill, and asphalt often seal, rather than destroy, the layers and fragile artifacts of earlier times. Architect Joe Schmidt reminded us that only the invention of the diesel-powered bulldozer made it possible to move and reorganize the soils of the city on a massive scale. The five-foot-deep foundations of City Hall required only narrow, hand-dug builder's trenches. Even on sites of modern construction, small areas undisturbed by the bulldozer are likely to be found, such as the privy at the Dock Street Theatre. The discovery in 2013 of unmarked graves at the Gaillard Municipal Auditorium, which was built in the 1960s, is another example of how undisturbed areas persist even on lots that have experienced major construction episodes.[2]

Just as our appreciation for the archaeological record has evolved over the decades, so too have the politics of managing that record. Archaeology has acquired many friends along the way. Support first came from the City, as revitalization efforts increased. Much of this revitalization involved federal funds and permits, making some archaeological work mandatory. A civic commitment to archaeology on a broader scale emerged from these projects, including support for developing a research design to guide further work. Construction projects that are not required to involve archaeological mitigation continue in and around the city. But a growing number of individuals and groups lobby for protection of below-ground remains.

The growing alliance between archaeology and historic preservation benefits both fields. Preservation organizations in Charleston—and elsewhere in the United States—were largely indifferent to archaeological study of the city's buried heritage until the late 1980s. Guided by broadminded program directors, Historic Charleston Foundation and the Preservation Society of Charleston embraced urban archaeological research and preservation and became their staunchest proponents. This partnership is critical for integrated preservation and interpretation of below-ground and aboveground resources. So too is the support of private property owners and community members, whose understanding and cooperation have grown through the years.

There is no denying the complexity of the archaeological record of urban environments. This complexity reflects the intricacy of urban life. Urban properties were, and are, multifunctional. We searched for evidence of commercial and craft activities distinct from residential activities, but such distinctions were rare. People lived everywhere, including at the Powder

Figure 12.2. View of Broad Street from the steeple of St. Michael's Episcopal Church, 2012. The Exchange Building is visible at the end of the street. (Photo by Katherine Pemberton, Courtesy of Historic Charleston Foundation.)

Magazine. Townhouses of wealthy merchants or planters housed many people, most of whom were not wealthy. An owner's family was likely out-numbered by resident slaves or servants, all living in the same constricted space. Social and physical distance were not equal. Further, the trash of all the different people living at these sites became mixed in the ground. This fact of urban life frustrated our attempts to discern status differences in the material or animal remains, despite the fact that social affiliations based on wealth, ethnicity, gender, and other social distinctions are often expressed through public culinary displays, food preparation, and material culture.[3]

Though we have just talked about "sites," the city *is* the site. All of our individual properties or "sites" are part of the larger, cohesive locus of human habitation, the urban environment, distinct from the nearby rural one. Further, all activities are part of the archaeological record of urban life. It is possible to learn much about life in a city even if the site's function, owner, occupant, and date of occupation are unknown and the excavations limited. Under this paradigm, fill from Atlantic Wharf is as informative as Miles Brewton's bottle seal from the Simmons-Edwards House.

We studied the city's buildings and open spaces in our examination of provisioning strategies. Urban spaces were filled with people and animals. Most of those animals fed the urban residents. We explored the sources of wild and domestic animals. Our rural sites illustrated the transportation of goods to market and the social connections facilitating economic exchange. Many goods and services linked the city with its rural neighbors and global markets. The merger of local and global provisions is characteristic of even the earliest Carolina deposits.

Returning to focus on cuisine and the earliest days of colonial Charleston, the evidence reminds us that this began as a self-sufficient colony where people tried many familiar ways to make a living and developed new ones. As Kathleen Deagan demonstrated for Spanish America, our study clearly indicates that a cuisine took shape that merged Native American, European, African, and Asian resources and traditions. The cuisine forged here, like those that emerged in other colonies, represents a new cultural form that cannot be traced back to a single ancestral tradition. It is a product of all the traditions present in the colony. The lowcountry cuisine made use of the local bounty as well as traditions and goods transported from elsewhere. In colonial settings where multi-group interactions occurred, new forms were the outcome of dynamic exchanges, reformations, and inventions. And Charleston's historic cuisine persists into the present century.[4]

In colonial settings that clearly involved multiple agents from multiple places, we can only guess at which traditions might prevail under which conditions. In the case of decisions related to animal use, geopolitical affiliation appears to have had little influence over how animals were used, prepared, and served. Instead, we see pragmatic decisions based on local social, economic, and environmental factors. The animal remains from

Charleston and its rural neighbors indicate that transformations in animal use by colonists occurred almost immediately, with later changes reflecting factors such as access to external markets, animal health, and the physical landscape. Moreover, each transformation was unique, as seen in the distinct differences between English Charleston and Spanish St. Augustine.

Foodways and cuisine were influenced by the environment, by the migration and mixing of different ethnic groups, and by regional, national, and global changes in the production, distribution, and consumption of foods. This merger of local and global elements is characteristic of even the earliest archaeological deposits. Archaeology demonstrates a relationship between the evolving urban landscape and resources available from local woods and waters. Archaeology also reflects the transatlantic connections of the port city, and the worldwide resources available to city residents. Charleston may have been on the frontier, but it was never isolated.

Our understanding of Charleston's cuisine derives from artifacts beyond those representing the foods served. Our study included the pottery used to prepare the foods, and the dishes from Europe and Asia used to serve the meals. We considered the accoutrements of dining and tea, including furnishings and clothing thought proper for shared social occasions. We examined the layout of rooms, houses, yards, and streets. We pondered the social message encoded in these elements.

The coast of Charleston was indeed bountiful. Charlestonians used their cattle and pigs, as well as their flocks of chickens, pigeons, and ducks, as a basis for their diet. Cattle, in particular, flourished in the pine forests and swamps of the lowcountry, and early colonists took advantage of that unexpected bounty. City dwellers also drew from the resources of the surrounding coast to expand and enliven their meals. Freshwater and marine fishes were commonly eaten, as were Canada geese, turkeys, alligators, and turtles. Archaeological research shows that the urban Charleston diet differed in some respects from the diet of their rural neighbors and even from that enjoyed in other coastal cities.

We have a composite archaeological signature of a vibrant, densely packed city, where people and animals carried on their activities in close proximity, where social distance did not equate to physical distance, and where multiple activities occurred simultaneously. If archaeology provides only a partial picture of city life, it provides one that differs from our traditional view of Charleston's past and is likely to continue surprising us.

APPENDIX 1

Reports for Charleston Sites

Unless listed separately, faunal reports are included in the general site report. All Charleston Museum *Archaeological Contributions* are available online at www.charlestonmuseum.org.

AIKEN-RHETT HOUSE

Zierden, Martha. "Aiken-Rhett House: Archaeological Research." Archaeological Contributions 31. Charleston, S.C.: The Charleston Museum, 2003.

Zierden, Martha, Jeanne Calhoun, and Debi Hacker. "Outside of Town: Preliminary Investigations of the Aiken-Rhett House." Archaeological Contributions 11. Charleston, S.C.: The Charleston Museum, 1986.

ATLANTIC WHARF

Zierden, Martha, and Elizabeth Reitz. "Excavations on Charleston's Waterfront: The Atlantic Wharf Garage Site." Archaeological Contributions 30. Charleston, S.C.: The Charleston Museum, 2002.

BEEF MARKET/CITY HALL

Calhoun, Jeanne, Elizabeth Reitz, Michael Trinkley, and Martha Zierden. "Meat in Due Season: Preliminary Investigations of Marketing Practices in Colonial Charleston." Archaeological Contributions 9. Charleston, S.C.: The Charleston Museum, 1984.

Zierden, Martha, and Elizabeth Reitz. "Archaeology at City Hall: Charleston's Colonial Beef Market." Archaeological Contributions 35. Charleston, S.C.: The Charleston Museum, 2005.

MILES BREWTON HOUSE

Zierden, Martha. "Archaeology at the Miles Brewton House, 27 King Street." Archaeological Contributions 29. Charleston, S.C.: The Charleston Museum, 2001.

CHARLES TOWN, MILLER SITE, JAMES LE SADE

Agha, Andrew. "Historical Archaeology at Old Towne Plantation, Miller Site Excavations Fall 2012–Summer 2013." Report on file, Charles Towne Landing State Historic Site, Charleston, S.C., 2013.

Beeby, Cicek, and David Jones. "Miller Site Excavations, Fall Field Season 2009." Report on file, Charles Towne Landing State Historic Site, Charleston, S.C., 2010.

Reitz, Elizabeth J., and Sarah G. Bergh. "Animal Remains from Two Early South Carolina Sites." Report on file, Zooarchaeology Laboratory, Georgia Museum of Natural History, University of Georgia, Athens, 2012.

Reitz, Elizabeth J., and Maran E. Little. "Vertebrate Remains from the Miller Site, 38Ch1-MS, Charles Towne Landing State Historic Site." Report on file, Charles Town Landing State Historic Site, Charleston, S.C., 2014.

CHARLESTON PLACE/CHARLESTON CENTER

Honerkamp, Nicholas, R. Bruce Council, and M. Elizabeth Will. "An Archaeological Investigation of the Charleston Convention Center Site, Charleston, South Carolina." Report on file, U.S. Department of the Interior, National Park Service, Atlanta, 1982.

Zierden, Martha, and Debi Hacker. "Charleston Place: Archaeological Investigation of the Commercial Landscape." Archaeological Contributions 16. Charleston, S.C.: The Charleston Museum, 1987.

DOCK STREET THEATRE

Zierden, Martha, Andrew Agha, Carol Colaninno, John Jones, Eric Poplin, and Elizabeth Reitz. "The Dock Street Theatre: Archaeological Discovery and Exploration." Archaeological Contributions 42. Charleston, S.C.: The Charleston Museum, 2009.

JULIANA DUPRE HOUSE

Reitz, Elizabeth J., and Joel A. Dukes. "Vertebrate Fauna from 40 Society Street and 72 Anson Street, Charleston, South Carolina." Report on file, The Charleston Museum, Charleston, S.C., 1993.

Zierden, Martha. "Field Report: Testing at 40 Society Street." Report on file, The Charleston Museum, Charleston, S.C., 1989.

EXCHANGE BUILDING/HALF MOON BATTERY

Herold, Elaine. "Archaeological Research at the Exchange Building, Charleston, S.C.: 1979–1980." Report on file, The Charleston Museum, Charleston, S.C., 1981.

Reitz, Elizabeth. "Vertebrate Fauna from the Charleston Exchange Building." Report on file, The Charleston Museum, Charleston, S.C., 1988.

Zierden, Martha, and Debi Hacker. "Examination of Construction Sequence at the Exchange Building." Archaeological Contributions 16. Charleston, S.C.: The Charleston Museum, 1986.

FIRST TRIDENT

Zierden, Martha, Jeanne Calhoun, and Elizabeth Pinckney. "An Archaeological Study of the First Trident Site." Archaeological Contributions 6. Charleston, S.C.: The Charleston Museum, 1983.

WILLIAM GIBBES HOUSE

Zierden, Martha, Jeanne Calhoun, Debi Hacker, and Suzanne Buckley. "Georgian Opulence: Archaeological Investigation of the Gibbes House." Archaeological Contributions 12. Charleston, S.C.: The Charleston Museum, 1986.

HEYWARD-WASHINGTON HOUSE

Herold, Elaine. "Preliminary Report on the Research at the Heyward-Washington House." Report on file, The Charleston Museum, Charleston, S.C., 1978.

Zierden, Martha. "Archaeological Testing and Mitigation at the Stable Building, Heyward-Washington House." Archaeological Contributions 23. Charleston, S.C.: The Charleston Museum, 1993.

Zierden, Martha, and Elizabeth Reitz. "Archaeology at the Heyward-Washington Stable: Charleston through the Eighteenth Century." Archaeological Contributions 39. Charleston, S.C.: The Charleston Museum, 2007.

HIERONYMOUS-ROPER HOUSE

Zierden, Martha, Kimberly Grimes, David Hudgens, and Cherie Black. "Charleston's First Suburb: Excavations at 66 Society Street." Archaeological Contributions 20. Charleston, S.C.: The Charleston Museum, 1988.

JACKSON HOUSE

Zierden, Martha, Elizabeth Reitz, and Barbara Ruff. "Archaeological Excavations at 70 Nassau Street: 1990–1991." Archaeological Contributions 47. Charleston, S.C.: The Charleston Museum, 2014.

KOHNE-LESLIE HOUSE

Reitz, Elizabeth J., and Joel A. Dukes. "Vertebrate Fauna from 40 Society Street and 72 Anson Street, Charleston, South Carolina." Report on file, The Charleston Museum, Charleston, S.C., 1993.

Zierden, Martha. "Field Report: Testing at 72 Anson Street." Report on file, The Charleston Museum, Charleston, S.C., 1992.

LODGE ALLEY/STATE STREET

Zierden, Martha, Jeanne Calhoun, and Elizabeth Paysinger. "Archaeological Investigations at Lodge Alley." Archaeological Contributions 5. Charleston, S.C.: The Charleston Museum, 1983.

MCCRADY'S TAVERN AND LONG ROOM

Zierden, Martha, Elizabeth Reitz, Michael Trinkley, and Elizabeth Paysinger. "Archaeological Excavations at McCrady's Longroom." Archaeological Contributions 3. Charleston, S.C.: The Charleston Museum, 1983.

MARY MUSGROVE'S COWPENS/GRANGE PLANTATION

Braley, Chad O. "Archaeological Data Recovery at the Cowpens/Grange Plantation Site (9CH137), Chatham County, Georgia." Report on file, Southeastern Archaeological Services, Inc., prepared for the Georgia Ports Authority, Savannah, through CH2M Hill/Lockwood Greene, Pooler, Ga., 2013.

Orr, Kelly, Elizabeth Reitz, and Gregory Lucas. "Vertebrate Remains from the Grange Plantation (9Ch137) Trading Post and Cowpens, Savannah, Georgia." Report on file, Zooarchaeology Laboratory, University of Georgia, Athens, 2008.

POST OFFICE/COURTHOUSE (MCKENZIE HOUSE)

Bastian, Beverly. "Historical and Archaeological Investigations at the United States Post Office/Courthouse Annex, Charleston, South Carolina." Report on file, National Park Service, Atlanta, Ga., 1987.

POWDER MAGAZINE

Zierden, Martha. "Archaeology at the Powder Magazine: A Charleston Site through Three Centuries." Archaeological Contributions 26. Charleston, S.C.: The Charleston Museum, 1997.

PRESIDENT STREET/MUSC

Zierden, Martha, and Robert Raynor. "The President Street Site: An Experiment in Public Archaeology." Archaeological Contributions 18. Charleston, S.C.: The Charleston Museum, 1988.

NATHANIEL RUSSELL HOUSE

Zierden, Martha. "Excavations in the Front Lawn: Nathaniel Russell House, 2003–2006." Archaeological Contributions 36. Charleston, S.C.: The Charleston Museum, 2006.

———. "Big House/Back Lot: An Archaeological Study of the Nathaniel Russell House." Archaeological Contributions 25. Charleston, S.C.: The Charleston Museum, 1996.

Zierden, Martha, Elizabeth Reitz, and Dan Weinand. "The Nathaniel Russell House: Initial Archaeological Testing." Archaeological Contributions 24. Charleston, S.C.: The Charleston Museum, 1995.

JOHN RUTLEDGE HOUSE

Zierden, Martha, and Kimberly Grimes. "Investigating Elite Lifeways through Archaeology: The John Rutledge House." Archaeological Contributions 21. Charleston, S.C.: The Charleston Museum, 1989.

ST. GILES KUSSOE/LORD ASHLEY

Agha, Andrew. "St. Giles Kussoe and 'The Character of a Loyal States-man': Historical Archaeology at Lord Anthony Ashley Cooper's Carolina Plantation." Report on file, Historic Charleston Foundation, Charleston, S.C., 2012.

Agha, Andrew, and Charles F. Philips Jr. "Archaeological Investigations at 38DR83a, St. Giles Kussoe House/Lord Ashley Settlement." Report on file, Brockington and Associates to Historic Charleston Foundation, Charleston, S.C., 2010.

SIMMONS-EDWARDS HOUSE

Zierden, Martha. "Excavations at 14 Legare Street, Charleston, South Carolina." Archaeological Contributions 28. Charleston, S.C.: The Charleston Museum, 2001.

SOUTH ADGER'S WHARF/LOWER MARKET

Butler, Nicholas, Eric Poplin, Katherine Pemberton, and Martha Zierden. "Archaeology at South Adger's Wharf: A Study of the Redan at Tradd Street." Archaeological Contributions 45. Charleston, S.C.: The Charleston Museum, 2012.

JAMES STOBO'S PLANTATION (WILLTOWN)

Webber, Jennifer J., and Elizabeth J. Reitz. Animal Use on the Eighteenth Century Frontier: Stobo Plantation, South Carolina. Report on file, Zooarchaeology Laboratory, Georgia Museum of Natural History, University of Georgia, Athens, 1999.

Zierden, Martha, Suzanne Linder, and Ronald Anthony. "Willtown: An Archaeological and Historical Perspective." Archaeological Contributions 27. Charleston, S.C.: The Charleston Museum, and Columbia: South Carolina Department of Archives and History, 1999.

VISITOR RECEPTION AND TRANSPORTATION CENTER

Grimes, Kimberly, and Martha Zierden. "A Hub of Human Activity: Archaeological Investigations of the Visitor's Reception and Transportation Center." Archaeological Contributions 19. Charleston, S.C.: The Charleston Museum, 1988.

OTHER SITES WITH FAUNAL STUDIES

Hamby, Theresa, and J. W. Joseph. "A New Look at the Old City: Archaeological Excavations of the Charleston County Judicial Center Site (38CH1708), Charleston, South Carolina." Technical Report 1192. Stone Mountain, Ga.: New South Associates, 2004.

Joseph, J. W., and Rita Folse Elliott. "Restoration Archaeology at the Charleston County Courthouse Site (38Ch1498)." Technical Report 194. Stone Mountain, Ga.: New South Associates, 1994.

Joseph, J. W., Theresa Hamby, and Jennifer Langdale. "The Vendue/Prioleau Project: An Archaeological Study of the Early Charleston Waterfront." Technical Report 772. Stone Mountain, Ga.: New South Associates, 2000.

Poplin, Eric, and Ed Salo. "Archaeological Investigations at 82 Pitt Street, Charleston, South Carolina: Final Report." Report on file, Historic Charleston Foundation, Charleston, S.C., 2009.

Trinkley, Michael, and Debi Hacker. "The Other Side of Charleston: Archaeological Survey of the Saks Fifth Avenue Location, Charleston, South Carolina." Research Series 45. Columbia, S.C.: Chicora Foundation, 1996.

———. "Life on Broad Street: Archaeological Survey of the Hollings Judicial Center Annex, Charleston, South Carolina." Research Series 192. Columbia, S.C.: Chicora Foundation, 1996.

APPENDIX 2

List of Sites Studied

Site Name	Deposit Date	Time Period	Status	Function
URBAN SITES				
Aiken-Rhett House	1818–1830	1820s–1850s	Upper class	Residential
Aiken-Rhett House	1830–1850	1820s–1850s	Upper class	Residential
Aiken-Rhett House	1850–1870	1850–1900	Upper class	Residential
Aiken-Rhett House	1870–1900	1850–1900	Upper class	Residential
Aiken-Rhett House	Early 20th century	1850–1900	Upper class	Residential
Atlantic Wharf	1790s–1820s	1750s–1820s	Public	Dump
Beef Market/City Hall	1692–1739	1710–1750s	Public	Market
Beef Market/City Hall	1739–1760	1710–1750s	Public	Market
Beef Market/City Hall	1760–1796	1750s–1820s	Public	Market
Beef Market/City Hall	Early 19th century	1820s–1850s	Public	City Hall
Brewton House (Brewton)	1750–1770	1750s–1820s	Upper class	Residential
Brewton House (Motte-Alston)	1775–1830	1820s–1850s	Upper class	Residential
Brewton House (Pringle-Frost)	1840s–1880	1850–1900	Upper class	Residential
Charleston Place	1730s–late 1800s	1820s–1850s	Moderate	Mixed
Dock Street Theatre	1736–1750s	1710–1750s	Public	Theater
Juliana Dupre House	Mid–late 1800s	1850–1900	Moderate	Residential
Exchange Building/Half Moon Battery	1750–1790	1750s–1820s	Public	Commercial
Exchange Building	Mid-19th century	1820s–1850s	Public	Commercial
Exchange Building	Late 19th century	1850–1900	Public	Commercial
First Trident	1740s	1710–1750s	Tannery	Commercial
First Trident	Colonial, 1740s–1790s	1750s–1820s	Moderate	Residential
First Trident	Federal, 1790s–1840s	1820s–1850s	Moderate	Residential

William Gibbes House	1772–1830s	Upper class	Residential
Heyward-Washington House	1730–1740	Upper class	Residential
Heyward-Washington House	1740–1750	Upper class	Residential
Heyward-Washington House	1750–1820	Upper class	Residential
Heyward-Washington House	Late 19th century	Upper class	Residential
Hieronymous-Roper House	1800–1870	Moderate	Residential
Jackson House	Mid- to late 1800s	Moderate	Residential
Kohne-Leslie House	Early to mid-1800s	Moderate	Residential
Kohne-Leslie House	Mid- to late 1800s	Moderate	Residential
Lodge Alley/State Street	18th century, 2nd half	Lower class	Mixed
Lodge Alley/State Street	19th century, 1st half	Lower class	Mixed
McCrady's Tavern	1720–1750	Public	Commercial
McCrady's Tavern and Long Room	1770s–1780s	Public	Tavern and Long Room
McCrady's Tavern	Early 19th century	Public	Tavern
Post Office (McKenzie House)	1725–1769	Upper class	Residential
Powder Magazine	1712–1750	Public	Civic
Powder Magazine	1751–1820	Public	Civic
Powder Magazine	1820–1850	Public	Civic
Powder Magazine	1851–1900	Public	Civic
President Street/MUSC	Mid-19th century	Moderate	Residential
President Street/MUSC	Late 19th century	Moderate	Residential
Russell House (pre-Russell)	1730–1808	Upper class	Residential
Russell House (Russell)	1808–1857	Upper class	Residential

(continued)

Appendix 2—*Continued*

Site Name	Deposit Date	Time Period	Status	Function
Russell House (Allston)	1857–1870	1850–1900	Upper class	Residential
Russell House (Sisters of Charity)	1870–1908	1850–1900	Public	School
Rutledge House	1730s–1760s	1710–1750s	Upper class	Residential
Rutledge House	1760s–1820s	1750s–1820s	Upper class	Residential
Rutledge House	Post-1820s	1820s–1850s	Upper class	Residential
Sanders House			Unknown	Urban
Simmons-Edwards (Brewton trash)	Late 1700s	1750s–1820s	Upper class	Residential
Simmons-Edwards House	1800–1880s	1820s–1850s	Upper class	Residential
Simmons-Edwards House	Late 1800s	1850–1900	Upper class	Residential
South Adger's Wharf	1710–1760	1710–1750s	Public	Dump/market
South Adger's Wharf	1760–1804	1750s–1820s	Public	Market
Visitor Reception and Transportation Center (VRTC)	1790s–1880s	1850–1900	Moderate	Mixed
RURAL SITES				
Cowpens, The	1732–1751	1750s–1820s		
Miller site/Le Sade	1670–1690s	1670–1700		
St. Giles Kussoe	1674–1683	1670–1700		
Stobo Plantation	1741–1781	1750s–1820s		

APPENDIX 3

Vernacular and Scientific Names for Plants and Animals

Vernacular Names	Scientific Names
TREES, SHRUBS, AND GRASSES	
Alders	*Alnus* spp.
American hollies	*Ilex opaca*
Bald cypresses	*Taxodium distichum*
Bayberries	*Morella caroliniensis*
Bearsfoots or hairy leafcups	*Smallanthus uvedalius*
Beeches	*Fagus grandifolia*
Black walnuts	*Juglans nigra*
Blackberries	*Rubus* spp.
Blackgums	*Nyssa sylvatica*
Blueberries	*Vaccinium* spp.
Cabbage palmettos	*Sabal palmetto*
Canarygrass	*Phalaris caroliniana*
Chinquapins	*Castanea pumila*
Cockleburs	*Xanthium strumarium*
Cordgrass	*Spartina patens*
Eastern redcedars	*Juniperus virginiana*
Fuzzybeans	*Strophostyles* spp.
Giant, river, or switchcanes	*Arundinaria* spp.
Goosefoots	*Chenopodium* spp.
Goosegrasses	*Eleusine* spp.
Grapes	*Vitis* spp.
Grasses	*Andropogon* spp., *Aristida* spp., *Panicum* spp.
Greenbriers	*Smilax* spp.
Groundnuts	*Apios* spp.
Hackberries	*Celtis* spp.

(*continued*)

Vernacular Names	Scientific Names
Hazelnuts	*Corylus* spp.
Hercules' clubs	*Zanthoxylum clava-herculis*
Hickories	*Carya glabra, C. pallida, C. tomentosa*
Knotweeds	*Polygonum* spp.
Laurel oaks	*Quercus laurifolia*
Live oaks	*Quercus virginiana*
Loblolly bays	*Gordonia lasianthus*
Longleaf pines	*Pinus palustris*
Magnolias	*Magnolia grandiflora*
Mulberries	*Morus* spp.
Oaks	*Quercus* spp.
Passionflowers or maypops	*Passiflora incarnata*
Persimmons	*Diospyros* spp.
Pigweeds	*Amaranthus* spp.
Pokeweeds	*Phytolacca americana*
Pond pines	*Pinus serotina*
Purslanes	*Portulaca* spp.
Red maples	*Acer rubrum*
Redbays	*Persea borbonia*
Saltgrasses	*Spartina* spp.
Saw palmettos	*Serenoa repens*
Slash pines	*Pinus elliottii*
Smartweeds	*Polygonum* spp.
Spanish moss	*Tillandsia usneoides*
Spurges	*Euphorbia* spp.
Sumacs	*Rhus* spp.
Sunflowers	*Helianthus annuus*
Swamp tupelos	*Nyssa biflora*
Sweetgums	*Liquidambar styraciflua*
Water tupelos	*Nyssa aquatica*
Wax myrtles	*Morella cerifera*
Widgeongrasses	*Ruppia maritima*
Wild onions and garlics	*Allium* spp.
Wild plums and cherries	*Prunus* spp.
Willows	*Salix* spp.
Yaupons	*Ilex vomitoria*

AMERICAN CULTIGENS

Beans	*Phaseolus vulgaris*
Corn or maize	*Zea mays*

Vernacular Names	Scientific Names
Peanuts	*Arachis hypogaea*
Peppers	*Capsicum* spp.
Potatoes	*Solanum tuberosum*
Sea Island cotton	*Gossypium barbadense*
Squashes	*Cucurbita pepo*
Sweetpotato	*Ipomoea batatas*
Tobacco	*Nicotiana* spp.
Tomatoes	*Solanum lycopersicum*
Upland cotton	*Gossypium hirsutum*

OLD WORLD CULTIGENS

Barley	*Hordeum vulgare*
Brassicas, broccoli, cauliflower, turnips, kale	*Brassica* spp.
Buckwheat	*Fagopyrum esculentum*
Indigo	*Indigofera tinctoria*
Okras	*Abelmoschus esculentus*
Oranges	*Citrus* spp.
Peaches	*Prunus persica*
Peas	*Pisum sativum*
Rice	*Oryza sativa*
Watermelon	*Citrullus* spp.
Wheat	*Triticum* spp.

WILD MAMMALS

Beavers	*Castor canadensis*
Black bears	*Ursus americanus*
Bobcats	*Lynx rufus*
Cottontails	*Sylvilagus floridanus*
Fox squirrels	*Sciurus niger*
Gray foxes	*Urocyon cinereoargenteus*
Gray squirrels	*Sciurus carolinensis*
Marsh rabbits	*Sylvilagus palustris*
Minks	*Neovison (Mustela) vison*
Mountain lions	*Puma (Felis) concolor*
Muskrats	*Ondatra zibethicus*
Opossums	*Didelphis virginiana*
Otters	*Lontra canadensis*
Rabbits	*Sylvilagus* spp.
Raccoons	*Procyon lotor*
Skunks	*Mephitis mephitis*

(continued)

Vernacular Names	Scientific Names
Squirrels	*Sciurus* spp.
White-tailed deer	*Odocoileus virginianus*
Wolves	*Canis lupus*
Woodrats	*Neotoma floridana*

WILD BIRDS

Black ducks	*Anas rubripes*
Blue-winged teals	*Anas discors*
Buzzards/vultures	*Cathartes* sp.
Canada geese	*Branta canadensis*
Coots and rails	Rallidae
Dabbling ducks	*Anas* spp.
Diving ducks	*Aythya* spp.
Doves and pigeons	Columbidae
Ducks	Anatinae
Ducks and geese	Anatidae
Geese	Anserinae
Great blue herons	*Ardea herodias*
Grebes	Podicipedidae
Gulls	Laridae
Hawks	*Buteo* spp.
Hawks and eagles	Accipitridae
Herons and egrets	Ardeidae
Herring gulls	*Larus argentatus*
Laughing gulls	*Leucophaeus (Larus) atricilla*
Mallards	*Anas platyrhynchos*
Mourning doves	*Zenaida macroura*
Passenger pigeons	*Ectopistes migratorius*
Pied-billed grebes	*Podilymbus podiceps*
Plovers	Charadriiformes
Quails	*Colinus virginianus*
Quails and turkeys	Phasianidae
Ring-necked pheasants	*Phasianus colchicus*
Sandpipers	Scolopacidae
Shovelers	*Anas clypeata*
Snowy egrets	*Egretta thula*
Terns	*Sterna* spp.
Turkeys	*Meleagris gallopavo*
Wood ducks	*Aix sponsa*

Vernacular Names	Scientific Names

TURTLES AND ALLIGATORS

Alligators	*Alligator mississippiensis*
Box turtles	*Terrapene carolina*
Chicken turtles	*Deirochelys reticularia*
Common cooters	*Pseudemys concinna floridana*
Cooters	*Pseudemys* spp.
Diamondback terrapins	*Malaclemys terrapin*
Green sea turtles	*Chelonia mydas*
Loggerhead sea turtles	*Caretta caretta*
Map turtles	*Graptemys* sp.
Mud and musk turtles	Kinosternidae
Mud turtles	*Kinosternon subrubrum*
Musk turtles	*Sternotherus odoratus*
Pond turtles	Emydidae
River cooters	*Pseudemys (Chrysemys) concinna*
Sea turtles	Cheloniidae
Slider turtles	*Trachemys* spp.
Snapping turtles	*Chelydra serpentina*
Softshell turtles	*Apalone* spp.
Yellow-bellied slider	*Trachemys scripta*

SHARKS, RAYS, AND BONY FISHES

Atlantic croakers	*Micropogonias undulatus*
Atlantic salmon	*Salmo* sp.
Atlantic sturgeons	*Acipenser oxyrinchus*
Bigeye jacks	*Caranx* sp.
Black drums	*Pogonias cromis*
Bluefishes	*Pomatomus saltatrix*
Bowfins	*Amia calva*
Bullhead catfishes	*Ameiurus* spp.
Cartilaginous fishes	Chondrichthyes
Catfishes	Siluriformes
Channel catfishes	*Ictalurus* sp.
Channel catfishes	*Ictalurus punctatus*
Codfishes	cf. Gadidae
Crevalle jacks	*Caranx hippos*
Dogfish sharks	Squaliformes
Drums	Sciaenidae
Eared sunfishes	*Lepomis* sp.

(continued)

Vernacular Names	Scientific Names
Flounders	*Paralichthys* spp.
Flounders	*Paralichthys lethostigma*
Freshwater catfishes	Ictaluridae
Gafftopsail catfishes	*Bagre marinus*
Gags	*Mycteroperca microlepis*
Gars	*Lepisosteus* spp.
Great white shark	*Carcharodon carcharias* (fossil)
Ground sharks	Carcharhiniformes
Groupers	Serranidae
Groupers	*Epinephelus* spp.
Grunts	*Haemulon* spp.
Hardhead catfishes	*Ariopsis felis*
Herrings	Clupeidae
Jacks	Carangidae
Kingfishes	*Menticirrhus* spp.
Largemouth basses	*Micropterus* spp.
Largemouth basses	*Micropterus salmoides*
Longnose gars	*Lepisosteus osseus*
Mackerels and tunas	Scombridae
Mullets	*Mugil* sp.
Parrotfishes	*Sparisoma* sp.
Perches	Percidae
Perch-like fishes	Perciformes
Pigfishes	*Orthopristis chrysoptera*
Porbeagles	*Lamna nasus*
Porcupinefishes	Diodontidae
Porgies	Sparidae
Queen triggerfishes	*Balistes vetula*
Red drums	*Sciaenops ocellatus*
Red snappers	*Lutjanus campechanus*
Redear sunfishes	*Lepomis microlophus*
Requiem sharks	Carcharhinidae
Rock sea basses	*Centropristis philadelphica*
Scups	*Stenotomus* spp.
Scups	*Stenotomus chrysops*
Sea basses/blackfishes	*Centropristis* spp.
Sea catfishes	Ariidae
Searobins	Triglidae
Searobins	*Prionotus* sp.
Seatrouts	*Cynoscion* spp.

Vernacular Names	Scientific Names
Sheepsheads	*Archosargus probatocephalus*
Skates and rays	Rajiformes
Snappers	Lutjanidae
Snappers	*Lutjanus* sp.
Spotted seatrouts	*Cynoscion nebulosus*
Spotted suckers	*Minytrema melanops*
Stingrays	Dasyatidae
Striped basses	*Morone* spp.
Striped basses	*Morone saxatilis*
Suckers	Catostomidae
Sunfishes	Centrarchidae
Thread herrings	*Opisthonema oglinum*
Yellow perches	*Perca flavescens*
Weakfishes	*Cynoscion* spp.

DOMESTIC MAMMALS

Cows	*Bos taurus*
European domestic rabbits	*Oryctolagus cuniculus*
Goats	*Capra hircus*
Domestic guinea pigs	*Cavia porcellus*
Pigs, swine, hogs	*Sus scrofa*
Sheep	*Ovis aries*
Sheep and/or goats	Caprinae
Domestic birds	
Chickens	*Gallus gallus*
Common pigeons, rock doves	*Columba livia*
Muscovy ducks	*Cairina moschata*

COMMENSAL ANIMALS

Black rats	*Rattus rattus*
Bluebirds	*Sialia sialis*
Bluejays	*Cyanocitta cristata*
Bobolinks	*Dolichonyx oryzivorus*
Cardinals	*Cardinalis cardinalis*
Carolina parakeet	*Conuropsis carolinensis*
Cats	*Felis catus*
Crows	*Corvus brachyrhynchos*
Deer mice	*Peromyscus* spp.
Dogs	*Canis familiaris*
Dogs, foxes, wolves	Canidae
Dogs, wolves	*Canis* spp.

(continued)

Vernacular Names	Scientific Names
Falcons	Falconidae
Finches and sparrows	Emberizidae
Flycatchers	Muscicapidae
Frogs and toads	Anura
Hispid cotton rats	*Sigmodon hispidus*
Horses	*Equus caballus*
Horses, mules, donkeys	*Equus* spp.
House mice	*Mus musculus*
Mockingbirds and thrashers	Mimidae
Moles	Talpidae
Non-poisonous snakes	Colubridae
Norway or brown rats	*Rattus norvegicus*
Old World rats	*Rattus* spp.
Perching birds	Passeriformes
Pit vipers	Crotalinae
Red-winged blackbirds	*Agelaius phoeniceus*
Rose-ringed parakeet	*Psittacula krameri*
Robins	*Turdus migratorius*
Screech owls	*Megascops (Otis) asio*
Southern toads	*Anaxyrus (Bufo) terrestris*
Spadefoot toads	*Scaphiopus holbrookii*
Toads	*Bufo* spp.
True frogs	*Rana* sp.

Note: The USDA Plants Database is used as the authority for vernacular and scientific names of plants, and the Integrated Taxonomic Information System is used as the authority for the names of animals. Some names were revised subsequent to the original zooarchaeological work. These name changes may not be reflected in this list.

APPENDIX 4

Charleston Artifact Assemblage

Artifact Categories	1680–1710	1710–1750	1750–1820	1820–1850	1850–1900
KITCHEN AND FOODWAYS					
Porcelain, Chinese, blue underglaze	8	304	3955	1199	945
Porcelain, Chinese, enameled	1	14	579	177	107
Porcelain, English		2	22		
Porcelain, Canton				29	112
Porcelain, Mazarine blue				1	2
Brown salt-glazed stoneware	61	123	98	143	97
Gray salt-glazed stoneware, miscellaneous	10	44	372	46	60
Rhenish stoneware	1	139	704	129	53
Nottingham stoneware	4	48	244	122	53
British brown stoneware	1	4	20		4
Slip-dipped white salt-glazed stoneware	18	27	167	4	1
White salt-glazed stoneware, molded		289	2293	296	250
Scratch blue stoneware		17	117	19	8
Littler's blue stoneware		1			
Elers ware			60	15	15
Black basalt ware			38	19	21
Stoneware bottle			14	1	
Stoneware, var.	6	28	245		
North Devon gravel-tempered ware	19	68	257		5
North Devon sgraffito slipware	2	14	391	9	5
Manganese Mottled ware	29	73	469	25	24
Slip-coated ware	1	11	35	2	4
Staffordshire slipware, combed and trailed	65	1096	5665	890	712
Buckley earthenware		31	125	19	14
Lead-glazed coarse earthenware	37	238	1970	389	374
Unglazed earthenware	2	10	135	112	123

(continued)

Artifact Categories	1680–1710	1710–1750	1750–1820	1820–1850	1850–1900
French green-glazed coarse earthenware	1	24	68	1	8
Saintonge wares	1	3	13		
Olive Jar	2	16	60	13	4
El Morro ware		1	33		
American red-bodied slipware		21	319	59	71
Mid-Atlantic earthenwares		4	81	13	13
Coarse earthenwares, miscellaneous		4	135		
Spanish wares; greyware	1		1	7	
Delftware, undecorated	58	512	1840	341	268
Delftware, decorated	49	296	2240	203	155
Faience, var.	1	3	47	11	7
Majolica, var.	1	3	25	1	
Astbury ware		5	104	14	15
Agate ware		14	144	32	9
Jackfield ware		9	129	19	29
Colono ware, var.	5	482	905	132	49
Colono ware, Yaughan	13	112	199	85	56
Colono ware, Lesesne	9	273	606	216	123
Colono ware, River Burnished	1	8	54	42	25
Native American pottery, historic period	8	28	98		1
Whieldon ware		41	234	39	38
Creamware		69	8017	3497	2252
Creamware, enameled		1	75	22	29
Creamware, transfer-printed		2	22	11	5
Creamware, other					2
Pearlware, undecorated			1585	1595	969
Pearlware, blue painted			499	420	258
Pearlware, polychrome painted			167	322	160
Pearlware, shell-edged		1	357	435	215
Pearlware, annular			272	413	327
Pearlware, transfer-printed			399	819	684
Whiteware, undecorated				1434	2289
Whiteware, painted				124	128
Whiteware, shell-edged				62	92
Whiteware, blue transfer-printed				510	672
Whiteware, other transfer-printed				208	208
Whiteware, sponged				34	28
Whiteware, stamped					2
Whiteware, annular				206	216
Whiteware, decaled					10
Whiteware, gilt					29
Whiteware, sprigged				11	7

Artifact Categories	1680–1710	1710–1750	1750–1820	1820–1850	1850–1900
Whiteware, flow blue				18	21
Whiteware, tinted				3	6
Yellow ware				58	119
Rockingham ware				22	43
Luster ware				28	12
Canary ware				1	4
Portobello ware				6	12
Stoneware, 19th-century, var.				314	191
Stoneware, albany-slipped				3	12
Stoneware, alkaline-glazed				12	23
Ginger beer bottle				5	9
White porcelain				135	662
White porcelain, gilt					16
Parian ware					3
Porcelain, soft-paste				2	7
Container glass, olive green	382	5124	22340	5824	5785
Pharmaceutical glass, aqua	14	148	1096	105	427
Container glass, aqua	14	283		852	584
Container glass, clear			2071	2743	5114
Container glass, amber				19	286
Container glass, brown				121	1451
Container glass, blue				60	395
Container glass, manganese				59	69
Milk glass				36	85
Table glass, var.	6	102	1346	490	537
Goblet		8	89	19	8
Tumbler		3	113	13	105
Cutlery		5	35	20	20
Kettle, iron		3	56	4	27
Tin can				51	1482
ARCHITECTURAL ITEMS					
Nail fragment	125	259	4856	3126	3731
Nail, unidentifiable	86	1663	9472	6346	8290
Nail, wrought	61	75	523	651	1009
Nail, machine cut		3	292	737	1849
Nail, wire				18	148
Nail, brass		1	29	36	86
Window glass, aqua	111	853	10140	4849	10658
Window glass, clear				1060	2400
Window glass, other				554	579
Spike		15	95	65	63
Hardware, miscellaneous		17	86	39	64

(*continued*)

Artifact Categories	1680–1710	1710–1750	1750–1820	1820–1850	1850–1900
Delft tile	3	7	250	27	194
Lead window came			1		10
ARMS AND MUNITIONS					
Musket ball, lead shot	2	14	61	20	63
Gunflint	1	8	21	12	16
Flint debitage	17	5	283	13	34
Percussion cap				3	5
Shell casing			5	13	36
CLOTHING AND SEWING					
Button, 1-hole bone		4	88	73	101
Button, 4-hole bone				17	182
Button, porcelain				12	214
Button, brass	3	12	109	79	86
Button, iron					11
Button, shell				9	94
Button, glass		5	23	1	3
Hook and eye			5	16	20
Glass bead		22	90	32	30
Buckle		6	45	14	24
Thimble		1	6	2	7
Straight pin		5	193	88	263
Scissors				1	3
Collar stud				2	19
Grommet					29
Lace bobbin			3	4	8
PERSONAL POSSESSIONS					
Toothbrush				7	31
Coin		1	17	17	28
Slate pencil		4	18	21	35
Parasol part			7	3	2
Fan		1	18	5	13
Pocket watch			3	4	3
Clock/watch					3
Paste jewel			5	3	2
Jewelry, miscellaneous			5	3	6
Wig curler		1	2	1	
Key			4	2	6
Eyeglass lens			1	2	3
Ruler				1	3
Comb				1	22

Artifact Categories	1680–1710	1710–1750	1750–1820	1820–1850	1850–1900
Musical instrument					2
Game piece (dice, domino, disc)			3	3	5
FURNITURE					
Upholstery tack		7	84	39	65
Furniture hardware, miscellaneous		1	48	44	65
Lamp hardware, miscellaneous				1	5
Lamp glass				9	76
Figurine			2	3	
Chandelier prism					2
TOBACCO PIPES					
Pipe stem, kaolin	125	992	5523	793	706
Pipe bowl, kaolin	50	195	873	138	95
Pipe, other				4	4
ACTIVITIES					
Barrel band (storage)	12	103	424	192	178
Tool, miscellaneous (construction, maintenance)		7	18	5	18
Equestrian (horseshoe, bit, saddle boss)	1	2	3	1	2
Fish/net weight (fishing)	1		4		2
Bale seal (shipping/mercantile)		7	5	6	3
Flower pot (gardening)		19	39	80	670
Toy, misc. (children's activities)			5	8	10
Marble		1	27	26	77
Doll			1	3	24
Lead, scrap (by-product)	2	10	38	14	9
Iron, scrap (by-product)		14	209	7	
Brass, scrap (by-product)	3	10	30		18

Note: Artifact tabulations do not include all Charleston sites. For more information, see the individual site reports (appendix 1). Sites included in each time period are: 1680–1710, Beef Market, South Adger's Wharf; 1710–1750, Beef Market, Dock Street Theatre, First Trident, Heyward-Washington House, McCrady's Tavern and Long Room, Powder Magazine, John Rutledge House, South Adger's Wharf; 1750–1820, Atlantic Wharf, Beef Market, Miles Brewton House, Exchange Building, William Gibbes House; Heyward-Washington House, Lodge Alley, McCrady's Tavern and Long Room, Powder Magazine, Nathaniel Russell House, John Rutledge House, Simmons-Edwards House, South Adger's Wharf; 1820–1850, Aiken-Rhett House, Beef Market, First Trident, William Gibbes House, Hieronymous-Roper House, Lodge Alley, McCrady's Tavern and Long Room, Powder Magazine, President Street, Nathaniel Russell House, John Rutledge House, Simmons-Edwards House; 1850–1900, Aiken-Rhett House, Miles Brewton House, Exchange Building, Heyward-Washington House, Hieronymous-Roper House, Jackson House, Powder Magazine, President Street, Nathaniel Russell House, Simmons-Edwards House, Visitor Reception and Transportation Center.

APPENDIX 5

Master Species List by MNI and Time Period

	1710–1750	1750–1820	1820–1850	1850–1900	Total
# of taxa (richness)	59	86	104	82	155
Total MNI	296	606	760	509	2171
Cows	46	75	110	45	276
Goats		3	4		7
Pigs	26	55	74	42	197
Sheep	1	6	4		11
Sheep and/or goats	26	23	30	24	103
Chickens	36	67	104	89	296
Common pigeons	2	5	7	5	19
Muscovy ducks	1	2	2		5
Beavers			1		1
Black bears	1				1
Fox squirrels			2		2
Minks		1			1
Muskrats		2			2
Opossums	3	3	7	5	18
Rabbits		4	3	1	8
Raccoons	3	2	1	3	9
Squirrels	1	3	4	2	10
White-tailed deer	7	18	28	8	61
Black ducks		2			2
Blue-winged teals			1		1
Buzzards/vultures			1		1
Canada geese	4	16	21	6	47
Coots and rails			1	1	2
Dabbling ducks	1	11	10	2	24
Diving ducks		1	2		3
Doves and pigeons	1	1			2
Ducks				1	1

(*continued*)

	1710–1750	1750–1820	1820–1850	1850–1900	Total
Ducks and geese	9	7	2	4	22
Geese		1			1
Grebes		1			1
Hawks and eagles				1	1
Herons and egrets				1	1
Herring gulls			1		1
Laughing gulls				1	1
Mallards		2	3	7	12
Mourning doves		1			1
Passenger pigeons			1	1	2
Plovers	1		1		2
Possible sandpipers				1	1
Possible turkeys				1	1
Quails	1	2	1	2	6
Quails and turkeys			1		1
Ring-necked pheasants			1		1
Sandpipers		2			2
Shovelers		1			1
Snowy egrets			1		1
Terns			2		2
Turkeys	11	16	30	16	73
Wood ducks		1		1	2
Alligators	1		1		2
Box turtles			1		1
Chicken turtles	2	4	5	3	14
Common cooters				2	2
Cooters	2	1	8	2	13
Diamondback terrapins	2	10	8	10	30
Loggerhead sea turtles			1		1
Map turtles			1		1
Mud and musk turtles		2	2		4
Pond turtles	2	3	1	3	9
River cooters			1	2	3
Sea turtles	6	7	6	2	21
Slider turtles	1	3	5	3	12
Snapping turtles		1	3		4
Softshell turtles		2	2	1	5
Unidentified turtles	1		1		2
Atlantic croakers	4	5	7	8	24
Atlantic salmon				1	1
Atlantic sturgeons		1	1	1	3
Bigeye jacks				1	1
Black drums	4	10	4	8	26
Bluefishes		2	3		5

	1710–1750	1750–1820	1820–1850	1850–1900	Total
Cartilaginous fishes	1	2	1		4
Catfishes		1		2	3
Channel catfishes			1		1
Channel catfishes		2		1	3
Codfishes			1		1
Crevalle jacks			1		1
Dogfish sharks			1	2	3
Drums	2		2		4
Eared sunfishes	1				1
Flounders	7	11	4	2	24
Flounders				1	1
Freshwater catfishes				1	1
Gafftopsail catfishes	6	13	12	6	37
Gags			3		3
Gars	2	3	2		7
Great white sharks			1		1
Ground sharks	2	2			4
Groupers		2			2
Groupers		2			2
Grunts		1		1	2
Hardhead catfishes	6	22	20	6	54
Herrings				1	1
Jacks		2		1	3
Kingfishes	2	2	1	1	6
Largemouth basses		1		1	2
Mackerels and tunas			1		1
Mullets	5	9	10	4	28
Parrotfishes		1			1
Perches	1		1		2
Perch-like fishes				1	1
Pigfishes		2	1	1	4
Porbeagles			1		1
Porcupinefishes		1			1
Porgies	1		1		2
Queen triggerfishes			1		1
Red drums	4	7	11	3	25
Red snappers			1		1
Redear sunfishes				1	1
Requiem sharks	1	1	3	1	6
Rock sea basses		5		1	6
Scups		9	8	4	21
Scups				3	3
Sea basses/blackfishes	7	18	17	15	57

(continued)

	1710–1750	1750–1820	1820–1850	1850–1900	Total
Sea catfishes			1		1
Searobins	1				1
Searobins		1			1
Seatrouts	5	8	8	5	26
Sheepsheads	2	5	9	8	24
Skates and rays	1				1
Snappers		1	2	1	4
Snappers				1	1
Spotted seatrouts		3	2		5
Stingrays			1		1
Striped basses		1	1	1	3
Thread herrings			1		1
Unidentified fishes			1		1
Black rats	3	8	2	3	16
Bluebirds				1	1
Bluejays		1			1
Cardinals			1		1
Cats	4	6	11	15	36
Deer mice		1	4		5
Dogs		4	3	9	16
Dogs, foxes, wolves	1				1
Dogs, wolves	2	1	1		4
Finches and sparrows		1		1	2
Flycatchers	1	1		1	3
Frogs and toads		1	8	2	11
Hispid cotton rats		1	2	1	4
Horses			8	2	10
Horses, mules, donkeys		1		1	2
House mice			2	3	5
Mockingbirds and thrashers			1		1
Non-poisonous snakes			1		1
Norway or Brown rats	6	3	20	1	30
Old World rats	11	52	34	74	171
Perching birds	1		2		3
Robins	2				2
Screech owls				1	1
Southern toads			3		3
Spadefoot toads	1	2	1		4
Toads		1		1	2
True frogs			1		1
Unidentified rodents	1				1

Note: The Minimum Number of Individuals (MNI) is an estimate of the lowest number of individuals of each species that would be necessary to explain the skeletal remains in the collection. See appendix 3 for scientific names.

APPENDIX 6

Richness, Number of Identified Specimens, MNI,
and Specimen Weight by Time Period

Site	Richness	NISP	MNI	Weight (gm)	Date of Deposits
1710–1750					
Beef Market/City Hall	8	1377	11	6440.14	1692–1739
Beef Market/City Hall	23	13007	36	23800.21	1739–1760
Dock Street Theatre	24	1748	51	1502.47	1736–1750s
First Trident	14	572	15	3268.90	1740s
Heyward-Washington House	12	606	16	2076.28	1730–1740
Heyward-Washington House	26	2296	34	4919.95	1740–1750
McCrady's Tavern	5	23	5	323.86	1720–1750
Post Office (McKenzie House)	19	2595	59	23339.27	1725–1769
Powder Magazine	19	1483	30	9741.49	1712–1750
Rutledge House	9	213	9	1226.33	1730s–1760s
South Adger's Wharf	16	1023	30	5292.03	1710–1760
1710–50 Totals		24943	296	81930.93	
1750–1820					
Atlantic Wharf	27	2826	65	9221.50	1790s–1820s
Beef Market/City Hall	23	15949	42	21159.42	1760–1796
Brewton House (Brewton)	26	2782	39	5090.25	1750–1770
Exchange Building/Half Moon Battery	4	57	5	374.40	1750–1790
First Trident	22	596	27	2956.12	1740s–1790s
Heyward-Washington House	28	2429	46	6767.83	1750–1820
Lodge Alley/State Street	17	2570	30	11827.12	18th century, 2nd half
McCrady's Tavern and Long Room	15	575	30	3852.87	1770s–1780s

Site					
Powder Magazine	19	1549	41	4025.41	1751–1820
Russell House (pre-Russell)	20	2023	31	15559.01	1730–1808
Rutledge House	19	2867	33	10298.28	1760s–1820s
Simmons-Edwards House (Brewton trash)	41	13083	140	47751.92	Late 1700s
South Adger's Wharf	31	3685	77	19928.74	1760–1804
1750–1820 Totals		50991	606	158812.87	
1820–1850					
Aiken-Rhett House	4	17	4	156.25	1818–1830
Aiken-Rhett House	20	531	29	767.72	1830–1850
Beef Market/City Hall	17	2900	21	6997.94	Early 19th century
Brewton House (Motte-Alston)	34	6076	62	16488.16	1775–1830
Charleston Place	51	11017	289	33604.98	1730s–late 1800s
Exchange Building	12	208	16	873.10	Mid-19th century
First Trident	33	4155	76	5091.40	Federal, 1790s–1840s
Gibbes House	17	1108	27	4393.73	1772–1830s
Kohne-Leslie House	6	142	6	388.78	Early to mid-1800s
Lodge Alley/State Street	10	500	14	2665.88	19th century, 1st half
McCrady's Tavern	6	84	8	629.51	Early 19th century
Powder Magazine	16	1078	27	6292.21	1820–1850
President Street/MUSC	6	148	6	296.18	Mid-19th century
Russell House (Russell)	22	3440	65	28811.18	1808–1857
Rutledge House	11	303	11	536.73	Post-1820s

(continued)

Appendix 6—*Continued*

Site	Richness	NISP	MNI	Weight (gm)	Date of Deposits
Simmons-Edwards House	40	5346	99	18231.74	1800–1880s
1820–50 Totals		37053	760	126225.49	
1850–1900					
Aiken-Rhett House	25	1585	48	4696.39	1870–1900
Aiken-Rhett House	6	56	6	129.04	1850–1870
Brewton House (Pringle-Frost)	43	7383	80	7512.12	1840s–1880
Dupre House	6	274	14	1079.59	Mid- to late 1800s
Exchange Building	6	37	6	200.90	Late 19th century
Heyward-Washington House	22	1502	35	3498.62	Late 19th century
Hieronymous-Roper House	9	429	19	2121.91	1800–1870
Jackson House	23	4206	153	5166.32	Mid- to late 1800s
Kohne-Leslie House	6	183	9	795.86	Mid- to late 1800s
Powder Magazine	16	1082	22	4259.53	1851–1900
President Street/MUSC	9	250	11	1114.40	Late 19th century
Russell House (Sisters of Charity)	10	331	11	1641.98	1870–1908
Simmons-Edwards House	23	1428	32	2848.47	Late 1800s
Visitor Reception and Transportation Center	22	1630	46	2953.66	1790s–1880s
1850–1900 Totals		21322	509	45576.37	
TOTAL URBAN CHARLESTON		134309	2171	412545.66	

Note: Richness refers to the number of taxa for which the Minimum Number of Individuals (MNI) is estimated. *NISP* refers to the number of identified specimens. See appendix 1 for references for each location.

NOTES

Chapter 1. Pots, Bones, and the Urban Landscape

1. Richard Barry, *Mr. Rutledge of South Carolina*, 44.

2. The term *lowcountry* refers to the coastal region of South Carolina, from the Atlantic Ocean to about 40 miles inland. According to Richard Porcher, the lowcountry begins where freshwater rivers first respond to tidal influence. The lowcountry environment and economy were dominated by plantations. See Kovacik and Winberry, *South Carolina*, 7; Porcher and Judd, *Market Preparation*, 1.

3. Time and space limit our ability to discuss Charleston in the larger contexts of the American urban experience and urban archaeological studies. To focus our Charleston study on foodways and animals, entire topics have been omitted. We have excavated and written extensively on landscapes and gardening but do not specifically discuss pleasure gardens in this volume, even though bone used as fertilizer was recovered and analyzed. We do not elaborate upon the anthropological theories that underlie our research, though astute colleagues will likely perceive our theoretical approach. Nor do we discuss the vagaries of the methods and materials featured in this volume; they are discussed at length in site reports and scholarly articles and would distract readers from the trajectory of the evolving urban environment.

4. Rothschild and Wall, *Archaeology of American Cities*; Staski, "Advances in Urban Archaeology."

5. Jackson, *Discovering the Vernacular Landscape*, 7–8.

6. Leone and Potter, *Recovery of Meaning*; see also O'Day et al., *Behaviour behind Bones*; King, *Archaeology, Narrative*.

7. Our examination of provisioning strategies follows the example provided for Williamsburg, Virginia, by Walsh et al., "Provisioning."

8. Arnott, *Gastronomy*; Douglas, "Deciphering a Meal," 249; Douglas, "Standard Social Uses"; see also Ferris, "Edible South"; Hooker, *Food and Drink*, 105–6, 113; Hooker, *Colonial Plantation Cookbook*, 19.

9. Armelagos, "You Are What You Eat"; Dennell, "Prehistoric Diet"; Farb and Armelagos, *Consuming Passions*, 190; Miracle and Milner, *Consuming Passions*.

10. Fenton and Kisban, *Food in Change*; Fisher, *Albion's Seed*, 199; Gabaccia, *We Are What We Eat*; Mennell et al., *Sociology of Food*.

11. Mintz, *Sweetness and Power*; see also Jochim, *Hunter-Gatherer Subsistence*.

12. Neither state existed during much of our study period, but a detailed description of changing boundaries and claims is beyond the scope of this volume.

13. For archaeology and ethnic affiliation, see Deagan, "Mestizaje"; Joseph and Zierden, *Another's Country*; Reitz et al., *Mission and Pueblo,* 20–29; VanDerwarker et al., "Farming and Foraging."

14. Agha, "St. Giles Kussoe," 5, 20–28; Lyon, *Enterprise of Florida,* 49–50; Waselkov and Gums, "Plantation Archaeology," 39, 63–97; see also Deagan, "Mestizaje"; Reitz and Scarry, *Reconstructing Historic Subsistence;* Silvia, "Native American."

15. See Bolton and Ross, *Debatable Land;* Wright, *Anglo-Spanish Rivalry.*

16. Each archaeological project is discussed in site reports listed in appendix 1. All site reports produced by The Charleston Museum are available online at www.charlestonmuseum.org.

Chapter 2. Urban Archaeology in the Historic City of Charleston

1. Salwen, "Archaeology in Megalopolis," 453; see also Cressey et al., "Core–Periphery"; Dickens, *Archaeology of Urban America;* Rothschild and Wall, *Archaeology of American Cities;* Salwen, "Foreword."

2. Honerkamp et al., "Archaeological Investigation."

3. Deagan, *Spanish St. Augustine;* Zierden and Calhoun, "Archaeological Preservation Plan."

4. Schiffer, "Toward a Unified Science; Schiffer, "Toward the Identification"; see also Fairbanks, "Backyard Archaeology."

5. South, *Method and Theory.*

6. D. Rosengarten et al., "Between the Tracks."

7. Deetz, "Prologue"; Handsman, "Class Histories," 6; Herman, *Town House;* Leone, "Interpreting Ideology." For an insightful discussion of interpretation of landscape, see King, *Archaeology, Narrative.*

8. For detailed discussion of zooarchaeological methods, see Reitz and Wing, *Zooarchaeology.*

Chapter 3. The Bountiful Coast

1. Hugh Talmage Lefler, ed., *A New Voyage to Carolina, by John Lawson,* 14–16.

2. Porcher and Raymer, *Guide to Wildflowers,* xxiii; Sanders and Anderson, *Natural History Investigations,* 12; VanDoran, *Travels of William Bartram.*

3. Edgar, *South Carolina,* 9; Kovacik and Winberry, *South Carolina,* 31; Reitz and Little, "Miller Site."

4. Frey and Howard, "Mesotidal"; Hubbard et al., "Role of Waves"; Kovacik and Winberry, *South Carolina,* 20; Porcher and Raymer, *Guide to Wildflowers,* xxiii.

5. Larson, *Aboriginal Subsistence Technology,* 35; Porcher, *Wildflowers of the Carolina Lowcountry,* 48–49; Porcher and Fick, *Sea Island Cotton,* 30; Shelford, *Ecology,* 56.

6. Lefler, *New Voyage,* 107; Porcher and Raymer, *Guide to Wildflowers,* 303; Stewart "What Nature Suffers," 73, 74, 238; VanDoran, *Travels of William Bartram,* 179–80.

7. Porcher and Raymer, *Guide to Wildflowers,* 303; Stewart, "What Nature Suffers," 238.

8. Porcher and Judd, *Market Preparation,* 28; see also Berlin, *Many Thousands Gone;*

Carney, *Black Rice*; Porcher and Fick, *Sea Island Cotton*; H. R. Smith, "Rich Swamps," 30–34, 41.

9. Clowse, *Economic Beginnings*; Edgar, *South Carolina*; Lefler, *New Voyage*; Silver, *New Face*.

10. Leland and Ressinger, "Ce Pais Tant Desiré," 2–33; "tigers and leopards" likely refers to the American panther and the bobcat, both later hunted as "beasts of prey." The black and white cat was, of course, a skunk.

11. Anderson, "Solid Sufficiency," 79; VanDoran, *Travels of William Bartram*, 232.

12. Lefler, *New Voyage*, 120–55.

13. Schorger, "Domestic Turkey"; Schorger, *Wild Turkey*; Speller et al., "Ancient mtDNA." Tame animals are individuals captured in the wild and raised in captivity. They may not reproduce in captivity and would return to the wild if able to do so. Feral animals were originally domestic but live as wild animals despite their domestic ancestry. Free-ranging animals are domestic animals supervised in some way, though that supervision may be minimal.

14. American Poultry Association, *Standards of Excellence*; Prestwood et al., "Parasitism," 160; South Carolina Society, *Report*.

15. Sprunt and Chamberlain, *South Carolina Bird Life*, 107, 112; American Poultry Association, *Standards of Excellence*.

16. Johnston, "Synanthropic Birds," 51, 61–62.

17. Bent, *Life Histories*, 388–99; Lefler, *New Voyage*, 50; Sprunt and Chamberlain, *South Carolina Bird Life*, 289–90.

18. Turtles are described in Carr, *Handbook of Turtles*; fishes are described in Dahlberg, "Ecological Study"; Dahlberg, *Guide to Coastal Fishes*, 28–31.

19. Richard Parkinson in Gray, *History of Agriculture*, 206.

20. Gray, *History of Agriculture*, 206; Towne and Wentworth, *Pigs*, 7–8; see also Laudonniere, *Three Voyages*, 23; Ribault, *Whole and True Discouerye*, 72.

21. Eckhard, *Digest*, 43; Waring, *History of Medicine*.

22. Rouse, *World Cattle III*; Rouse, *Criollo*; see also Arnade, "Cattle Raising"; Bushnell, "Menéndez Marquéz"; Cáceres, December 12; García, *Dos antiguas*, 206; Griñán, *Relación*; Hann, "Translation," 200; Reitz and Ruff, "Morphometric Data." See chapter 5 for more detailed discussion.

23. Bonner, *Georgia Agriculture*; Thompson, *History of Livestock*, 211; Williamson and Payne, *Introduction*, 19.

24. Stoudemire, *Natural History*, 18; LaFebvre and deFrance, "Guinea Pigs"; Newsom and Wing, *On Land and Sea*, 204–5; Pigière et al., "New Archaeozoological Evidence"; Wing, "Domestication."

25. Clayton, "Muscovy Duck"; Donkin, *Muscovy Duck*, 90–93; Serjeantson, *Birds*, 302; Stahl, "Exploratory Osteological Study."

26. Cáceres, December 12.

27. Hawes, "Pigeons"; Serjeantson, *Birds*, 304–10.

28. Odum and Barrett, *Fundamentals*, 514.

29. Deagan and Cruxent, *Archaeology at La Isabela*, 146; Reitz and Little, "Miller Site"; Reitz and Scarry, *Reconstructing Historic Subsistence*.

30. Hess, *Carolina Rice Kitchen*, 107, F3–4.

Chapter 4. Development of Charleston and the Lowcountry

1. Based on Charles F. Kovacik and John J. Winberry, *South Carolina*, 7, 18.

2. Ribault, *True Discouerye*.

3. Waselkov, "French Colonial Archaeology."

4. Braund, *Deerskins and Duffels*; Martin, "Southeastern Indians"; Merrell, *Indians' New World*.

5. Clowse, *Economic Beginnings*; Edgar, *South Carolina*, 48, 133; Fraser, *Charleston!*; Weir, *Colonial South Carolina*. For a discussion of lessons learned from earlier colonies, see Kupperman, *Jamestown Project*, 2–3.

6. Bates and Leland, *French Santee*; Clowse, *Economic Beginnings*, 88–89; Dunn, *Sugar and Slaves*; Edgar, *South Carolina*; Van Ruymbeke, "Huguenots"; Wood, *Black Majority*.

7. Waddell, *Indians of the South*, 4–6.

8. Lord Anthony Ashley Cooper's correspondence with Indian agent Henry Woodward suggests some subterfuge in maintaining the Proprietors' monopoly. See Agha, "St. Giles Kussoe," 22–23; Fagg, "St. Giles Seigniory;" Lesser, *South Carolina Begins*, 38.

9. Martin, "Southeastern Indians," 310; see also Bowne, *Westo Indians*; Braund, *Deerskins and Duffels*; Gallay, *Indian Slave Trade*; Snell, "Indian Slavery."

10. V. W. Crane, *Southern Frontier*; Lefler, *New Voyage*; Marcoux, *Pox, Empire*, 33, 49–50; Ramsey, *Yamasee War*.

11. Deagan and McMahon, *Fort Mose*; Dunbar, "Colonial Carolina Cowpens"; Otto, "Origins of Cattle-Ranching," "Livestock-Raising"; Stewart, "Whether Wast"; Wood, *Black Majority*.

12. Harmon and Snedeker, "Archaeological Record of Tar and Pitch"; Kovacik and Winberry, *South Carolina*, 70.

13. Carney, *Black Rice*; Chaplin, *Anxious Pursuit*; Edelson, *Plantation Enterprise*; H. R. Smith, "Rich Swamps."

14. Berlin, *Many Thousands Gone*; Kovacik and Winberry, *South Carolina*, 75.

15. Hart, *Building Charleston*, 22; Mathews, "Contemporary View," 153; Poston, *Buildings of Charleston*, 48; Salley, *Records*, 105; Weir, "Charles Town circa 1702," 67.

16. Butler, "Timeline," 201; Leland and Ressinger, "Ce Pais Tant Desiré."

17. Clowse, *Economic Beginnings*, 163; Rogers, *Charleston*; Weir, "Charles Town circa 1702," 66. Wales, Ireland, and Scotland joined with England to become Great Britain in 1707.

18. Braund, *Deerskins and Duffels*; Piker, *Four Deaths*, 6, 250, 299n2; Silver, *New Face*, 94; Waselkov, "Seventeenth-Century Trade."

19. Fraser, *Charleston!* 55, 135; Goldfield, *Cotton Fields*.

20. Butler, "Timeline"; Calhoun, *Scourging Wrath*; Fraser, *Lowcountry Hurricanes*; Herold, "Archaeological Research at the Exchange Building"; *South Carolina Gazette*, September 19, 1752.

21. Lounsbury, *Statehouse to Courthouse*, 14; Savage and Leath, "Buying British"; Weir, *Colonial South Carolina*; see also Joseph, "From Colonist to Charlestonian."

22. Lounsbury, *Statehouse to Courthouse*, 16; Saunders, "'As regular and fformidable,'" 213; Weir, "Charles Town circa 1702." For a discussion of wharf construction, see Joseph et al., "Vendue/Prioleau."

23. Fraser, *Charleston!*, 151; Lefler, *New Voyage*; Rogers, *Charleston*; Taylor, *South Carolina Naturalists*.

24. Borick, *Gallant Defense*; Fraser, *Charleston!*; *Royal Gazette*, July 6, 1780, and September 19, 1780; Shepherd, "Going Up the Country"; Wallace, *South Carolina*, 294.

25. Porcher and Fick, *Sea Island Cotton*.

26. Kovacik and Winberry, *South Carolina*, 72–74; Porcher and Judd, *Market Preparation*.

27. Poston, *Buildings of Charleston*, 197; Powers, *Black Charlestonians*.

28. Fraser, *Reminiscences*, 12–13.

29. Edgar, *South Carolina*; Kelly, *America's Longest Siege*; Rogers, *Charleston*.

30. T. Rosengarten, "Southern Agriculturalist."

31. Fraser, *Charleston!*, 197–98.

32. Powers, *Black Charlestonians*, 11, 17, 37; D. Rosengarten et al., "Between the Tracks."

33. Greene et al., *Slave Badges*; Singleton, "Slave Tag."

34. Powers, *Black Charlestonians*, 31; Robertson, *Denmark Vesey*.

35. Goldfield, "Pursuing the American Dream," 67; Williams, *Charleston's Water*.

36. Edgar, *South Carolina*, 284; Kovacik and Winberry, *South Carolina*, 120; Severens, *Antebellum Architecture*; Waddell, *Charleston in 1883*, xii.

37. Tennant family papers in D. Rosengarten et al., "Between the Tracks," 132; see also T. Rosengarten, *Tombee*, 86.

38. Côté, *Mary's World*; McInnis, *Politics of Taste*, 329; D. Rosengarten et al., "Between the Tracks."

39. Powers, *Black Charlestonians*, 103, 133; see also Harris, *Deep Souths*; Williamson, *After Slavery*.

40. Edgar, *South Carolina*, 379; Harris, *Deep Souths*; T. Rosengarten, *Tombee*; Severens, *Antebellum Architecture*; Waddell, *Charleston in 1883*.

41. Kovacik and Winberry, *South Carolina*, 117; H. R. Smith, "Rich Swamps," 286; H. R. Smith, "Land of Cypress and Pine," 13.

42. Harris, *Deep Souths*; McKinley, *Stinking Stones*, 75–88; Shick and Doyle, "Phosphate Boom."

43. For descriptions of hurricanes and their aftermath, see Doar, *Rice and Rice Planting*; Dusinberre, *Them Dark Days*; Fraser, *Lowcountry Hurricanes*. For discussion of the earthquake and its effects, see Edgar, *South Carolina*; Harris, *Deep Souths*; Powers, *Black Charlestonians*, 265; Stockton, *Great Shock*; Williams and Hoffius, *Upheaval in Charleston*.

44. Waddell, *Charleston in 1883*; Williams, *Charleston's Water*, 43.

45. Hutchisson and Greene, *Renaissance in Charleston*; Severens, *Charleston Renaissance*; Weyeneth, *Historic Preservation*, 2, 20; Lapham, "Notes."

46. Bland, *Preserving Charleston's Past*; Donaldson, "Charleston's Racial Politics," 187.

47. See Upton, "City as Material Culture," 53–54.

48. Zierden and Herman, "Charleston Townhouses"; see also Haney, "In Complete Order," 36; Herman, *Town House*.

Chapter 5. Settlement

1. Based on Andrew Agha, "St. Giles Kussoe and 'The Character of a Loyal States-man,'" and *Calendar of State Papers*, vol. 7.

2. Edgar, *South Carolina*; South, *Archaeological Pathways*; Camunas in Stoner and South, *Exploring 1670 Charles Town*; Weir, *Preface*.

3. Agha, "Miller Site"; Jones and Beeby, "Miller Site Excavations"; South, *Archaeological Pathways*, 40–45; South and Hartley, "Deep Water"; Shaftesbury Papers, 448 in Agha and Philips, "Archaeological Investigations."

4. Shaftesbury Papers, 446, 448 in Agha and Philips, "Archaeological Investigations."

5. South and Hartley, "Deep Water." For their survey, South and Hartley relied on the presence of North Devon wares to indicate seventeenth-century occupations.

6. Hurry et al., "Telling Time."

7. Nöel Hume, *Guide to Artifacts*; Julie King, personal communication, 2014.

8. Deagan, *Artifacts of the Spanish Colonies*, vol. 1, 96; Deagan, "Material Assemblage"; Deagan, "Eliciting Contraband"; King, "Ceramic Variability"; Skowronek, "Empire and Ceramics."

9. Nöel Hume, *Guide to Artifacts*.

10. Stoner, "Towne"; Stoner and South, *Exploring 1670 Charles Town*; see also Agha, "St. Giles Kussoe."

11. Nöel Hume, *Glass*.

12. Marcoux, "Glass Trade Beads."

13. Marcoux, "Using Diversity."

14. Reitz and Waselkov, "Vertebrate Use." For a Spanish colonial example, see Deagan, "Mestizaje"; Deagan, *Spanish St. Augustine*.

15. Wood, *Strange New Land*.

16. Pavao-Zuckerman, "Vertebrate Subsistence"; Pavao-Zuckerman, "Culture, Contact and Subsistence"; Reitz and Little, "Miller Site"; Reitz et al., *Mission and Pueblo*.

17. Orr and Lucas, "Rural–Urban Connections"; Reitz and Bergh, "Animal Remains"; Reitz and Little, "Miller Site"; Reitz and Waselkov, "Vertebrate Use."

18. Nairne, "Letter," 46 in Brooks et al., *Living on the Edge*, 46; Porcher and Raymer, *Guide to Wildflowers*, 53. Porcher notes that the livestock industry depended on a variety of native plants, particularly salt hay (*Spartina patens*), a "high marsh plant of the maritime strand." See also Anderson, *Creatures of Empire*; Arnade, "Cattle Raising"; Bushnell, "Menéndez Marquéz"; Dunbar, "Colonial Carolina Cowpens"; Groover and Brooks, "Catherine Brown Cowpen"; Stewart, *"What Nature Suffers,"* 74; Stewart, "Whether Wast."

19. Nairne, "Letter," 46 in Brooks et al., *Living on the Edge*, 34; see also Otto, "Origins of Cattle-Raising"; Otto, "Livestock-Raising."

20. Agha and Phillips, "Archaeological Investigation"; Dunbar, "Colonial Carolina Cowpens"; Groover and Brooks, "Catherine Brown Cowpen"; Otto, "Origins of Cattle-Ranching"; Otto, "Livestock-Raising"; Rowland et al., *History of Beaufort County*, 87; Stewart, "Whether Wast"; Wood, *Black Majority*, 31.

21. Brooks et al., *Living on the Edge*; Dunbar, "Colonial Carolina Cowpens"; Hann, *Apalachee*; Haygood, "Cows, Ticks, and Disease"; McTavish et al., "New World Cattle"; Otto, "Livestock-Raising"; Reitz and Ruff, "Morphometric Data"; Rouse, *World Cattle III*; Rouse, *Criollo*, 73–77, 89–90; Stewart, "Whether Wast"; Stewart, *"What Nature Suffers,"* 72; Thompson, *History of Livestock Raising*.

22. Gremillion, "Human Ecology"; Groover and Brooks, "Catherine Brown Cowpen";

Stewart, *"What Nature Suffers,"* 73. The term *cowpen* may refer to different types of open-range stock-raising habits elsewhere.

23. Bierer, *History of Animal Plagues*, 6, 8; Haygood, "Cows, Ticks, and Disease"; Stewart, "Whether Wast."

Chapter 6. Raiding and Trading

1. Based on Edward R. McCrady, *History of South Carolina*, 398, and Katherine Saunders, "'As regular and fformidable,'" 204.

2. Dunbar, "Colonial Carolina Cowpens"; see Gallay, *Indian Slave Trade*, 49.

3. Edgar, *South Carolina*, 136; Harmon, *Trade and Privateering*, 83; Mathews, "Contemporary View," 13; see also Deagan, "Eliciting Contraband"; Halbirt, "La Ciudad."

4. Arnade, *Siege of St. Augustine*; Fraser, *Charleston!*; Moore, "1702 Siege"; Taylor, *American Colonies*; Waterbury, "Firestorm and Ashes"; Weir, *Colonial South Carolina*.

5. Cheves, *Collections*, 183; see Crane, *Southern Frontier*, 3; Wright, *Anglo-Spanish Rivalry*.

6. Butler, "Timeline."

7. Herold, "Archaeological Research at the Exchange Building"; Lapham, "Notes"; Saunders, "As regular and fformidable."

8. Similar large cypress piles from the city gate and ravelin on the landward side were exposed by construction of the Judicial Center; two were retrieved and conserved by New South Associates in 1999. New South also recorded a portion of the moat during this construction episode. Most of the archaeological deposits at that site are from later in the eighteenth century. See Hamby and Joseph, "New Look."

9. Davis, "Public Powder Magazines."

10. Deetz, *Flowerdew Hundred*, 4; South, *Method and Theory*, 105; see also Gibb and King, "Gender, Activity Areas, and Homelots"; "Diagnostic Artifacts," www.chesapeake archaeology.org.

11. Anthony, "Colono Wares"; Drucker and Anthony, *Spiers Landing*; Nöel Hume, "Indian Ware"; South, "Palmetto Parapets"; Wheaton and Garrow, "Acculturation"; see also DeCorse, "Oceans Apart"; Ferguson, *Uncommon Ground*; Ferguson, "Medicine and Hygiene"; Ferguson, "Cross."

12. Anthony, "Tangible Interaction"; Cooper and Steen, "Potters"; Ferguson, *Uncommon Ground*.

13. Agha, "St. Giles Kussoe"; Brilliant, "Colonoware"; Marcoux, "Using Diversity"; see also Anthony, "Tangible Interaction"; Brilliant, "Colonoware, Creolization"; Cooper and Steen, "Potters"; Steen, "Stirring the Ethnic Stew."

14. Deagan, "Eliciting Contraband," 106, 112; Halbirt, "La Ciudad"; Harmon, *Trade and Privateering*, 2.

15. Edgar, *South Carolina*, 136, 139–44.

16. Joseph et al., "Vendue/Prioleau," 5; Stevens, *Journals*.

17. Edgar, *South Carolina*, 131; Halbirt, "Apocalypse," 41.

18. Reitz et al., *Mission and Pueblo*; Reitz and Waselkov, "Vertebrate Use"; Zierden and Reitz, "Eighteenth-Century Charleston."

19. Fraser, *Charleston!*, 24; Lisa O'Steen in Hamby and Joseph, "New Look," 189–90;

Journal of the Commons House of Assembly, November 20, 1706–February 8, 1706/7; *South Carolina Gazette,* November 5, 1744.

20. Hann, "Translation"; Boyd et al. in Milanich, *Florida Indians,* 174; see also Bushnell, "Menéndez Marquéz"; Stewart, "Whether Wast."

21. Salley, *Records; Calendar of State Papers,* vol. 23, 200; Nairne, "Letter."

22. Decker et al., "Worldwide Patterns of Ancestry"; Fussell, "Size of English Cattle"; Fussell, "Animal Husbandry," pts. 1 and 2; Leavitt, "Attempts"; McTavish et al., "New World Cattle"; Periam, *American Farmer's Pictorial Cyclopedia,* 540–48; Rouse, *World Cattle I,* 281; Rouse, *World Cattle II,* 1026–127; Rouse, *World Cattle III,* 351–53, 361–62; Rouse, *Criollo,* 7, 288; Thompson, *History of Livestock Raising,* 3; Trow-Smith, *History of British Livestock Husbandry,* 45–58, 70–72, 90; Youatt, *Cattle,* 95.

23. Agha, "St. Giles Kussoe," 11–12, 15, 19–20; Cook, "Domestic Livestock"; Decker et al., "Worldwide Patterns of Exportation"; Rouse, *World Cattle III,* 358–61; Rouse, *Criollo;* Thompson, *History of Livestock Raising;* Wood, *Black Majority,* 31.

24. Reitz and Ruff, "Morphometric Data"; Rouse, *World Cattle III,* 14–15; Rouse, *Criollo.*

25. Rouse, *Criollo,* 186; Thompson, *History of Livestock Raising,* 65.

26. Benson, *Peter Kalm's Travels,* 55–56; see also Cook, "Domestic Livestock."

27. Armitage, "Hertfordshire Cattle"; Armitage, "System for Ageing and Sexing the Horn Cores"; Armitage, "Use of Bone"; Armitage, "Post-Medieval Cattle Horn Cores"; Armitage and Clutton-Brock, "System for Classification"; Armitage et al., "Early Agricultural Land Drains." Horn cores occasionally were used as fill to improve drainage.

28. Decker et al., "Worldwide Patterns of Ancestry"; McTavish et al., "New World Cattle."

Chapter 7. Supplying the Early City

1. Based on John James Audubon, *Ornithological Biography,* and plate 1, "Wild Turkey, John James Audubon's *Birds of America, National Audubon Society,* www.audubon.org/birds-of-america/wild-turkey.

2. Edgar, *South Carolina,* 52.

3. Carney, *Black Rice;* Weir, *Colonial South Carolina;* Wood, *Black Majority.*

4. Lounsbury, *Illustrated Glossary; South Carolina Gazette,* December 12, 1761.

5. Merrens, *Colonial South Carolina Scene,* 282; Poston, *Buildings of Charleston,* 155–56.

6. Honerkamp and Fairbanks, "Site Formation Processes."

7. Joseph, "Meeting at Market"; Joseph and Elliott, "Restoration Archaeology," 89.

8. Fraser, *Charleston!,* 60; Poston, *Buildings of Charleston,* 180.

9. Crosby, *Columbian Exchange;* Crosby, *Ecological Imperialism;* Jones, "Palynological Evidence."

10. Bates and Leland, *Proprietary Records;* Herold, "Preliminary Report," 4.

11. *South Carolina Gazette,* Jan. 26, 1740.

12. Ramsey, *Yamasee War;* see also Green et al., "Yamasee in South Carolina," 202; Jon Marcoux, personal communication, June 2014; Marcoux, *Pox, Empire;* Mason, Ocmulgee; Pavao-Zuckerman, "Deerskins and Domesticates"; Southerlin et al., "Return of the Yamasee"; Sweeney, "Investigating Yamasee Identity"; Waselkov et al., "Archaeological Excavations."

13. Herold, *Preliminary Report,* 5.

14. Herman, "Charleston Single House," 38; Herman, *Town House.*

15. Hamby and Joseph, "New Look"; Joseph, "Colonist to Charlestonian," 224; Joseph, "Agriculture in Colonial Charleston"; Shlasko, "Frenchmen and Africans"; Wheaton and Garrow, "Acculturation."

16. Joseph, "Colonist to Charlestonian," 229; Joseph, "Agriculture in Colonial Charleston."

17. Wood, *Black Majority*, 319–24. For various interpretations, see also M. Smith, *Stono.*

18. Deagan and Landers, "Fort Mose"; Wood, *Black Majority.*

19. Anthony, "Tangible Interaction"; Berlin, *Many Thousands Gone*, 65–67, 145.

20. Ferguson, "Cross"; Russell, "Material Culture and African American Spirituality"; Stine et al., "Blue Beads."

21. Berlin, *Many Thousands Gone*; Deagan and Landers, "Fort Mose"; Thornton, "African Dimensions," 1102; Wood, *Black Majority*, 314.

22. Braley, "Archaeological Data Recovery"; Braund, *Deerskins and Duffels*; Hahn, *Life and Times of Mary Musgrove*; Hahn, "'Indians that live about Pon'"; Piker, *Four Deaths.*

23. Braley, "Archaeological Data Recovery"; Swanton, *Indians*, 314.

24. Bonnie Gums, personal communication, 2001; Joseph, "Colonist to Charlestonian"; Waselkov, "French Colonial Archaeology"; see also Deagan, *Artifacts of the Spanish Colonies*, vol. 1.

25. For comparative archaeological assemblages, see Beaudry et al., "Vessel Typology"; Brown et al., "Shields Tavern Site"; Luckenbach, "Ceramics"; Rockman and Rothschild, "City Tavern."

26. Morgan, *Slave Counterpoint.*

27. The term *taxon* (plural: *taxa*) refers to a group of animals that includes one or more different species. These groups may not be strict taxonomic categories such as species, genus, or family, but they do have functional value, such as "wild taxa," which may include all wild animals regardless of taxonomic affiliation. See chapter 2 for a brief explanation of individuals and meat, or Reitz and Wing, *Zooarchaeology*, for a detailed discussion.

28. Armitage and McCarty, "Turtle Remains"; Rogers, *Papers of Henry Laurens*, 4; Taylor, *Hoppin' John's*, 145.

29. Booth, *Hung, Strung, and Potted*, 85–87; Carson, *Colonial Virginia Cookery*, 182–90; Hilliard, *Hogmeat and Hoecake*, 191; Nöel Hume, *Food*, 18; see also Walsh et al., "Provisioning."

Chapter 8. Townhouse Life

1. Based on Josiah Quincy, qtd. in Côté, *Mary's World*, 19.

2. Green, *Rise of Urban America*; Rogers, *Charleston*, 74; Weir, *Colonial South Carolina.*

3. Herman, "Charleston Single House"; Zierden and Herman, "Charleston Townhouses."

4. Côté, *Mary's World*; Shepherd, "Going Up the Country."

5. Bland, *Preserving Charleston's Past*; Côté, *Mary's World.*

6. Côté, *Mary's World*, 17, 19; Simons and Lapham, *Charleston, South Carolina*, 44.

7. *City Gazette and Daily Advertiser*, August 13, 1795; McPherson Family File, S.C. Historical Society.

8. *South Carolina Gazette*, September 14, 1773.

9. Salley, *Records*, #510, S.C. 1780–1781, 7–8.

10. Herman, "Charleston Single House," 38–41; Severens, *Antebellum Architecture*, 7.

11. Carp, "Changing Our Habitation"; Herman, *Town House*; Zierden and Herman, "Charleston Townhouses."

12. McInnis, "Idea of Grandeur," 33; see also Bushman, *Refinement of America*; Carp, "Changing Our Habitation"; Chappell, "Housing a Nation"; Herman, *Town House*; McInnis, *Politics of Taste*, 31; McInnis and Mack, *Pursuit of Refinement*, 31, 33; Sweeney, "High-Style Vernacular," 15.

13. Nash, "Domestic Material Culture"; Savage, *Nathaniel Russell House*, 4; Savage and Iseley, *Charleston Interior*; Savage and Leath, "Buying British."

14. Calhoun et al., "Geographic Spread"; Martin, "Consumption, Commodities"; Martin, *Buying into the World of Material Goods*.

15. Carson, *Ambitious Appetites*; Martin, "Fashionable Sugar Dishes"; Martin, "Consumption, Commodities"; Martin, *Buying into the World of Material Goods*; Roth, *Tea Drinking*.

16. Hudgins, "Staffordshire"; Nöel Hume, *Guide to Artifacts*, 123; South, "John Bartlam."

17. Towner, *Creamware*, 139.

18. *South Carolina Gazette*, October 13, 1770.

19. Brad Rauschenberg and John Bivins, personal communication, 1990; see South, "John Bartlam"; Hudgins, "Staffordshire."

20. D. Rosengarten, *Row upon Row*, 18; also D. Rosengarten et al., *Grass Roots*.

21. Heath, "Cowrie Shells, Global Trade"; Herman, "Poetics of Urban Space"; Stine et al., "Blue Beads." Barbara Heath has suggested that cowrie shells are most closely associated with port cities and may have served as currency in the African trade, rather than as charms.

22. Anthony, "Tangible Interaction"; Crane, "Colono Wares"; Ferguson, *Uncommon Ground*; Isenbarger, "Potters, Hucksters, and Consumers"; Joseph, "Colonoware for the Village."

23. Gregorie, *Notes on Sewee Indians*, 21.

24. Ferguson, "Lowcountry Plantations," 188; Joseph, "Colonoware for the Village"; Riggs et al., "Catawba Pottery"; Steen, "Archaeology of the Settlement Indians."

25. Burton, *Antique Sealed Bottles*; Duncan, *Atlantic Islands*, 36–39; Hancock, *Oceans of Wine*, 391, 395; Keel and Kowal, "Charles Pinckney's Snee Farm."

26. Garrett, *At Home*, 73, 92. Dan Ksepka is curator of science at the Bruce Museum, Greenwich, Connecticut. Dwight Williams is director of Cypress Gardens in Berkeley County, South Carolina. Laurie Reitsema is assistant professor of anthropology at University of Georgia. Daniel Thomas is curator at the National Museum of Natural History. Bruce Manzano is professor of anthropology at University of Kentucky. Nicolas Laracuente is review coordinator at Kentucky Heritage Council.

27. Garrett, *At Home*, 73, 92; *Charleston Courier*, 1808; Lefler, *New Voyage*, 148; *South Carolina Gazette and Daily Advertiser*, May 4, 1785; VanDoran, *Travels of William Bartram*, 245.

28. Côté, *Mary's World*; Herman, *Town House*; Zierden and Herman, "Charleston Townhouses."

29. Reitz and Wing, *Zooarchaeology*, 216–19, 223–24.

30. Bowen, "Faunal Remains"; *City Gazette and Daily Advertiser*, 1794; Jameson,

"Purity and Power"; Paston-Williams, *Art of Dining*, 271; *South Carolina Gazette*, 1744; Zierden and Calhoun, "Urban Adaptation."

31. Hooker, *Food and Drink*; Hooker, *Colonial Plantation Cookbook*; Paston-Williams, *Art of Dining*.

32. D. Rosengarten et al., "Between the Tracks"; Walsh et al., "Provisioning"; Zierden and Calhoun, "Urban Adaptation."

33. The process of killing and butchering carcasses into primary, secondary, and tertiary units is culturally patterned but also conforms to the morphology of the animal. Primary butchery is primarily intended to dismember the carcass. Secondary and tertiary butchery subdivides portions into smaller units of meat. Secondary and tertiary butchery are related to the number of people to be fed, how the meat will be prepared (e.g., roasted, boiled, fried, or stewed), the size of the cooking vessel, and how the meat will be served. See Reitz and Wing, *Zooarchaeology*, 126–32, 272–75.

34. *South Carolina Gazette*, October 10, 1773; *Southern Agriculturist* 9, (1836), 165.

Chapter 9. The Commercial City

1. Based on Herold and Thomas, "History of the Charleston Center Site," 55–59, 123–26.

2. Calhoun et al., "Geographic Spread."

3. Rogers, *Charleston*.

4. Mazyck, *Guide to Charleston*, 38–43.

5. Dickens, *Archaeology of Urban America*; Salwen, "Foreword."

6. Borchert, *Alley Life*, 17–23; Bridenbaugh, *Cities in Revolt*, 227–28.

7. *South Carolina Gazette*, April 5, 1770; *Charleston City Directory*, 1790.

8. Salley, *President Washington's Tour*, 17; Charleston County Register Mesne Conveyance Office, book C-7: 387.

9. Honerkamp, "Households or Neighborhoods"; Honerkamp and Fairbanks, "Site Formation Processes."

10. *South Carolina Weekly Gazette*, October 4, 1783.

11. *Columbian Herald*, May 11, 1786.

12. *City Gazette and Daily Advertiser*, August 18, 1791; see also Armitage, "Hertfordshire Cattle"; Maag, "Cattle Raising," 70.

13. *South Carolina Weekly Gazette*, October 4, 1783.

14. Edwards, *Ordinances*, 39; Eckhard, *Digest of Ordinances*, 137.

15. McInnis, *Politics of Taste*, 184; Morgan, *Slave Counterpoint*; T. Rosengarten, *Tombee*; USDA, *Development of Trucking*; see also Kidd, "Truck Farming," 3-1. Kidd defines truck farming as "those 'quick-harvest' fruits and vegetables of 'a perishable nature,' brought to market by wagon, rail, or motorized vehicle."

16. Bresee, *Sea Island Yankee*; see also Frazier, *James Island*; Morgan, *Slave Counterpoint*, 250–51. None of these are European crops; most were originally domesticated in the Americas or Asia.

17. Crane, "Colono Wares"; Isenbarger, "Potters, Hucksters, and Consumers"; Joseph, "Colonoware for the Village."

18. *South Carolina Gazette* 1732 in Crane, "Colono Wares," 129–30; Espenshade, *River of Doubt*; Joseph, "Meeting at Market."

19. *City Gazette and Daily Advertiser*, May 22, 1790; Morgan, *Slave Counterpoint*, 55.

Chapter 10. The Crowded City

1. Based on Carrie Albee, "Historical Timeline, Aiken-Rhett House," the Cheves-Middleton Papers, and the *Diary of J. B. Grimball*. For details on the foods available in the Charleston markets, see Shields, *Southern Provisions*, chapter 8.

2. Garrett, "Introduction," 5; Poston, *Buildings of Charleston*, 198; Waddell, *Charleston in 1883*.

3. Edgar, *South Carolina*, 273, 284; Goldfield, *Cotton Fields and Skyscrapers*, 86; Greb, "Charleston, South Carolina Merchants," 18.

4. Pease and Pease, "Blood-Thirsty Tiger"; Severens, *Antebellum Architecture*, 267.

5. Wade, *Slavery in the Cities*.

6. Poston, *Buildings of Charleston*, 463. William Hieronymous operated Hieronymous and O'Brien Livery Stables on Church Street.

7. Weyeneth, *Historic Preservation*, 55.

8. Poston, *Buildings of Charleston*, 422; Shields, *Southern Provisions*, 197.

9. Poston, *Buildings of Charleston*, 389; Simons and Thomas, "Architectural Guide."

10. Buck, "Aiken-Rhett House"; Graham et al., "Architectural Development."

11. Paston-Williams, *Art of Dining*, 229–31.

12. Faux, *Memorable Days*, 43.

13. Charleston District Court of Equity, 1783–1868.

14. Edgar, *South Carolina*, 329; Killens, *Trial Record*; Lofton, *Denmark Vesey's Revolt*; Robertson, *Denmark Vesey*.

15. Hamilton, *Account*, 25; Killens, *Trial Record*, 82; see also Lofton, *Denmark Vesey's Revolt*.

16. Jackson, *Discovering the Vernacular Landscape*, 7–8; Kryder-Reid, "'As Is the Gardener'"; Shackel and Little, *Historical Archaeology*; Stilgoe, *Common Landscape*, 3; Upton, "City as Material Culture."

17. Reinhard, "Pollen Analysis"; Reinhard, "Analysis of Soils."

18. Herman, "Poetics of Urban Space"; Zierden and Herman, "Charleston Townhouses," 222.

19. Reinhard, "Pollen Analysis"; Trinkley, "Ethnobotanical Samples"; Trinkley, "Ethnobotanical Analysis"; Weir, *Colonial South Carolina*, 44.

20. Herman, "Slave and Servant Housing," 97; T. Rosengarten, "In the Master's Garden," 18; see also Upton, "White and Black Landscapes."

21. African American residents of these urban compounds often found ways to circumvent restrictions and continued to find some measure of privacy and even independence within urban spaces. See Herman, "Slave and Servant Housing"; McInnis, *Politics of Taste*, 168.

22. Herman, "Slave and Servant Housing," 88, 92; McInnis, *Politics of Taste*, 106; see also Buck in Graham et al., "Architectural Development"; Herman, *Town House*, 149–54.

23. A. Smith, *Charleston Sketchbook*; see also Zierden and Herman, "Charleston Townhouses."

24. Graham et al., "Architectural Development"; Herman, "Poetics of Urban Space."

25. Greene et al., *Slave Badges*, 22, 29; Singleton, "Slave Tag"; see also Wade, *Slavery in the Cities*.

26. Miller, "Revised List"; Nöel Hume, *Guide to Artifacts*.

27. Carson, *Ambitious Appetites*, 101; Paston-Williams, *Art of Dining*.

28. Clark, *South Carolina*, 161.

29. Hooker, *Colonial Plantation Cookbook*; Rhett, *Two Hundred Years*; South Carolina Institute, *Premium List*, 11–12.

30. Doar, *Rice and Rice Planting*, 27; Hess, *Carolina Rice Kitchen*, 50, F 3–4. Eliza Perroneau Mathewes' recipe appears in the *Carolina Rice Cook Book* (1901) compiled by Louisa Cheves Smythe Stoney for the South Carolina Interstate and West Indian Exposition. It was reprinted by Karen Hess from a copy at the South Caroliniana Library, University of South Carolina, Columbia. For a discussion of this publication, see Taylor, *Hoppin' John's*.

31. Shannon and Weaver, *Mathematical Theory*, 14; Sheldon, "Equitability Indices." Diversity is estimated using MNI or biomass in the Shannon-Weaver Index, and equitability is measured using the Sheldon Index. Diversity values can range from essentially zero to five; equitability ranges from essentially zero to one. See Reitz and Wing, *Zooarchaeology*, 245–47.

32. D. Rosengarten et al., "Between the Tracks."

33. Poplin and Salo, "Archaeological Investigations at 82 Pitt Street."

34. Armitage, "Use of Bone," 157; Armitage, "Gazetteer," 202–9; Baker and Worley, *Animal Bones*, 10; Fletcher, *Gardens of Earthly Delights*, 230; "Shakespeare's Curtain Theatre," museumoflondonarchaeology.org.uk/NewsProjects/CurtainTheatre 2012.

35. Cruickshank and Burton, *Life in the Georgian City*.

36. Honerkamp et al., "Archaeological Investigation of the Charleston Center Site"; Honerkamp and Council, "Individual versus Corporate Adaptations."

Chapter 11. Landscape Changes

1. South Carolina Society for the Improvement of Domestic Poultry, *Report of the Executive Committee*, 8.

2. Harris, *Deep Souths*; T. Rosengarten, *Tombee*; Severens, *Antebellum Architecture*, 265.

3. Mazyck, *Guide to Charleston*, 38, 43; South Carolina Institute, *Premium List*, 38; see also Stoney, *This Is Charleston*, 47. For the cause of the 1861 fire, see Ferrara, "Moses Henry Nathan," and research by Katherine Pemberton, Historic Charleston Foundation.

4. Williams and Hoffius, *Upheaval in Charleston*; descriptions of progressive efforts in the 1880s from ongoing research by Susan Williams.

5. For discussion of efforts to plant after the Civil War, see Côté, *Mary's World*, 314. For postwar occupation of the Miles Brewton House, see Côté, *Mary's World*, 327.

6. Côté, *Mary's World*, 354–58. For the history of Susan Pringle Frost, see Bland, *Preserving Charleston's Past*.

7. Banov, *As I Recall*, 7; Stockton, "Historical Background," 22.

8. Susan Williams, personal communication, 2015.

9. Fraser, *Charleston!*, 304. For legislation relating to drainage, see Dingle, "Sewerage and Drainage"; for legislation relating to filling, see Lebby, *Digest of Acts of the Assembly*.

10. Williams, *History of Charleston's Water*.

11. *City Yearbooks*, 1887, 65.

12. For comments on privies, see *City Yearbooks*, 1887, 1905; for discussions of urban livestock, see *City Yearbooks*, 1912, 182.

13. Barnes, *Diseases and Human Evolution*, 242, 252, 255–56; Waldron, *Paleopathology*, 111–13.

14. Privy vaults were convenient disposal areas, following a long tradition in Charleston and many other cities. Cisterns, in contrast, are often filled with clean sand or remain unfilled; perhaps Charlestonians had uses for nonpotable water or did not rely entirely on the municipal water system.

15. In 1807 the City designated the new, consolidated market as the "Centre Market." David Shields reports that by 1820 Charlestonians began to refer to it as the "Charleston Market," the name used today. See Shields, *Southern Provisions*, 167.

16. Leland, *Charleston*, 37; Poston, *Buildings of Charleston*, 395–96, 339.

17. Mazyck in Waddell, *Charleston in 1883*, 18; Rogers, *Charleston*, 87; *Southern Agriculturalist* 9 (1836), 167; South Carolina Institute, *Premium List*. We are indebted to Susan Williams for bringing this remarkable document to our attention; see also Stockton, *Great Shock*; Waddell, *Charleston in 1883*; Williams and Hoffius, *Upheaval in Charleston*, 115.

18. See Rogers, *Charleston*; the Duke of Saxe-Weimar reported in 1826, "The market consists of five houses . . . the most beautiful tropical fruit therein arranged, oranges from Florida, pistachios, and large excellent pine apples from Cuba. . . . Upon the roofs of the market house sat a number of buzzards, who are supported by the offals," 87; for analysis of "Charleston Square," see Shields and Mitchell, "Nat Fuller's Feast"; Raskin, "Illustrated."

19. South Carolina Institute, *Premium List*, 58.

20. Rogers, *Charleston*, 87; see also Clark, *South Carolina*, 104.

21. Merrens, *Colonial South Carolina Scene*, 284; "d" is the notation for the English penny.

22. Berlin, *Slaves without Masters*, 218–19; Bishop et al., "We Are in Trim;" Foner, *Nothing but Freedom*; McKinley, *Stinking Stones*; Morgan, *Slave Counterpoint*; D. Smith, *Charlestonian's Recollections*, 64.

23. D. Smith, *Charlestonian's Recollections*, 64; An extensive discussion of the postbellum fish market is found in Shields, *Southern Provisions*. Analysis of the catch of Charleston's mosquito fleet is in Bishop et al., "We Are in Trim."

24. Butler, "New Archaeology"; McCord, *Statutes*; see also Shields, *Southern Provisions*, 185.

25. Morgan, *Slave Counterpoint*, 241; T. Rosengarten, *Tombee*, 131, 601.

26. Adger letter 1873 in Brown, "Research Report"; Haney, "In Complete Order," 30.

27. Haney, "In Complete Order"; Horlbeck Brothers, *Day Book*, 3.

28. Edwards, *Ordinances*, 178–79, in Greene et al., *Slave Badges*, 64.

29. See Johnston, "Synanthropic Birds," 49; Luniak, "Synurbanization," 51; McKinney, "Urbanization."

Chapter 12. Archaeology in the City, Archaeology of the City

1. Herman, "Poetics"; Jackson, *Discovering the Vernacular Landscape*, 7–8; Upton, "City as Material Culture."

2. Kropf, "Dozens of Graves Found at Gaillard"; Kropf, "Gaillard Graveyard Remains."

3. Deagan, "Colonial Origins"; House, *Family Cookery*; O'Day et al., *Behaviour behind Bones*; Pavao-Zuckerman and Loren, "Presentation Is Everything"; Reitz, "Zooarchaeological Analysis"; Reitz and Scarry, *Reconstructing Historic Subsistence*.

4. Deagan, "Transculturation," 27, 35; Deagan, "Colonial Origins"; see also Ferris, "Edible South"; Shields, *Southern Provisions*; Taylor, *Hoppin' John's*.

REFERENCES

Agha, Andrew. "Miller Site Excavations Fall 2012–Summer 2013." Report on file, Charles Towne Landing State Historic Site, Charleston, S.C., 2012.

———. "St. Giles Kussoe and 'The Character of a Loyal States-man': Historical Archaeology at Lord Anthony Ashley Cooper's Carolina Plantation." Report on file, Historic Charleston Foundation, Charleston, S.C., 2012.

Agha, Andrew, and Charles F. Philips Jr. "Archaeological Investigations at 38DR83a, St. Giles Kussoe House/Lord Ashley Settlement." Report on file, Brockington and Associates to Historic Charleston Foundation, Charleston, S.C., 2010.

Albee, Carrie. "Historical Timeline, Aiken-Rhett House." Report on file, Historic Charleston Foundation, Charleston, S.C., 2001.

American Poultry Association. *American Standard of Excellence*. [Buffalo, N.Y.]: The Association, 1874.

Anderson, Jay Allan. "'A Solid Sufficiency': An Ethnography of Yeoman Foodways in Stuart England." PhD diss., Department of Folklore and Folklife, University of Pennsylvania, 1971.

Anderson, Virginia DeJohn. *Creatures of Empire: How Domestic Animals Transformed Early America*. New York: Oxford University Press, 2004.

Anthony, Ronald W. "Colono Wares." In *Home Upriver: Rural Life on Daniels Island*, edited by M. Zierden, L. Drucker, and J. Calhoun, 7-22–7-51. Report on file, South Carolina Department of Highways and Public Transportation, Columbia, 1986.

———. "Tangible Interaction: Evidence from Stobo Plantation." In *Another's Country*, edited by J. W. Joseph and M. Zierden, 45–64. Tuscaloosa: University of Alabama Press, 2002.

Armelagos, George J. "You Are What You Eat." In *Paleonutrition: The Diet and Health of Prehistoric Americans*, edited by K. D. Sobolik, 235–44. Center for Archaeological Research Occasional Paper 22. Carbondale: Southern Illinois University, 1994.

Armitage, Philip L. "Gazetteer of Sites with Animal Bones Used as Building Material." In *Diet and Crafts in Towns: The Evidence of Animal Remains in the Roman to the Post-Medieval Periods*, edited by D. Serjeantson and T. Waldron, 201–23. British Archaeological Reports British Series 199. Oxford: B.A.R., 1989.

———. "Hertfordshire Cattle and London Meat Markets in the 17th and 18th Centuries." *London Archaeologist* 8, no. 8 (1978):217–23.

———. "Post-Medieval Cattle Horn Cores from the Greyfriars Site, Chichester, West Sussex, England." *Circaea* 7, no. 2 (1990):81–90.

———. "A System for Aging and Sexing the Horn Cores from British Post-Medieval Sites (17th to Early 18th Century) with Special Reference to Unimproved British Longhorn Cattle." In *Aging and Sexing Animal Bones from Archaeological Sites*, edited by B. Wilson, C. Grigson, and S. Payne, 37–54. British Archaeological Reports British Series 109. Oxford: B.A.R., 1982.

———. "The Use of Bone as Building Material in Post-Medieval Britain." In *Diet and Crafts in Towns: The Evidence of Animal Remains in the Roman to the Post-Medieval Periods*, edited by D. Serjeantson and T. Waldron, 147–60. British Archaeological Reports British Series 199. Oxford: B.A.R., 1989.

Armitage, Philip L., and Juliet Clutton-Brock. "A System for Classification and Description of the Horn Cores of Cattle from Archaeological Sites." *Journal of Archaeological Science* 3 (1976):329–48.

Armitage, Philip L., Richard Coxshall, and John Ivens. "Early Agricultural Land Drains in the Former Parishes of Edmonton and Enfield." *London Archaeologist* 3, no. 15 (1980):217–23.

Armitage, Philip L., and Colin McCarty. "Turtle Remains from a Late 18th Century Well at Leadenhall Buildings." *London Archaeologist* 4, no. 1 (1980):8–16.

Arnade, Charles W. "Cattle Raising in Spanish Florida." *Agricultural History* 35, no. 3 (1961):3–11.

———. *The Siege of St. Augustine in 1702*. Gainesville: University of Florida Press, 1959.

Arnott, Margaret L., editor. *Gastronomy: The Anthropology of Food and Food Habits*. Mouton: The Hague, 1975.

Audubon, John James. *Ornithological Biography, or an Account of the Habits of the Birds of the United States of America; Accompanied by Descriptions of the Objects Represented in the Work Entitled the Birds of America, and Interspersed with Delineations of American Scenery and Manners*. Philadelphia: Judah Dobson, 1831.

Baker, Polydora, and Fay Worley. *Animal Bones and Archaeology: Guidelines for Best Practice*. London: English Heritage, 2014.

Banov, Leon. *As I Recall: The Story of the Charleston County Health Department*. Columbia, S.C.: R. L. Bryan, 1970.

Barnes, Ethne. *Diseases and Human Evolution*. Albuquerque: University of New Mexico Press, 2005.

Barry, Richard. *Mr. Rutledge of South Carolina*. New York: Duell, Sloan and Pearce, 1942.

Bates, Susan B., and H. Cheves Leland. *French Santee: A Huguenot Settlement in Colonial South Carolina*. Baltimore: Otter Bay Books, 2014.

———. *Proprietary Records of South Carolina, Volume 3: Abstracts of the Records of the Surveyor General of the Province, Charles Town, 1678–1698*. Charleston, S.C.: History Press, 2007.

Beaudry, Mary, Janet Long, Henry M. Miller, Fraser D. Neiman, and Garry W. Stone. "A Vessel Typology for Early Chesapeake Ceramics: The Potomac Typological System." *Historical Archaeology* 17, no. 1 (1983):18–43.

Benson, Adolph, editor. *Peter Kalm's Travels in North America: The English Version of 1770*. New York: Wilson-Erickson, 1937.

Bent, Arthur Cleveland. 1932. *Life Histories of North American Gallinaceous Birds*. New York: Dover, 1963.

Berlin, Ira. *Many Thousands Gone: The First Two Centuries of Slavery in North America, 1685–1815*. Lincoln: University of Nebraska Press, 1998.

———. *Slaves without Masters: The Free Negro in the Antebellum South*. New York: Oxford University Press, 1974.

Bierer, Bert W. 1939. *History of Animal Plagues of North America*. Washington, D.C.: United States Department of Agriculture, 1974.

Bishop, James M., Glenn Ulrich, and Henrietta S. Wilson. "'We Are in Trim to Due It': A Review of Charleston's Mosquito Fleet." *Reviews in Fisheries Science* 2, no. 4 (1994):331–46.

Bland, Sidney. *Preserving Charleston's Past, Shaping Its Future: The Life and Times of Susan Pringle Frost*. Columbia: University of South Carolina Press, 1999.

Bolton, Herbert E., and Mary Ross. *The Debatable Land*. New York: Russell and Russell, 1968.

Bonner, James C. *A History of Georgia Agriculture, 1732–1860*. Athens: University of Georgia Press, 1964.

Booth, Sally S. *Hung, Strung, and Potted: A History of Eating in Colonial America*. New York: Carlson N. Potter, 1971.

Borchert, James. *Alley Life in Washington: Family, Community, Religion, and Folklife in the City, 1850–1870*. Chicago: University of Illinois Press, 1980.

Borick, Carl. *A Gallant Defense: The Siege of Charleston, 1780*. Columbia: University of South Carolina Press, 2003.

Bowen, Joanne. "Faunal Remains and Urban Household Subsistence in New England." In *The Art and Mystery of Historical Archaeology: Essays in Honor of James Deetz*, edited by A. Yentsch and M. Beaudry, 267–81. Boca Raton, Fla.: CRC Press, 1992.

Bowne, Eric E. *The Westo Indians: Slave Traders of the Early Colonial South*. Tuscaloosa: University of Alabama Press, 2005.

Braley, Chad O. "Archaeological Data Recovery at the Cowpens/Grange Plantation Site (9CH137), Chatham County, Georgia." Report on file, Southeastern Archaeological Services, Inc. Prepared for the Georgia Ports Authority, Savannah, Georgia, through CH2M Hill/Lockwood Greene, Pooler, Ga., 2013.

Braund, Kathryn E. Holland. *Deerskins and Duffels: The Creek Indian Trade with Anglo-America, 1685–1815*. Lincoln: University of Nebraska Press, 1993.

Bresee, Clyde. *Sea Island Yankee*. Columbia: University of South Carolina Press, 1986.

Bridenbaugh, Carl. *Cities in Revolt: Urban Life in America 1743–1775*. New York: Alfred A. Knopf, 1955.

Brilliant, Brooke. "Colonoware: Pots, People, and the Process of Creolization." Paper presented at the 24th annual meeting of the Society for Historical Archaeology, Austin, Tx., 2011.

———. "Colonoware, Creolization, and Interactions between African Americans and Native Americans during the Colonial Period in the South Carolina Lowcountry." MA thesis, Department of Anthropology, University of South Carolina, 2011.

Brooks, Richard D., Mark D. Groover, and Samuel C. Smith. *Living on the Edge: The Archaeology of Cattle Raisers in the South Carolina Backcountry*. Savannah River Archaeological Research Paper 10. Columbia: South Carolina Institute of Archaeology and Anthropology, 2000.

Brown, C. Allan. "Research Report on the History of the Grounds of No. 14 Legare." Report on file, Historic Charleston Foundation and Glenn Keyes Architects, Charleston, S.C., 2001.

Brown, Gregory, Thomas Higgins, David Muraca, Kathleen Pepper, and Roni Polk. "Archaeological Investigations of the Shields Tavern Site, Williamsburg." Report on file, Colonial Williamsburg Foundation, Williamsburg, Va., 1990.

Buck, Susan L. "The Aiken-Rhett House: A Comparative Architectural Paint Study." PhD diss., Department of Art Conservation, University of Delaware, 2003.

Burton, David. *Antique Sealed Bottles 1640–1900: And the Families That Owned Them.* London: Antique Collectors Club, 2014.

Bushman, Richard. *The Refinement of America: Churches, Houses, Cities.* New York: Alfred A. Knopf, 1992.

Bushnell, Amy. "The Menéndez Marquéz Cattle Barony at La Chua and the Determinants of Economic Expansion in Seventeenth-Century Florida." *Florida Historical Quarterly* 56, no. 4 (1978):407–31.

Butler, Nicolas. "New Archaeology in Charleston: The South Adger's Wharf Dig." Lecture presented to the Faculty Seminar, College of Charleston, Charleston, S.C., 2008.

———. "Timeline of Events for the Walled City." In *Archaeology at South Adger's Wharf,* by Nicolas Butler, Eric Poplin, Katherine Pemberton, and Martha Zierden, 201–10. Archaeological Contributions 45. Charleston, S.C.: The Charleston Museum, 2010.

Cáceres, A. de. December 12, 1574. Archivo General de las Indias, 54-2-2, Santo Domingo 124. Manuscript Photostat. J. T. Connor Papers, reel 2, P. K. Yonge Library of Florida History, University of Florida, Gainesville.

Calendar of State Papers, Colonial Series America and West Indies. Vol. 7, 1669–74. Edited by W. Noel Sainsbury. Preserved in Her Majesty's Public Record Office. http://www.british-history.ac.uk/cal-state-papers/colonial/america-west-indies/vol7.

———. *Calendar of State Papers, Colonial Series, America and West Indies.* Vol. 23, 1706–1708. Edited by Cecil Headlam. Preserved in Her Majesty's Public Record Office. http://www.british-history.ac.uk/cal-state-papers/colonial/america-west-indies/vol23.

Calhoun, Jeanne A. *The Scourging Wrath of God: Early Hurricanes in Charleston, 1700–1804.* Leaflet no. 29. Charleston, S.C.: The Charleston Museum, 1983.

Calhoun, Jeanne, Martha Zierden, and Elizabeth Paysinger. "The Geographic Spread of Charleston's Mercantile Community, 1732–1767." *South Carolina Historical Magazine* 86, no. 3 (1985):182–220.

Carney, Judith A. *Black Rice: The African Origins of Rice Cultivation in the Americas.* Cambridge: Harvard University Press, 2001.

Carp, Benjamin. "Changing Our Habitation: Henry Laurens, Rattray Green, and the Revolutionary Movement in Charleston's Domestic Spaces." In *Material Culture in Anglo-America,* edited by D. S. Shields, 285–309. Columbia: University of South Carolina Press, 2009.

Carr, Archie. *Handbook of Turtles.* Ithaca, N.Y.: Cornell University Press, 1952.

Carson, Barbara G. *Ambitious Appetites: Dining, Behavior, and Patterns of Consumption in Federal Washington.* Washington, D.C.: American Institute of Architects Press, 1990.

Carson, Jane. *Colonial Virginia Cookery*. Williamsburg, Va.: Colonial Williamsburg Foundation, 1968.

Chaplin, Joyce E. *An Anxious Pursuit: Agricultural Innovation and Modernity in the Lower South, 1730–1815*. Chapel Hill: University of North Carolina Press, 1993.

Chappell, Edward A. "Housing a Nation: The Transformation of Living Standards in Early America." In *Of Consuming Interest: The Style of Life in the Eighteenth Century*, edited by C. Carson, R. Hoffman, and P. Albert, 167–232. Charlottesville: University Press of Virginia, 1994.

Charleston City Directory. Charleston Library Society, Charleston, S.C.

Charleston County Register of Mesne Conveyance Office, Charleston, S.C.

Charleston Courier. 1803–72. Microfilm, Charleston County Library, Charleston, S.C.

Charleston District Court of Equity. 1783–1868. Records on file, South Carolina Department of Archives and History, Columbia, S.C.

Cheves, Langdon. *Collections of the South Carolina Historical Society, Volume V*. Richmond, Va.: William Ellis Jones, Book and Job Printer, 1897.

Cheves–Middleton Papers. South Carolina Historical Society, Charleston, S.C.

City Gazette and Daily Advertiser. 1787–1833. Charleston Library Society, Charleston, South Carolina, and NewsBank and/or American Antiquarian Society, 2004, Worcester, Mass.

City Yearbooks, City of Charleston. The Charleston Museum Archives, Charleston, S.C., 1880–1915.

Clark, Thomas D. *South Carolina: The Grand Tour 1780–1865*. Columbia: University of South Carolina Press, 1973.

Clayton, G. A. "Muscovy Duck." In *Evolution of Domesticated Animals*, edited by I. L. Mason, 340–44. London: Longman, 1986.

Clowse, Converse D. *Economic Beginnings in Colonial South Carolina, 1670–1730*. Columbia: University of South Carolina Press, 1971.

Columbian Herald. 1784–96. www.gencaologybank.com. NewsBank and/or American Antiquarian Society, 2004, Worcester, Ma.

Cook, Peter W. "Domestic Livestock of Massachusetts Bay 1620–1725." In *The Farm*, edited by P. Benes, 109–25. Deerfield, Mass.: Dublin Seminar for New England Folklife, 1988.

Cooper, Margaret, and Carl Steen. "Potters of the South Carolina Lowcountry: A Material Culture Study of Creolization." Paper presented at 31st annual meeting of the Society for Historical Archaeology, Atlanta, Ga., 1998.

Côté, Richard N. *Mary's World: Love, War, and Family Ties in Nineteenth-Century Charleston*. Mt. Pleasant, S.C.: Corinthian Books, 2000.

Crane, Brian. "Colono Wares and Criollo Ware Pottery from Charleston, South Carolina and San Juan, Puerto Rico in Comparative Perspective." PhD diss., Department of American Civilization, University of Pennsylvania, 1993.

Crane, Verner W. *The Southern Frontier, 1670–1732*. New York: W. W. Norton, 1981.

Cressey, Pamela, John Stephens, Steven Shephard, and Barbara Magid. "The Core–Periphery Relationship and the Archaeological Record in Alexandria, Virginia." In *Archaeology of Urban America*, edited by R. S. Dickens, 143–74. New York: Academic Press, 1982.

Crosby, Alfred. *The Columbian Exchange: Biological and Cultural Consequences of 1492*. Westport, Conn.: Praeger, 1972.

———. *Ecological Imperialism: Biological Expansion of Europe, 900–1900.* Cambridge: Cambridge University Press, 1986.

Cruikshank, Dan, and Neil Burton. *Life in the Georgian City.* London: Viking, 1990.

Dahlberg, Michael D. "An Ecological Study of Georgia Coastal Fishes." *Fish. B-NOAA* 70, no. 2 (1972):323–53.

———. *Guide to Coastal Fishes of Georgia and Nearby States.* Athens: University of Georgia Press, 1975.

Davis, Nora. "Public Powder Magazines at Charleston." Charleston, S.C.: City of Charleston Yearbook, 1942.

Davis, Simon J. M. *The Archaeology of Animals.* New Haven: Yale University Press, 1987.

Deagan, Kathleen. *Artifacts of the Spanish Colonies of Florida and the Caribbean, 1500–1800.* Vol. 1, *Ceramics, Glassware, and Beads.* Washington, D.C.: Smithsonian Institution Press, 1987.

———. *Artifacts of the Spanish Colonies of Florida and the Caribbean, 1500–1800.* Vol. 2, *Portable Personal Possessions.* Washington, D.C.: Smithsonian Institution Press, 2002.

———. "Colonial Origins and Colonial Transformations in Spanish America." *Historical Archaeology* 37, no. 4 (2003):3–13.

———. "Eliciting Contraband through Archaeology: Illicit Trade in Eighteenth-Century St. Augustine." *Historical Archaeology* 41, no. 4 (2007):98–116.

———. "The Material Assemblage of 16th Century Spanish Florida." *Historical Archaeology* 12 (1983):25–50.

———. "Mestizaje in Colonial St. Augustine." *Ethnohistory* 20, no. 1 (1973):55–65.

———. *Spanish St. Augustine: The Archaeology of a Colonial Creole Community.* New York: Academic Press, 1983.

———. "Transculturation and Spanish American Ethnogenesis: The Archaeological Legacy of the Quincentenary." In *Studies in Culture Contact,* edited by J. G. Cusick, 23–43. Occasional Papers 25. Carbondale: Southern Illinois University Center for Archaeological Investigation, 1998.

Deagan, Kathleen, and José María Cruxent. *Archaeology at La Isabela: America's First European Town.* New Haven: Yale University Press, 2002.

Deagan, Kathleen, and Jane Landers. "Fort Mose: Earliest Free African-American Town in the United States." In *I, Too, Am America: Archaeological Studies of African American Life,* edited by T. Singleton, 261–82. Charlottesville: University Press of Virginia, 1999.

Deagan, Kathleen, and Darcie A. MacMahon. *Fort Mose: Colonial America's Black Fortress of Freedom.* Gainesville: University Press of Florida, 1995.

Decker, Jared E., Stephanie D. McKay, Megan M. Rolf, Jae Woo Kim, Antonio Molina Alcalá, Tad S. Sonstegard, Olivier Hanotte, Anders Götherström, Christopher M. Seabury, Lisa Praharani, Masroor Ellahi Babar, Luciana Correia de Almeida Regitano, Mehmet Ali Yildiz, Michael P. Heaton, Wan-Sheng Liu, Chu-Zhao Lei, James M. Reecy, Muhammad Saif-Ur-Rehman, Robert D. Schnabel, and Jeremy F. Taylor. "Worldwide Patterns of Ancestry, Divergence, and Admixture in Domesticated Cattle." *PloS Genetics* 10, no. 3 (2014): e1004254.

Decker, Jared E., Stephanie D. McKay, Megan M. Rolf, Jae Woo Kim, Antonio Molina Alcalá, Tad S. Sonstegard, Olivier Hanotte, Anders Götherström, Christopher M. Seabury, Lisa Praharani, Masroor Ellahi Babar, Mehmet Ali Yildiz, Michael P. Heaton,

Wan-Sheng Liu, James M. Reecy, Muhammad Saif-Ur-Rehman, Robert D. Schnabel, and Jeremy F. Taylor. "Worldwide Patterns of Exportation, Admixture and Selection in Domesticated Cattle." In *Evolutionary Relationships and Signatures of Selection in Cattle Established Using Genome-Wide Single Nucleotide Polymorphism*, 159–239. PhD diss., Genetics Area Program, University of Missouri, Columbia, 2012.

DeCorse, Christopher. "Oceans Apart: Africanist Perspectives on Dispora Archaeology." In *I, Too, Am America: Archaeological Studies of African American Life*, edited by T. Singleton, 132–55. Charlottesville: University Press of Virginia, 1999.

Deetz, James. *Flowerdew Hundred: The Archaeology of a Virginia Plantation, 1619–1864.* Charlottesville: University Press of Virginia, 1993.

———. "Prologue: Landscapes as Cultural Statements." In *Earth Patterns: Essays in Landscape Archaeology*, edited by W. Kelso and R. Most, 1–6. Charlottesville: University Press of Virginia, 1990.

Dennell, Robin W. "Prehistoric Diet and Nutrition: Some Food for Thought." *World Archaeology* 11 (1979):121–35.

Diary of J. B. Grimball. Charleston, S.C., WPA State Historical Project #165-33-7999. Copied from original manuscript in possession of the family. Special Collections, Addlestone Library, College of Charleston, Charleston, S.C.

Dickens, Roy S. *Archaeology of Urban America: The Search for Pattern and Process.* New York: Academic Press, 1982.

Dingle, James Hervey. "Sewerage and Drainage with a Review of the Tidal System of Charleston." PhD diss., Cornell University, 1892.

Doar, David. *Rice and Rice Planting in the South Carolina Low Country.* Contributions 8, Charleston, S.C.: The Charleston Museum, 1970 (1936).

Donaldson, Susan V. "Charleston's Racial Politics of Historic Preservation: The Case of Edwin A. Harleston." In *Renaissance in Charleston*, edited by J. Hutchisson and H. Greene, 176–98. Athens: University of Georgia Press, 2003.

Donkin, R. A. *The Muscovy Duck, Cairina moschata domestica.* Rotterdam: A. A. Balkema, 1989.

Douglas, Mary. "Deciphering a Meal." In *Implicit Meanings: Essays in Anthropology*, edited by M. Douglas, 249–75. Boston: Routledge and Kegan Paul, 1975.

———. "Standard Social Uses of Food: Introduction." In *Food and the Social Order: Studies of Food and Festivities in Three American Communities*, edited by M. Douglas, 1–39. New York: Russell Sage Foundation, 1984.

Drucker, Lesley M., and Ronald W. Anthony. *The Spiers Landing Site: Archaeological Investigations in Berkeley County, South Carolina.* Research Studies Series 10. Columbia, S.C.: Carolina Archaeological Services, 1979.

Dunbar, Gary S. "Colonial Carolina Cowpens." *Agricultural History* 35, no. 3 (1961):125–30.

Duncan, T. Bentley. *Atlantic Islands: Madeira, the Azores, and the Cape Verdes in Seventeenth-Century Commerce and Navigation.* Chicago: University of Chicago Press, 1972.

Dunn, Richard. *Sugar and Slaves: The Rise of the Planter Class in the English West Indies, 1624–1713.* New York: W. W. Norton, 1972.

Dusinberre, William. *Them Dark Days: Slavery in the American Rice Swamps.* New York: Oxford University Press, 1996.

Eckhard, George B. *A Digest of the Ordinances of the City Council of Charleston . . . from the year 1783 to October 1844 . . . to Which are Annexed the Acts of the Legislature Which Relate Exclusively to the City of Charleston.* Charleston, S.C.: Walter and Burke, 1844.

Edelson, Max. *Plantation Enterprise in Colonial South Carolina.* Cambridge: Harvard University Press, 2006.

Edgar, Walter. *South Carolina: A History.* Columbia: University of South Carolina Press, 1998.

Edwards, Alexander. *Ordinances of the City Council of Charleston.* Charleston: WP Young, 1802.

Espenshade, Christopher T. "A River of Doubt: Marked Colonoware, Underwater Sampling and Questions of Inference." *African Diaspora Archaeology Network Newsletter (On-Line)*, March, 2007.

Fagg, Daniel W. "St. Giles Seigniory: The Earl of Shaftesbury's Carolina Plantation." *South Carolina Historical and Genealogical Magazine* 71 (1970):117–23.

Fairbanks, Charles H. "Backyard Archaeology as a Research Strategy." *Conference on Historic Sites Archaeology Papers* 11 (1977):133–39.

Farb, Peter, and George Armelagos. *Consuming Passions: The Anthropology of Eating.* New York: Washington Square Press, 1980.

Faux, William. *Memorable Days in America.* New York: AMH Press, 1969 (1823).

Fenton, Alexander, and Eszter Kisban. *Food in Change: Eating Habits from the Middle Ages to the Present Day.* Edinburgh: John Donald Publishers, in association with the National Museum of Scotland, 1986.

Ferguson, Leland. "'The Cross Is a Magic Sign': Marks on Eighteenth-Century Bowls from South Carolina." In *I, Too, Am America: Archaeological Studies of African American Life*, edited by T. Singleton, 116–31. Charlottesville: University Press of Virginia, 1999.

———. "Lowcountry Plantations, the Catawba Nation, and River Burnished Pottery." In *Studies in South Carolina Archaeology: Essays in Honor of Robert L. Stephenson*, edited by A. Goodyear and G. Hanson, 185–91. Anthropological Studies 9. Columbia: South Carolina Institute of Archaeology and Anthropology, 1989.

———. "Medicine and Hygiene: Expanding Interpretations of African American Pottery from South Carolina Plantations." Paper presented at the 28th annual meeting of the Society for Historical Archaeology, Washington, D.C., 1995.

———. *Uncommon Ground: Archaeology and Early African America, 1650–1800.* Washington, D.C.: Smithsonian Institution Press, 1992.

Ferrara, Marie. "Moses Henry Nathan and the Great Charleston Fire of 1861." *South Carolina Historical Magazine* 104 (2003):258–80.

Ferris, Marcie Cohen. "The Edible South: Introduction to a Special Issue." *Southern Cultures* 15, no. 4 (2009):3–27.

Fisher, David Hackett. *Albion's Seed: Four British Folkways in America.* New York: Oxford University Press, 1989.

Fletcher, John. *Gardens of Earthly Delight: The History of Deer Parks.* Oxford: Windgather Press, 2011.

Foner, Eric. *Nothing but Freedom: Emancipation and Its Legacy.* Baton Rouge: Louisiana State University Press, 1983.

Fraser, Charles. *Reminiscences of Charleston, Lately Published in the Charleston Courier, and Now Revised and Enlarged by the Author.* Charleston, S.C.: John Russell, 1854.

Fraser, Walter J. *Charleston! Charleston! The History of a Southern City.* Columbia: University of South Carolina Press, 1989.

———. *Lowcountry Hurricanes: Three Centuries of Storms at Sea and Ashore.* Athens: University of Georgia Press, 2006.

Frazier, Eugene. *James Island: Stories from Slave Descendants.* Charleston, S.C.: History Press, 2006.

Frey, Robert W., and James D. Howard. "Mesotidal Estuarine Sequences: A Perspective from the Georgia Bight." *Journal of Sedimentary Petrology* 56 (1986):911–24.

Fussell, G. E. "Animal Husbandry in Eighteenth Century England, Part 1: Cattle." *Agricultural History* 11 (1937):96–116.

———. "Animal Husbandry in Eighteenth Century England, Part 2: Sheep, Swine, Horses, and Poultry." *Agricultural History* 11 (1937):189–214.

———. "The Size of English Cattle in the Eighteenth Century." *Agricultural History* 3 (1929):160–81.

Gabaccia, Donna R. *We Are What We Eat: Ethnic Foods and the Making of Americans.* Cambridge: Harvard University Press, 1998.

Gallay, Alan. *The Indian Slave Trade: The Rise of the English Empire in the American South, 1670–1717.* New Haven: Yale University Press, 2002.

García, Genaro, editor. *Dos antiguas relaciones de La Florida.* Mexico City: J. Aguilar Vera, 1902.

Garrett, Elisabeth Donaghy. *At Home: The American Family 1750–1870.* New York: Harry N. Abrams, 1990.

Garrett, Wendell. "Introduction." In *In Pursuit of Refinement: Charlestonians Abroad, 1740–1860.* Columbia: University of South Carolina Press and Gibbes Museum of Art, 1999.

Gibb, James G., and Julia A. King. "Gender, Activity Areas, and Homelots in the 17th-Century Chesapeake Region." *Historical Archaeology* 25, no. 4 (1991):109–31.

Goldfield, David R. "Pursuing the American Dream: Cities in the Old South." In *The City in Southern History*, edited by B. Brownell and D. Goldfield, 52–90. Port Washington, N.Y.: Kennikat Press, 1977.

———. *Cotton Fields and Skyscrapers: Southern City and Region, 1607–1980.* Baton Rouge: Louisiana State University Press, 1982.

Graham, Willie, Carl Lounsbury and Orlando Ridout V. "Architectural Development Overview: Aiken Rhett House, 48 Elizabeth Street." Report on file, Historic Charleston Foundation, Charleston, S.C., 2003.

Gray, Lewis Cecil. *History of Agriculture in the Southern United States to 1860.* Washington, D.C.: Carnegie Institution, 1933.

Greb, Gregory Allen. "Charleston, South Carolina Merchants, 1815–1860: Urban Leadership in the Antebellum South." PhD diss., Department of History, University of California–San Diego, 1978.

Green, Constance M. *The Rise of Urban America.* New York: Harper and Row, 1965.

Green, William, Chester B. DePratter, and Bobby Southerlin. "The Yamasee in South Carolina: Native American Adaptation and Interaction along the Carolina Frontier." In *Another's Country: Archaeological and Historical Perspectives on Cultural Interactions in the Southern Colonies*, edited by J. W. Joseph and M. Zierden, 13–29. Tuscaloosa: University of Alabama Press, 2002.

Greene, Harlan, Harry S. Hutchins Jr., and Brian E. Hutchins. *Slave Badges and the Slave-Hire System in Charleston, South Carolina, 1783–1865*. Jefferson, N.C.: McFarland, 2004.

Gregorie, Anne K. *Notes on Sewee Indians and Indian Remains of Christ Church Parish, Charleston County, South Carolina*. Contributions 5. Charleston, S.C.: The Charleston Museum, 1925.

Gremillion, Kristen J. "Human Ecology at the Edge of History." In *Between Contacts and Colonies*, edited by C. B. Wesson and M. A. Rees, 12–31. Tuscaloosa: University of Alabama Press, 2002.

Griñán, Pedro Sánchez. *Relación*. MSS 11.265:1725, 1792, 1900. Translated by J. M. Belmonte. Manuscript on file, Historic St. Augustine Preservation Board, St. Augustine, Fla., 1757.

Groover, Mark D., and Richard D. Brooks. "The Catherine Brown Cowpen and Thomas Howell Site: Material Characteristics of Cattle Raisers in the South Carolina Backcountry." *Southeastern Archaeology* 22 (2003):92–111.

Hahn, Steven C. "'The Indians that live about Pon Pon': John and Mary Musgrove and the Making of a Creek Indian Community in South Carolina, 1717–1732." In *Creating and Contesting Carolina*, edited by M. LeMaster and B. J. Wood, 343–66. Columbia: University of South Carolina Press, 2013.

———. *The Life and Times of Mary Musgrove*. Gainesville: University Press of Florida, 2012.

Halbirt, Carl. "The Apocalypse of 1702: Archaeological Evidence of Moore's Siege." St. Augustine: *El Escribano* 39 (2002):29–44.

———. "La Ciudad de San Augustin: A European Fighting Presidio in Eighteenth-Century La Florida." *Historical Archaeology* 38, no. 3 (2004):33–46.

Hamby, Theresa, and J. W. Joseph. "A New Look at the Old City: Archaeological Excavations of the Charleston County Judicial Center Site (38CH1708), Charleston, South Carolina." Stone Mountain, Ga.: New South Associates Technical Report 1192, 2004.

Hamilton, James, Jr. *An Account of the Late Intended Insurrection among a Portion of the Blacks in This City*. Charleston: Published by the Authority of the Corporation of Charleston, 1822.

Hancock, David. *Oceans of Wine: Madeira and the Emergence of American Trade and Taste*. New Haven: Yale University Press, 2009.

Handsman, Russell G. "Class Histories, Self-Doubt and the Archaeology of Presented Landscapes." Paper presented at the 20th annual meeting of the Society for Historical Archaeology, Savannah, Ga., 1987.

Haney, Gina. "In Complete Order: Social Control and Architectural Organization in the Charleston Back Lot." MA thesis, Department of Architectural History, University of Virginia, 1996.

Hann, John H. *Apalachee: The Land between the Rivers*. Gainesville: University Press of Florida, 1988.

———. "Translation of Alonso de Leturiondo's Memorial to the King of Spain." *Florida Archaeology* 2 (1986):165–225.

Harmon, Joyce. *Trade and Privateering in Spanish Florida, 1762–1763*. St. Augustine, Fla.: St. Augustine Historical Society, 1969.

Harmon, Michael A., and Rodney J. Snedeker. "The Archaeological Record of Tar and Pitch Production in Coastal Carolina." In *Carolina's Historical Landscapes*, edited by L. Stine, M. Zierden, L. Drucker, and C. Judge, 145–60. Knoxville: University of Tennessee Press, 1997.

Harris, J. William. *Deep Souths: Delta, Piedmont and Sea Island Society in the Age of Segregation*. Baltimore: Johns Hopkins University Press, 2001.

Hart, Emma. *Building Charleston: Town and Society in the Eighteenth-Century British Atlantic World*. Charlottesville: University of Virginia Press, 2010.

Hawes, R. O. "Pigeons." In *Evolution of Domesticated Animals*, edited by I. L. Mason, 351–56. London: Longman, 1984.

Haygood, Tamara Miner. "Cows, Ticks, and Disease: A Medical Interpretation of the Southern Cattle Industry." *Journal of Southern History* 52, no. 4 (1986):551–64.

Heath, Barbara. "Buttons, Beads, and Buckles: Contextualizing Adornment within the Bounds of Slavery." In *Historical Archaeology, Identity Formation, and the Interpretation of Ethnicity*, edited by M. Franklin and G. Fesler, 47–70. Williamsburg, Va.: Colonial Williamsburg Research Publications, 1999.

———. "Cowrie Shells, Global Trade and Local Exchange: Piecing Together the Evidence. *Historical Archaeology*. In press.

Herman, Bernard L. "The Charleston Single House." In *The Buildings of Charleston*, by Jonathan Poston, 37–41. Columbia: University of South Carolina Press, 1997.

———. "A Poetics of Urban Space." In *Material Culture in Anglo-America: Regional Identity and Urbanity in the Tidewater, Lowcountry, and Caribbean*, edited by D. Shields, 191–201. Columbia: University of South Carolina Press, 2009.

———. "Slave and Servant Housing in Charleston, 1770–1820." *Historical Archaeology* 33, no. 3 (1999):88–101.

———. *Town House: Architecture and Material Life in the Early American City, 1780–1830*. Chapel Hill: University of North Carolina Press, 2005.

Herold, Elaine. "Archaeological Research at the Exchange Building, Charleston, S.C.: 1979–1980." Report on file, The Charleston Museum, Charleston, S.C., 1981.

Herold, Elaine, and Elizabeth Thomas. "History of the Charleston Center Site." Report on file, The Charleston Museum, Charleston, S.C., 1981.

Hess, Karen. *The Carolina Rice Kitchen: The African Connection*. Columbia: University of South Carolina Press, 1992.

Hilliard, Sam B. *Hogmeat and Hoecake: Food Supply in the Old South*. Carbondale: Southern Illinois University Press, 1972.

Honerkamp, Nicholas. "Households or Neighborhoods: Finding Appropriate Levels of Research in Urban Archaeology." Paper presented at the 20th annual meeting of the Society for Historical Archaeology, Savannah, Ga., 1987.

Honerkamp, Nicholas, and R. Bruce Council. "Individual versus Corporate Adaptations in Urban Contexts." *Tennessee Anthropologist* 9, no. 1 (1984):22–31.

Honerkamp, Nicholas, R. Bruce Council, and M. Elizabeth Will. "An Archaeological Investigation of the Charleston Center Site, Charleston, South Carolina." Report on file, U.S. Department of the Interior, National Park Service, Atlanta, 1982.

Honerkamp, Nicholas, and Charles H. Fairbanks. "Definition of Site Formation Processes in Urban Contexts." *American Archeology* 4, no. 1 (1984):60–66.

Hooker, Richard J. *A Colonial Plantation Cookbook: The Receipt Book of Harriott Pinckney Horry, 1770.* Columbia: University of South Carolina Press, 1984.

———. *Food and Drink in America: A History.* Indianapolis: Bobbs-Merrill, 1981.

Horlbeck Brothers. *Day Book, 1824–1828.* Charleston, S.C.: South Carolina Historical Society.

House, R. *Family Cookery, Combining Elegance and Economy.* London: J. Bailey, 1800. Winterthur, Del.; Winterthur Library, Printed Book and Periodical Collections.

Hubbard, Dennis K., George D. Oertel, and Dag Nummedal. "The Role of Waves and Tidal Currents in the Development of Tidal-Inlet Sedimentary Structures and Sand Body Geometry: Examples from North Carolina, South Carolina, and Georgia." *Journal of Sedimentary Petrology* 49 (1979):1073–92.

Hudgins, Lisa. "Staffordshire in America: The Wares of John Bartlam at Cain Hoy, 1765–1770." *Ceramics in America* (2009):69–80.

Hurry, Silas, Meta Janowitz, Henry Miller, and Bly Straube. "Telling Time in the Seventeenth Century." Poster produced by URS Archaeology Laboratory, Burlington, N.J., and Council for Northeast Historical Archaeology, 2000

Hutchisson, James M., and Harlan Greene. *Renaissance in Charleston: Art and Life in the Carolina Low Country, 1900–1940.* Athens: University of Georgia Press, 2003.

Isenbarger, Nicole. "Potters, Hucksters, and Consumers: Placing Colonoware within the Internal Slave Economy Framework." MA thesis, Department of Anthropology, University of South Carolina, 2006.

Jackson, James Brinckerhof. *Discovering the Vernacular Landscape.* New Haven: Yale University Press, 1984.

Jameson, Robert. "Purity and Power at the Victorian Dinner Party." In *The Archaeology of Contextual Meaning,* edited by I. Hodder, 54–65. Cambridge: Cambridge University Press, 1987.

Jochim, Michael A. *Hunter–Gatherer Subsistence and Settlement: A Predictive Model.* New York: Academic Press, 1976.

Johnston, Richard F. "Synanthropic Birds of North America." In *Avian Ecology and Conservation in an Urbanizing World,* edited by J. M. Marzuff, R. Bowman, and R. Donelly, 49–67. Boston: Kluwer Academic, 2001.

Jones, David, and Cicek Beeby. "Miller Site Excavations: Fall Field Season 2009." Report on file, Charles Towne Landing Historic Site, Charleston, S.C., 2010.

Jones, John. "Palynological Evidence of Eighteenth Century Dietary Patterns." In *The Dock Street Theatre,* edited by M. Zierden, 71–80. Archaeological Contributions 42. Charleston, S.C.: The Charleston Museum, 2009.

Joseph, J. W. "Agriculture in Colonial Charleston: Landuse, Landscape, and the Lost Colonial City." *South Carolina Antiquities* 39 (2007):18–33.

———. "Colonoware for the Village—Colonoware for the Market." *South Carolina Antiquities* 36 (2004):72–86.

———. "From Colonist to Charlestonian: The Crafting of Identity in a Colonial Southern City." In *Another's Country: Archaeological and Historical Perspectives on Cultural Interactions in the Southern Colonies,* edited by J. W. Joseph and Martha A. Zierden, 215–34. Tuscaloosa: University of Alabama Press, 2002.

———. "Meeting at Market: The Intersection of African American Culture, Craft, and

Economy and the Landscape of Charleston, South Carolina." *Historical Archaeology* 50, no. 1 (2016):94–113.

Joseph, J. W., and Rita Folse Elliott. "Restoration Archaeology at the Charleston County Courthouse Site (38Ch1498)." Technical Report 194. Stone Mountain, Ga.: New South Associates, 1994.

Joseph, J. W., Theresa Hamby, and Jennifer Langdale. "The Vendue/Prioleau Project: An Archaeological Study of the Early Charleston Waterfront." Technical Report 772. Stone Mountain, Ga.: New South Associates, 2000.

Joseph, J. W., and Martha A. Zierden, editors. *Another's Country: Archaeological and Historical Perspectives on Cultural Interactions in the Southern Colonies.* Tuscaloosa: University of Alabama Press, 2002.

Journal of the Commons House of Assembly. Columbia: Historical Commission of South Carolina and South Carolina Department of Archives and History.

Keel, Bennie C., and Amy C. Kowal. "The Archaeology of Charles Pinckney's Snee Farm: A Summary of Fieldwork 1987–1999." Accession 943. Tallahassee, Fla.: National Park Service Southeast Archaeological Center, 2014.

Kelly, Joseph. *America's Longest Siege: Charleston, Slavery, and the Slow March toward the Civil War.* New York: Overlook Press, 2013.

Kidd, Shawn. "Truck Farming on the Eastern Shore: 1880–1950. In *Eating Delmarva: Agricultural Transformations in Wicomico County, 1880–2004,* by Michael Lewis. http://faculty.salisbury.edu/~mllewis/Agriculture/chapter_three.htm. Accessed January 25, 2014.

Killens, James O., editor. *The Trial Record of Denmark Vesey.* Boston: Beacon Press, 1970.

King, Julia A. *Archaeology, Narrative, and the Politics of the Past: The View from Southern Maryland.* Knoxville: University of Tennessee Press, 2012.

———. "Ceramic Variability in 17th Century St. Augustine, Florida." *Historical Archaeology* 18, no. 2 (1984):75–82.

Kovacik, Charles F., and John J. Winberry. *South Carolina: A Geography.* Boulder, Colo.: Westview Press, 1987.

Kropf, Schuyler. "Dozens of Graves found at Gaillard," *Post and Courier,* February 15, 2013.

———. *Post and Courier,* "Gaillard Graveyard Remains Determined to Be African-American." November 22, 2013.

Kryder-Reid, Elizabeth. "'As Is the Gardener, So Is the Garden': The Archaeology of Landscape as Myth." In *Historical Archaeology of the Chesapeake,* edited by P. Shackel and B. Little, 131–48. Washington, D.C.: Smithsonian Institution Press, 1994.

Kupperman, Karen Ordahl. *The Jamestown Project.* Cambridge: Belknap Press of Harvard University Press, 2007.

LaFebvre, Michelle J., and Susan D. deFrance. "Guinea Pigs in the Pre-Columbian West Indies." *Journal of Island and Coastal Archaeology* 9 (2014):16–44.

Lapham, Samuel. "Notes on the Granville Bastion, 1704." *South Carolina Historical and Genealogical Magazine* 26 (1925):224.

Larson, Lewis H. Jr. *Aboriginal Subsistence Technology on the Southeastern Coastal Plain during the Late Prehistoric Period.* Gainesville: University Press of Florida, 1980.

Laudonniere, Rene. *Three Voyages.* Translated by Charles E. Bennett. Gainesville: University Press of Florida, 1975.

Leavitt, Charles T. "Attempts to Improve Cattle Breeds in the United States, 1790–1860." *Agricultural History* 7, no. 2 (1933):51–67.

Lebby, Robert. *Digest of Acts of the Assembly of South Carolina and Ordinances of the City of Charleston, Relative to the Health Department.* Charleston: Daily Republican Office, 1870.

Lefler, Hugh Talmage, editor. *A New Voyage to Carolina, by John Lawson.* Chapel Hill: University of North Carolina Press, 1967.

Leland, Cheves, and Dianne Ressinger. "Ce Pais Tant Desire, This Much Longed-for Country." *Transactions of the Huguenot Society of South Carolina* 110 (2006):2–33.

Leland, Isabella G. *Charleston: Crossroads of History.* Woodland Hills, Calif.: Windsor Publications and Charleston Trident Chamber of Commerce, 1980.

Leone, Mark P. "Interpreting Ideology in Historical Archaeology: Using the Rules of Perspective in the William Paca Gardens in Annapolis, Maryland." In *Ideology, Power, and Prehistory*, edited by D. Miller and C. Tilley, 25–35. Cambridge: Cambridge University Press, 1984.

Leone, Mark P., and Parker B. Potter Jr. *The Recovery of Meaning: Historical Archaeology in the Eastern United States.* Washington, D.C.: Smithsonian Institution Press, 1988.

Lesser, Charles H. *South Carolina Begins: The Records of a Proprietary Colony, 1663–1721.* Columbia: South Carolina Department of Archives and History, 1995.

Lofton, John. *Denmark Vesey's Revolt: The Slave Plot That Lit a Fuse to Fort Sumter.* Kent, Ohio: Kent State University Press, 1964.

Lounsbury, Carl. *An Illustrated Glossary of Early Southern Architecture and Landscape.* New York: Oxford University Press, 1994.

———. *From Statehouse to Courthouse: An Architectural History of South Carolina's Colonial Capitol and Charleston County Courthouse.* Columbia: University of South Carolina Press, 2001.

Luckenbach, Al. "Ceramics from the Edward Rumney/Stephen West Tavern, London Town, Maryland, circa 1725." In *Ceramics in America 2002*, edited by R. Hunter, 130–52. Hanover, N.H.: Chipstone Foundation and University Press of New England, 2002.

Luniak, Maciej. "Synurbization–Adaptation of Animal Wildlife to Urban Development." In *Proceedings of the 4th International Urban Wildlife Symposium*, edited by W. Shaw, L. K. Harris, and L. Vandruff, 50–55. Tucson: University of Arizona, 2004.

Lyon, Eugene. *The Enterprise of Florida.* Gainesville: University Press of Florida, 1976.

Maag, James. "Cattle Raising in Colonial South Carolina." MA thesis, Department of History, University of Kansas, 1964.

Marcoux, Jon B. "Glass Trade Beads from the English Colonial Period in the Southeast, ca. A.D. 1607–1783." *Southeastern Archaeology* 31, no. 2 (2012):157–84.

———. *Pox, Empire, Shackles, and Hides: The Townsend Site, 1670–1715.* Tuscaloosa: University of Alabama Press, 2010.

———. "Using Diversity in Native American Pottery Assemblages to Document Population Movements in the Early Carolina Indian Trade: A Preliminary View from Charleston." Paper presented at the 47th meeting of the Society for Historical Archaeology, Quebec, Canada, 2014.

Martin, Ann Smart. *Buying into the World of Material Goods: Early Consumers in Backcountry Virginia.* Baltimore: Johns Hopkins University Press, 2008.

———. "Consumption, Commodities, and Cultural Identity in Eighteenth-Century Virginia." Paper presented at the 28th annual meeting of the Society for Historical Archaeology, Washington, D.C., 1995.

———. "'Fashionable Sugar Dishes, Latest Fashion Ware': The Creamware Revolution in the Eighteenth-Century Chesapeake." In *Historical Archaeology of the Chesapeake*, edited by P. Shackel and B. Little, 169–88. Washington, D.C.: Smithsonian Institution Press, 1994.

Martin, Joel. "Southeastern Indians and the English Trade in Skins and Slaves." In *The Forgotten Centuries: Indians and Europeans in the American South, 1521–1704*, edited by C. Hudson and C. Tesser, 304–25. Athens: University of Georgia Press, 1994.

Mason, Carol. *The Archaeology of Ocmulgee Old Fields, Macon, Georgia.* Tuscaloosa: University of Alabama Press, 2005.

Mathews, Maurice. "A Contemporary View of Carolina in 1680." *South Carolina Historical Magazine* 55 (1954):153–59.

Mazyck, Arthur. *Guide to Charleston, Illustrated.* Charleston, S.C.: Walker, Evans and Cogswell, 1875.

McCord, David J. *The Statutes at Large of South Carolina.* Columbia: A. S. Johnston, 1840.

McCrady, Edward R. *The History of South Carolina under the Proprietary Government.* New York: Russell and Russell, 1897.

McInnis, Maurie D. "An Idea of Grandeur: Furnishing the Classical Interior in Charleston, 1815–1840." *Historical Archaeology* 33 no.3 (1999):32–47.

———. *The Politics of Taste in Antebellum Charleston.* Chapel Hill: University of North Carolina Press, 2005.

McInnis, Maurie D., and Angela Mack, editors. *In Pursuit of Refinement: Charlestonians Abroad, 1740–1860.* Columbia: University of South Carolina Press and Gibbes Museum of Art, 1999.

McKinley, Shepherd W. *Stinking Stones and Rocks of Gold: Phosphate, Fertilizer, and Industrialization in Postbellum South Carolina.* Gainesville: University Press of Florida, 2014.

McKinney, Michael L. "Urbanization as a Major Cause of Biotic Homogenization." *Biological Conservation* 127 (2006):247–60.

McPherson Family File, South Carolina Historical Society (SCHS), Charleston, S.C.

McTavish, Emily J., Jared E. Decker, Robert D. Schnabel, Jeremy F. Taylor, and David M. Hillis. "New World Cattle Show Ancestry from Multiple Independent Domestication Events." *Proceedings of the National Academy of Sciences* 2013 110, no. 15 (2013): E1398-E1406.

Mennell, Stephen, Ann Murcott, and Anneke van Otterloo. *The Sociology of Food: Eating, Diet and Culture.* New York: Sage Publications / International Sociological Association, 1992.

Merrell, James. *The Indians' New World: The Catawba and Their Neighbors.* Lincoln: University of Nebraska Press, 1992.

Merrens, H. Roy. *The Colonial South Carolina Scene: Contemporary Views, 1697–1774.* Columbia: University of South Carolina Press, 1977.

Milanich, Jerald T. *Florida Indians and the Invasion from Europe.* Gainesville: University Press of Florida, 1998.

Miller, George L. "A Revised List of CC Index Values for Classification and Economic Scaling of English Ceramics from 1787 to 1880." *Historical Archaeology* 25, no. 1 (1991):1–25.

Mintz, Sidney. *Sweetness and Power.* New York: Viking Penguin, 1985.

Miracle, Preston T., and Nicky Milner. *Consuming Passions and Patterns of Consumption.* Oxford: Oxbow Books, 2002.

Moore, Gregory A. "The 1702 Siege of St. Augustine: English Miscalculation or Spanish Good Fortune?" *El Escribano* 39 (2002):16–28.

Morgan, Philip D. *Slave Counterpoint: Black Culture in the Eighteenth-Century Chesapeake and Lowcountry.* Chapel Hill: University of North Carolina Press, 1998.

Museum of London. "Shakespeare's Curtain Theatre Unearthed in East London." http://www.theguardian.com/culture/2012/jun/06/shakespeare-curtain-theatre-shoreditch-east-lonfon.

Nairne, Thomas. "A Letter from South Carolina" (1710). Reprinted in *Selling a New World: Two Colonial South Carolina Promotional Pamphlets*, edited by J. P. Greene. Columbia: University of South Carolina Press, 1989.

Nash, R. C. "Domestic Material Culture and Consumer Demand in the British Atlantic World: Colonial South Carolina, 1670–1770." In *Material Culture in Anglo-America*, edited by D. Shields, 221–66. Columbia: University of South Carolina Press, 2009.

National Audubon Society. "John James Audubon's Birds of America. http://www.audubon.org/birds-of-america.

Newsom, Lee A., and Elizabeth S. Wing. *On Land and Sea: Native American Use of Biological Resources in the West Indies.* Tuscaloosa: University of Alabama Press, 2004.

Nöel Hume, Audrey. *Food.* Colonial Williamsburg Archaeological Series 9. Williamsburg: Colonial Williamsburg Foundation, 1978.

Nöel Hume, Ivor. *Glass in Colonial Williamsburg's Archaeological Collections.* Colonial Williamsburg Archaeological Series 1. Williamsburg: Colonial Williamsburg Foundation, 1969.

———. *A Guide to Artifacts of Colonial America.* New York: Alfred A. Knopf, 1969.

———. "An Indian Ware of the Colonial Period." *Quarterly Bulletin of the Archaeological Society of Virginia* 17, no. 1 (1962):1–12.

O'Day, Sharyn J., Wim Van Neer, and Anton Ervynck. *Behaviour behind Bones: The Zooarchaeology of Ritual, Religion, Status, and Identity.* Oxford: Oxbow Books, 2004.

Odum, Eugene P., and Gary W. Barrett. *Fundamentals of Ecology.* 5th ed. Belmont, Calif.: Thomson Brooks/Cole, 2005.

Orr, Kelly L., and Gregory S. Lucas. "Rural–Urban Connections in the Southern Colonial Market Economy: Zooarchaeological Evidence from the Grange Plantation (9Ch137) Trading Post and Cowpens." *South Carolina Antiquities* 39 (2007):1–17.

Otto, John S. "Livestock-Raising in Early South Carolina, 1670–1700: Prelude to the Rice Plantation Economy." *Agricultural History* 61, no. 4 (1987):13–24.

———. "The Origins of Cattle-Ranching in Colonial South Carolina, 1670–1715." *South Carolina Historical Magazine* 87, no. 2 (1986):117–24.

Paston-Williams, Sara. *The Art of Dining: A History of Cooking and Eating.* London: National Trust, 1993.

Pavao-Zuckerman, Barnet. "Culture, Contact and Subsistence Change at Fusihatchee (1EE191)." PhD diss., Department of Anthropology, University of Georgia, 2001.

———. "Deerskins and Domesticates: Creek Subsistence and Economic Strategies in the Historic Period." *American Antiquity* 72, no. 1 (2007):5–33.

———. "Vertebrate Subsistence in the Mississippian–Historic Transition." *Southeastern Archaeology* 19, no. 2 (2000):135–44.

Pavao-Zuckerman, Barnet, and Diana D. Loren. "Presentation Is Everything: Foodways, Tablewares, and Colonial Identity at Presidio Los Adaes." *International Journal of Historical Archaeology* 16 (2012):199–226

Pease, Jane H., and William H. Pease. "The Blood-Thirsty Tiger: Charleston and the Psychology of Fire." *South Carolina Historical Magazine* 79, no. 1 (1978):281–95.

Periam, Jonathan, and A. H. Baker. *The American Farmer's Pictorial Cyclopedia of Live Stock.* St. Louis, Mo.: N. D. Thompson, 1882.

Pigière, Fabienne, Wim Van Neer, Cécile Ansieau, and Marceline Denis. "New Archaeozoological Evidence for the Introduction of the Guinea Pig to Europe." *Journal of Archaeological Science* 39 (2012):1020–24.

Piker, Joshua. *The Four Deaths of Acorn Whistler: Telling Stories in Colonial America.* Cambridge: Harvard University Press, 2013.

Poplin, Eric, and Ed Salo. "Archaeological Investigations at 82 Pitt Street, Charleston, South Carolina: Final Report." Report on file, Historic Charleston Foundation, Charleston, S.C., 2009.

Porcher, Richard D. *Wildflowers of the Carolina Lowcountry and Lower Pee Dee.* Columbia: University of South Carolina Press, 1995.

Porcher, Richard D., and Sarah Fick. *The Story of Sea Island Cotton.* Layton, Utah: Wyrick, 2005.

Porcher, Richard D., and William R. Judd. *The Market Preparation of Carolina Rice: An Illustrated History of Innovations in the Lowcountry Rice Kingdom.* Columbia: University of South Carolina Press, 2014.

Porcher, Richard D., and Douglas A. Raymer. *A Guide to the Wildflowers of South Carolina.* Columbia: University of South Carolina Press, 2001.

Poston, Jonathan. *The Buildings of Charleston: A Guide to the City's Architecture.* Columbia: University of South Carolina Press and Historic Charleston Foundation, 1997.

Powers, Bernard E. Jr. *Black Charlestonians: A Social History, 1822–1885.* Fayetteville: University of Arkansas Press, 1994.

Prestwood, Annie K., Forest E. Kellogg, and Gary L. Doster. "Parasitism among Wild Turkeys in the Southeast." In *Proceedings of the Third National Wild Turkey Symposium,* Austin, Texas Chapter Wildlife Society, edited by L. Halls, 27–32, 1975.

Ramsey, William L. *The Yamasee War: A Study of Culture, Economy, and Conflict in the Colonial South.* Lincoln: University of Nebraska Press, 2008.

Raskin, Hanna. "Illustrated Nat Fuller Bio Released prior to Sunday Feast." *Post and Courier* (Charleston, S.C.), April 7, 2015.

Reinhard, Karl. "Analysis of Soils from 14 Legare Street: A Microfossil Survey." In *Excavations at 14 Legare Street,* edited by M. Zierden, appendix 2. Archaeological Contributions 28. Charleston, S.C.: The Charleston Museum, 2001.

———. "Pollen Analysis of the Miles Brewton House." In *Archaeology at the Miles Brewton House,* edited by M. Zierden, 197–210. Archaeological Contributions 29. Charleston, S.C.: The Charleston Museum, 2001.

Reitz, Elizabeth. "Zooarchaeological Analysis of a Free African Community: Gracia Real de Santa Teresa de Mose." *Historical Archaeology* 28, no. 1 (1994):23–40.

Reitz, Elizabeth J., and Sarah G. Bergh. "Animal Remains from Two Early South Carolina Sites." Report on file, Zooarchaeology Laboratory, Georgia Museum of Natural History, University of Georgia, Athens, 2012.

Reitz, Elizabeth J., and Maran E. Little. "Vertebrate Remains from the Miller Site, 38Ch1-MS, Charles Towne Landing State Historic Site." Report on file, Charles Towne Landing State Historic Site, Charleston, S.C., 2014.

Reitz, Elizabeth, Barnet Pavao-Zuckerman, Dan C. Weinand, Gretchen Duncan, and David Hurst Thomas. *Mission and Pueblo of Santa Catalina de Guale, St. Catherines Island, Georgia: A Comparative Zooarchaeological Analysis.* Anthropological Papers of the American Museum of Natural History 91. New York: American Museum of Natural History, 2010.

Reitz, Elizabeth, and Barbara Ruff. "Morphometric Data for Cattle from North America and the Caribbean prior to the 1850s." *Journal of Archaeological Science* 21 (1994):699–713.

Reitz, Elizabeth, and C. Margaret Scarry. *Reconstructing Historic Subsistence with an Example from Sixteenth-Century Spanish Florida.* Special Publication Series 3. N.J.: Society for Historical Archaeology, 1985.

Reitz, Elizabeth, and Gregory Waselkov. "Vertebrate Use at Early Colonies in the Southeastern Coasts of Eastern North America." *International Journal of Historical Archaeology* 19 (2015):21–45.

Reitz, Elizabeth, and Elizabeth S. Wing. *Zooarchaeology.* 2nd ed. Cambridge: Cambridge University Press, 2008.

Rhett, Blanche Salley. *Two Hundred Years of Charleston Cooking.* Columbia: University of South Carolina Press, 1976 (1930).

Ribaut, Jean. *The Whole and True Discouery of Terra Florida.* Edited by J. T. Conner. Deland: Florida State Historical Society, 1927.

Riggs, Brett H., R. P. Stephen Davis, and Mark R. Plane. "Catawba Pottery in the Post-Revolutionary Era: A View from the Source." *North Carolina Archaeology* 55 (2006):60–88.

Robertson, David. *Denmark Vesey: The Buried History of America's Largest Slave Rebellion and the Man Who Led It.* New York: Alfred A. Knopf, 1999.

Rockman, Diana Diz., and Nan A. Rothschild. "City Tavern, Country Tavern: An Analysis of Four Colonial Sites." *Historical Archaeology* 18, no. 2 (1984):112–21.

Rogers, George C. *Charleston in the Age of the Pinckneys.* Columbia: University of South Carolina Press, 1980.

Rogers, George C., editor. *The Papers of Henry Laurens, Volume 4: September 1, 1763–August 31, 1765.* Columbia: University of South Carolina Press, 1974.

Rosengarten, Dale. *Row upon Row: Sea Grass Baskets of the South Carolina Lowcountry.* Columbia: University of South Carolina Press and McKissick Museum, 1986.

Rosengarten, Dale, Theodore Rosengarten, and Enid Schildkrout. *Grass Roots: African Origins of an American Art.* New York: Museum for African Art, 2008.

Rosengarten, Dale, Martha Zierden, Kimberly Grimes, Ziyadah Owusu, Elizabeth Alston, and Will Williams III. "Between the Tracks: Charleston's East Side during the Nineteenth Century." Archaeological Contributions 17. Charleston, S.C.: The Charleston Museum, 1987.

Rosengarten, Theodore. "In the Master's Garden." In *Art and Landscape in Charleston and the Lowcountry*, by John Beardsley. Washington, D.C.: Spacemaker Press, 1998.

———. "The Southern Agriculturist in an Age of Reform." In *Intellectual Life in Antebellum Charleston*, edited by M. O'Brien and D. Moltke-Hansen, 279–94. Knoxville: University of Tennessee Press, 1986.

———. *Tombee: Portrait of a Cotton Planter*. New York: William Morrow, 1986.

Roth, Rodris. *Tea Drinking in 18th-Century America: Its Etiquette and Equipage*. Contributions from the Museum of History and Technology, Bulletin 225. Washington, D.C.: Smithsonian Institution, 1961.

Rothschild, Nan, and Diana Wall. *The Archaeology of American Cities*. Gainesville: University Press of Florida, 2014.

Rouse, John E. *The Criollo*. Norman: University of Oklahoma Press, 1977.

———. *World Cattle I: Cattle of Europe, South America, Australia, and New Zealand*. Norman: University of Oklahoma Press, 1970.

———. *World Cattle II: Cattle of Africa and Asia*. Norman: University of Oklahoma Press, 1970.

———. *World Cattle III: Cattle of North America*. Norman: University of Oklahoma Press, 1973.

Rowland, Lawrence S., Alexander Moore, and George C. Rodgers Jr. *The History of Beaufort County, South Carolina, Volume I, 1514–1861*. Columbia: University of South Carolina Press, 1996.

Royal Gazette, 1780–1782. Microfilm on file, Special Collections, Addlestone Library, College of Charleston, Charleston, S.C.

Russell, Aaron E. "Material Culture and African American Spirituality at the Hermitage." *Historical Archaeology* 31, no. 2 (1997):63–80.

Salley, Alexander S. *President Washington's Tour through South Carolina in 1791*. Columbia: State Printing Co., 1932.

———. *Records in the British Public Record Office Relating to South Carolina, 1663–1684*. Columbia: State Printing Co., 1928.

Salwen, Bert. "Archaeology in Megalopolis: Updated Assessment." *Journal of Field Archaeology* 5 (1978):453–59.

———. "Foreword: Archaeology of Urban America." In *Archaeology of Urban America*, edited by R. S. Dickens Jr., xiii–xvii. New York: Academic Press, 1982.

Sanders, Albert E., and William D. Anderson Jr. *Natural History Investigations in South Carolina from Colonial Times to the Present*. Columbia: University of South Carolina Press, 1999.

Saunders, Katherine. "'As regular and fformidable as any such woorke in America': The Walled City of Charles Town." In *Another's Country*, edited by J. W. Joseph and M. Zierden, 198–214. Tuscaloosa: University of Alabama Press, 2002.

Savage, J. Thomas. *Nathaniel Russell House*. Charleston, S.C.: Historic Charleston Foundation, 1989.

Savage, J. Thomas, and N. Jane Iseley. *The Charleston Interior*. Greensboro, N.C.: Legacy, 1995.

Savage, J. Thomas, and Robert A. Leath. "Buying British: Merchants, Taste, and Charleston Consumerism." In *In Pursuit of Refinement*, edited by M. McInnis and A. Mack, 55–64. Columbia: University of South Carolina Press, 1999.

Schiffer, Michael B. "Toward a Unified Science of the Cultural Past." In *Research Strategies in Historical Archaeology*, edited by S. South, 13–40. New York: Academic Press, 1977.

———. "Toward the Identification of Formation Processes." *American Antiquity* 48, no. 4 (1983):675–706.

Schorger, A. William. "The Domestic Turkey in Mexico and Central America in the Sixteenth Century." *Wisconsin Academy of Sciences, Arts and Letters* 52 (1963):133–52.

———. *The Wild Turkey: Its History and Domestication*. Norman: University of Oklahoma Press, 1966.

Serjeantson, Dale. *Birds*. Cambridge: Cambridge University Press, 2009.

Severens, Kenneth. *Charleston: Antebellum Architecture and Civic Destiny*. Knoxville: University of Tennessee Press, 1988.

Severens, Martha. *The Charleston Renaissance*. Spartanburg, S.C.: Sealand Press, 1998.

Shackel, Paul, and Barbara Little. *Historical Archaeology of the Chesapeake*. Washington, D.C.: Smithsonian Institution Press, 1994.

Shannon, Claude E., and Warren Weaver. *The Mathematical Theory of Communication*. Urbana: University of Illinois Press, 1949.

Sheldon, Andrew L. "Equitability Indices: Dependence on the Species Count." *Ecology* 50 (1969):466–67.

Shelford, Victor E. *Ecology in North America*. Urbana: University of Illinois Press, 1974.

Shepherd, Rebecca. "Going Up the Country: A Comparison of Elite Ceramic Consumption Patterns in Charleston and the Carolina Frontier." MA thesis, Department of Anthropology, University of South Carolina, 2014.

Shick, Tom W., and Don H. Doyle. "The South Carolina Phosphate Boom and the Stillbirth of the New South, 1867–1920." *South Carolina Historical Magazine* 86 (1985):1–31.

Shields, David S. *Southern Provisions: The Creation and Revival of a Southern Cuisine*. Chicago: University of Chicago Press, 2015.

Shields, David S., and Kevin Mitchell. "Nat Fuller's Feast: The Life and Legacy of an Enslaved Cook in Charleston." *Lowcountry Digital History Initiative*. http://ldhi.library.cofc.edu/exhibits/show/nat_fuller. Accessed April 21, 2015.

Shlasko, Ellen. "Frenchmen and Africans in South Carolina: Cultural Interaction on the Eighteenth-Century Frontier." In *Another's Country*, edited by J. W. Joseph and M. Zierden, 133–44. Tuscaloosa: University of South Carolina Press, 2002.

Silver, Timothy. *A New Face on the Countryside: Indians, Colonists, and Slaves in South Atlantic Forests, 1500–1800*. Cambridge: Cambridge University Press, 1990.

Silvia, Diane E. "Native American and French Cultural Dynamics on the Gulf Coast." *Historical Archaeology* 36, no. 1 (2002):26–35.

Simons, Albert, and Samuel Lapham Jr. *Charleston, South Carolina*. The Octagon Library of Early American Architecture, vol. 1. New York: American Institute of Architects Press, 1927.

Simons, Albert, and W. H. Johnson Thomas. "An Architectural Guide to Charleston, South Carolina, 1700–1900." Manuscript on file, Historic Charleston Foundation, Charleston, S.C., 1968.

Singleton, Theresa A. "The Slave Tag: An Artifact of Urban Slavery." *South Carolina Antiquities* 16 (1984):41–68.

Skrowonek, Russell. "Empire and Ceramics: The Changing Role of Illicit Trade in Spanish America." *Historical Archaeology* 26, no. 1 (1992):109–18.

Smith, Alice R. Huger. *A Charleston Sketchbook, 1796–1806: Forty Watercolor Drawings of the City and Surrounding Country, By Charles Fraser.* Charleston, S.C.: Carolina Art Association, 1959.

Smith, Hayden R. "In the Land of Cypress and Pine: An Environmental History of the Santee Experimental Forest, 1683–1937." U.S. Department of Agriculture Forest Service, General Technical Report SRS-115, Asheville, N.C., 2012.

———. "Rich Swamps and Rice Grounds: The Specialization of Inland Rice Culture in the South Carolina Lowcountry, 1670–1861." PhD diss., Department of History, University of Georgia, 2012.

Smith, D. E. Huger. *A Charlestonian's Recollections, 1846–1913.* Charleston, S.C.: Carolina Art Association, 1950.

Smith, Mark M. *Stono: Documenting and Interpreting a Southern Slave Revolt.* Columbia: University of South Carolina Press, 2005.

Snell, William R. "Indian Slavery in Colonial South Carolina, 1671–1795." PhD diss., Department of History, University of Alabama, 1973.

South, Stanley A. *Archaeological Pathways to Historic Site Development.* New York: Kluwer Plenum, 2002.

———. "John Bartlam: Staffordshire in Carolina." Research Manuscript Series 231. Columbia: South Carolina Institute of Archaeology and Anthropology, 2004.

———. *Method and Theory in Historical Archaeology.* New York: Academic Press, 1977.

———. "Palmetto Parapets: Exploratory Archaeology at Fort Moultrie, South Carolina, 38Ch50." South Carolina Institute of Archaeology and Anthropology Anthropological Studies 1. Columbia: South Carolina Institute of Archaeology and Anthropology, 1974.

South, Stanley A., and Michael Hartley. "Deep Water and High Ground: Seventeenth Century Low Country Settlement." South Carolina Institute of Archaeology and Anthropology Research Manuscript Series 166. Columbia: South Carolina Institute of Archaeology and Anthropology, 1980.

South Carolina Gazette. 1732–67. Microfilm on file, Special Collections, Addlestone Library, College of Charleston and Charleston County Library, Charleston, S.C.

South Carolina Gazette and Daily Advertiser. 1783–85. http://www.genealogybank.com/explore/newspapers/all/usa/south-carolina/charleston.

South Carolina Institute. *Premium List, Fair of 1870.* Charleston, S.C.: Walker, Evans and Cogswell, 1870.

South Carolina Society for the Improvement of Domestic Poultry. *Report of the Executive Committee.* Charleston, S.C.: Thomas H. Hays, 1852.

South Carolina Weekly Gazette. 1783–86. http://www.genealogybank.com/explore/newspapers/all/usa/south-carolina/charleston.

Southerlin, Bobby, Dawn Reid, Connie Huddleston, Alana Lynch, and Dea Mozingo. "Return of the Yamasee: Archaeological Data Recovery at Chechesy Old Field, Beaufort County, South Carolina." Report on file, Chechessee Land and Timber Company, Okatie, S.C., 2001.

Southern Agriculturist. "Part III. Miscellaneous Intelligence" 9 (1836):165. Charleston: A. E. Miller, 1828–39. Microfilm, Addlestone Library, College of Charleston, Charleston, S.C.

Speller, Camilla F., David V. Burley, Robyn P. Woodward, and Dongya Y. Yang. "Ancient mtDNA Analysis of Early 16th Century Caribbean Cattle Provides Insight into Founding Populations of New World Creole Cattle Breeds." *PloS ONE* 8 (2013):569–84.

Sprunt, Alexander Jr., and E. Burnham Chamberlain. *South Carolina Bird Life.* Columbia: University of South Carolina Press, 1970.

Stahl, Peter W. "An Exploratory Osteological Study of the Muscovy Duck (*Cairina moschata*)(Aves: Anatidae) with Implications for Neotropical Archaeology." *Journal of Archaeological Science* 32 (2005):915–29.

Staski, Edward. "Advances in Urban Archaeology." In *Advances in Archaeological Method and Theory, Volume 5,* edited by M. Schiffer, 97–150. New York: Academic Press, 1982.

Steen, Carl. "An Archaeology of the Settlement Indians of the South Carolina Lowcountry." *South Carolina Antiquities* 44 (2012):19–34.

———. "Stirring the Ethnic Stew in the South Carolina Backcountry: John de la Howe and Lethe Farm." In *Historical Archaeology, Identity Formation, and the Interpretation of Ethnicity,* edited by M. Franklin and G. Fesler, 93–120. Williamsburg, Va.: Colonial Williamsburg Research Publications, 1999.

Stevens, Michael E. *Journals of the House of Representatives, 1792–1794.* Columbia: University of South Carolina Press, 1988.

Stewart, Mart A. *"What Nature Suffers to Groe," Life, Labor, and Landscape on the Georgia Coast, 1680–1920.* Athens: University of Georgia Press, 1996.

———. "Whether Wast, Deodand, or Strayd: Cattle, Culture, and the Environment in Early Georgia." *Agricultural History* 65, no. 3 (1991):1–28.

Stilgoe, John R. *Common Landscape of America 1580–1845.* New Haven: Yale University Press, 1982.

Stine, Linda, Melanie Cabak, and Mark Groover. "Blue Beads as African American Cultural Symbols." *Historical Archaeology* 30, no. 3 (1996):49–75.

Stockton, Robert P. *The Great Shock: The Effects of the 1886 Earthquake on the Built Environment of Charleston, South Carolina.* Easley, S.C.: Southern Historical Press, 1986.

———. "Historical Background of the Survey Area—Charleston Neck." Report on file, City of Charleston, Charleston, S.C., 1985.

Stoner, Michael J. "The Towne before the City: The Caribbean Influence at 1670 Charles Town." *South Carolina Antiquities* 38 (2006):67–83.

Stoner, Michael J., and Stanley A. South. *Exploring 1670 Charles Town: 39CH1A/B Final Archaeology Report.* Research Manuscript Series 230. Columbia: South Carolina Institute of Archaeology and Anthropology, 2001.

Stoney, Samuel Gaillard. *This Is Charleston: A Survey of the Architectural Heritage of a Unique American City.* Charleston, S.C.: Carolina Art Association, 1976 (1944).

Stoudemire, Sterling A., editor. *Natural History of the West Indies, by Gonzalo Fernandez de Oviedo y Valdes.* Chapel Hill: University of North Carolina Press, 1959.

Swanton, John. *Indians of the Southeastern United States.* Bulletin No. 137, Bureau of American Ethnology. Washington, D.C.: Smithsonian Institution, 1946. Reprint, Clair Shores, Mich.: Scholarly Press, 1977.

Sweeney, Alexander Y. "Investigating Yamasee Identity: Archaeological Research at Poco-taligo." MA thesis, Department of Anthropology, University of South Carolina, 2003.

Sweeney, Kevin M. "High-Style Vernacular: Lifestyles of the Colonial Elite." In *Of Consuming Interest: The Style of Life in the Eighteenth Century*, edited by C. Carson, R. Hoffman, and P. J. Albert, 1–58. Charlottesville: University Press of Virginia, 1994.

Taylor, Alan. *American Colonies*. Penguin History of the United States. New York: Viking Penguin, 2001.

Taylor, David. *South Carolina Naturalists: An Anthology, 1700–1860*. Columbia: University of South Carolina Press, 1998.

Taylor, John Martin. *Hoppin' John's Lowcountry Cooking: Recipes and Ruminations from Charleston and the Carolina Coastal Plain*. New York: Bantam Books. 1992.

Tennant Family Papers, South Caroliniana Library, Columbia, S.C.

The Shaftesbury Papers. "The Shaftesbury Papers, South Carolina Historical Society." Charleston, S.C.: Home House Press, 2010.

Thompson, James W. *History of Livestock Raising in the United States, 1607–1860*. Washington, D.C.: Report of the U.S. Department of Agriculture, 1942.

Thornton, John. "African Dimensions of the Stono Rebellion." *American Historical Review* 96, no. 4 (1991):1101–13.

Towne, Charles W., and Edward N. Wentworth. *Pigs: From Cave to Cornbelt*. Norman: University of Oklahoma Press, 1950.

Towner, Donald. *Creamware*. Boston: Faber and Faber, 1978.

Trinkley, Michael. "Analysis of Ethnobotanical Samples." In *Meat in Due Season,* by Jeanne Calhoun, Elizabeth Reitz, Michael Trinkley, and Martha Zierden, 88–94. Archaeological Contributions 9. Charleston, S.C.: The Charleston Museum, 1984.

———. "Ethnobotanical Analysis of Samples from the Gibbes House." In *Georgian Opulence,* by Martha Zierden, Suzanne Buckley, Jeanne Calhoun and Debi Hacker, 98–107. Archeological Contributions 12. Charleston, S.C.: The Charleston Museum, 1987.

Trow-Smith, Robert. *A History of British Livestock Husbandry, 1700–1900*. London: Routledge and Kegan Paul, 1959.

Upton, Dell. "The City as Material Culture." In *The Art and Mystery of Historical Archaeology: Essays in Honor of James Deetz*, edited by M. Beaudry and A. Yentsch, 51–74. Boca Raton, Fla.: CRC Press, 1992.

———. "White and Black Landscapes in Eighteenth-Century Virginia." In *Material Life in America, 1600–1860,* edited by Robert Blair St. George, 357–69. Boston: Northeastern University Press, 1988.

USDA. *Development of Trucking Interests*. U.S. Department of Agriculture Yearbook. Washington, D.C.: Government Printing Office, 1901.

VanDerwarker, Amber M., Jon B. Marcoux, and Kandace D. Hollenbach. "Farming and Foraging at the Crossroads: The Consequences of Cherokee and European Interaction through the Late Eighteenth Century." *American Antiquity* 78 (2013):68–88.

VanDoran, Mark, editor. *Travels of William Bartram*. New York: Dover, 1955.

Van Ruymbeke, Bertrand. "The Huguenots of Proprietary South Carolina: Patterns of Migration and Integration." In *Money, Trade, and Power: The Evolution of Colonial South Carolina's Plantation Society*, edited by J. Greene, R. Brana-Shute, and R. Sparks, 26–48. Columbia: University of South Carolina Press, 2001.

Waddell, Gene. *Charleston in 1883*. Easley, S.C.: Southern Historical Press, 1983.

———. *Indians of the South Carolina Lowcountry 1562–1751*. Spartanburg, S.C.: Reprint Company, 1980.

Wade, Richard C. *Slavery in the Cities: The South, 1820–1860*. New York: Oxford University Press, 1964.

Waldron, Tony. *Paleopathology*. Cambridge: Cambridge University Pres, 2009.

Wallace, David Duncan. *South Carolina: A Short History, 1520–1948*. Columbia: University of South Carolina Press, 1961.

Walsh, Lorena, Ann Smart Martin, and Joanne Bowen. "Provisioning Early Chesapeake Towns, the Chesapeake: A Multidisciplinary Case Study." Colonial Williamsburg Foundation Report to the National Endowment for the Humanities. Williamsburg, Va.: Colonial Williamsburg Foundation, 1997.

Waring, Joseph. *A History of Medicine in South Carolina, 1670–1825*. Columbia: South Carolina Medical Association, 1964.

Waselkov, Gregory A. "French Colonial Archaeology at Old Mobile: An Introduction." *Historical Archaeology* 30, no. 1 (2002):3–12.

———. "Seventeenth-Century Trade in the Colonial Southeast." *Southeastern Archeology* 8, no. 2 (1989):17–33.

Waselkov, Gregory A., John Cottier, and Craig T. Sheldon. "Archaeological Excavations at the Early Historic Creek Indian Town of Fusihatchee (Phase 1, 1988–1989)." Report on file, Auburn University and University of South Alabama, 1990.

Waselkov, Gregory A., and Bonnie L. Gums. "Plantation Archaeology at Rivière aux Chiens, ca. 1725–1848." Archaeological Monograph 7. Mobile: University of South Alabama, Center for Archaeological Studies, 2000.

Waterbury, Jean Parker, editor. "Firestorm and Ashes: The Siege of 1702." *El Escribano* 39, 2002.

Weir, Robert M. "Charles Town circa 1702: On the Cusp." *El Escribano* 39 (2002):65–79.

———. *Colonial South Carolina: A History*. Millwood, N.Y.: KTO Press, 1983.

———. *Preface to the Reprint: The Shaftesbury Papers*. Charleston, S.C.: Home House Press, 2010.

Weyeneth, Robert R. *Historic Preservation for a Living City: Historic Charleston Foundation, 1947–1997*. Columbia: University of South Carolina Press, 2000.

Wheaton, Thomas, and Patrick Garrow. "Acculturation and the Archaeological Record in the Carolina Lowcountry." In *The Archaeology of Slavery and Plantation Life*, edited by T. Singleton, 239–59. New York: Academic Press, 1985.

Williams, Susan Millar, and Stephen G. Hoffius. *Upheaval in Charleston: Earthquake and Murder on the Eve of Jim Crow*. Athens: University of Georgia Press, 2011.

Williams, Theresa W., editor. *A History of Charleston's Water, 1823–2010: The Development of a Public Water and Wastewater System*. Charleston, S.C.: Charleston Water System Archives and Records Management, 2010.

Williamson, Joel. *After Slavery: The Negro in South Carolina during Reconstruction, 1861–1877*. Chapel Hill: University of North Carolina Press, 1965.

Williamson, Grahame, and William F. A. Payne. *An Introduction to Animal Husbandry in the Tropics*. London: Longman, 1978.

Wing, Elizabeth S. "Domestication of Andean Mammals." In *High Altitude Tropical Bio-*

geography, edited by F. Vuillemier and M. Monasterio, 262–64. Oxford: Oxford University Press, 1986.

Wood, Peter A. *Black Majority: Negroes in Colonial South Carolina from 1670 through the Stono Rebellion*. New York: Alfred A. Knopf, 1975.

———. *Strange New Land: Africans in Colonial America*. New York: Oxford University Press, 2003.

Wright, J. Leitch. *Anglo-Spanish Rivalry in North America*. Athens: University of Georgia Press, 1971.

Youatt, William. *Cattle*. New York: A. O. Moore, 1859.

Zierden, Martha, and Jeanne Calhoun. "Urban Adaptation in Charleston, South Carolina, 1730–1820." *Historical Archaeology* 29, no. 1 (1986):29–43.

———. "An Archaeological Preservation Plan for Charleston, South Carolina." Archaeological Contributions 8. Charleston, S.C.: The Charleston Museum, 1984.

Zierden, Martha, and Bernard L. Herman. "Charleston Townhouses: Archaeology, Architecture, and the Urban Landscape, 1750–1850." In *Landscape Archaeology: Reading and Interpreting the American Historical Landscape,* edited by R. Yamin and K. Metheny, 193–227. Knoxville: University of Tennessee Press, 1996.

Zierden, Martha A., and Elizabeth J. Reitz. "Eighteenth-Century Charleston: Aftermath of the Siege." *El Escribano* 39 (2002):113–31.

INDEX

McGee, Peter, 94

McInnis, Maurie, 159, 198, 216

McKinley, Shepherd, 69

McPherson, John, 152–53

MeadWestvaco (MWV), 79

Meat, 140, 199, 221; bones, 171–72; Charleston cut, *173*; class and, 172; consumption, 171, 173, 180; cultural values and, 175; cuts of, 172, *173*, 175, *176*, *177*, *178*; diet, 224; distribution, 175; domestication of, 141; markets, 173; nutrition and, 10; sources of, 173, 175, 224, 225; status and, 175; value of, 172. *See also* Butchering; Slaughter

Medical University of South Carolina, 237

Medicine containers, 103, 104

Meeting Street, 20, 182–84, *185*, 237, 255, 257

Memorial to the King of Spain (Leturiondo), 110

Menus, 8, 205; "Ball Supper," *221*; dinner party, 222; foodways and, 9

Mercantilism, 157, 188

Merchants, 54, 55, 59, 64, 106, 122, 182, 185

Mice, 52

Middle class, 224; artisans, 237; growth of, 253

Middleton, Frances Kinloch, 205

Middleton-Pinckney House, 70

Military artifacts, 101, 258–59, 286

Milk, 49, 80, 87

Miller, John, 17, 76, 94, 97

Miller Site, 76–77, 86, 274

Milner, John, Jr., 126, 128, 129, 150

Milner, John, Sr., 126, 128

Mines, phosphate, 69

Minimum Number of Individuals (MNI), 31, 294–96, 309n31. *See also* Zooarchaeology

Missroon House, 93–94

MNI. *See* Minimum Number of Individuals

Mobile, 66

Monkeys, 167

Moore, James B., 56, 92, 107, 115, 257

Morgan, Philip, 198, 199

Mortality rates, 60

Mortar, 80

Mose. *See* Gracia Real de Santa Teresa de Mose

Mosquito fleet, 246, *247*

Motte, Rebecca, 64, 94, 97, 147

Mules, 48

Mullets, 47, 108, 139, 246

Multifunction sites, 22

Municipal government, 240

Municipal services, 239–42

Muscovy duck, 50, 106, 140, 190

Musgrove, John, 135

Musgrove, Mary, 117, 133, *134*, 135, 257

Musicians, 124

Mutton, 140, 205, 222

MWV. *See* MeadWestvaco

Nails, 238, 285

Nairne, Thomas, 87, 110

Nassau Street, 236

National Forest System, 69

National Park Service, 19

National Society of Colonial Dames, 100–101

Native Americans, 12, 34, 37, 53; Africans and, 131; animal use of, 84–85; cattle and, 87; cowpens and, 141; farmers, 41; hunting of, 39; influence of, 127; population of, 108; pottery of, 102–5, 126, 133, 164, 284; role in urban life, 102; settlers and, 58; slavery of, 85, 110, 132; trade with, 58, 61, 75–76, 91, 131, 135

Naval stores, 59, 98, *98*, 116

Neck, Charleston, 64, 66, 67–68, 183, 205, 206, 210

Negro Act, 130

New Orleans, 66

New South Associates, 122, 129

Nöel Hume, Ivor, 103

Noisette, Philip, 213

Nutrition, 8–11

Ocmulgee, 127

Oglethorpe, James, 135

Old Mobile, 55

Old Town Plantation, 76

Old World cultigens, 39, 277–78

MARTHA A. ZIERDEN is curator emeritus of historical archaeology at The Charleston Museum. She is coeditor of *Another's Country: Archaeological and Historical Perspectives on Cultural Interactions in the Southern Colonies* and editor of *Charleston in the Context of Trans-Atlantic Culture.*

ELIZABETH J. REITZ, professor of anthropology at the University of Georgia, is the coauthor of seven books, including *Zooarchaeology* and *Case Studies in Environmental Archaeology.*